T0320017

Future Challenges in Evaluating and Managing Sustainable Development in the Built Environment

Future Challenges in Evaluating and Managing Sustainable Development in the Built Environment

Edited by

Peter S. Brandon
Patrizia Lombardi
Geoffrey Q. Shen

WILEY Blackwell

This edition first published 2017
© 2017 by John Wiley & Sons Ltd

Registered Office
John Wiley & Sons Ltd, The Atrium, Southern Gate, Chichester, West Sussex, PO19 8SQ,
United Kingdom.

Editorial Offices
9600 Garsington Road, Oxford, OX4 2DQ, United Kingdom.
The Atrium, Southern Gate, Chichester, West Sussex, PO19 8SQ, United Kingdom.

For details of our global editorial offices, for customer services and for information about
how to apply for permission to reuse the copyright material in this book please see our website at
www.wiley.com/wiley-blackwell.

The right of the author to be identified as the author of this work has been asserted in accordance with the
UK Copyright, Designs and Patents Act 1988.

All rights reserved. No part of this publication may be reproduced, stored in a retrieval system, or
transmitted, in any form or by any means, electronic, mechanical, photocopying, recording or otherwise,
except as permitted by the UK Copyright, Designs and Patents Act 1988, without the prior permission of
the publisher.

Designations used by companies to distinguish their products are often claimed as trademarks. All brand
names and product names used in this book are trade names, service marks, trademarks or registered
trademarks of their respective owners. The publisher is not associated with any product or vendor
mentioned in this book.

Limit of Liability/Disclaimer of Warranty: While the publisher and author(s) have used their best efforts
in preparing this book, they make no representations or warranties with respect to the accuracy or
completeness of the contents of this book and specifically disclaim any implied warranties of
merchantability or fitness for a particular purpose. It is sold on the understanding that the publisher is not
engaged in rendering professional services and neither the publisher nor the author shall be liable for
damages arising herefrom. If professional advice or other expert assistance is required, the services of a
competent professional should be sought.

Library of Congress Cataloging-in-Publication data applied for

ISBN: 9781119190714

A catalogue record for this book is available from the British Library.

Wiley also publishes its books in a variety of electronic formats. Some content that appears in print may
not be available in electronic books.

Cover image: Flying explorations over the city – Charlie Lombardi
Cover design: Wiley

Set in 10/12.5pt Minion by SPi Global, Pondicherry, India
Printed and bound in Malaysia by Vivar Printing Sdn Bhd

10 9 8 7 6 5 4 3 2 1

Contents

List of Contributors

Matar Alzahmi
Thinklab, University of Salford, Salford,
M5 4WT, UK

Andrew Basden
Business School, University of Salford,
Salford, M5 4WT, UK

Sara Biscaya
Architecture, University of Salford, Salford,
M5 4WT, UK

Peter S. Brandon
School of the Built Environment,
University of Salford, Salford,
M5 4WT, UK

Ian Cooper
Eclipse Research Consultants, Cambridge,
CB4 2JD, UK

Stephen Curwell
Heys Environmental, Oldham, OL3 5RL, UK

Manila De Iuliis
Municipality of Santo Stefano al Mare, 18010
Santo Stefano al Mare, Italy

Chrisna du Plessis
Department of Architecture, University of
Pretoria, Pretoria, 0028, South Africa

Terrence Fernando
Thinklab, University of Salford, Salford,
M5 4WT, UK

Carlos T. Formoso
Building Innovation Research Unit,
Federal University of Rio Grande do Sul,
Porto Alegre, Brazil

Ghassan Aouad
Applied Science University, East Al-Ekir,
Bahrain

Kaichen Goh
Department of Construction Management,
Universiti Tun Hussein Onn Malaysia,
Johor, Malaysia

Peter Hibberd
The Joint Contracts Tribunal, London EC1N
6TD, UK

Anton Ianakiev
School of Architecture, Design and the Built
Environment, Nottingham Trent University,
Nottingham, NG1 4FQ, UK

Tuba Kocaturk
Department of Architecture, University of
Liverpool, Liverpool, L69 7ZN, UK

Dezhi Li
Department of Construction and Real Estate,
Southeast University, 210018, Nanjing, China

Patrizia Lombardi
Interuniversity Department of Regional and
Urban Studies and Planning, Politecnico di
Torino, Torino, 10125, Italy

Luciana I.G. Miron
Building Innovation Research Unit,
Federal University of Rio Grande do Sul,
Porto Alegre, Brazil

Margaret K.Y. Mok
Department of Building and Real Estate,
The Hong Kong Polytechnic University,
Hong Kong, China

Trevor Mole
Property Tectonics, Manchester,
M27 8UX, UK

Sidney Newton
Faculty of Built Environment,
The University of New South Wales,
Sydney, NSW 2052, Australia

Giulia Sonetti
Interuniversity Department of Regional
and Urban Studies and Planning,
Politecnico di Torino, Torino, 10125, Italy

Srinath Perera
School of Computing, Engineering &
Mathematics, Western Sydney University,
Penrith, NSW 2751, Australia

John Ratcliffe
The Futures Academy, Taplow, SL6 0GA, UK

Marjan Sarshar
School of Architecture, Design and the Built
Environment, Nottingham Trent University,
Nottingham, NG1 4FQ, UK

Geoffrey Q. Shen
Department of Building and Real Estate,
The Hong Kong Polytechnic University,
Hong Kong, China

Alison Stacey
Economic Development, Nottingham City
Council, Nottingham, NG2 3NG, UK

Michele Florencia Victoria
Department of Architecture and Built
Environment, Northumbria University,
Newcastle upon Tyne, NE1 8ST, UK

Jay Yang
School of Civil Engineering and
Built Environment, Queensland University
of Technology, Brisbane,
QLD 4001, Australia

Tan Yigitcanlar
School of Civil Engineering and
Built Environment, Queensland
University of Technology, Brisbane,
QLD 4001, Australia

Acknowledgements

The authors of this book wish to express their sincere gratitude to Professor Hisham Elkadi, Head of the School of the Built Environment at the University of Salford, for his generous support of the August 2015 workshop in Cheshire, UK, on which this book is based.

Apart from providing a platform for deliberating each chapter of the book and making necessary amendments, the workshop also provided an opportunity to celebrate Professor Peter Brandon's remarkable achievements in education and research within the built environment over the past 40 years, particularly in the field of construction economics and management, information technology applied to construction and the evaluation of sustainable development.

Peter Brandon was appointed the UK's first Professor of Quantity and Building Surveying at the University of Salford, where many of the authors of this book have worked or studied. In the first five years of his time at Salford, he helped to raise the research performance of the School to the highest level attainable under the UK's Research Assessment Exercise, and in 2003 became Pro Vice Chancellor for research. In 2006 Professor Brandon led the University to the highest rise in the league tables of any university and, few years, later has been awarded an OBE in the HM The Queen's Birthday Honours List.

In addition to his academic career at Salford, Professor Brandon has held many major posts related to surveying and construction in the UK, including Chair of the Construction and Built Environment Panel of the Science and Engineering Research Council, Inaugural Chair of the Research Committee of the Royal Institution of Chartered Surveyors, Chair of the Built Environment Panel of the UK's Research Assessment Exercise in 1996 and 2001 and Chair of the Ross Priory Group (incorporating all the major research organisations in the Built Environment in the UK) and many others. He has also been on a number of committees and delegations of the Higher Education Funding Councils and has toured the Institutional bodies of Vice Chancellors and Senior University staff in Europe addressing the subject of Research Quality Assessment.

Last but not least, our sincere thanks are due to Ms Hanneke Van-Dijk without whose dedicated support and professional services the workshop would not have been such a great success. We would also like to thank Ms Federica Borio for her help in the preparation of this book.

Chapter 1
Initiative and Obsolescence in Sustainable Development

Peter S. Brandon

School of the Built Environment, University of Salford, Salford, M5 4WT, UK

1.1 Introduction

There comes a time within every academic discipline or topic where we need to stop and take stock, consider the future and recognise that some of our cherished ideas must die. We can no longer persevere with the norms we have enjoyed in our research and we must think anew about discarding those which no longer have anything to offer, regenerating those which still have potential and exploring the horizon for new insights which will give us encouragement in the future. It is the history of scientific discovery and is often referred to as a paradigm shift (Kuhn, 1962).

Sustainable Development has been a latent factor in emerging research for a very long time although not always made explicit as such. Since the concept was formalised largely through the concerns about pollution, climate change and non-renewable resources. It has become almost a cliché. After more than 50 years of international focus it has become an umbrella term which encompasses many different things for many different people. The underlying concept of intergenerational justice (not penalising future generations by what we do today) permeates all discussion. However this important notion can give rise to everything from making people happy to conserving the planet to planning resilience to disaster and much more. This creates difficulties in establishing a vocabulary for communication of ideas and determining where to focus attention in research and application. Each focus has different ideas and different processes and often their own language. The temptation is to retreat into reductionism and, by so doing, ignore the dependencies between the complex variables which go to make up a sustainable environment. While we focus on climate change we may miss the importance of social cohesion. If we focus on energy production we may miss the side effects of other pollutants which are just as dangerous. If we concentrate on crime in a community we may miss the underlying problems of design of buildings which enable people to live together in harmony. If we focus on conservation we may play down the impact on the economy by which we maintain our style of living.

Future Challenges in Evaluating and Managing Sustainable Development in the Built Environment,
First Edition. Edited by Peter S. Brandon, Patrizia Lombardi and Geoffrey Q. Shen.
© 2017 John Wiley & Sons Ltd. Published 2017 by John Wiley & Sons Ltd.

These examples of inter-dependencies are reflected in the way we classify and structure the subject. They are also prevalent in what we measure and how we assess performance. Measurement and assessment enables us, or should enable us, to determine whether we are making progress in the field and also challenges us to make explicit what we mean by sustainable development. We cannot measure if we are not able to define the term explicitly.

This book attempts to shine light on some of these issues within the Built Environment. This admittedly is a subset of the whole subject of sustainability. It is however a significant sector dealing as it does with the quality of life (in accommodation for most human activity), the heavy use of scarce resources (including energy) and the transport and movement of people and goods across the globe. The subject, by its very nature, is concerned with the future and how we should design and shape it. What cities do we want to live in? What relationship do we want between ourselves? How do we want to travel? How do we protect ourselves against future possibilities of failure? What level of comfort do we want to achieve and how will we achieve it? How do we create harmony in all aspects of life? The list is endless but vital to our understanding of how and what we bequeath to future generations.

The book has been divided into three sections, each with experienced and knowledgeable authors who are leading thinkers in that field. The grouping is:

- Section 1 – World Views and Values
- Section 2 – Design and Evaluation Tools and Technology
- Section 3 – Engaging with Practice, Stakeholders and Management.

These groupings are important for a number of reasons. First, the world view helps us identify the lens by which we view the problem. Do we use the economy as the key feature by which we view and evaluate all others or is there something else? It would seem in most Western nations the economy would be the pre-eminent concern but is it right? Second, the growing use of information and other technologies in design is allowing us to communicate effortlessly between each other and promote ideas to much larger groups. Will this allow us to democratise decision making or will it lead to autocratic rule demanded by the controller of the machine? As artificial intelligence begins to make inroads into our decision making, upon whose values and whose world view will it be based? These are not trivial questions but must be addressed if we are to seek a sustainable future. Third, we need to devise methods by which the future thinkers can link with existing practice to create a seamless development so there is not a divide between theory and practice which has been the downfall of so many bright ideas. Here we have included, for example, a case study in Chapter 13 by Trevor Mole which illustrates how a small professional firm is engaging with the subject within its business plan. It is not an academic paper but it demonstrates that the subject can provide competitive advantage.

Some will argue that science is a major factor in understanding sustainable development. One feature of science is that we use the existing paradigm to build our accepted knowledge for as long as it meets the need of the problem it seeks to understand or seeks to solve. There is a natural inclination to give up what we know to move forward into a new way of thinking. John Brockman (Brockman, 2015) edited a book which is entitled

'*This idea must die*'. It contains 165 short essays by a varied group of authors, spelling out what current ideas should be jettisoned within the natural sciences because they are blocking progress. Similarly there may be a requirement for us even at this stage of sustainable development to challenge our current thinking and decide which paths should continue and which should stop!

This book attempts to identify problems caused by existing methods and provide a challenge for the future. Paradoxically it uses active researchers to explain from their own research what these challenges might be and what ideas might be left on the junk heap of discarded imagination.

1.2 Section 1: World views and values

At the heart of any debate about the future is the lens through which we focus and view the whole problem. If we feel that little can be done without ensuring that economic development continues unabated then our prism is the economy. If we think that conservation of all non-renewable resources is key then we will look at preservation as being the key factor, that is, we do not want to leave future generations with an absence of key resources. On the other hand, if we consider that religion is central then we seek out the precepts of a religion and its beliefs and adhere to these at all costs. If we think that science and technology will eventually resolve our problems then that is where we put our effort.

It may be hard to harmonise these broadly and firmly held views (and others) but if we are to seek a global consensus then we shall have to try and seek common ground.

The root of the world view can be seen in its definition of sustainable development. Perhaps the most well known and well used definition is the WCED Brundtland Commission (WCED, 1987) which states the following:

'Sustainable Development is development that meets the needs of the present without compromising the ability of future generations to meet their own needs'.

This definition does not attempt to define the needs of the present or the needs of the future, both of which are difficult to assess. If we cannot define our present needs without compromise then what chance have we of understanding future needs? This definition is often quoted but the real world view it represents is seen in the next paragraph of the report which says:

'In essence sustainable development is a process of change in which exploitation of resources, the direction of investments, the orientation of technical developments and institutional change are all in harmony and enhance current and future potential to meet human needs and aspirations'.

Now we see a shift towards what many people would say would be the predominately Western view of development although it does leave scope for others. It does not talk about sharing or making sacrifices for future generations. It appears to be the sort of statement large global companies would want to make to secure their future. The statement may be right but who has the power to implement and what will be their priorities? It may be that we all have to make sacrifices even for selfish reasons to avoid social conflict but will the people with power really choose this world view? It is an enormous agenda just to find the harmonious common ground.

So what is a world view? At the heart of a discussion on sustainable development must be the very essence of the attitudes and beliefs which influences our thinking. One definition of a world view is as follows:

'A comprehensive view or personal philosophy of human life and the universe' (Collins, 2000)

Others have enlarged upon this definition and Wikipedia has suggested:

'A World View is the fundamental cognitive orientation of an individual or society encompassing the entirety of the individual or society's knowledge and point of view. A World View can include natural philosophy, formative, existential and normative postulates; or themes values and ethics … additionally it refers to the framework of ideas and beliefs forming a global description through which an individual, group or culture watches and interprets the world and interacts with it'.

Probably it is the latter part of the last statement which is most pertinent to this book. In particular it is the way in which we interpret the world and how this interpretation allows us to interact with it which is important. In fact professional knowledge and skill within the design and construction professions is largely based on the way we interpret and act upon our understanding of the built environment.

Leo Apostel (1925–1995) was a Belgium philosopher who was interested in bridging the gap between exact science and the humanities (Anon, 2015). He suggested that a 'world view' is an ontology or a descriptive model of the world and should comprise six elements, namely:

1. An explanation of the world
2. A futurology answering the question 'Where are we heading?'
3. Values, answers to ethical questions such as 'What shall we do?'
4. A praxeology or methodology or theory of action
5. An epistemology or theory of knowledge 'What is true or false?'
6. An aetiology (the study of causation) as it should contain an account of its own building blocks, its origins and construction on which it is based.

These six facets give us an indication of what we should be addressing when we explore and challenge the issues related to Sustainable Development. This book is mainly concerned with item two, futurology examining where we are heading. Since Sustainable Development covers such a wide range of subject matter this is not a trivial matter. It is not surprising, that in general debate, one or more of these characteristics is missing. Andrew Basden in Chapter 19 uses the work of the Dutch philosopher Herman Dooyeweerd to provide a framework for discussion which is outlined by Brandon and

Lombardi (2011). The Dooyeweerd approach to the cosmos (Dooyeweerd, 1955) is gaining momentum and may assist in dealing with the inter-dependencies between various aspects of what make development sustainable.

In this book, John Ratcliffe (Chapter 2) calls on his vast knowledge and experience in considering sustainability futures to examine the changes that are likely to happen to cities. Chrisna du Plessis (Chapter 3) uses her renowned knowledge of examining sustainable development in developing countries to challenge the prevailing views of sustainable development, while Patrizia Lombardi (Chapter 4), through her extensive work on evaluating sustainable development, focuses on the post carbon city and whether resilience has a part to play in future assessments. Finally, Ian Cooper (Chapter 5) reflects on the outcomes of the successful European BEQUEST network – one of the pioneer projects in the field – where he had a key role in analysing the methods by which sustainability in the built environment was evaluated. All these chapters reflect on the persistence of current world views and those which should replace them.

It is unlikely that we will ever get a full and complete World View defined but our explanation and recognition of what World View we are using may help us to understand our limitations and may help us appreciate others. Even within a single world view we find a large number of unintended consequences caused by not taking a holistic view of the problem. For example the Aswan Dam in Egypt, built to stop flooding of the river Nile and to generate hydroelectric power, has also stopped the natural deposition of silt during the annual flood. The farmers now require artificial fertiliser, which leads to pollution of the river as the fertiliser seeps out from the land. One solution provides another problem! If it is a problem within one world view then it is likely to be a greater problem when more than one view is seeking to be harmonised with others.

1.3 Section 2: Design and evaluation tools and technology

The recognition of a world view influences our view of how we should act to realise development of that view in practice. To achieve this we need a series of tools which enable us to act in a sensible and structured way. These tools allow us to communicate and build knowledge as a community. They can vary from paper-based calculations derived from measurements and evaluations, to technical support, all in the form of solutions to various aspects of the physical built environment. These might include innovation in heat storage, passive design for energy reduction, extraction of materials, dealing with pollution and in fact the list could go on forever! Alternatively they might be more abstract issues which deal with qualitative judgements, feelings and emotions which are difficult to assess. Our way of handling this complexity is to build models with different levels of granularity to address different levels of knowledge and hopefully at some time we can bring them together to deal with the interdependence they have upon each other. Gaining harmony among the myriad of models is probably one of the most difficult and challenging things we seek to achieve, as it is in real life. A decision in one area can have repercussions in any number of different areas and in ways which are not always predictable. Nevertheless the way forward must be to strive for models which give us a better picture of the world as we observe it and which can be inter-related.

The introduction of information and communication technologies (ICT) has provided a springboard from which real advances in integration and computation can take place. The limitations of the human mind are gradually being overtaken by the computing power of the machine. We are not yet at a stage where we can realistically claim artificial intelligence is available but the signs are there for massive improvement in the next 50 years. This development raises all sorts of ethical and moral questions regarding the delegation of authority. At what point do we delegate authority to the machine on issues which affect human lives? The truth is that we are already delegating much of human decision making to machines and to some extent we are happy to do so. It is expedient for us because human beings do not have the capability to deal with very large scale problems involving masses of data. At the moment the machine models our thinking once we have given the parameters and inputs it requires. However the modelling process within the machine is largely a model of our own form of reasoning. As time goes on then the machine may well develop its own form of reasoning following the evolution which we have given it in the form of its architecture and software. It will have its own equivalent of DNA and it may be difficult for mere humans to understand what has developed. Booth, the Chief Scientist of IBM, saw the development of software intelligence developing in three stages (Booth, 2007): first, transparency in the development of the model, second, dependence on the machine to write software and then, third, what he called 'the rise of the machine'. His prediction for these stages was three 10-year developments running sequentially.

Already developments are taking place where the machine is required to solve common problems in engineering and design. We cannot design and build the designs created by, say Frank Gehry and others, without the use of the computer. In medicine we are jacking microprocessors into the human brain to compensate for hearing and sight loss. It is not too big a step before we use the machine for enhancement of the brain rather than repair. It may be difficult to know whether it is the human aspect of the brain or the model in the microprocessor which is influencing our decisions. There are serious ethical and moral problems associated with such advancements.

The danger is that it becomes expedient for us to allow the machine to take decisions. If we do not have the means by which we can challenge its decisions or we choose not to worry about such issues then we can find ourselves in a situation where we are reliant on the intelligence of the machine alone. It may be difficult for us to design intelligent machines which are challengeable and they may become 'black boxes' to most people. We are then in the hands of the machine or an elite human population which has power to control both us and the machine. This sounds like science fiction but we are slowly moving to this threshold by default. In the context of sustainable development where we might not be able to understand our current human needs nor those of future generations we are placing human beings in a precarious position. When we create these models we build in the programmers view of what 'values' the machine should hold and we find that other programmers adopt the same routines until one person's values get embedded so deep that we cannot clearly identify the source, let alone challenge the content. In addition values and knowledge need to evolve and change over time and this becomes more difficult as the models are adopted and extended. One postulated solution to this problem is to allow the machine to learn of itself using the routines embedded by humans which by themselves may have built in bias and prejudice. Unfortunately if the machine can change these learning processes on its own then there is likely to be a loss of transparency in the process. How will we be able to democratically change what the machine has determined? Will there still be scope for dialogue?

These are not trivial issues and they are magnified by attempting to use these tools for a subject with so many interdependent variables such as in Sustainable Development. It may be easy to write a program that calculates heat loss. However when we try and look at the reasons why we are concerned about this issue, namely the cost and nature of fossil fuel, then it becomes an extremely complex situation for which most of our current models are ill prepared. The political ramifications, the competitors in the market, the prevailing economic models, the geopolitical alliances, the pollutants in the fuel, the comfort level expected by users, the transport requirements, consideration of the needs of future generations and so on; we can see that we are dealing with a much larger universe of issues, many of which are changing with time and possibly values. Inevitably many of the variables will be qualitative and almost by definition will require human judgement. We then have the problem of which human, or humans, do we model to make these judgements? This is a gross simplification of the problem but it illustrates a few of the difficulties we would face.

This book cannot deal with a problem of this magnitude and the issues raised in Section 2 are more immediate and the models created are heavily constrained. Nevertheless they outline the direction of flow within the research community towards new tools to enable us to be for effective and efficient in our decision making.

Section 2 has a wide variety of chapters by significant authors engaged in the development of tools. Tuba Kocaturk (Chapter 10) addresses the role of design in shaping a sustainable future using ICT through 'digital ecosystems'. Sidney Newton (Chapter 6), Sara Biscaya and Ghassan Aouad (Chapter 7) and Marjan Sarsha et al. (Chapter 11) look at tools that might provide new approaches. Srinith Perera and Michele Victoria (Chapter 8) look at evaluating carbon in sustainable development and Terence Fernando and Marta Alzhami (Chapter 9) examine the tools used in disaster management, an extreme form of instability.

Although computer technology will dominate this area of modelling for many years to come it is not just the architecture, capacity and speed which will have impact. It is also the type of measurement, the source data and the assumptions in such models which will influence our behaviour. This is true even without the computational power of machines. Bentivegna (1997) in his chapter on the *Limitations of Environmental Evaluations* suggests that:

> 'Environmental evaluation is still a controversial question because its theoretical and empirical outcomes do not yet allow generally valid results. Therefore they need to be put into practice cautiously. Moreover, when environmental evaluation is used in decision making within public decision processes, its intrinsic limitations are magnified by its multi-functional task.'

There is evidence that there have been major errors in prediction caused by incorrect assumptions in relatively simple measures. If this is true for simple evaluation it is even more true when the whole of the factors contributing to Sustainable Development are taken into account. The number of variables and the number of permutations coupled with the uncertainty and fuzziness of the data leads to vast potential for error. At the present time there is considerable interest in integrating large data sets and trying to solve big data problems. One specific area is the integration of computer systems throughout a city in order to take a more holistic view of any problem relating to the sustainability of the city and/or the community. The Salford University Thinklab[1] has been using such major data sets for many years in matters such as crime detection and flooding and in social aspects such as employment, health and planning.

The fact that we can put information into a machine and we can model aspects of city structure and life does not mean that we will get a sensible result. The assumptions in the models and structure of the data lead to a combination which can only increase the uncertainty of the results. Nevertheless the process should be evolutionary. Providing appropriate feedback is available, the systems can be modified to improve performance and over a long period of time this process may be enhanced by computer self learning. It may be that we can create an intelligent digital ecosystem as suggested by Tuba Kocaturk in Chapter 10 of this book. In such a system the dependencies between variables must be made explicit and quantified and the modelling of the process of change over time must be modelled too.

At the moment we have a long way to go before we can rely on these systems. We do not have robust models, we do not have a significant understanding of inter-dependence and we do not have the robust feedback mechanisms needed to modify the system as the physical and community systems change. It is a massive multi-disciplinary research agenda. To approach such a task we do need a robust world view structure which will allow all disciplines to contribute, from the humanities and the arts to the engineering and science communities and from the social sciences to the designers of the physical attributes of the built environment. Whichever structure and approach is adopted it must also include a method of challenging the results and understanding its argument otherwise the computer and its models can become an oppressive tool operated by an elite. Some of the early work on knowledge-based systems provided ideas for such a democratic approach (Brandon *et al.*, 1996) but the problems tended to be formulaic and the arguments rudimentary whereas the real world is difficult to define in these terms. The result was useful but too simple for further development.

Section 2 of this book gives some insights into current thinking within members of the research community engaging with these problems. It will be interesting to observe how far these ideas can be taken in the foreseeable future.

1.4 Section 3: Engaging with practice, stakeholders and management

Once our current and future world views have been established and once we have considered how technology can provide the tools by which we can support sustainability it is important that we consider the manner in which we can expedite any change through

---

[1] The Thinklab is a laboratory at Salford University developing the use of ICT in a hitech environment to address the needs of cities and particularly their future sustainability.

practice. If we need to go from one paradigm to another we must be prepared to take our fellow practitioners on the journey. It is often the implementation which slows down the whole process. This implementation inevitably requires communication, education and sometimes regulation and a legal framework for it to be successful. Bright ideas remain hidden because these factors are not addressed within the practice of professional and other interest groups. There is inertia to change which can delay acceptance and implementation for decades and even longer. Even now in the climate change agenda there are still those, expert and non-expert, who refuse to believe that human intervention is the cause of changes in greenhouse gases and must be remedied. Gore (2006) in his book '*An Inconvenient Truth*' addresses a readership of perceived sceptics in an attempt to convince them that we need a shift in our thinking. It is part of the communication and education that needs to prevail to exercise change. Albert Einstein was aware of this in his own domain of physics and drew attention to the fact that we often look for solutions to a problem within those ideas which caused the problem in the first place! Hence the solutions fail. James Lovelock (2000) in his book '*Homage to Gaia*' outlined his struggle to develop a theory that would redefine how we see the Earth and come to terms with what it means to be a responsible 'child' of Earth. It was this struggle which played a major part in establishing the Green Movement which is a significant aspect of sustainable development. These leaders were or are in the vanguard of change and though they would not claim perfection in their thinking they adjust the social attitudes and willingness of peoples to change that which is necessary for a revolution in human thought.

The practitioners then follow with their response to the challenge of the thinkers once the thinkers message is beginning to influence the world. The problem for many small firms is 'how to begin to immerse themselves in the new paradigm'. For many it is a question of timing. Engaging too quickly may mean that the markets (within a Western view of economic activity) may not be receptive to a new idea. On the other hand move too late and your competitors are leaving you behind. To them in it can be a matter of life or death within a commercial environment. In this book Trevor Mole (Chapter 13) explains how his medium sized building surveying firm is tackling the issue in a very pragmatic and practical way. His clientele are open and willing to change and his commercial antenna is such that he knows he has to provide new products and new processes to suit their requirements. This response provides him with a competitive edge.

These practitioners also work within a professional environment, often facilitated by a professional Institution which seeks to set standards and encourage education on sustainability matters. In the Built Environment most of the professional institutions are encouraging various approaches to Sustainable Development. They have limited powers to enforce a view but they have a great opportunity to promulgate new ideas through their education and research activities. They have a major impact on attitudes within their membership to any new paradigm. They have power through the organisations and bodies they support. For example in this book Peter Hibberd (Chapter 16) outlines how the UK Joint Contracts Tribunal have attempted to bring aspects of sustainable development into their Standard Forms of Contract for the Industry. (As Chair of the JCT he has a unique insight into the current thinking on the issue.) It is unlikely that his would have happened if it were not for the groundwork done by the Thinkers and the Educators related to Property and Construction.

Important issues arise when addressing the engagement of practice and these link back to the 'world view' of practice and the tools that are available to them. The delay in implementation of ideas very often arises because the technology that is needed for implementation has not developed or been made available at an economic cost for general acceptance.

Implementation research is a key investment for any idea. Lester Thorow (1971) in his book '*The Zero Sum Society*' suggested that there are three major forms of research and he used the analogy of road building to illustrate the purpose of each. The first he described as 'Scientific Research' where the researcher scours the horizon and explores the terrain to find new ways across the landscape. The second he called 'Engineering Research' where the researcher addresses the problem of 'How to get from where we are to where we want to be; and the third was 'Implementation Research' (although he did not call it by this name) where the researcher finds out whether it is possible to adopt the engineers solution at a reasonable cost and in reasonable time to get a return on the investment. Very often the cost of the implementation research far exceeds the cost of the other two. These three types of research address the why, how and when of progress.

The chapters in the third section of this book embrace the views of those who are attempting to bring sustainable development to the forefront of practice. These include the Institutions such as the Joint Contracts Tribunal (Chapter 16, by Hibberd) and firms such as Property Tectonics (Chapter 13, by Mole) as well as researchers working in combined teams with practitioners. The recognition of identifying our values (Chapter 12, by Shen and Mok; Chapter 14, by Formosa and Miron) is important in this field as we shift from our present view of practice to that of the future. Within practice there is the question of how we integrate sustainable development in urban environments (Chapter 15, by Curwell) and with reference to urban transport systems and infrastructure (Chapter 17, by Yang *et al.*). Permeating all the chapters is the important issue of time and our understanding of the multiple horizons within which we work (Chapter 18, by De Iuliis). Time is critical to our conceptual thinking engaging our world view but is often ignored. We need to address what we mean and over what period when we evaluate sustainable development (Schwartz, 1991; Brand, 1999).

If Sustainable Development is to continue to be an important theme then the relevance to practice is essential and we need to take all stakeholders on the journey!

1.5 Initiative and obsolescence

Having considered the world view that is appropriate to progress, the tools that can enable the view to be realised and the means by which we can make it a reality we then need to address how we identify ideas that are most likely to achieve positive results and those which are no longer pertinent to achieving progress. Neither are easy to achieve. We know there is massive investment in our current models, not only in monetary terms but in education, research and belief systems. If we are to change then the investment must change too and there will almost certainly be inertia to anything that requires these aspects to be challenged. Ideas which have been held for considerable lengths of time will need to be ditched to allow new models to emerge. Some will be embedded in history, in markets, in belief systems and attitudes which may be centuries old. They do not fall easily! It is probably easier to postulate something new than to let go of the old. What ideas are we prepared to let die?

In this book the death of ideas is not made explicit but rather implicit in the discussions which follow in the text. The problem is that most authors will have sought a reductionist approach which allows them to handle a complex problem through a focus on part of sustainability and it is usually a simplification. This is understandable. Virtually all researchers take this approach in order to be able to achieve an output which is accessible to their clientele and acceptable to the research community within the time that is available before their money runs out! However there must come a point when the inter-dependence between models and ideas needs to be addressed as a whole in order to gain the harmony that sustainability demands.

In the author's view and in the context of evaluating sustainable development certain principles should be adopted for examining the models and systems which we might develop to achieve sustainable development. These should be (Brandon and Lombardi, 2011):

- *Holistic:* They should encompass all the key aspects needed to establish Sustainable Development.
- *Harmonious:* They should endeavour to balance or be used to balance the criteria upon which sustainability will be judged and particularly the inter-dependence between all the contributing factors.
- *Habit forming:* They should be a natural tool to all concerned and encourage good habits.
- *Helpful:* They should assist in the process of evaluation and not confuse matters by further complexity or conflict.
- *Hassle-free:* They should be able to be used by a wide range of people, both expert and non-expert (although at different levels) and the results and limitations should be easy to communicate and explain.
- *Hopeful:* They should point towards a possible solution and not leave the user in a state where there appears to be no answer.
- *Human:* They should seek solutions which by their nature assist the development of human beings without pain, suffering and undue anxiety.

Of course it is much easier to say these things and rather more difficult to achieve them. They represent aspirations but nevertheless they provide a check list for any future approach. The first two items in the list are key to addressing sustainable development and the remainder outline the importance of recognising the human and social requirements if such a system is to be adopted and used.

If we relate this to the main sections of the book we can probably say that:

- *World View:* This represents the biggest challenge facing us today. We have made progress in recent years in recognising at an international level the importance of sustainable development in terms of climate change. The Leaders of the world have committed themselves to the reduction of greenhouse gas emissions to avoid global warming. However this is only part of the change in world view that needs to be addressed and there is far less unanimity about all the other issues such as pollution, population control, mutual sacrifice for mutual benefit and a re-prioritisation of values to assist the whole human race. This is not a trivial issue and it will take much political, scientific and sharing of belief before a world view can be established. Present value and belief systems have taken centuries to develop and it would be difficult and optimistic to expect change in much shorter time periods. However the growth in exchange of knowledge and the way in which social media now permeates large parts of the world can give us a realistic expectation of faster change. This informal method of education coupled with formal approaches may well be the best way of changing viewpoints and may be preferable to imposition.

- *ICT Design and Evaluation:* These tools contain within them the power to reveal new discoveries, new ideas and new methodologies. The development in artificial intelligence, providing it is controlled for the benefit of human kind (and we understand what does benefit humans both now and in the future), has the possibility of enhancing our own capability to solve problems. Perhaps the biggest issue we face, at least in seeking harmony, is dealing with the interdependence between events and decision-making. The past has seen us limited by a sharp focus resulting in a myopic view of each sub-problem and a reductionist view resulting in sub-optimisation. If the ICT tools now dealing with Big Data can be harnessed then it may be possible to unite the different perspectives to the same problem from different viewpoints. However it will not deal with the resolution unless a true world view can be developed.

- *Engaging with Practice:* In the shorter term practice and professional judgement must be engaged to assist in the journey to a sustainable future. Those who earn their keep by making judgements now need to act wise to the needs of sustainable development and recognise the implications of their judgements for the longer term. A realistic approach has to be communicated simply and positively. A good example in the past has been the Three Ls concept (Long life, Loose fit, Low energy) put forward by Sir Alex Gordon in a lecture to the RIBA in 1974 which was a useful mantra for architects and building professionals to adopt as they went through the process of designing and creating a new building. However the process of building is a complex social organisation engaging many hundreds of specialists, as well as clients, and they work together in a position of trust. Socially there needs to be good faith and the avoidance of an inequality of knowledge and power to ensure that all move forward together in harmony.

Ceric (2015) quotes Ostrom in her recent book on '*Trust in Construction Projects*' as follows:

'A central question has overshadowed the thinking of social scientists at least since the work of Thomas Hobbes(1588–1679): how do communities of individuals sustain agreements that counteract individual temptations to select short term, hedonistic actions when all parties would be better off if each party selected actions leading to higher group and individual returns? In other words how do groups of individuals gain trust?'

This question could be easily placed at the door of all those concerned with sustainable development. What sacrifices are we prepared to make now in order to ensure that future generations are not disadvantaged leading to social breakdown, poverty and potentially the end of a species (see Rees, 2003). It lies at the root of our understanding of sustainable development. We can develop technology and persuade governments to adopt limited gains but if we are not prepared to look beyond the present and sacrifice where this is required then sustainability is an illusion. To do this then we must develop trust between all participants.

1.6 Final statement

This book is intended to encourage new thinking and new developments as we test the underlying concepts of sustainable development in the built environment. It can only do this if we, as a research and practice community, are prepared to challenge the status quo and engage together in developing new ideas which will encourage us all to work together for mutual benefit. May this book provide a stimulus!

References

Anon (2015) The biography and work of L. Apostel (1925–1995), *Wikipedia* (accessed 11 July 2015).

Brockman, J. (2015) *This Idea Must Die*, Harper Perennial, New York.

Collins (2000) *Collins English Dictionary (21ˢᵗ Century Edition)*, Collins, London.

Brand, S. (1999) *The Clock of the Long Now*, Basic Books, New York.

Brandon, P., Basden, A., Hamilton, I., Stockley, J. (1996) *Expert Systems; The Strategic Planning of Construction Projects*, RICS Publishing, London.

Brandon, P., Lombardi, P. (2011) *Evaluating Sustainability in the Built Environment*, John Wiley & Sons, Ltd/Blackwell, Oxford, UK.

Booth, G. (2007) *Turing Lecture*, Manchester University, Available: http://www.bcs.org/serverphp?show=ConWebDoc 10367 (accessed 11 April 2007).

Bentivegna, V. (1997) Limitations in environmental evaluations. In: *Evaluation of the Built Environment for Sustainability* (eds P.S. Brandon, P. Lombardi, V. Bentivegna), Spon, London, pp. 25–38.

Ceric, A. (2015) *Trust in Construction Projects*, Routledge, London.

Dooyeweerd, H. (1955) *A New Critique of Theoretical Thought*, Prestbyterian and Reformed Publishing Company, Philadelphia.

Gore, A. (2006) *An Inconvenient Truth: The Planetary Emergency of Global Warning and What We Can Do about It*, Rodale, New York.

Kuhn, T.S. (1962) *The Structure of Scientific Revolutions*, University of Chicago Press, Chicago.

Lovelock, J. (2000) *Homage to Gaia*, Souvenir Press, London.

Thorow, L. (1971) *The Zero Sum Society*, Basic Books, New York.

Gordon, A. (1974) *Three Ls Concept – Long Life, Loose Fit, and Low Energy*, RIBA, London.

Rees, M. (2003) *Our Final Century: Will the Human Race Survive the Twenty First Century*, Arrow Books, London.

Schwartz, P. (1991) *The Art of the Long View: Planning for the Future in and Uncertain World*, Doubleday, New York.

WCED (1987) *Our Common Future*, WCED Brundtland Commission, United Nations, New York.

Section 1
World Views and Values

Chapter 2
Cities of Tomorrow: Five Crucibles of Change

John Ratcliffe
The Futures Academy, Taplow, SL6 0GA, UK

'The ideas which are here expressed laboriously are extremely simple and should be obvious. The difficulty lies not in the new ideas, but in escaping from the old ones, which ramify, for those brought up as most of us have been, into every corner of our minds'. (John Maynard Keynes)

2.1 Exordium

2.1.1 The global context

We live at a time of monumental change that includes troubled and turbulent globalisation, mounting quantities of information and regulation, the growing hegemony of science and technology and the discordant clash of civilizations. These changes call for new ways of thinking and learning – at school, by government, in business, within communities and among the professions. There must also be changes in the rules of the game as they affect the economy in general and the built environment in particular.

The spirit of this work is based on the premise that a new mindset, reinforced by fresh ways of thinking about the future, is needed by all those involved in conceiving, designing, funding, constructing, occupying and managing the world's cities of tomorrow so as to face the challenges, and grasp the opportunities, that lie ahead over the new few decades.

At the global scale, there is growing recognition that humankind is on a non-sustainable course which could lead to 'grand-scale catastrophes' (e.g. Lovelock, 2006; Rees, 2003). At the same time, however, we are unlocking formidable new capabilities. This could be humanity's last century, or a century that sets the world on a new course towards a spectacular future. Echoing the warnings of Paul Hawken and Amory and Hunter Lovins (2000) and their promotion of 'natural capitalism' as a fundamental change in the way of doing business, the global economy seems to be outgrowing the capacity of the earth to

Future Challenges in Evaluating and Managing Sustainable Development in the Built Environment,
First Edition. Edited by Peter S. Brandon, Patrizia Lombardi and Geoffrey Q. Shen.
© 2017 John Wiley & Sons Ltd. Published 2017 by John Wiley & Sons Ltd.

support it. We are consuming renewable resources faster that they can regenerate: forests are shrinking, grasslands are deteriorating, water tables are falling, fisheries are collapsing and soils are eroding. On top of this, there is climate change, rising and moving populations, an increasingly polarised world, perverse subsidies by governments, impending energy and water wars, failed nations, shanty cities and false accounting for the GDP measure that ignores natural capital. Throughout, there is also the uncertainty of new technologies more powerful than the sum of their parts. Indeed, it is possible to think that we have become like the sorcerer's apprentice, having started something we can barely control!

2.1.2 The city dilemma

City building has become the ultimate expression of mankind's ingenuity. The twenty-first century, moreover, is set to be the century of cities, for cities are moving centre stage, with both the commercial and cultural world increasingly being characterised by cities rather than by countries. Though the world's cities differ significantly, they should all espouse one particular key ambition – to pursue a path of sustainable urban development – enhancing their quality of life and economic competitiveness while reducing both social exclusion and environmental degradation. Cities of all sizes, locations and conditions face this dilemma – and share the need to develop new processes of policy formulation and decision-making to reconcile their quandary.

Further, as one of humanity's primary predicaments, the accelerating process of urbanization presents multiple pressing problems that are intensely complex, deeply uncertain and latently lasting a generation or more. Failing to understand and address these intricate, ambivalent and enduring dilemmas could result in systemic breakdowns with major consequences for the civic societies concerned. Political policy makers and professional urban planners alike need the structured capability to sense, explore, envision and prepare for how the future may emerge and to use those insights in formulating strategy, plans and operations for the communities they serve. This, of course, is Strategic Urban Foresight.

2.1.3 City planning and futures thinking

City planning and futures studies are both chiefly concerned with the needs and expectations of tomorrow. Each activity deals with ambiguous, multifaceted and contentious issues, for which the outcomes are complex and uncertain. Their common purpose is to provide a 'better future', while avoiding undesirable risks. City planning and futures studies both share ethical dilemmas of representation and manipulation from the way they operate, and the methodological difficulties of balancing a wide range of information, techniques, participants and attitudes. Despite these similarities, the way of thinking about and addressing the future by the city planning profession differs greatly from the one practised by futurists. A 'futures' approach constitutes a much more effective platform for collaborative planning, helping to develop agreed solutions and ensuring that the ownership of those solutions is embedded in the community so that they have a greater chance of successful implementation.

For some time, it has been recognised that the prevailing planning approach towards the future is inadequate and a slow shift towards new ways of thinking and acting about the future of cities has been observed. Various criticisms have been levelled at prevailing planning practice, which include the following:

- Ineffective mechanisms to deal with the complexity and uncertainty of urban environments.
- Widespread short-term orientation of planning.
- Inadequacy of the 'predict and provide' model, which reinforces the present conditions and makes it more difficult to consider alternative future options.
- Lack of a comprehensive integration of physical planning with economic and social development.
- Limited collaboration of stakeholders from different sectors.
- Paucity of real community participation.
- Failure to provide visionary and innovative solutions.
- Being reactive rather than proactive towards the future.

The recognition of these failures of current planning practice has led to a search for and adoption of new and more imaginative future-oriented approaches. Over recent years, The Futures Academy has developed a futures methodology – Prospective Through Scenarios – which aims to integrate futures thinking into city planning. This 'prospective' method employing 'scenario' techniques enables the forward view. That is, it provides interpretative or propositional knowledge about the future, up-dates this regularly, assesses the quality of emerging understandings and uses them for a range of socially useful purposes. Also, it provides a 'map of the future' and supplies policy-makers and others with views, images and alternatives about city futures in order to inform and future-proof decisions in the present. There are a number of reasons why it is important to adopt futures methods into city planning:

- Extending thinking beyond the conventional and fostering more forward thinking as a result.
- Forcing thoughts and stimulating conversations about the future.
- Helping to identify assumptions about the future that might require examination, testing and subsequent modification.
- Encouraging people to have regard to the positive possibilities and opportunities that tomorrow might hold, as well as the potential threats and disasters.
- Making more intelligent decisions today concerning the future by focusing the mind on the most important questions that must be resolved in order to formulate better policy.
- Inspiring people to 'think outside the box'.
- Widening perspectives and increasing the number of options available for exercising more deliberate decision-making towards positive change.
- Preparing for and managing change better by enhancing the capacity to learn.

- Making response times to actual future events much shorter and reactions more relevant.
- Fostering active participation in strategic thinking leading to decision-making.

The adoption of futures methods into city planning offers a rigorous, comprehensive and integrated approach towards urban stewardship, relying more on intuition, participation and adaptability. It also enables the development of preferred visions of urban futures through mobilisation – bringing together and facilitating the networking of key stakeholders and sources of knowledge. What follows is distilled from that approach.

2.1.4 A sense of foresight

Over the past few decades, futures thinking and foresight studies have progressively been employed to inform and influence urban policy. The performance, however, has been extremely patchy and partial. Proselytizers of a 'prospective' process within the public realm of urban affairs are constantly faced in practice by barriers to effective strategic long-term thinking. These include: the dominant focus on electoral, legislative and budgetary cycles; the paucity of political support and poor stakeholder engagement; institutional inertia and compartmentalisation of function and responsibility; and incompatibility of timescales and inadequacy of experience and expertise.

Moreover, whilst the academic 'cognoscenti' of the futures and foresight field produce an extensive theoretical literature on the pros and cons of different methodologies and devise ever more sophisticated refinements to techniques, a sensible and systematic appraisal of workaday approaches, with guidelines as to their application, impacts and effectiveness, remains largely lacking, or at best superficial. But even the most relevant, reliable and robust foresight frameworks, constructed and conducted by experienced consultants, are of little use or significance if the organisational culture and capacity to absorb and apply them is enfeebled. The overriding goal, therefore, is not just an awareness of the potential of futures studies and strategic urban foresight, but the embedding of it in the societal mindset and civic capabilities of the communities engaged.

By far the greatest challenge of all, therefore, is the embedding of futures thinking into the urban agencies, authorities, organisations and communities concerned.

2.2 Disquisition

Contemplating our cities of tomorrow is, of course, a complex affair. It requires drawing on a wide range of information sources, anticipating emerging issues, identifying unintended consequences, involving all concerned and getting a sense of the big picture. Strategic foresight, thus, becomes the pre-eminent methodology for thinking about and planning for the future. Strategic foresight is having a view of what can be done by communities and organisations today to positively influence tomorrow. It is the ability to create and maintain a high-quality, coherent and functional forward view and to use the insights arising in organisationally useful ways. Above all, it is about thinking, debating and shaping the future.

Central to foresight, however, is the concept that trends matter and weak signals count. Setting up a rigorous, systematic and sensitive process for spotting and acting on emerging trends and detecting seemingly unimportant things that could ultimately have profound impacts is a prerequisite for the successful modern municipal organisation. The five 'crucibles of change' that follow have surfaced during the course of the past few years in a succession of strategic urban foresight studies and describe the major forces where stresses and tensions will be greatest. But they also identify where opportunities for innovation and change will arise. Organisations that understand them will be best equipped to anticipate and respond to their own advantage. Others ignore them at their peril.

1. Quality of Life: people, places and profiles.
2. Competitiveness: creativity, knowledge and enterprise.
3. Sustainability: resilience, responsibility and readiness.
4. Connectivity: communications, infrastructure and facilities.
5. Governance: values, vision and leadership.

2.2.1 Quality of life: People, places and profiles

When it comes to 'quality of life' as an 'ideal' for building tomorrows cities, it was Leonard Hobhouse, an Edwardian liberal and radical thinker, who insisted that: 'An ideal is as necessary to the reformer as the established fact is to the conservative'. The ideal, perhaps, is to view the city as a kind of 'liberal republic', in which independent, capable individuals have the power to determine and create their own version of 'a good life' and a 'good society'.

Social cohesion

Successive scenario exercises conducted by The Futures Academy over the past 20 years around built environment futures have identified a recurring 'pivotal uncertainty' that describes the onset of civil strife and the breakdown of law and order in the inner-city as a result of worsening social exclusion and increasing marginalisation among large parts of the local populace. An inventive scare story, perhaps, but so too was the threat of urban terrorism a decade or so ago and, in 'scenario-speak', terrorism has moved from being a 'wildcard', through the 'pivotal uncertainty' stage, then to being a 'significant trend', and finally now forms a 'context shaper' in most scenario exercises. The collapse of established order is most evident in some of the mega-cities of the developing world. Frustrations with poverty and unemployment can, however, breed hopelessness, unfulfilled expectations and boredom in almost any city context, and whole areas can be changed into virtual ghettos with self-reinforcing cycles of deprivation and disorder practically anywhere. Tackling terrorism will seem relatively straightforward compared with controlling the tumult of a city's own citizens.

Social disruption threatens cities economic prosperity and social stability, as well as constituting a personal tragedy for those affected. Exclusion takes many forms: children without real prospects for their future; low educational attainment; isolation; homelessness or inadequate housing; high levels of debt; limited access to transport and essential services, including information and communication services; limited access to police and justice; poor health; and lack of citizens' rights. It also has many secondary symptoms, such as social fragmentation, civil disorder, a growth in racial tension, youth alienation and delinquency, crime and policing problems, drug abuse and mental health problems. All these factors have encouraged the development of segregated cities where certain distressed neighbourhoods have become locked out of wider social and economic development. Such social disorder is a mounting cost to society as a whole and a serious drain on the local as well as national economy.

Exclusion and culture

Detailed studies of social exclusion in localities throughout Europe, reinforced by findings from The Futures Academy, have indicated that the broad processes of such exclusion are roughly similar:

- Stigmatisation of the areas based both on the presence of specific groups within them (minority ethnic groups, migrants and the unemployed) and on the physical signs of neglect;
- Spatial concentration of stigmatised groups, whether through public or private sector housing processes;
- Subtle local social processes, which contained the aspirations and affective focus of everyday life within the neighbourhoods, whether the neighbourhood was in an isolated peripheral position or an enclave within the central urban area;
- The presence of specific groups and conflicts in the neighbourhood which disrupted social relationships within it (mental illness and substance abuse, in particular, generated high levels of fear and anxiety).

To these must surely be added the lawlessness engendered by the drug culture dominating more and more areas of cities. In all the neighbourhoods examined, however, the social bases of conflict were similar: young versus old, minority ethnic versus ethnic nationals, newcomers versus long established residents. Clearly, a new set of pro-active strategies to overcome these divisions is necessary.

Portentously, and perhaps a little pompously, it can be claimed that rediscovering the importance of open and direct dialogue between cultures will be one of mankind's major challenges in the years to come.

Authenticity and distinctiveness

Cities should acknowledge the unique identity they possess, play to their strengths, be authentic, avoid direct copying from others and seek to be best in class at something.

Though distinctiveness is something of an elusive concept, every village, town or city has distinctive assets. There has, however, been widespread debate over the past couple of decades about the apparent process of homogenisation that has happened to towns and cities. The expression 'cloneliness' has been coined to describe how cities have become more and more alike – identical chain shops, similar restaurants and common commercial designs. This reduction in locally owned business can also result in economic weakness as money flows out of an area to distant corporate headquarters and local needs no longer determine decision-making.

While these trends towards homogenisation are troubling, there are growing signs that cities are seeking to be distinctive. They recognise that, by striving for distinctiveness and developing their own unique assets, specialisms and character, they can enhance their profile.

Distinctiveness in itself, however, is not a solution. It must also be authentic, for when an ill-conceived marketing campaign falters, or a 'flash' landmark building fails, the results can actually be counter-productive.

Decent affordable housing

Common to all The Futures Academy city visioning exercises over the years, and familiar to anyone concerned with community planning and development, is the continuing call for decent and affordable housing. It is fundamental to the health and well-being of citizens, and to the smooth functioning of economies; nevertheless, around the world, in developing and advanced economies alike, cities are struggling to meet that basic quality of life requirement. It has been estimated that, if current trends in urbanisation and income growth persist, by 2025 the global affordable housing gap could affect one in three urban dwellers, or about 1.6 billion people (McKinsey Global Institute, 2014). Four actions used in concert could, however, reduce the cost of affordable housing by 20–50% and narrow the gap: unlocking land supply; reducing construction costs; improving operations and maintenance; and lowering financing costs for buyers and developers (McKinsey Global Institute, 2014). Policy makers, working with the private sector and local communities, need to set clear aspirations for housing throughout their cities.

Asset-based community development

A defining influence upon the work of The Futures Academy was a masterclass given in Dublin by John McKnight of Chicago for The Futures Academy on the use of asset-based community development (ABCD) as an approach that seeks to identify and deploy the innate strengths within communities as a means of enhancing the quality of life therein (Kretzman and McKnight, 1993). The process of ABCD starts by assessing the resources of a community through a 'capacity inventory' or, more generally, by exploring with citizens the types of skills and experience that are locally available. Then the communities are supported to discover what they care enough about to act upon. And, finally, individuals, agencies, associations and institutions all come together to determine how everyone can collaborate to achieve the goals set. At the core of ABCD is its focus on social relationships as assets. In this way, not only is it a practical application of the concept of social capital, but it also lends itself to incorporations within a broader process of Strategic Urban Foresight.

2.2.2 Competitiveness: Creativity, knowledge and enterprise

As commonly averred, cities have one crucial resource – their people. Creativity, knowledge and enterprise are fast replacing location and accessibility as the prime determinants of growth. Thus, with the common challenge for cities across the world being 'competitiveness', and the key to competitiveness being entrepreneur-ship, successful cities of the future will be those that engender an environment in which creative and innovative individuals and organisations can gather, grow and thrive.

A creative milieu

There has been an enormous ballyhoo about the notion of 'creative cities' over the past decade or so. Much debate has raged around its various meanings and practical applica-tions in academic and policy circles alike. It is tempting to suggest that we all know what we mean by a 'creative city'; you know one when you see one; and the forces at play in generating a creative milieu are beyond the jurisdiction or judgement of planners, politicians or other property professionals. This, however, would be grudging, glib and gratuitous. Creativity, in all likelihood, is at the core of building tomorrows cities. Conventionally, the 'creative city' is a term increasingly used in various parts of the world to describe an interrelated series of industries and activities, mostly linked to the 'new economy' of information and culture. In some circles, it is also used to describe imagina-tive approaches to continuous planning and problem solving related to a wide range of challenges facing cities today. Key concepts comprise networks that support perpetual learning and innovation, bottom-up development practices, the use of futures think-ing, and attention to the cultural industries and new media as leading forces in urban regeneration.

It can be argued that human cleverness, desires, motivations, imagination and crea-tivity are replacing location, natural resources and market access as urban resources. And that ultimately, it is the creativity of those who live in and run cities that will determine future success. Nevertheless, creativity is not something that can simply be imported into the city on the backs of peripatetic computer hackers, skateboarders, gays and assorted bohemians, but must be developed organically through the com-plex interweaving of relations of production, work and social life in specific urban contexts.

The knowledge village concept

Successor to the 'scenario parks', 'technopoles' and 'digital hubs' of the late twentieth century, a new species of urban cluster is emerging in cities around the world that aims to promote creativity, innovation and knowledge within a high-quality living and working environment. Called the 'knowledge village', such an approach would develop human, social, physical and technological capital to promote specific business sectors (e.g. health, media, bio-nanotechnology, design/arts) through inter-organisational and cross-industry collaboration. It would be based on the creation of a mediated environment, including ambient technologies, digital systems and networked places. Above all, knowledge village development would also seek to optimise the links and activities between industry, business and academe – national, regional and global.

Encouraging the entrepreneur

The future is no longer the preserve of conventional economic theories, traditional management models or ready-made mass ideologies, with all the passivity and lack of personal responsibility these concepts imply. This century, it is argued, will belong to the individual and the achiever, to those capable of exercising their independence, responsibility, professionalism and initiative, whatever their role in government, business, civic affairs, the voluntary sector, industry, or society at large. Fostering and promoting a spirit of enterprise, therefore, becomes an imperative part of this future. All the actors are involved – economic, social, cultural, educational and political – at one level or another. It is not simply a matter of encouraging the spirit of enterprise, but also of creating a framework conducive to project generation and development. Moreover, learning systems in the city as a whole, must concentrate upon 'shaping people' not merely 'spreading knowledge'.

Clusters as catalysts

The popular buzz-word in the field of innovation, specialisation and the city is 'clusters'. The propensity for certain types of economic activity – manufacturing and service alike – to gather together in dense locational clusters appear to have been intensifying in recent decades. This current quest for mutual proximity on the part of all manner of economic agents is mainly a strategic response to heightened economic competition which, in many sectors of the economy, has intensified uncertainty and placed an even higher premium on learning and innovation. Clustering enables firms to respond to these challenges by allowing them greater levels of operational flexibility and by enhancing their innovative capacities.

It should be appreciated, however, that the concept of clusters focuses not so much on the agglomeration of a single industry, but on the externalities across industries. Such externalities, in the form of a range of productive relationships between business, industries, universities, trade associations, services, cultural activities, leisure facilities, local government agencies and other civic institutions, take on great importance in the context of modern city competition. Moreover, a cluster is much more than simply an economic organisation facilitating production efficiency. The essence of a cluster lies just as much in the exchange of insights, knowledge and technology, and in offering a structure that offers the incentives and flexibility to innovate and specialise.

Global infrastructure crisis

Severe underinvestment, a lack of high-level strategic vision and a paucity of robust finance models have all contributed to a crisis in global infrastructure where the world probably invests about half of what it should. A recent backlash against some ill-conceived and poorly operated private finance initiatives (PFIs) and public private partnerships (PPPs) has almost certainly worsened the situation.

Nevertheless, every successful competitive city aspires to deliver high-quality infra-structure. Infrastructure – the physical facilities and supportive systems which engender economic activity – that is well maintained, reliable, safe, resilient and customer friendly. Worldwide, the investment required to close the infrastructure gap is staggering – estimated by the OECD to be in the region of 70 trillion Euros. Addressing the infra-structure crisis, however, is more than just about money. It is about such issues as: policy goals and objectives; trade-offs among resources; asset performance; rehabilitation and replacement strategies; programme delivery; and, of course, finance and funding. Governments around the world, at country and city level, many of which have neglected public infrastructure for decades, now need to plan and invest on an unprecedented scale to provide adequate energy, transportation, water, waste, sanitation and other services for their growing populations.

2.2.3 Sustainable cities: Resilience, responsibility and readiness

The past decade has witnessed an explosion in the literature surrounding sustainability in general and, more particularly, how the process of urbanism in the built environment can meet human needs and ensure city sustainability. This demands new approaches to how we understand, plan, design, build, use and manage our cities. For it has been held that:

> 'Cities are the convenient remedy to the inconvenient truth'.

Rediscover the city

We should start thinking of cities as the solution to the global challenges we face rather than the problem. As the economic drivers of our societies, cities concentrate people, pro-duction, transport and consumption, thereby encapsulating most of these challenges. What do we need to do? First, we need a new mindset to unleash the potential that our cities hold to become drivers of sustainability and replace the outmoded paradigms of the industrial age. Second, we must adopt an holistic approach, understanding that our cities are complex adaptive systems where all the challenges we face are interconnected. And third, we must develop the concept of bringing the city back to nature, creating greater awareness of the need for resource reduction and motivate city users to become more self-sufficient in all they do.

In achieving these aims we need to redefine city value. High quality of life and sus-tainable living are dependent on each other. Urban life must attract residents, tourists, investors, students, companies and cultural events. But this must all be done with social, environmental, and economic sustainability as the overarching set of values. This will require involving everyday experts. Including all city users in the process of city planning is crucial to attaining urban sustainable development. Participatory citizenship must be encouraged, because city users of all kinds are the real experts on city life.

Integrate environmental thinking

Attaining the acme of 'smart growth' has become a watchword for cities around the world; and the way city leaders integrate environmental imperatives into economic decision-making is vital to achieving such smart growth. The optimum approach to environmentally aware growth recognises the costs of degrading the environment and thereby integrates environmental goals into the planning process (e.g. Vancouver, Copenhagen, Singapore). Planning, designing and constructing infrastructure in an environmentally conscious way and using a combination of participation, pricing, regulation and information campaigns to encourage citizens to safeguard resources can help reach such goals (McKinsey, 2013).

Sustainable growth will, therefore, depend upon investment in infrastructure that reduces emissions, waste production and water use; as the way we build and renovate our cities will determine their ecological sustainability for decades to come. Improving existing infrastructure, developing green districts and making the most of scarce land resources by building high-density communities can all help (McKinsey, 2013). Above everything else, however, there is the need to develop future-proofed urban strategies and insist on opportunity for all.

Is 'Transition Engineering' perhaps the way? Conceivably, given the ubiquitous and increasingly equivocal use of the term 'sustainability', it is timely to advance the notion and operation of 'Transition Engineering' (Krumdieck, 2013). The basic idea is that sustainability becomes an element of standard practice in the same way that safety engineering has evolved over the past 100 years. Transition Engineering is proposed as the general practice of changing existing engineering systems to reduce the risks of unsustainable resource use or pollution. The engineering professions, at some point in the future, will take up transition engineering as part of common convention and usage with accompanying discipline-specific methods, techniques and procedures. The history of safety engineering shows that the transition to safety was initiated through conscientious engineering, not through policy leadership or economic signals. Similarly, it is suggested that currently practising engineers can conscientiously begin the project of 'transition' towards reducing unsustainable risks because society values survive and can adapt to change. You do not need to engineer for sustainability, you need to engineer to reduce and eliminate the risks of unsustainability!

Redistribute urban decision-making

Climate change, pollution and carbon emissions are no respecters of geographical or administrative borders. Anything that takes place in one city, country or region inevitably affects its immediate – and sometimes distant – surroundings. It is also important to encourage surrounding communities and hinterlands to supply the food, water, power and other resources necessary to sustain the long-term viability of cities.

No city administration can meet the growing urban challenges on its own. Social, economic and environmental conditions are all interwoven and interdependent through time and across space. Any sustainable city, therefore, needs to employ new decision-making processes to ensure careful coordination and proper attention. This, in turn, requires new administrative frameworks to support urban development at a metropolitan level, covering a wide geographical area. Additionally, better communications between central and local government are needed, as well as a broader commitment towards the objectives of sustainable planning. Any new urban development body must, therefore, also develop and strengthen a city's relations with the surrounding areas through business partnerships, investment consortia, collaborative planning and joint strategy formulation.

Any new metropolitan governance system must ensure local–national co-ordination and bring together decision-making bodies from all sectors, and at all scales, to safeguard different interests and protect long-term viability, but without adding to existing bureaucracy. The competitive advantage of cities will rely more and more on a shared strategy that deals effectively with conflicting interests, whilst building upon a large-scale vision and a capacity for allocating a limited amount of resources in a way that supports the well-being of the public in general.

De-design urban planning

Buildings and urban landscapes are fundamental in the creation of liveable and competitive cities that attract residents, visitors and investments. Yet architecture and design that focuses narrowly on aesthetics and buildings as isolated bodies fall far short of the requirements for sustainable city development. The advent of 'green buildings' has, in part, been a response to this. But much more 'out of the box' thinking is called for to fulfil the full potential of architecture and design in challenging conventional notions about city development.

'De-designing' city planning is about focusing on the people and the environment, and on the processes, rather than on the buildings and the design itself. Sustainable design is fundamentally 'green', but it should also actively encourage and motivate sustainable behaviour. This makes it crucial to reframe the goals and roles of designers and architects.

Thus, the new mission for designers and city planners should be motivating sustainable living. When contemplating a new project, architects and designers must get together with transport planners, politicians, the business community and experts on health, the environment and other fields to integrate the many aspects of living, working, educating and recreating that motivate a sustainable lifestyle. They must learn to take a much wider perspective, aiming for a more citizen-centred design approach and avoiding 'over designing', where design takes priority over human needs. Instead, design should contribute to the humanity of cities, involving citizens and based on their values and needs.

Promote corporate urban responsibility

Cities account for about 80% of all carbon dioxide emissions worldwide. Industrial activities and business life play a large part in this and, thereby, have a critical role in influencing future sustainable city development. As key stakeholders there should be a clear commitment from commerce to a shared vision and action plan addressing city sustainability. This should be based on a new understanding and partnership between public and private sectors, with collaboration and co-operation being the watchwords rather than rules and regulations.

For most companies and industries there is a high level of self-interest in corporate urban responsibility as cities provide the critical mass in terms of workforce for their operations and provide the quality of life through affordable housing, accessible infra-structure and good social, recreational, medical and educational services that are critical to survive global competition. Further, it is a win–win situation in bringing together the interests of a city's business life and public well-being. Private sector commitment to the goal of sustainable development is crucial to the effective implementation of sustainable city planning. But companies in the private sector must feel they are part of the decision-making process concerning future city developments, so that they can also be held to have a shared responsibility for the outcome. The public and private sectors should evolve a joint 'urban code of conduct' with a sustainable, holistic objective.

As part of all this, it is necessary to motivate corporate urban responsibility by constructing a functional framework of green incentives that reflect market demands and build on market mechanisms. For:

> 'If you say "stop polluting", nothing will happen. But if you create a market for sustainable behaviour, businesses will see the potential and then take action' (Chris Steins, Director, Urban Insight, Los Angeles).

To promote such responsibility we need to embrace chaos, crisis and change. Sustainable city development is not only about the long-term prevention of future threats to our urban way of life, such as natural disasters. It is also about ensuring that our cities can deal with the more general consequences of risk and uncertainty. Sudden changes in the world economy, virulent pandemics, technological breakthroughs or new social phenomena might happen at any time, and we need to be able to adapt to these changes immediately. Tackling unpredictability requires long-term strategy as well as short-term flexibility and adaptability.

Sustainable strategies, of course, have to possess flexibility, so city administrative struc-tures need to be organised and prepared for rapid decision-taking and immediate action in crisis situations. Master plans for long-term visions have to be broken down into short-term goals, creating incentives and making the changes evident to the people involved and the outside world. Furthermore, aiming for adaptability we should dispense with the idea that our cities should be 'climate proof' and instead channel thinking and resources into making them 'climate adaptive'. Some climate changes, such as rising water levels and temperatures are unavoidable. Wherever possible, moreover, we need to turn risks into opportunities by learning from the lessons of the past – and the knowledge and experience of others.

In addition, we need new mindsets, new institutional frameworks, new partnerships and new strategies. We also need more highly skilled, courageous and passionate urban leaders to initiate and carry forward the goal of sustainable city development. There has to be a new class of leader across the world's cities who have sustainability at the top of their urban agenda.

2.2.4　Connectivity: Communications, infrastructure and facilities

Arguably, the main message to those responsible for shaping the cities of tomorrow and creating better urban environments is simple – 'Never forget the basics'! Making a city 'clean, green and safe' and 'well connected all round' are the paramount virtues for city leaders, planners, developers and managers alike.

The focus, therefore, should be on well connected cities – in every way. In a global economy, of course, connectivity in terms of communications is of great import as a critical driver of competitiveness: air, high-speed trains and information and communication technology (ICT) interconnectivity are all important. Plugged-in cities are also innovative cities. But not forgetting the words of Aristotle:

> 'A city should be built to give its inhabitants security and happiness'

Smart development

The notion of 'smart development' itself derives from the 'smart growth movement' which, at its core, is defined as being about ensuring that neighbourhoods, towns, cities and regions accommodate growth in ways that are economically sound, environmentally responsible and socially supportive of community liveability. In other words, growth that supports that quality of life.

It was probably the Urban Land Institute (ULI), with whom The Futures Academy extensively collaborated a decade or so ago, which pioneered the concept of smart growth aligned to the doctrine of smart development and, in doing so, identified a set of common features that should shape policy and practice. These can usefully be summarised as follows:

- *Collaborating on Solutions*, establishing a shared approach between developers, environmentalists, civic organisations, public officials and local citizens as to how future growth can best be accommodated.
- *Mixing Land Uses*, so as to achieve several smart growth simultaneously by attracting homeowners of various income levels, providing a range of local employment opportunities and reducing travel needs.
- *Encouraging Brownfield Redevelopment and Infill Development*, which fulfils a prime aim of smart growth by revitalising the neglected part of towns, cities and older neighbourhoods.

- *Building Master-planned Communities*, most usually on Greenfield areas adjacent to the urban fringe, and taking the form of long-term, multi-phased projects that combine a comprehensive mix of land uses and are held together by unifying design and service elements.
- *Conserving Open Spaces*, the value of which is fast being recognised by developers who find that the incorporation of natural features, cycling paths, play areas and additional footpaths makes their schemes more marketable.
- *Providing Transportation Options*, for though the car retains its allure to most occupiers, there is rapidly becoming a growing interest in other choices such as light and heavy rail systems, expanded bus services and bike and pedestrian paths, which all enhance mobility and improve the quality of life.
- *Offering Housing Opportunities*, because the lack of affordable accommodation contributes significantly to the jobs/housing imbalance facing many major towns and cities. This may be due to several factors such as opposition to higher-density development, restricted residential land designation or a desire to attract jobs over homes. Properly planned and designed, however, there is a realisation that mixed income housing schemes can be both attractive and profitable.
- *Lowering Barriers and Providing Incentives* is a key principle of smart growth and development and distinguishes it from traditional growth management policies in that it combines incentives, disincentives and conventional planning techniques to promote a pattern of development that achieves economic; environmental and quality of life objectives.
- *Using High-quality Design Techniques* is also a central component of smart development as it can help alleviate public opposition to new proposals. By employing design techniques such as integrated land uses, mixed housing types, open space protection, and a pedestrian-oriented environment, developers can create new places that are actively supported, rather than opposed, by neighbourhood groups and local authorities.

The smart growth movement, through smart development, has the potential to build stronger towns, sustainable regions and more inclusive communities. It is a movement still in its infancy, but it could help us build the better cities of tomorrow.

Intelligent cities

There are various meanings to the term 'intelligent city', including: the virtual reconstruction of cities; urban development based on ICT; urban environments with embedded ICT; territories that bring innovation systems and ICTs within the same locality; and cities characterised by a high capacity for learning, knowledge creation and innovation. All of these meanings apply according to condition and circumstance. However, it is the concept that is important; and to get a better sense of the concept of the intelligent city it is sometimes helpful to draw an analogy with the natural world, seeing the city as an organism, monitoring its various component systems and responding to potential or actual changes of state in order to maintain equilibrium.

Transit-oriented development

Whilst not new, transit-oriented development (TOD) has come to prominence over the past decade or so as city suburbs seek a solution to their future well-being. Consequently, a renewed interest is being shown worldwide in public transit use and public transit investment; and the realisation is growing that a substantial market exists for a new form of walkable, mixed-use urban development around new rail or other forms of public transport. Such TODs have the potential to provide residents with improved quality of life and reduced household transportation expenses while providing cities, and city regions, with stable mixed-income neighbourhoods that reduce environmental impacts and provide real alternatives to traffic congestion. The hope or hype, however, sometimes exceeds the progress or the promise.

Big data and the digital city

As much as the Internet has already changed the world, it is the Web's next phase that will have the greatest impact upon the future of cities, revolutionising the way we live, work, play and learn. The next phase, which some call the Internet of Things and others the Internet of Everything, is the intelligent connection of people, processes, data and artifacts. Digitally smart cities are seen as those that integrate information communications technology across three or more functional areas to enrich the lives of its citizens. Creative platforms and killer apps have already helped reduce traffic, parking, congestion, energy consumption and crime. They have also generated revenue and lowered costs for city residents and visitors (Chambers and Elfrink, 2014).

The future city, indeed, has been envisaged as comprising constellations of instruments across many scales that are connected through multiple networks which provide continuous data regarding the movements of people and materials and the status of various structures and systems (Batty, 2012). As such, the digitally instrumented city offers the promise of an objectively measured, real-time analysis of urban life and infrastructure.

As digitally enhanced cities become increasingly embedded with all kinds of infrastructure and networks, devices, sensors and activators, so the volume of data produced by them grows exponentially, providing rich streams of information about cities and their citizens. Such big data have been described as: 'varied, fine-grained, indexical, dynamic and relational, enabling real-time analysis of different systems and to interconnect data across systems to provide detailed views of the relationships between data' (Kitchin, 2013). For citizens, such data and subsequent analysis offer insights into city life, aiding everyday living and decision-making as well as empowering alternative visions for future city developments. For governments, big data and integrated analysis and control centres promise more efficient and effective municipal management and civic regulation. And, for corporations, big data analytics present new, long-term business opportunities as key players in city governance (Kitchin, 2013). The next decade will surely witness the reality of the real-time city throughout the world.

2.2.5 Governance: Values, vision and leadership

A new paradigm is emerging – one with a fresh spirit of collaborative, democratic decision-making. Central to this is a shift from 'government' to 'governance'. This concept of governance relates to a new array of arrangements for collaboration and partnership between government organisations, business associations and community groups of various kinds.

The challenges of city governance

Cities across the world are facing a range of challenges. To begin with, there is economic globalisation, economic restructuring, competition between cities and the restructuring of welfare states, all of which basically lie beyond their control. Then there are: the budgetary limitations which have reduced the level of public resources available for urban investment; the processes of administrative decentralisation and regionalisation bringing increased responsibilities for cities; the changing relationships between the public and private sectors in the provision of services and utilities of all kinds; the growing polarisation in incomes, employment quality and job security; the fragmentation of the labour market, the decline in manufacturing and the rise in service sector industries; and the increased pressure from the supra-national bodies for financial convergence and orthodoxy. On top of all this, social and cultural changes are taking place which generate additional demands on city governments to provide better environments and a generally higher quality of life. Governance itself, with all its complexity, uncertainty and changeability, is the key challenge that faces all cities and city regions.

As powers, responsibilities and resources are increasingly devolved downwards to cities, there is currently an indication that certain spheres of governance will move more significantly to the global space. Treaty systems to deal with such global lawlessness as cross-border drug trafficking, cybercrime, hostage taking, financial fraud and corruption will extend their reach. And, at the city level, it is likely that greater collaboration between major cities, non-governmental agencies and global corporations will grow, often usurping the role of nation states.

Central to the notion of governance, however, is the concept of 'social capital', the harnessing of which can be viewed as perhaps the greatest challenge of all. Social capital has increasingly been used to express the capacities available within the wider social context upon which governance activity, business initiative and cultural life can draw. It has become one of the most popular expressions to describe an attitude, approach or model towards governance that reverses traditional notions of the behaviour of institutions.

Values and vision

In exploring and determining a vision for a city it is important to establish the 'values' concerning utility, security, order and beauty that are held by the various communities comprising the citizenry, actual and aspirational, to agree upon an 'identity' for the city capitalising upon its cultural, social, economic, physical and historic strengths and to recognise the need for effective 'branding' of that identity and those values. This will involve defining themes, considering options and setting strategies. It might also include the production of such instruments as charters, declarations or manifestos to act as a rallying point. Landmark events such as major sporting events, international conferences or entertainment festivals can also alter perceptions about a city and showcase its virtues.

It is, of course, for each city to establish its own set of values. The creation of any kind of template contradicts the very purpose.

Voguish though it be, the 'vision thing' is vital. It must, however, be a shared vision, understood and subscribed to by most of the citizenry. All too often, such vision statements are conjured up by politicians or professionals working in relative isolation, or compiled remotely from a lexicon of conceptual whiz-words and phrases pilfered from other exercises conducted elsewhere, then surreptitiously processed through a charade of public consultation. Anyone involved in the formulation of 'mission statements' in the corporate world will know the stratagem. The vision for a city cannot be 'bought off the rack'.

Any urban strategist, with a firm commitment to furthering the cause of sustainable city development, would avow the concepts, methods and techniques to be found in the futures field. Here, such approaches as 'foresighting' and the 'prospective', supported by tried and tested techniques like environmental scanning, strategic conversations, scenario planning and futures workshops, provide a formidable framework and an adjustable set of tools to help communities explore and determine possible and preferred futures.

Visioning processes, drawn from the futures field, represent the main way in which citizens can be involved in the imagination and, less often, the construction of the future. The principle behind such visioning methods is that future images can affect present behaviours, guiding choice and influencing decisions. This approach focuses on 'desirables' and emphasises 'values', giving people the opportunity and the instruments to consider, comprehend and construct those images collectively. It aims, moreover, to examine ways in which those images or visions can be turned into reality. First, by selecting only the most striking and salient images and, then, by framing solid and visible strategies for action.

Doing more with less

It has been argued that successful cities secure all the revenues due to them, explore investment partnerships among a range of other agencies, corporations and institutions across the sectors and make radical and rational organisational changes that promote efficiency in both management structures and the cost of operations. Effective city leaders have also discovered that, if well designed and properly executed, public–private partnerships can be an essential element in sustaining the competitiveness and resilience of their cities, delivering lower-cost, higher-quality infrastructure and services (McKinsey, 2013). To do this, furthermore, successful city leaders must win support for change, building talented and committed teams of civil servants and forging a stake-holder consensus with the local population and business community. There is also a growing trend for alliances to be developed between previously competing cities, regions and agencies in a new collaborative spirit of 'co-opetition'.

City leadership, partnership and empowerment

No evaluation of the visionary process would be complete without mention of 'leaders' and 'leadership'. It is a subject that has spawned a myriad publications over recent years. In essence, however, municipal leadership is all about articulating a vision, harnessing the power of new ideas and mobilising civic energy. The effective civic leader will:

- Search for meaning and know what to do in a situation in which others may be wringing their hands. He or she must be a believer.
- Understand the issues and see the big picture.
- Craft a vision.
- Be a people person, sensitive to the feelings, needs, and wants of others, willing to give credit to others, adept at human relations and ready to validate each and every other person's authenticity.
- Include others in the decision-making process.
- Avoid the acute angle that polarises and mediate among conflicting viewpoints, always searching for ways that produce growth.
- Help others to understand the importance of civility in the art of public life.
- Learn from failure, accept mistakes and take risks, as necessary, to promote creative problem solving.
- Follow through on good ideas and have the courage and persistence to stand one's ground.
- Celebrate and appreciate.

Experience shows that changing the municipal mindset is the greatest challenge of all facing city leaders in achieving good governance.

A global parliament of mayors

In facing the most perilous challenges of our time – climate change, extreme poverty, international crime, civil disorder, adequate shelter, and the discordant clash of cultures – the nation states of the world appear generally dysfunctional and sometimes even paralysed. The past tendency to consider social, economic, environmental, technological and political issues in national terms, however, is giving way to a new paradigm of global governance where the planet might be ruled by cities. Indeed, the very nature of the city encourages local municipalities to view the world in practical terms, in stark contrast to the ideological strife and sovereign rivalry of countries (Katz and Bradley, 2013).

Across the world, hundreds of mayors are already collaborating to build a global network to shift the balance of power and create a new force in urban and regional governance that will transform the cities of tomorrow. Many, more formal organisations are emerging – Metropolis, Global Mayors Foundation, CEOs for Cities, World Cities Summit and The Compact of Mayors – where elected civic leaders share their experiences and aspirations. Moreover, a Global Parliament of Mayors has been proposed (Barber, 2013) and a blueprint for an inaugural pilot prepared for late 2015. Here, it is hoped that, regardless of political affiliation, locally elected leaders can collectively exhibit a non-partisan and pragmatic style of governance that is lacking in national and international halls of power. Echoing the immortal words of former New York mayor Fiorello la Guardia:

'There is no Democratic or Republican way of fixing a sewer.'

2.3 Propositum

Manifestly, there is a mighty global metamorphosis underway around today's cities as they plan and prepare for the prospects of tomorrow. Urban societies across the world are boldly leading change from dead-end 'business as usual' tactics towards transformative strategies that are essential for creating a flourishing and sustainable urban future. There might be a long way to go, but hearteningly the evidence is starting to show that at least the era of denial has ended. What role, therefore, has futures thinking and foresight methodology got to play in forging a better tomorrow?

2.3.1 How should we think and behave?

Getting people to change their minds about things that matter is perhaps the biggest challenge of them all. A global project conducted a few years ago suggested that mindsets in city governance would have to change in the following directions and dimensions (Ratcliffe *et al.*, 2009):

- *Strategically.* The art of the long and wide view needs to be cultivated more assiduously, with a better understanding of the driving forces of change and a clearer vision of the chosen path towards a preferred future.
- *Systematically.* Perhaps the biggest breakthrough in how we comprehend the built environment and guide change, in the organisations that contribute towards its stewardship, is to be gained from systems theory and systems thinking. All participating agencies and disciplines should be better versed.
- *Creatively.* Everyone has creative capacities, but all too often they are stifled or suppressed. As the precursor to innovation, itself the salvation for sustainability, there is a need to develop and exploit the creative capacities across and within city communities and institutions.
- *Responsibly.* As we enter the 'age of sustainability' we also enter the 'age of responsibility' – individually, corporately and collectively. Lapsing for a moment into a somewhat

sentimental family homily, my own mother used to say 'if everyone swept outside their own front door, the whole town would be clean'!

- *Intergenerationally*. A perspective based on the sharing of information, thoughts, feelings, experiences and skills across and between generations can enrich all of us and is, at heart, the central core of civility.

Thinking is one thing – acting is entirely another. With varying emphases between the regions of the world, there was agreement among participants that we would have to nurture altered modes of behaviour in the following spheres:

- *With Values*. Determining the right set of values at every level – individual, group, community, corporation, city, region and global – is at the root of everything, however patent or pretentious it might sound. It came to the fore, sometimes surprisingly so, at all the workshops.
- *With Responsibility*. Repetitious but fundamental, the role that responsible behaviour, especially within the corporate sectors of the built environment, is the active or operational face of establishing values. Rapid change is taking place, superficial at first, but increasingly sincere and significant.
- *With Cross-disciplinarity*. Whether inter-, multi- or trans-disciplinary, the complex nature of built environment issues demands such an approach.
- *With Discretion*. Not just generally exercising more and better judgement as what to build where, but also ensuring greater flexibility and adaptability in planning, design, financing, construction, servicing, management and use.
- *With Foresight*. Following in the footsteps of science and technology, the built environment disciplines and agencies are beginning to develop a capacity for critical thinking concerning long-term developments, to foster debate and decision-making across broader constituencies and to acquire an appreciation of how to shape a preferred future – the capacity of foresighting.

Arguably, there has probably never been a period in human history when strategic foresight has been more needed – whether for cultures, countries, corporations or communities – let alone cities – for these are extraordinary times.

2.3.2 Futures and foresight: hindrance and help

Addressing the challenge posed at the outset of this piece of embedding futures thinking into the outlook for cities, a framework of factors respectively impeding and facilitating the progress of 'prospective' planning has emerged from the scores of projects conducted by The Futures Academy over the past decade or so. These are described very briefly below.

The most common obstacles to the effective generation of a strategic foresight culture can be summarised as follows:

1. Overcoming inherent resistance to change at all levels and across all sectors.
2. Convincing organisations, and their leaders, that long-term thinking is possible, credible and productive.

3. Extracting organisations away from a reliance on facts, forecasts and formalities.
4. Building an understanding of, and confidence in, what futures thinking and the discipline of foresight can accomplish.
5. Getting people to think, act and plan outside their roles and compartments.
6. Encouraging policy-makers to think beyond electoral, budgetary and legislative cycles.
7. Forging a shared vision and basis of trust between stakeholders.
8. Aligning futures and foresight activity with political and planning cycles.
9. Over-elaborating the futures methodology and foresighting techniques.
10. Using the wrong consultants, experts and facilitators – lacking in urban empathy and experience.

In a similar way, the most important ingredients to success in establishing both a philosophy and a practice of prospective thinking and planning can be summarised as follows:

1. Establish a continuous horizon scanning facility.
2. Found a forum where all the stakeholders can meet to think, talk, plan and act – creatively and differently – together.
3. Ensure the commitment of leadership throughout the system. Appreciating that effective leaders are not always the most obvious.
4. Identify 'champions' at different levels across all agencies involved to promote the cause of strategic urban foresight.
5. Invoke feelings of both crisis and opportunity to elicit change.
6. Recognise that different kinds of futures activity work in different circumstances, contexts, timeframes and institutional arrangements.
7. Be seen to deliver competitive advantage to the city and its sectors.
8. Select a few 'quick hits' of successful achievement to sponsor support for a futures approach.
9. Forge an alliance with a local university or business school to develop executive training and other community based programmes in futures studies and strategic urban foresight.
10. Collaborate with 'remarkable' people and 'visionary' agencies.

Quintessentially, however, the embedding of futures thinking in urban policy is predominantly about leadership, as leadership itself is about the future. The critical credo, therefore, for enlightened leadership through strategic foresight, to which we should all aspire, is to:

- Create a civic democracy of ideas.
- Amplify the municipal imagination.
- Dynamically reallocate city resources.
- Aggregate the collective wisdom of communities.
- Minimise the drag of old mental urban models.
- Give everyone the chance to take part.

Remembering, all the while, that no one person knows best in everything and that it is no longer possible to figure it all out from the top. It maybe magniloquent, moreover, but a memorable epilogue suggests that the future of humanity is inextricably bound with the triumph of tomorrows cities, for they must audaciously play a more prominent part in shaping policy across the entire spectrum of governance on both national and international stages. This, most of all, demands 'enlightened leadership' through 'strategic foresight'.

'Cities with imagination and dynamic leadership have the capacity to help solve some of our world's most urgent problems' (George Ferguson, Mayor of Bristol, UK; European Green Capital 2015).

References

Barber, B. (2013) *If Mayors Ruled the World: Dysfunctional Nations, Rising Cities*, Yale University Press, New Haven.

Batty, M. (2012) Smart cities of the future. *European Physical Journal Special Topics* **214**, 481–518.

Chambers, J., Elfrink, W. (2014) *The Future of Cities*, Council on Foreign Relations, Washington, D.C.

Hawken, P., Lovins, A., Lovins, H. (1999) *Natural Capitalism: Creating the Next Industrial Revolution*, Earthscan, London.

Katz, B., Bradley, J. (2013) *The Metropolitan Revolution*, Brookings Institution Press, Washington, D.C.

Kitchin, R. (2013) *The Real-Time City? Big Data and Smart Urbanism*, Smart Urbanism Conference, University of Durham, Durham.

Kretzman, J., McKnight, J. (1993) *Building Communities from the Inside Out*, ACTA Publications, Chicago.

Krumdieck, S. (2013) Transition engineering: planning and building the sustainable world. *The Futurist*, July/August.

Lovelock, J. (2006) *The Revenge of Gaia: Why the Earth Is Fighting Back – and How We Can Still Save Humanity*, Allen Lane, London.

McKinsey Global Institute (2013) *How to Make a City Great*, MGI Report. Available at: www. mckinsey.com/~/media/mckinsey/global%20themes/urbanization/how%20to%20make% 20a%20city%20great/how_to_make_a_city_great.ashx (accessed 15 March 2016).

McKinsey Global Institute (2014) *Tackling the World's Affordable Housing Challenge*. MGI Report. Available at: http://www.mckinsey.com/global-themes/urbanization/tackling-the-worlds-affordable-housing-challenge (accessed 15 March 2016).

Ratcliffe, J., O'Brien, G., Brodowitz, D. (2009) *Built Environment Foresight 2030: The Sustainable Development Imperative*, The Futures Academy. Available at: www.thefuturesacademy.co.uk/ sites/default/files/BEF%202030-FINAL.pdf (accessed 15 March 2016).

Rees, M. (2003) *Our Final Century?: Will the Human Race Survive the Twenty-first Century?* Heinemann, London.

Chapter 3
Going Beyond Sustainability: Changing Views, Changing Ways

Chrisna du Plessis

Department of Architecture, University of Pretoria, Pretoria, 0028, South Africa

3.1 Introduction

In 2014 the usually conservative World Bank published a report entitled *Turn Down the Heat: Confronting the New Temperature Normal*. This document warns that 'even with very ambitious mitigation action, warming close to 1.5 °C above pre-industrial levels by mid-century is already locked-in to the Earth's atmospheric system and climate change impacts such as extreme heat events may now be unavoidable'; furthermore, without rapid changes to policy and practice, there is a 40% likelihood that average global temperatures will be at least 4 °C warmer by the end of the century, ending all hope of meeting development goals, something which will already be very difficult with the locked-in warming of 1.5 °C (World Bank, 2014). In the same year the Fifth Assessment Report of the Intergovernmental Panel on Climate Change (IPCC) adjusted the scales for possible changes in average surface temperature for the Arctic regions from a maximum of 7 °C in the Fourth Assessment Report, to a maximum of above 11 °C change in the average for the period 2081–2100 relative to the average temperature in the period 1986–2005 (IPCC, 2014). Add to this the overshoot of several other critical planetary boundaries (Steffen *et al.*, 2015) and the possible effects of feedback as result of these changes on the global social-ecological system, and humankind is facing a frightening future.

It is becoming clear that 50 years of chasing the sustainable development goals of reducing negative environmental impacts, without obstructing accepted patterns of technological and economic development, have failed. While there has been tremendous advancement in the development of tools and technologies to reduce environmental impact, resulting in a booming 'green' economy, the fact is that these tools have not been particularly effective in slowing down the by now inevitable crash of the global ecosystem, let alone save the world from the effects of a rapidly deteriorating environment. There is a growing realisation that, despite large gains in technological innovation and

Future Challenges in Evaluating and Managing Sustainable Development in the Built Environment,
First Edition. Edited by Peter S. Brandon, Patrizia Lombardi and Geoffrey Q. Shen.
© 2017 John Wiley & Sons Ltd. Published 2017 by John Wiley & Sons Ltd.

policy and regulatory development, these efforts are too little too late and we are by no means reducing the negative impacts of consumption-based industrialised human development in any meaningful way. The sustainable development project has largely failed.

The Triple Bottom Line model of People, Planet and Profit used to shape sustainability strategies does little more than allowing politicians and big business to play facetious and disingenuous number games with indicators and targets, many of which are set somewhat arbitrarily through political horse-trading and tightly bounded cost–benefit analyses, instead of real systemic and scientific understanding. For example, the 2 °C limit to global warming agreed to during COP21 in Paris will have devastating consequences for human well-being and the global economy (World Bank, 2014), but is considered the only politically acceptable target. And in the confusing smoke and mirrors game of international development, climate change denial, political posturing, big business agendas and competing civil society interests it is easy to lose sight of the fact that the world we want (as decided at Rio + 20 and described in the Sustainable Development Goals) is not possible in the world we are creating.

The sad truth is that the world we are creating holds little possibility of a peaceful, equitable and thriving future; and we need to come to terms with the fact that everything we know about the ecosystems we depend on, and therefore the world that is possible to us, is already changing in ways we cannot predict. To quote Winston Churchill (1936): 'we have passed the time of procrastination and baffling delays … we are now in the period of consequences'. It is becoming clear that 'sustainability' is not enough. The standard responses of mitigation, efficiency and reducing negative impacts are nothing but a gradual application of the brakes to a juggernaut already on the edge of the cliff, while what is required is a radical alteration of course. To deal with the consequences of our current social and economic development models we will need to go beyond sustainability. Buckminster Fuller famously claimed that one cannot change things by fighting an existing reality; instead one should create an alternative model that makes the existing reality obsolete. Therefore, instead of trying to be less bad, perhaps we need to focus not only on how human activities can respond and adapt to these consequences, but can have a positive impact and help to heal and regenerate the world. This chapter explores what this would require.

3.2 What lies beyond sustainability?

Reed (2007) describes an evolutionary trajectory of environmentally responsible design that moves from fragmentary approaches (high performance, green) that reduce negative impact, to a whole systems approach that aims to build the evolutionary potential of the whole system (integrating ecological and social systems) and its capability to regenerate and co-evolve through healthy and mutually beneficial relationships. He sees these levels of the trajectory not as mutually exclusive, but rather as nested – thus increasing efficiency and reducing negative impacts are fundamental conditions of creating a built environment with a net positive impact – with sustainability as a neutral position, the baseline of what needs to be achieved to maintain the health of the planet's living systems and their ability to continue supporting human life. He argues that sustainability is the point of equilibrium that divides a degenerative system from a regenerative system. When sustainability is seen as a transition point, instead of a goal to be achieved, it introduces a game-shifting change of perspective, allowing us to construct a narrative we can use to orchestrate a systemic shift. This narrative uses a very simple device – that of a threshold or boundary line with one set of conditions below the line and another above the line, with the threshold representing a step change in thinking brought about by a shift in worldview, as described in Figure 3.1.

Below the line we find the status quo of a degenerating global social–ecological system. The environmental conditions discussed above are but one symptom; similar symptoms can be seen in the struggling global economy, in the multiple refugee crises and in the growing political and religious intolerance resulting in an increasingly fearful and exploitative world. Escaping this downward spiral is becoming increasingly difficult as the various forces at play introduce feedback loops that strengthen the downward direction. The Syrian refugee crisis is a good illustration of how the interactions between factors such as climate change, a global economic recession and religious fundamentalism can destabilise an entire region, causing ripples across the globe.

The dominant narratives below the line are that of survival, scarcity, competition and fear. At the root of these narratives lies a worldview characterised by division – divisions between organic and inorganic systems, mind and matter, the individual and the community, and humans and nature. It furthermore sees the world as the sum of autonomous parts following predictable paths and causal relationships which are to be studied and developed independently and manipulated to serve human purposes; and when it deals with systems, it tends to use simpler levels of systems thinking appropriate to mechanical systems. This view of reality is referred to as the mechanistic worldview (Capra, 1997; Rees, 1999) and, while it has been tremendously successful in revealing the workings of the observable aspects of the universe and has allowed tremendous

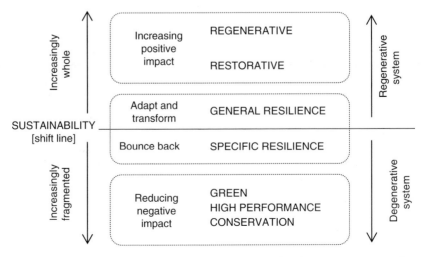

Figure 3.1   Shifting from degenerative to regenerative development. Source: Adapted from Reed, B. 2007. Reproduced with permission of Taylor and Francis group.

technological advances, it is also at the heart of the current global environmental and socio-economic crises.

Largely a product of this worldview, the mainstream sustainability discourse is stuck in a reductionist, steady-state model of the world in which the needs of people and planet are seen as competing with each other in a space defined by a largely neo-liberal capitalist economic system based on resource exploitation, represented by the third 'p' of profit and prosperity. In this view, the economy is considered an autonomous entity feeding on human and natural 'resources', instead of as the processes of exchange determined by the relationships between the various actors and components of the global social–ecological system. Strategies and initiatives, such as green assessment or rating systems, and policy instruments, such as the Sustainable Development Goals, perpetuate the divisions and competition in the system. This view of sustainability therefore maintains the Enlightenment habit of reducing a complex system to its individual components, and in the process it misses the interdependencies in the system that keeps it healthy and flourishing.

Spanning the threshold is the concept of resilience. Whereas the focus of sustainability is on increasing efficiency and effectiveness, reducing negative impacts and balancing competing demands, the resilience discourse acknowledges that large scale system change is now inevitable and that we best prepare for it so as to maintain the functional integrity of the global social–ecological system. The below the line resilience approach is to focus on the efficiency and optimisation of one aspect of the system so that it can absorb specific short-term perturbations or 'pulse disturbances', such as an environmental or social disaster, and bounce back to its original condition. This is referred to as specific resilience (Walker and Salt, 2006) and it exhibits the focus on the parts of the system and maintaining equilibrium that is characteristic of below the line thinking.

While developing specific resilience is critical to maintaining the function of physical or social infrastructure in a city, overall sustainability can only be achieved through the development of general resilience. This aims to build the adaptive capacity of the system as a whole by increasing the options available to the system to maintain its functional integrity during both fast (pulse) and slow (or press) disturbances or to transform the system, changing the way it functions and increasing its capacity to function under different conditions (Walker and Salt, 2006). This may mean deliberately moving the system into a different regime so as to release the inherent potential that has been trapped through the perverse resilience of higher-level systems such as the economy, political regimes or technological infrastructure biases. The goal no longer is merely to live within our means, but to ensure we develop the capacity for adaptation in all our systems, even if that means the transformation of these systems or their replacement with entirely new systems. This is the first step towards moving above the line to create a regenerative system.

Above the line, the questions are not how to reduce negative impact or adapt to the inevitable radical changes coming, although both of these aspects remain important. The questions asked are: first, how do we regenerate our social–ecological systems so that life can flourish in them; and second, how do we contribute to making a positive impact – not just doing less harm, but doing more good? The regenerative development discourse is concerned with healing fractured systems, bringing about new life and new ways of being. Instead of trying to slow down or bowing to the inevitable, its aim is to fix the current mess and replace it with a healthy and abundant world in which all living beings can thrive. It aims to heal some of the divisions created by the Enlightenment: the division between individual and community, between humans and the community of life and between the interior and exterior dimensions of existence.

Regenerative development is characterised by whole systems thinking – an understanding that the world is an interconnected and interdependent living system created through a complex and adaptive web of flows and relationships between all the various entities that make up the structure of the system. This way of thinking is rooted in what has been termed the ecological or whole systems worldview (Lazlo, 1987; Goldsmith, 1988; Capra, 1997; Elgin and Le Drew, 1997).

There are three key aspects to the ecological worldview (Du Plessis, 2009). The first is the recognition of wholeness. This worldview describes a fundamentally unified world consisting of multiple interdependent conditions of being, nested in levels of increasing complexity and consciousness in which everyone and everything is interconnected at scales ranging from local to global, sub-atomic to cosmic. This understanding of an interconnected, interdependent and integrated (whole) world reveals the non-duality of self and non-self, with that which is traditionally seen as separate from the self instead seen as an extension of the self. In other words, the individual is not separate from its environment. The second aspect is the importance of relationship as creative principle. This living world is co-created and co-evolves through interactive processes between biotic and abiotic agents at many scales within and between levels of existence. The third aspect is the acceptance of the world as constantly changing, inherently unpredictable and ultimately impermanent.

The implication of an interconnected and interdependent world is that humankind can no longer see itself as separate from nature, instead we are nature – our atoms, our cells, even our thoughts and emotions are inextricably woven into the fabric of the cosmos. What we see as our bodies and our artefacts are but merely knots in the flows of exchange that creates the world. From here, one can argue that, if we are part of nature, we are subject to its laws and we are participating in and co-evolving through its processes. This encourages and allows transformative practices of co-creation and regeneration, which not only opens up new strategies for living and being that works with the flows and processes of nature, but also fosters a value system of interdependence, responsibility and resilience to guide these strategies. At a practical level, this translates into a necessary transformation of both practice and practitioner – a changing worldview also changing the way in which we create a built environment that can have a positive impact and help heal and regenerate the world. The next sections in this chapter will explore these transformations in more detail.

3.3 Changing views: Transforming story, transforming thought

To change the way we do things, we need first to change the way we think about what we do and why we do it. This requires that we change the narratives which guide decision-making and structure the paradigms of business, technology and economy. The power of narrative as an agent of change is a recurring motif in the discourse of regenerative development. Charles Eisenstein argues that the power of working with changing narratives allows both the disruption of the old by opening up the flaws and inconsistencies of the current story and the presentation of a vision of a new and irresistible future (Eisenstein, 2013). Thomas Berry proposes that 'we are in trouble just now because we do not have a good story' – our old story about how the world works and how we fit into it is no longer working and we need to develop a new story (Berry, 1990). The ecological worldview represents a different set of narratives about how the world works and our place and purpose in it. Shifting from the mechanistic worldview to the ecological worldview brings about changes in key themes of our development narrative that will allow us also to shift from a degenerative narrative to a regenerative narrative.

3.3.1 Shifting from negative to positive

The first critical change in our thinking is to shift from negative to positive narratives. The sustainability discourse is steeped in negative narratives: limited resources, a deteriorating environment, inequitable socio-economic structures and the destructive nature of humankind. While these narratives are supported by empirical evidence, they not only disempower, but engage the primitive fight, flight or freeze response, resulting in behaviours which exacerbate the problems experienced. Reframing the narratives to express hope instead of fear disengages the reptilian brain and engages the problem-solving powers of the pre-frontal cortex. For example, by reframing the question of how to deal with resource scarcity to how do we generate abundance, the fear of scarcity and how this will impact on our personal survival is diminished, which allows us to open up to collaborative and mutually supportive solutions which would not be possible in a world of aggressive competition for limited resources where it is each man for himself. However, the most important positive change in our narrative is that humans can be a force for good – that we can play a positive role in the development, regeneration and evolution of the global social–ecological system.

3.3.2 Change is to be embraced, not feared

The second necessary shift in our thinking is to accept that change is the essence of life, that life continues to evolve and that disruptive change is the essence of evolution. The systems of which we are part are in constant flux: cells in our bodies die to be replaced by others, economies go boom and bust, religions grow and disappear, civilisations rise and fall, rivers change their course, sea levels rise and fall as climatic conditions change, mountains arise and are eroded, continents shift and collide, stars are born and die. Whenever there is a change, there is the opportunity for that which is dysfunctional or no longer appropriate or effective, to be replaced by something different and hopefully better. The metaphor of the Adaptive Cycle proposes that systems follow a cycle of change that goes through phases of rapid growth, conservation, release and reorganization (Holling and Gunderson, 2002). During the conservation phase the system becomes more regulated and efficient and new ways of doing becomes difficult as potential gets tied up in existing structures. The very rigidity of the system makes it more vulnerable to external shocks and internal pressures which can trigger a collapse. Such a system collapse can allow the rebuilding of the system in a different way with new operating rules, new structures and new dynamics.

Working from a regenerative paradigm, system collapses are embraced as a means of breaking open dysfunctional, but highly resilient systems that perpetuate a degenerative system, and replacing these with systems that are regenerative in nature. The twenty-first century will see a number of disruptive changes in ecosystem functions which may lead to the collapse of social structures such as local and even global economic systems. While these will come at no small hardship, as cities like Detroit and Greensburg are illustrating, disaster can bring opportunity for reinvention that can move the social–ecological system away from degenerative system states, introducing practices and structures that can bring new life and support a positive developmental pathway.

3.3.3 Rethinking the meaning of development

The third important narrative change is in our interpretation of development. Current narratives equate development with notions of material progress in technology, standards of living and levels of education – all measured according to very narrow standards originating in the industrialising societies of Western Europe and North America with their Enlightenment heritage of rationalism, humanism and the scientific method. The widespread encouragement of these standards negates the importance of other measures of development found in different cultural and social contexts that are more concerned with the development of human well-being through maintaining healthy social and spiritual relationships, such as the Bhutanese Happiness Index. What is necessary is a return from understanding development as progress to the dictionary meaning of development which has to do with unfolding of latent potential into actual mature or complex states – in other words, evolution. This is a process that cannot be measured according to pre-determined targets because it is essentially unpredictable and its outcomes emerge from complex contextual dynamics.

At an individual level, the focus on developing potential shifts personal ambitions from having the most one can get, to being the best human being one can be – a shift that can bring about far-reaching changes in consumption patterns and social behaviours. At larger scales, seeing development as the process of bringing forth potential in local social-ecological systems, without linking this to specific notions of how that potential will manifest in that particular context, allows context-appropriate solutions to emerge that builds the potential of the whole living system. It does, however, require a much deeper engagement with stakeholders than is usual in most planning, development and design practices (Hes and Du Plessis, 2015). In the built environment this different perspective of development also switches the conversation from focusing on the value that is being created for the investor, developer or client, to thinking about what value is being created for the wider system within which the project is situated and how the development can contribute to growing the creative potential within that system so that it can continue to evolve.

3.3.4 Context rules

One of the main pursuits of the Enlightenment has been the discovery of universal truths, of general rules that govern behaviour. This need for generalisation cascaded down into the management tools of checklist-based performance indicators used to assess buildings, people and ecosystems irrespective of their particular characteristics or the contexts within which they operate. This often results in assessment systems which make it easy for companies and developers to follow the letter, but not the spirit of sustainability, by checking technical performance boxes with no consideration of the ethical boundaries being crossed.

Understanding the world as constantly created by a multiplicity of complex contextual dynamics introduces the fourth shift in thinking from clear and definite rules of the binary 'if this, then that' variety, to the more murky 'it depends …' What is regenerative in one context may not work in another, and it may have the opposite effect in a third context. Regenerative development and design initiatives need to work from place: considering the natural and social history of the place, the available potential and the local values. It is about 'seeing how life works in this place, seeing how this community works, seeing how your organisation works and what each is valuing for its own survival and its own ability to thrive' (Joel Glanzberg, pers. comm.). The success of a project or organisation can only be measured in terms of how it responds to the needs and values of its context and how it contributes to the flourishing of life in that context.

3.3.5 Impact is not always negative

Every organism on the planet has an impact – all extract nutrients and water, all release waste products, all take up space and all alter their immediate environment to some extent. To strive for zero impact therefore does not make sense. Whatever we do will require resources, will create waste and will change the shape of our immediate environment. How we do this is what differentiates degenerative processes from regenerative processes. Approaches like biomimicry (Benyus, 2002) and cradle to cradle (McDonough and Braungart, 2002) provide nature-inspired strategies for most of our currently degenerative practices, such as seeing waste as a resource, setting up symbiotic systems of food production or industrial manufacturing, allocating resources to that which supports life, not destroying life and taking only what you need. However, a regenerative paradigm requires more: it requires that more is put back into the system than what was taken out, that the development initiative increases the creative potential and capacity for evolution in the system.

In the built environment this can be achieved through the building project's engagement with site in a way which allows for an increase in biodiversity and strengthening of ecosystem functions such as cleaning and retention of water or climate management. There are already numerous examples around the world of buildings or infrastructure projects which do exactly that, for example the Khoo Teck Puat hospital in Singapore (Kishnani, 2012). The more difficult change in practice is for individual building projects to be considered as part of a larger social–ecological system in which they collaborate with other buildings to create a precinct, a neighbourhood and a city that enhances life and grow potential in both the ecological and social aspects of the system. On a physical level this can include: simple design approaches that blur the boundaries between public and private space such as sensitive street interfaces which provide protection against weather; turning interstitial spaces into pocket parks for rest and connecting to nature or small public squares for social engagement or informal trading; or opening parts of the building to the community after hours. Having a net positive impact requires looking differently at the boundary between the object of building and the system within which it is embedded.

3.3.6 It is not about the building

Interviewing over 50 regenerative design and development practitioners and thinkers, Hes and Du Plessis (2015) found one common theme was paramount: regenerative practice is not about the performance of the object (e.g. building, road, bridge, park), but about how the process of designing and delivering that object acts as a catalyst for change and developing potential. They found examples of building projects leading to larger positive systemic change ranging from a tourist resort in Mexico (Playa Viva) which restored the estuary in which it is situated and created many new economic opportunities for the local community to a supermarket which stimulated a local food production strategy and regenerated the local agricultural economy (Brattleboro Co-op in Vermont), or to a post-disaster reconstruction intervention that changed the values of an entire town (Greensburg in Kansas). The big change in thinking is to not see the building (or other infrastructure object) as something that is fixed and separate, but rather as 'a place where the flows of energy, people, materials, ideas and so forth come together' which allows the practitioner to intervene in that web of dynamics in a way that enables the system to manifests its full potential (Ben Haggard, pers. comm.). For this to be successful though, the way development and design happens, as well as the role of the built environment practitioner, has to change dramatically.

3.4 Changing self: Transforming knowledge into wisdom

What Charles Eisenstein calls the paradox of separation suggests that the world can only change if the majority of the billions of people living on the planet change their behaviour but that, as individuals, their choices make little difference (Eisenstein, 2013). However, the ecological worldview suggests that we are not separate and that change can only happen if individuals start changing. Understanding that we live in a world where there is no real separation between the self (the individual I) and the extended self (that what is not I) and where new system behaviours emerge from the small interactions between individual agents in the system, the necessity of change at an individual level as a catalyst for larger systems change is indisputable. It is therefore no surprise that, within the regenerative discourse, the need for personal development and transformation is seen as a vital component of creating a better world, interweaving personal transformation and the transformation of practice. As Bill Reed (pers. comm.) puts it: 'It's not just about making ourselves better people, it's that the work I want to do in the world is requiring me to face this thorny issue'.

One of the most common themes that emerged from the interviews undertaken by Hes and Du Plessis (2015) was the level of conscious engagement with self necessary to be effective in doing regenerative work. This engagement took many forms ranging from meditative practices to structured reflection on the progress of a project and the practitioner's role in that process; at its core is the development of wisdom.

As Emblemsvåg and Bras (2000) argue, 'modern society is facing a serious dilemma: we are increasing our rational knowledge rapidly, but we are not gaining the wisdom to use it to the best for all mankind'. Modern society places great value on the acquisition of knowledge, but there is a fundamental difference between being knowledgeable and being wise. As Einstein (quoted in Bierly *et al.*, 2000) proposed: 'One can have the clearest and most complete knowledge of what is, and yet not be able to deduct from that what should be the goal of our human aspirations'. Batchelor (2001) suggests that 'wisdom does not refer to an accumulation of knowledge, but to an experiential understanding that enables you to make a radical shift in your perceptions and habits'. This understanding is developed by exploring and integrating different kinds of knowledge to reveal a richer picture of the reality being experienced and then using this knowledge and its consequences for the well-being of the world. Malan and Kriger (cited in Bierly *et al.*, 2000) suggest that wisdom develops from interactions with the environment (experience) which leads to learning and eventually, to wisdom through a self-reflection of these experiences. However, 'wisdom is not merely a result of inquiring and reflecting on the relationship between self and society, but it is also the embodiment of action taken to transform self and society towards a better whole' (Bierly *et al.*, 2000).

Trowbridge (2005), drawing on numerous cross-cultural studies of what people consider as wisdom, identifies a number of qualities inherent in a wise person. These include good judgement, reflectiveness, insight, ability to deal with difficult and complex problems, openness to experience, relativistic thinking, critical thinking, self-knowledge, knowledge of limits, humility, self-control, a broad and deep knowledge and experience, benevolence, empathy, compassion, a concern for the common good, a reduction of self-centredness and increased transpersonal awareness.

There are several aspects to developing these qualities of wisdom necessary to become a regenerative practitioner. The first is to adopt a transdisciplinary approach that acknowledge that there are many ways of knowing and many sources of knowledge, each with its own way of validation, and that all of these are needed to make sense of the world. Knowledge can be derived from many different sources, including: different epistemologies (e.g. rational, empirical, relational); different methods suitable to different dimensions of existence (e.g. observation, reason and contemplation); different kinds of knowledge (e.g. scientific, intuitive, instrumental, ethical); different levels of reality (e.g. quantum, macrophysical, spiritual); subjective sources such as human interior experience; and the wider ecology of mind (Du Plessis, 2009). The wise practitioner draws on all these forms of knowledge to make sense of the context within which he is working and living in order to 'choose and apply the appropriate knowledge in a given situation' (Bierly *et al.*, 2000), resulting in actions which will support the ability of the whole to thrive and evolve.

The second aspect is to make time for reflection. Reflective practices allow us to connect with both the self and the extended self, developing and deepening our transpersonal awareness. Reflection cultivates awareness of our own inner states and how these influence our actions and responses to the social and environmental dynamics that shape our outer states and our relationship with the extended self. It prompts us to test our actions against our values to make sure that we continue to act with integrity. And it allows us to stand back and consider the changing environment and how a course of action should be adapted in response to new knowledge and changes. Reflective practices also enable the third aspect of developing wisdom: to be vulnerable to the world. Qualities such as empathy, compassion and a concern for the common good can only be developed by opening the self to the world, including being honest about own agendas of ego and self-interest.

The fourth aspect of developing wisdom is to not shy away from the mental effort involved in dealing with complex systems and situations and the challenges of a new way of working in a world that is very different from the below the line world. Modern society, with its very short attention span and pressure on quick delivery and increasing productivity, encourages not only lazy thinking, but also an almost pathological need to avoid thinking. There is no time for deep thinking about a problem, its systemic causes and the consequences of suggested solutions; no time for deep stakeholder engagement to come to solutions that add value to the broader system and allow its potential to be developed; no time to appreciate the nuances and complexities that enrich our physical, intellectual and spiritual engagement with self and the extended self. Thinking is replaced by superficial guidelines, checklists and bulleted strategies that reduce the need to think, treating every problem as essentially the same irrespective of its context. The result is inappropriate, even destructive, development 'interventions' and an a-contextual built environment that provides little connection to the spirit of place and contributes even less to the health and well-being of the systems within which it is situated.

Working on these four aspects encourages the healing of the divisions between individual and community, between humans and the community of life and between the body and soul or the interior and exterior dimensions of existence that is necessary to heal and regenerate the world. When combined with the changed narratives discussed above, it encourages a number of changes in the practices of design and development.

3.5 Changing ways: Transforming practice

Working from an ecological worldview with the objective of enabling the living system within which one is working to increase its health, manifest more potential and continue to evolve, requires game-changing shifts in practice, which in turn require changes in the roles and relationships of the built environment professions and in how these professions are educated.

3.5.1 From consultation and collaboration to co-creation

Integrated design and delivery (IDD) and building information management systems (BIM) are becoming commonplace in high-performance building and require increasing levels of collaboration between members of the professional team throughout the design and construction process. However, regenerative development and design requires a different level of collaboration that is about developing reciprocal relationships to maintain and grow the health and potential of the larger system, and co-creating a shared vision of what the full potential of the system could be and how the project can contribute to achieving this vision. This means: first, a change on who is called on to collaborate; and second, the purpose and process of collaboration change. Developing design solutions that would grow the potential of the system means including the community and the natural systems of the place itself as partners in the design process (Hes and Du Plessis, 2015). Ensuring that this collaboration is effective would require the inclusion of other sources of knowledge and creativity in the design and development process. Ecologists, botanists, hydrologists and geologists become more than the passive providers of site reports, actively participating in developing design solutions that would build on the potential of the place and enrich the system. Sociologists, anthropologists and even psychologists assist in developing deeper project briefs and more meaningful processes of engagement with the community. Engaging with indigenous sources of knowledge and history of place ensures that solutions evolve from the potential of place.

The scope of collaboration depends on the scale of the project, with projects involving neighbourhood or precinct development requiring a different level and process of collaboration than a building. However, there are four things all projects need to consider in designing their collaboration process. The first is that the project is a system that exists at but one level of a set of nested systems. For example, a building sits within a precinct, which sits within a neighbourhood in a city. Its development and design process should include collaboration with other buildings in the precinct to see how it can contribute to the precinct's ability to provide conditions in which all its inhabitants can thrive, as well as considering its contribution to large system scales (e.g. feeding into the energy grid), which requires collaboration with role players sitting at higher levels of the system. Second, the goal of collaboration is to co-create a vision of what this place can be if it reaches its full potential. This is an on-going and iterative process which starts during the development of the project brief and continues after the professional team departs; and it provides a sense of ownership and fellowship amongst participants that will support an enduring product and continual co-creation and evolution in response to changing circumstances. Third, it is worthwhile creating platforms that will invite those voices that are frequently excluded (e.g. children, the elderly, the homeless, informal traders), as these bring different perspectives that can lead to novel and innovative solutions from which new potential can emerge (Hes and Du Plessis, 2015). Collaborative processes structured in a way that supports these requirements and outcomes also require a change in the role of the development or design consultant.

3.5.2 Changing role of the practitioner

A co-creative development and design process fundamentally changes the role of the design consultant. The first change is the shift from an expert-driven design culture to a co-creative design culture in which 'the design consultant becomes a matchmaker, mediator and facilitator of the dialogue between all parties, including the ecological systems of the place' (Hes and Du Plessis, 2015) in order to develop a brief based on shared values and not just practical requirements. The second change in the role of the consultant is to that of storyteller and vision-holder responsible for identifying the narratives that shape the place, presenting these to the participants in a way that allows them to situate their own narratives within this larger narrative, and guiding them to developing a different narrative for a better future. Third, the regenerative practitioner is responsible for mentoring the stakeholder team, leading them into an ecological worldview, helping them to develop not just new mental models, but 'a new mind' (Mang and Reed, 2012). These changes in practice requires not just the conscious engagement with self as discussed above, but also real change in how practitioners are educated.

3.5.3 Changing education for a regenerative built environment

Educating the regenerative built environment practitioners of the future means more than teaching them about resource efficiency, community engagement and site analysis, although these remain important tools. What is needed is a transformational approach to education that will develop a new relational worldview to replace the mechanistic one that has created an unsustainable and degenerative development model. It requires the development of a range of skills such as ecological and community literacy, commons thinking, [complex] systems thinking and futures thinking (Stibbe, 2009) and the development of what Paul Murray (2010) calls the sustainable self. This includes the adoption of reflective practices to manage emotional well-being and cultivate self-awareness, developing a personal value system that aligns with the ecological worldview (Du Plessis, 2013), and developing the ability to think about the self in relationship to the extended self.

The second major change required is to shift from disciplinary to transdisciplinary education. As discussed above, regenerative design and development requires the participation of a number of disciplines that are not traditionally seen as built environment disciplines in the development of the project brief, in its design and in its implementation and continued operation. It is not practical to expect of the design practitioner to have all of the skills that would lead to a meaningful engagement with site and community and allow the level of innovation required. Instead, it is necessary to develop collaborative educational strategies between built environment and other disciplines that would allow students to develop the skills necessary to function as members of a team that can facilitate the kind of projects that would shift us from a degenerative world to a regenerative one.

3.6 Conclusions

This chapter set out to explore how we can change the meta-narrative of sustainability from a focus on the negative, divisive narratives of a degenerative system to a focus on the positive, co-creative narratives of a regenerative system by going beyond sustainability. It is suggested that this approach allows us to shift the conversation to developing a vision of an alternate future in which our social-ecological systems are regenerated so that life can flourish in them, with humans making a positive impact, contributing to developing, growing and evolving the potential in the system. The proposed regenerative development discourse is concerned with healing fractured systems, bringing about new life and new ways of being that not only fix the current mess we have made of the global social-ecological system, but also replace it with a healthy and abundant world in which all living beings can thrive. To be able to do this, it is necessary to shift to an ecological worldview that heals the divisions between self and extended self, between humans and nature and between mind, matter and spirit. This encourages and allows transformative practices of co-creation and regeneration, which not only open up new strategies for living and being that works with the flows and processes of nature, but also foster a value system of interdependence, responsibility and resilience to guide these strategies. At a practical level, this translates into a necessary transformation of both practice and practitioner – a changing worldview also changing the way in which we create a built environment that can have a positive impact and help heal and regenerate the world.

Changing the meta-narrative, that is the worldview guiding actions and values, also changes a number of key narratives:

- Humans have the potential to be a force of good.
- Disruptive changes in the system represent an opportunity for introducing new structures and ways of doing.
- Development is not about progress, but about the continuous unfolding of potential.
- There are no universal guidelines and indicators for regenerative design and development – these have to emerge from contextual dynamics and respond to ecological worldview values.
- Impact is not always negative.
- Built environment practice is not about delivering an object, but about facilitating the object's potential as catalyst for wider systemic change.

These changes in worldview and narratives further call for different ways of engaging with the problems of built environment practice, requiring: more meaningful processes of collaboration and changes in the role of the practitioner; increased transdisicplinary work in both practice and education; development of a range of non-traditional skills; and conscious self-development of the practitioner. The challenge for the future is to develop the processes, tools and pedagogies that will enable and support this evolution towards regenerative built environment practice that engages with the development of the world from a place of wisdom.

Acknowledgements

The financial assistance (Grant no. 78649) of the National Research Foundation (NRF) of South Africa toward research is hereby acknowledged. Opinions expressed and conclusions arrived at are those of the authors and cannot necessarily be attributed to the NRF.

References

Batchelor, M. (2001) *Meditation for Life*. Frances Lincoln, London.

Benyus, J.M. (2002) *Biomimicry: Innovation Inspired by Nature*, 3rd edn. HarperCollins Perennial, New York.

Berry, T. (1990) *The Dream of the Earth*. Sierra Club Books, San Francisco.

Bierly, P.E. Kessler, E.H., Christensen, E.W. (2000) Organized learning, knowledge and wisdom. *Journal of Organizational Change Management* **13**(6), 595–619.

Capra, F. (1997) *The Web of Life*. Flamingo, London.

Churchill, W.S. (1936) *The Locust Years*. Speech to the House of Commons, 12 November. Available at: http://www.churchill-society-london.org.uk/Locusts.html (accessed on 12 November 2015).

Du Plessis, C. (2009) *An approach to studying urban sustainability from within an ecological worldview*. PhD thesis, University of Salford, Salford.

Du Plessis, C. (2013) Using the long lever of value change. In: *Motivating Change: Sustainable Design and Behaviour in the Built Environment* (eds R. Crocker, S. Lehmann). Routledge Earthscan, Oxford, pp. 92–108.

Emblemsvåg, J, Bras, B. (2000) Process thinking – a new paradigm for science and engineering. *Futures* **32**, 635–654.

Eisenstein, C. (2013) *The More Beautiful World our Hearts Know is Possible*. North Atlantic Books, Berkeley.

Elgin, D., Le Drew, C. (1997) *Global Consciousness Change: Indicators of an Emerging Paradigm*. Millennium Project, San Francisco.

Goldsmith, E. (1988) The way: an ecological worldview. *The Ecologist* **18**(4/5). Available at: http://www.edwardgoldsmith.com/page138.html (accessed 29 Jan 2008).

Hes, D., Du Plessis, C. (2015) *Designing for Hope: Pathways to Regenerative Sustainability*. Earthscan/Routledge, New York.

Holling, C.S., Gunderson, L.H. (2002) Resilience and adaptive cycles. In: *Panarchy. Understanding Transformations in Human and Natural Systems* (eds L.H. Gunderson, C.S. Holling). Island Press, Washington, D.C., pp. 25–62.

IPCC (2014) *Climate Change 2014 Synthesis Report: Summary for Policy Makers*. Intergovernmental Panel on Climate Change, Geneva.

Kishnani, N. (2012) *Greening Asia. Emerging Principles for Sustainable Architecture*. BCI Asia, Singapore.

Lazlo, E. (1987) *Evolution: The Grand Synthesis*. Shambala, Boston.

Mang, P., Reed, B. (2012) Designing from place: a regenerative framework and methodology. *Building Research and Information* **40**(1), 23–38.

McDonough, W., Braungart, M. (2002) *Cradle to Cradle*. North Point Press, New York.

Murray, P. (2011) *The Sustainable Self: a Personal Approach to Sustainability Education*. Earthscan, London.

Reed, B. (2007) Shifting from "sustainability" to regeneration. *Building Research and Information* **35**(6), 674–680.

Rees, W.E. (1999). Achieving sustainability: Reform or transformation? In: *The Earthscan Reader in Sustainable Cities* (ed. D. Satterthwaite). Earthscan, London, pp. 25–52.

Steffen, W., Richardson, K., Rockström, J., *et al.* (2015) Planetary boundaries: guiding human development on a changing planet. *Science* **347**, 6219; *doi: 10.1126/science.1259855.*

Stibbe, A. (ed.) (2009) *The Handbook of Sustainability Literacy: Skills for a Changing World*. Green Books, Dartington.

Trowbridge, R.H. (2005) *The Scientific Approach of Wisdom*. PhD thesis, Union Institute and University, Cincinnati.

Walker, B.H., Salt, D. (2006) *Resilience Thinking. Sustaining Ecosystems and People in a Changing World*. Island Press, Washington, D.C.

World Bank (2014) *Turn Down the Heat: Confronting the New Climate Normal*. World Bank, Washington, D.C.

Chapter 4

Transition Towards a Post Carbon City – Does Resilience Matter?

Patrizia Lombardi and Giulia Sonetti
Interuniversity Department of Regional and Urban Studies and Planning, Politecnico di Torino, Torino, 10125, Italy

'May you live in interesting times' (Chinese curse)

4.1 Introduction

Current reports on the state of the world and the levels of consumption show that very little progress has been done in the field of sustainable development in cities (UNEP, 2012; IPCC, 2014). Currently, cities consume 75% of natural resources and about 67–76% of energy. In Europe, the finding is even more important (IEA, 2008). Moreover, considering energy vulnerability, the availability and price of energy is particularly crucial for cities which totally import their primary energy. Furthermore, cities are responsible for the majority of the world's greenhouse gas (GHG) emissions (71–76%).

Although sustainable development and climate change have been debated for more than three decades, a consensus is still far away (Adams, 2006). The debate has certainly stimulated carbon reduction policies, leading to a relative decoupling in some industries; but these again were offset by ever continuing growth. Both in terms of availability of renewable resources and in terms of the environmental impacts of our consumption and production, we are pushing beyond the limits, leading to acceleration of extinction rates, ocean acidification, loss of clean potable water and so on (Rockström *et al.*, 2009; Loorbach, 2014).

According to a number of scholars (Adams, 2006; Krumdieck, 2013; Loorbach; 2014) in the climate debate, originating from the 1970s, sustainability has become an element of 'standard practice' and therefore has become part of the problem. In particular, Loorbach (2014), points out that we have developed dominant societal regimes based upon (past) problem solving through central (government) planning and control, based on cheap fossil resources and linear modes of innovation. These regimes, on the

Future Challenges in Evaluating and Managing Sustainable Development in the Built Environment,
First Edition. Edited by Peter S. Brandon, Patrizia Lombardi and Geoffrey Q. Shen.
© 2017 John Wiley & Sons Ltd. Published 2017 by John Wiley & Sons Ltd.

foundations of modernity, are dependent on sustaining an unsustainable status quo – he called them a 'problem–industrial complex' – and, therefore, are systemically unsustainable in a fundamental way.

The Post Carbon City (PCC) has recently emerged as a concept as it emphasises the process of transformation, a shift in paradigm, which is necessary in order to respond to the multiple challenges of climate change, ecosystem degradation, social equity and economic pressures.

Energy and climate are essential issues, at the same time as a long-term target (reduction of GHG) and short-term requirements (resilience with regards to oil price rises and supply disruption). Cities are here understood not only as local authorities but as complex, adaptive, social–ecological systems, including a local ecosystem of inhabitants, companies, public utilities and local governments.

According to the EU POCACITO project (2013) – *POst CArbon CIties of TOmorrow* – 'foresight for sustainable pathways towards liveable, affordable and prospering cities in a world context' (SSH.2013.7.1-1), the concept of the 'post carbon city' implies a paradigm shift about the relationships between energy, climate change and city. Post carbon cities must reach a massive reduction of GHG emissions by a factor in 2050 of four compared to 1990, a near self-sufficiency in carbon fossil fuels – oil, gas, coal – and develop the capacity to adapt to climate change. This implies the establishment of new types of cities that are zero-carbon as well as environmentally, socially and economically sustainable (EU Pocacito project, 2013).

The 'capacity of an urban system to absorb disturbance and reorganise while undergoing change so as to still retain essentially the same function, structure, identity, and feedbacks' is named urban resilience (Walker *et al.* 2004). This chapter argues that this concept of urban resilience should be appropriately applied to the study of this transition toward PCC since it derives from the observation that a given ecosystem may exist in multiple stable states, as systems evolve and adapt through time. It also enquiries about the key role of the human factor – that is the ability of stakeholders – in the adaptive capacity of urban systems to improve resilience (Folke *et al.*, 2005).

Methods in this study used literature reviews and case studies analysis taken from the MILESECURE-2050 (Multidimensional Impact of the Low-carbon European Strategy on Energy Security, and Socio-Economic Dimension up to 2050 Perspective) (2012) project of the European Union. This collaborative research has revealed that policy-makers may be ignoring the human factor in energy transition to the detriment of rapid and significant change across Europe. This implies significantly less emphasis on technology and on top-down planning and more emphasis on the enabling of both individuals and social groups to articulate themselves and participate in the energy transformation.

This chapter is organised as follows. The next section focuses on the relations between cities and climate change and introduces the concept of post carbon city. Section 4.3 discusses the concept of sustainable development and current approaches to achieve it in cities. It argues that resilient thinking approaches are more appropriate than current efficiency approaches for dealing with transitions toward post carbon city. Finally, it presents a number of case studies derived from an analysis developed by MILESECURE-2050. Section 4.4 provides final remarks and further developments of this study.

4.2 Cities and climate change

In industrialised, emerging and middle economies, cities are bearing a considerable responsibility in sustainable development and climate change. On one hand, population growth creates pressure on: urban economic system (financing of infrastructures, financing of public services), social system (health impacts, air pollution and noise pollution; employment; social integration and quality of life); environment (resource consumption, especially energy and land use). On the other hand, urban areas are exposed and vulnerable to climate change. Indeed, they can be struck by direct impacts of climate change: global warming, change in precipitation patterns, higher frequency and intensity of extreme events (heat waves, floods, droughts, etc.) or sea rise. These expected risks are extremely likely to increase, and will be borne by local authorities which will have to face their cost (ESPON, 2010) and to adapt to them.

In addition, cities are becoming the focal point of climate change mitigation strategies because they are able to respond to disturbances in their external environments in addition to internal environments (Evans 2008).

This is made clear in Figure 4.1 where it can be seen that the city plays a very significant role at the interface between policy and enabling action. While we need to act in each layer of the triangle, a useful focus for sustainable development in the first instant could well be the city and its environs. This would combine policy with action and is likely to have the greatest impact.

Cities, not only as local authorities but also as a local ecosystem of inhabitants, companies, public utilities and local governments, are today recognised at the international level for their key role in the fight against climate change. As pointed out by

Figure 4.1 Who does own the problem? The key role of the city (Source: Brandon and Lombardi, 2011).

Vidalenc *et al.* (2014), cities are recognised to play a key role in delivering sustainable development in the context of the built environment, as follows:

- Cities play an institutional role on land and urban planning through regulation, which allows setting up a long term vision on what they will look like in the future.
- Cities can make use of their economic and financial power, by differentiating taxation with reference to land use may for giving incentives to change behaviours (e.g. alleviating urban sprawl, promoting energy retrofitting of buildings and/or energy savings, etc.).
- Cities are able to organise urban metabolism through public transportation and local mobility management, or make coherent and sustainable choices thanks to their competence in social housing, urban heating and natural hazard protection.
- Cities can implement technological solutions at a wider scale. As an example, in energy systems, electric vehicle deployment requires some new infrastructures that cannot be developed without a strong commitment from local authorities. Clearly, the private sector influences many of the above triggers.

Drawing support from associations or active networks such as Local Governments for Sustainability in the 1990s, Climate Alliance and Energy Cities, some cities voluntarily became involved in climate plans, energy-transition experiments, eco-district projects and, more recently, 'resilient cities' (Emelianoff and Mor, 2013). Some of these initiatives and experiments have become symbolic, but the movement has far higher aspirations

The Covenant of Mayors for sustainable local energy was launched in 2008, under the leadership of the European Commission (2012). It requires signatory cities to submit, within one year, an energy action plan for reducing its CO_2 emissions by at least 20% by 2020.

Recently, a new conceptualisation of the post carbon city has emerged which recognises the ability of cities to act and react to climate change (Evans, 2008; Chatterton, 2013).

According to Gruenig and Livingston (2015), cities are political powers and, in the continued absence of a global climate agreement, the ability of cities will be of critical importance in transforming the global energy regime by breaking the carbon cartel and establishing the way toward a post carbon tomorrow. Examples can be found in: Frankfurt am Main (Germany), Lisbon (Portugal), São Paulo (Brazil), Nice (France), Guangzhou (China), Houston (Texas, USA).

The post carbon builds upon issues beyond GHG emissions, energy conservation and climate change, adding a broader set of concerns including economic justice, behaviour change, wellbeing, mutualism, land ownership, the role of capital and the state and self management (EU Pocacito project, 2013). Post carbon cities are committed to reach the targets posed by the European Commission in 2011, launching the Energy Roadmap – *Roadmap for moving to a competitive low-carbon economy in 2050* (European Commission, 2011). This involves a cut in the EU greenhouse emissions by 80% by 2050 (compared with 1990 levels) entirely through measures taken within Europe. To achieve this, intermediate GHG cuts of 25% by 2020, 40% by 2030 and 60% by 2040 would be needed. This implies the establishment of new types of cities that are *low carbon* as well as environmentally, socially and economically sustainable.

According to the European Commission (2011), '*In a low-carbon society we will live and work in low-energy, low-emission buildings with intelligent heating and cooling systems. We will drive electric and hybrid cars and live in cleaner cities with less air pollution and better public transport*'. This could be achieved through European Union legislation, relevant subsidies and investment strategies which aim to contrast a multitude of issues which range from climate change to the expected depletion of fossil fuels, from issues of energy poverty to security of energy supply and from highly volatile energy prices to the new energy-related geopolitical realities (Pearson *et al.*, 2014).

According to MILESECURE-2050 (2012), the low carbon society have to be considered as a process by nature that it is not the mere result of intentional actions but the product of the interaction of multiple intended and unintended elements, partly attributable to operational level but, in part, directly attributable to the cognitive level (i.e. representational, such as cultural factors and stereotypes) and to pre-cognitive processes (i.e. non-representational factors, such as emotions and affects) in an all-defining complex of 'societal processes' (see Figure 4.2).

More specifically, the MILESECURE-2050 project aimed to understand and overcome the political, economic and behavioural trends that led Europe to its difficulties in reducing fossil fuel consumption and in diversifying its energy balance at rates which guarantee European energy security in the next years, reduce the threat of climate change and diminish the risk of an energy gap in the coming decades. In doing so, the

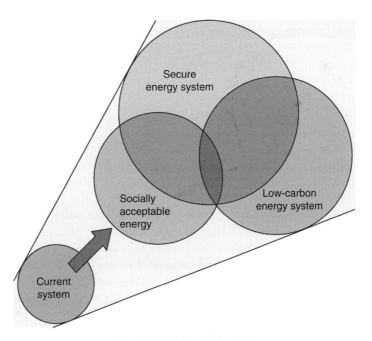

Figure 4.2   Societal process (MILESECURE-2050, 2012).

study has assumed a number of methodological concepts from the transition management theory, the path dependency theory and the vision of creative destruction developed by Schumpeter (1994). Such theories are relevant to examine transitional societal processes based on technological changes and how these changes impact the transitional processes.

In particular, the process towards a post carbon city is the aggregation of a number of underlying transitions and incremental processes of experimentation, break-through, institutionalisation, behavioural and cultural change. These processes are mainly driven, in our Western democracies, by distributed control, renewable resources and systemic innovation. Loorbach (2014) says that it is a 'socio-economic revolution', representing a 'fundamental power shift away from powerful elites controlling resources, money and power towards diverse and distributed forms of collaboration between professionals and citizens'. It is made up by a growing number of both citizens and professionals as individuals that increasingly decide to develop an alternative currency, produce their own energy, get their food from the farm, collectively organise care and set up a collective pension fund. The MILESECURE-2050 research project has identified and analysed a large number of case studies and experiences incorporating the basic features of a more complex transition to environmentally sustainable ways of producing, consuming, and distributing energy, as illustrated in the next Section 4.3 below.

4.3 Approaches to sustainable development

Since Rachel Carson's '*Silent Spring*' in 1962 and the Club of Rome report (Meadows *et al.*, 1972), the environmental concerns about the impacts of our economies have increasingly grown, helping to clean up industries and to create public awareness. However, current reports on the state of the world and levels of consumption show that very little progress has been done in the field of sustainable development in cities (IPCC, 2014).

The International Union for Conservation of Nature (Adams, 2006) identifies some of the possible reasons as the elasticity of the concept, the 'three pillars' model implying falsely that trade-offs are always possible between the different dimensions, and the problem of metrics as a result of the desire to set targets and measure progress. There are numerous other reasons cited by critics – weak political will, conflict between the growth imperative and the notion of limits on consumption, failure to communicate the reality and urgency of the problem, individual self-interest and so on.

According to Adams (2006) and Loorbach (2014), there is a profound paradox here. On the one hand, the twenty-first century is widely heralded as the era of sustainability, with a rainbow alliance of government, civil society and business devising novel strategies for increasing human welfare within planetary limits. On the other hand, the evidence (IPCC, 2014; UNEP, 2012) is that the global human enterprise rapidly becoming *less* sustainable and not more.

There is no agreed way of defining the extent to which sustainability is being achieved in any policy programme. Sustainability and sustainable development are effectively ethical concepts, expressing desirable outcomes from economic and social decisions. The term 'sustainable' is therefore applied loosely to policies to express this aspiration, or to imply that the policy choice is 'greener than it might otherwise be' (e.g. the idea of a 'sustainable road building programme'). Everywhere the needs of achieving sustainable development are ignored in practical decisions. Often sustainable development ends up being development as usual, with a brief embarrassed genuflection towards the desirability of sustainability. The important matter of principle therefore becomes a victim of the desire to set targets and measure progress.

Analysts agree that one reason for the widespread acceptance of the idea of sustainable development is precisely this looseness (Adams, 2006; Drexhage and Murphy, 2010). The concept can be used to cover very divergent ideas; currently in fact environmentalists, governments, economic and political planners and business people use 'sustainability' or 'sustainable development' to express sometimes very diverse visions of how economy and environment should be managed. 'The Brundtland definition was neat but inexact. The concept is holistic, attractive, elastic but imprecise. The idea of sustainable development may bring people together but it does not necessarily help them to agree goals. In implying everything sustainable development arguably ends up meaning nothing (Adams, 2006).

The conventional understanding of sustainable development, based on the 'three pillars' model, is flawed because it implies that trade-offs can always be made between environmental, social and economic dimensions of sustainability. However, in practice, development decisions by governments, businesses and other actors do allow trade-offs and put greatest emphasis on the economy above other dimensions of sustainability. This is a major reason why the environment continues to be degraded and development does not achieve desirable equity goals.

The three 'pillars' cannot be treated as equivalents. First, the economy is an institution that emerges from society: these are in many ways the same, the one a mechanism or set of rules created by society to mediate the exchange of economic goods or value. The environment is different, since it is not created by society. Thinking about trade-offs rarely acknowledges this. Second, the environment underpins both society and economy. The resources available on earth and the solar system effectively present a finite limit on human activity. Effective limits are often much more specific and framing, in that the capacity of the biosphere to absorb pollutants, provide resources and services is clearly limited in space and time. In many areas (e.g. warm shallow coastal waters adjacent to industrialised regions) that capacity is close to its limits (Adams, 2006).

An alternative view is proposed by Hart (2002) and later by Brandon and Lombardi (2005). As represented in Figure 4.3, the dimensions are nested – economy within society and both economy and society within the environment. This approach nests the sustainable development dimensions as three concentric circles – economy within society and both economy and society within the environment. In fact, economics is a part of, only exists within and was invented by, the human realm. Thus, it is appropriately positioned within the society dimension. This recognises that a city, or an urban system is a socio-ecological system, allowing to take better decisions based on appropriate understanding of the trade-offs between elements.

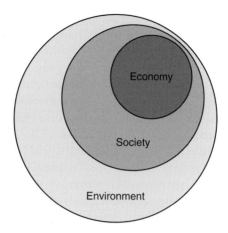

Figure 4.3   Model of Sustainable development (Hart, 2002).

According to this view, the following assumptions can be made:

- Socio-ecological systems are linked: one impacts upon another and society is depending on the environment.
- Socio-ecological systems are complex adaptive systems.
- There is no certainty of determined outcomes and the behaviour in the long term is unpredictable.
- Expertise can help in putting attention to observable thresholds, but it is not sufficient to infer the cause–effect relation.

The above assumptions are clearly in contrast or, at least, in contradiction with current business strategy with regard to sustainability. This is dominated by an eco-efficiency approach, defined as the 'increasing of productive output while using fewer resources' (Schmidheiny, 1992). The result is almost universally seen as advantageous to both the economy and the environment, as well as encouraging sustainability. From a strategic business perspective, the eco-efficiency approach allows measurable objectives that are consistent with a continuous improvement philosophy or quality-focused management culture; eco-efficiency is therefore convenient within the frames of current theory and magnitudes of business economics.

Despite all the benefits of eco-efficiency, we have now realised that these improvements can bring price reductions that in turn may provoke increased consumption. Talking about environmental sustainability, this is the well known 'rebound effect', that is the phenomenon by which improved efficiency on an intensive (or per product) basis creates new demands for products that adversely impact the environment on an extensive basis (total consumption; Lombardi and Trossero, 2013). From a broader systems perspective, eco-efficiency may have counter-intuitive effects regarding longterm sustainability (Alcott, 2005), reducing flexibility, increasing externalisation and losing spare capacity, in a word, decreasing resilience.

Resilience can be defined as the adaptive capacity of urban systems: the 'capacity of an urban system to absorb disturbance and reorganise while undergoing change so as to still retain essentially the same function, structure, identity, and feedbacks' (Walker *et al.* 2004). It is the ability of stakeholders – that is, the human actors – to improve its resilience (Berkes and Jolly, 2002; Berkes *et al.* 2002, Folke *et al.* 2002, 2005, 2010; ; Foxon *et al.*, 2009) to fluctuating environmental and socio-economic pressures, such as long-term changes in urban resident demographics, city and rural migration patterns and potential city health concerns.

Resilience thinking involves exploring interacting hierarchies of nested systems: higher-level systems are driven by slow variables and lower-level systems are driven by fast-changing variables.

Currently, most urban resilience research focuses on the societal capacity to respond and adapt to natural disaster events. These processes, oriented around maintaining security and stability, are most often viewed from a short-term engineering resilience perspective, referring to the time needed for a system to return to a stable equilibrium state. However, there is an increasing interest in exploring how to incorporate approaches around longer-term systemic transformation (incorporating risk mitigation within the recovery processes).

The main criticism of the engineering 'bouncing back' perspective relates to the probability that old and unsustainable urban patterns will be maintained. The need to return to a stable state prevails over possible transformation and a long-term view, which sustainable development requires. A generalised example of a hidden 'lock-in' (mainstreaming old patterns of consumption) is the dependency on energy consumption and its consolidation through installing air conditioning when adapting buildings to increasing temperatures.

According to the different possible long-term scenarios related to any short-term decision, building resilience in social–ecological systems never fully removes vulnerabilities, but it can alter the configuration of system resources and capacities, which implies a shift in the space and time of system vulnerabilities.

The new resilience-thinking approach may make some processes poor in terms of eco-efficiency, but supportive of a systemic and wide sustainability overview (Korhonen and Seager, 2008), since resilience, for social–ecological systems, is then related to: (i) the magnitude of shock that the system can absorb and remain within a given state; (ii) the degree to which the system is capable of self-organisation; and (iii) the degree to which the system can build capacity for learning and adaptation. Management can destroy or build resilience, depending on how the social–ecological system organises itself in response to management actions (Ernstson *et al.*, 2010). Thus resilience, for social–ecological systems, can be defined as the capacity of a system to cope with change, either through persistence, adaptation or transformation.

The study of the transition towards future production and consumption systems that involve not only a more efficient usage resources but also a resilience building among communities requires the presence of innovative case studies. In Europe there are a number of case studies representing 'anticipatory experiences of energy transition' (AEs). These are about 1500 cases (but 90 have been deeply analysed by the MILESECURE-2050 project (Lombardi and Gruenig, 2016) which have developed environmentally sustainable ways of producing, consuming and transporting energy.

Such experiences have been understood as already existing 'parts' of a future post carbon society allowing to focus on concrete factual elements and not mere hypotheses. Examples can be found in:

- Eva-Lanxmeer, a social–ecological district of 24 ha that has been built on a former farmland surrounding a protected drinking water extraction area;
- Vitoria-Gasteiz (Spain), providing an integrated model to regulate traffic, access and urban space organisation through the definition of so-called superblocks;
- Copenhagen's Green Structure Plan named the Five Finger Plan, to control urban development and to ensure that people are always able to access to open space, parks and undeveloped, natural areas on a regional scale.

AEs have incorporated the basic features of a more complex transition to an environmentally sustainable society and that anticipate the basic features of a broader and more complex transition to environmentally sustainable ways of producing, consuming and distributing energy. Their anticipatory character may be assimilated to their ability, at the present time, to take decisions and develop practical solutions to resolve issues related to the future (Lombardi and Gruenig, 2016; Lombardi, 2015).

The main result of the analysis of AEs is that energy transition does not seem to present itself as a gradual change. In fact, it does not take the form of the mere penetration into society of new greener and efficient technologies (technological drive); nor it is 'merely' the introduction of new rules or restrictions that citizens must accept (normative drive or consent drive); neither it consists only in new attitudes toward consumption (and savings) to be interiorised by the population (ethical or lifestyle drive). Each of the above drives is present in the experiences considered, but all three are based on a vision of change in which both the social and the anthropological/individual dimensions are relegated to a function of 'acceptance' of measures and decisions that come from the outside.

Although these visions of energy transition recognise the importance of social and anthropological impacts and feedback, they tend to consider the human factor as a mere receptor, not an agent of change. Therefore, what is actually lacking is the perspective of human agency, as a constitutive element of the transformation of the energy systems.

In short, the human factor becomes the driver of energy transition in at least three distinct levels:

1. The set-up of energy production and consumption becomes more visible and closer to citizens. In this framework we witness citizens gaining ownership of the means of energy production, the spread of new technical skills, the activation of social networks for the installation and maintenance of low-carbon technologies.
2. The energy issue becomes a direct interest of citizens who actively participate in the regulation, orientation, management (also in economic terms) and monitoring of measures and policies of energy transition.
3. There is a strong personal effort on the energy transition through an intense emotional involvement; a highest attention to several aspects of everyday life (food, waste

collection, energy consumption, body care and health); an increased use of physical effort in the field of mobility (but not only), that is through the use of bicycles or with an increased inclination to move on foot or by public transport.

4.4 Concluding remarks

This chapter has argued that a paradigm shift is necessary in order to progress toward sustainable development in cities. This is related to urban resilience defined as 'capacity of an urban system to absorb disturbance and reorganise while undergoing change so as to still retain essentially the same function, structure, identity, and feedbacks' (Walker *et al.* 2004). The resilience approach is critical to build redundancy into a certain interpretative model, as it comes with the classical adaptive cycle, encouraging a look at the whole figure (reorganisation, conservation, release, exploitation) of the system.

In this perspective, urbanisation could be seen as a way of human life following climate stabilisation/permanent agriculture/permanent settlement, scaling-up the manipulation of nature, rather than coping with its dynamic challenges. The rapid technology advancement made humans incredibly adapting, but here comes the paradox of urban resilience: cities have been designed to remove or minimise environmental disturbances (see Alberti and Marzluff, 2004). The benefits of urban inhabitants and cities derive from ecosystem processes including, for instance, improved water and air quality, storm protection, flood mitigation, sewage treatment, micro-climate regulation, recreation and health values (Collier *et al.*, 2013). Such 'ecosystem services' are inextricably linked to ecological processes whose negative outcomes, though, are often externalised by omitting the local environmental impacts due to the production/disposal phases, or by addressing the external cost to unequal financial instruments.

The resilience approach demonstrates the importance of living with disturbances when a city is likely to be unpredictably tackled by climate change effects, and therefore it favours the blooming of self-organised tools and measures to face the quick change. When the urban community is well self-organised and can rely on traditional knowledge about coping with changes without external help, resilience increases and the disaster/ emergency response gives better outcomes. This concept implies significantly less emphasis on technology and top-down planning and more emphasis on the human factor in the analysis of energy transition.

The study of the transition towards future production and consumption systems that involve not only a more efficient usage of resources but also resilience-building among communities requires the presence of innovative case studies. From this perspective, it could therefore be the case of a critical evaluation of the radical innovation and the strategic rethinking needed by universities.

The concept of a 'Living Laboratory' scales down the length of the urban border condition to that of the campus and takes students, teachers and administrative staff as 'citizens' of this portion of the city; the support of private industries and governmental task forces fosters the role of the university in the co-creation of sustainable life conditions. The vast partnerships among universities and between academia and its environment (thanks to a European-funded project for advanced education schemes, collaborative research, consultations with local government for urban reforms or real estate development projects, industry-preferred test beds or within society through economic exchanges, as will be specified in the following paragraphs) lead many universities to assume a highly ambitious role of collaborating with diverse social actors to create societal transformations in the goal of sustainability. This is also seen as part of the so-called 'third mission' of universities which refers to a further goal to add to the universities traditional teaching and research missions: the perceived need to engage with societal demands and link the university with its socio-economic context. The transition towards sustainable universities will help in understanding the further resilience and sustainability management of the wider urban environment.

As with any other urban district, different campus plans do influence the sustainability performance of the overall city – this is the main aspect to consider when scaling sustainability evaluations from building to neighbourhood. However, when investing in the social dimension of the energy transition problem, the wellbeing, land use, mobility, social equity, urban economic sustainability, energy sources and infrastructure are special factors in a campus community (Sonetti, 2015).

Of course, this scale-up is not costless: decision-making at urban level requires complex methods to evaluate different features and to guarantee sustainability and resilience for a large number of stakeholders. In the case of a University the stakeholders are far from homogeneous: short-stay students (for one month or one year) to long-stay ones (five years or more) to permanent staff and daily visitors. This community is difficult to target in terms of differentiated strategy and communication level. Plus, the quadruple helix approach (Lombardi, 2011) highlights problems related to the simultaneous satisfaction of all the stakeholders interplaying with the university as a place of knowledge transfer, urban node and varied social actors: decision makers/urban planners, investors/developers/construction companies, designers (engineers, architects), grant managers, building owners, SMEs/IT solutions providers, citizens, and finally students, professor, peer universities, research centres, not to mention the legislative (regional and ministerial) compliances.

In this perspective, some of the criteria for a resilient city seem to be applicable to the campus dimension even without the disaster response, with the hypothesis that resilient community building as a fertile ground for user behaviour leverages for energy reduction in the university campus. Institutions now have the responsibility, more than ever before, to integrate sustainable development and resilience requirements into all their teaching, research, community engagement and campus operations to make a difference into the race to innovate a new urban and citizen paradigm toward a low carbon society.

Acknowledgements

MILESECURE-2050 and POCACITO are two European Union collaborative projects which have received funding from the European Commission in the Seventh Framework SSH Programme.

References

Adams, W.M. (2006) *The Future of Sustainability: Rethinking the Environment and Development in the Twenty-First Century*, Report of the IUCN Renowned Thinkers Meeting, 29–31 January, 27/05/06. Available at: http://cmsdata.iucn.org/downloads/iucn_future_of_sustanability.pdf (accessed 7 March 2016).

Alberti, M., and Marzluff, J.M. (2004) Ecological resilience in urban ecosystems: Linking urban patterns to human and ecological functions, *Urban Ecosystems* **7**, 241–265.

Alcott, B. (2005) Jevons' paradox, *Ecological Economics* **54**(1), 9–21.

Berkes, F., and Jolly, D. (2002) Adapting to climate change: Social–ecological resilience in a Canadian western arctic community, *Ecology and Society* **5**.

Berkes, F., Colding, J., Folke, C. (eds) (2002) *Navigating Social–Ecological Systems: Building Resilience for Complexity and Change*, Cambridge University Press, Cambridge.

Brandon, P.S., Lombardi, P. (2005) *Evaluating Sustainable Development in the Built Environment*, 2nd edn, Wiley-Blackwell, London.

Chatterton P. (2013) Towards an agenda for post-carbon cities. Lessons from Lilac, the UK's first ecological, affordable cohousing community. *International Journal of Urban and Regional Research* **37**(5).

Collier, M.J., Nedović-Budić, Z., Aerts, J., Connop, S., Foley, D., Foley, K., Verburg, P. (2013) Transitioning to resilience and sustainability in urban communities. *Cities* **32**, S21–S28.

Drexhage J., Murphy D. (2010) *Sustainable development: from Brundtland to Rio 2012*, Background Paper, United Nations Headquarters, New York, September 2010. Available at: http://www.un.org/wcm/webdav/site/climatechange/shared/gsp/docs/GSP1-6_Background%20on%20Sustainable%20Devt.pdf (accessed 7 March 2016).

Emelianoff, C., Mor, E. (2013) Société postcarbone: les villes pionnières. *Futuribles* **392**, 27–41.

Ernstson H., van der Leeuw S., Redman C.L., Meffert D.J., Davis G., Alfsen C., Elmqvist T. (2010) Urban transitions: on urban resilience and human-dominated ecosystems, *Ambio* **39**(8), 531–545.

ESPON (2010). *Scientific Dialogue on Cities, Rural Areas and Rising Energy Prices.* First ESPON 2013 Scientific Report. ESPON, Luxembourg.

EU Pocacito project (2013) *POst CArbon CIties of TOmorrow.* Available at: www.POCACITO.eu (accessed 7 March 2015).

European Commission (2011) *Communication from the Commission to the European Parliament, the Council, the European Economic and Social Committee, and the Committee of the regions. A roadmap for moving to a competitive low carbon economy in 2050.* Available at: http://eur-lex.europa.eu/legal-content/EN/TXT/?uri=celex%3A52011DC0112 (accessed 7 March 2015).

European Commission (2012) *Work Programme 2013, Cooperation, Theme 8, Socio-Economic Sciences And Humanities.* SSH.2013.7.1-1. *Post-carbon Cities in Europe: A Long-term Outlook.* European Commission, Bruxelles.

Evans, G. (2008) Transformation from "carbon valley" to a "post-carbon society" in a climate change hot spot: the coalfields of the Hunter Valley, New South Wales, Australia. *Ecology and Society* **13**(1), 39.

Folke, C., Carpenter, S., Elmqvist, T., Gunderson, L., Holling, C.S., Walker, B. (2002) Resilience and sustainable development: building adaptive capacity in a world of transformations. *Ambio* **31**(5), 437–440.

Folke, C., Carpenter, S.R. Walker, B. Scheffer, M. Chapin, T., Rockström J. (2010) Resilience thinking: integrating resilience, adaptability and transformability. *Ecology and Society* **15**(4), 20.

Folke, C., Hahn, T., Olsson, P., Norberg, J. (2005) Adaptive governance of social–ecological systems. *Annual Review of Environment and Resources* **30**, 441–473.

Foxon, T.J., Reed, M.S., Stringer, L.C. (2009) Governing long-term social–ecological change: What can the resilience and transitions approaches learn from each other? *Environmental Policy and Governance* **19**(1), 3–20.

Gruenig, M., Livingston, D. (2015) The future of power in a post-carbon society, *The American Institute for Contemporary German Studies* **61** AICGS Policy Report.

Hart, K. (2002) World society as an old regime. *Elite Cultures: Anthropological Perspectives*, **2002**, 22–36.

IEA (2008) *World Energy Outlook*. OECD/International Energy Agency, Paris.

IPCC (2014) Summary for policymakers. In: *Climate Change 2014: Mitigation of Climate Change. Contribution of Working Group III to the Fifth Assessment Report of the Intergovernmental Panel on Climate Change* (eds O. Edenhofer, R. Pichs-Madruga, Y. Sokona, E. Farahani, S. Kadner, K. Seyboth, A. Adler, I. Baum, S. Brunner, P. Eickemeier, B. Kriemann, J. Savolainen, S. Schlömer, C. von Stechow, T. Zwickel, J.C. Minx). Intergovernmental Panel on Climate Change/Cambridge University Press, Cambridge.

Korhonen, J., Seager, T.P. (2008) Beyond eco-efficiency: a resilience perspective. *Business Strategy and the Environment* **17**(7), 411–419.

Lombardi, P. (2015) Local experiences in energy transition. *Energia, Ambiente e Innovazione ENEA*, Speciale **I-2015**, 55–59.

Lombardi, P., Trossero, E. (2013) Beyond energy efficiency in evaluating sustainable development in planning and the built environment. *International Journal of Sustainable Building Technology and Urban Development* **4**(4), 274–282.

Lombardi, P. (2011) New challenges in the evaluation of smart cities. *Network Industries Quarterly* **13**, 8–10.

Lombardi, P., Gruenig, M. (eds) (2016) *Low-carbon Energy Security from a European Perspective*. Elsevier, Amsterdam, The Netherlands.

Loorbach, D. (2014) *To Transition! Governance Panarchy in the New Transformation*. Inaugural Address on 31 October, Faculty of Social Science EUR, Erasmus University, Rotterdam.

Meadows, D.H., Meadows, D.L., Randers, J., and Behrens, W.W. III (1972) *Limits to Growth*. New American Library, New York.

MILESECURE-2050 (2012) *Multidimensional Impact of the Low-carbon European Strategy on Energy Security, and Socio-Economic Dimension up to 2050 Perspective*. Deliverable 2.2. Available at: http://www.milesecure2050.eu/en/public-deliverables (accessed 7 March 2016).

Pearson A., Gruenig M., Prahl A., Caiati G., Efthimiadis T., Sitko I. (2014) *Report on drivers of societal processes of energy transition*, SSH.2012.2.2-2, Deliverable 3.1, MILESECURE-2050. Available at: http://www.milesecure2050.eu/en/public-deliverables (accessed 7 March 2016).

Rockström, J., Steffen, W., Noone, K., *et al.* (2009) Planetary boundaries: exploring the safe operating space for humanity. *Ecology and Society* **14**(2), 32.

Schmidheiny, S. (1992) The business logic of sustainable development. *Columbia Journal of World Business* **27**(3/4), 18–24.

Schumpeter, J. (1994) *History of Economic Analysis*. Cambridge University Press, Cambridge.

Sonetti, G. (2015) *What if We Adopt a Resilience Thinking Approach in the Urban Governance for Emission Reduction? Observations from a University Campus Case Study*. Paper presented at the ERSA 2015 conference. Available at: http://www-sre.wu.ac.at/ersa/ersaconfs/ersa15/e150825aFinal01295.pdf (accessed 7 March 2016).

UNEP (2012) *Global Initiative for Resource Efficient Cities*. United Nations Environmental Programme, Vienna.

Vidalenc, E., Rivière, A., Theys, J. (2014) *Cities as key players for the transition towards a post-carbon society: A French perspective*, French Ministry for Ecology, Sustainable Development and Energy, Foresight Report. Available at: http://www.developpement-durable.gouv.fr/IMG/pdf/VPC_English_FINAL.pdf (accessed 7 March 2016).

Walker, B., Holling, C.S., Carpenter, S.R., Kinzig, A. (2004) Resilience, adaptability and transformability in social–ecological systems. *Ecology and Society* **9**, 16–20.

Chapter 5
Sustainable Urban Development – Where Are You Now?

Ian Cooper
Eclipse Research Consultants, Cambridge, CB4 2JD, UK

'Much of the work in a civilised community rests upon the assumption that the show is good for a long run. The drama of the present tends to move in a given direction only when it receives the double impact of the past and the future, and if the past be too frightful for remembrance or the future too cloudy for anticipation, the present ceases to move in any particular direction, and teeters fitfully about from point to point' Lewis Mumford (1921).

5.1 Introduction

This chapter charts the progress of sustainable urban development (SUD) since the Building Environmental Quality Evaluation for Sustainability through Time (BEQUEST) Network produced the first framework (2001) for trying to put this complex idea into practice. This opportunity is used to:

- Look back at the BEQUEST Network and comment on its legacy
- Track how SUD has diffused since then, particularly as a policy imperative, and
- Comment on how this concept is now being framed.

The chapter raises three questions:

1. What is meant now by the term SUD?
2. What framings and tools are being offered for implementing SUD?
3. And is SUD still relevant and useful as a focus for research in today's circumstances?

As a result, this chapter is primarily concerned with the unfolding history of SUD as an idea over the past quarter of a century.

Future Challenges in Evaluating and Managing Sustainable Development in the Built Environment,
First Edition. Edited by Peter S. Brandon, Patrizia Lombardi and Geoffrey Q. Shen.
© 2017 John Wiley & Sons Ltd. Published 2017 by John Wiley & Sons Ltd.

5.2 Establishing the BEQUEST network

In 1995, attempting to evaluate the sustainability of the built environment was novel – an intriguing idea still in its infancy, [although Elkins *et al.* (1991) has already used the term 'sustainable urban development' four years earlier]. A workshop on evaluating the sustainability of the built environment was arranged in Florence to:

- serve as forum for exchanging information between interested parties (primarily, at that stage, academics)
- develop collaboration and interaction between the different disciplines involved in the production of the built environment.

Contributions to this workshop were captured by its three organisers in a set of proceedings (Brandon, Lombardi and Bentivegna, 1997). This was the first in a series of publications on SUD directly co-produced by the members of the community of interest it assembled. Perhaps the workshop's most significant outcome was a decision to call together a 'group of experts' to discuss the need for joint action on SUD at an international level. This meeting resulted in a successful bid for funding for a 'concerted action' entitled Building Environmental Quality Evaluation for Sustainability through Time (BEQUEST). This was supported by the European Union Research Directorate, under the Human Dimensions of Environmental Change theme of its fourth Framework Programme, between 1998 and 2001. The network of interested parties it gathered together was charged not just with building bridges between the different disciplines involved but with constructing a platform that all of the participants could share when seeking to assess SUD. Because of this underlying motivation, the concerted action emphasised creating consensus – stressing development of a common language and construction of a shared analytical framework for SUD. Given the infancy of SUD as an inter-disciplinary endeavour at this point, this was an extremely high ambition – to deliver a multi-professional consensus around the assessment of urban sustainability (Cooper, 2002).

5.3 Building the BEQUEST team

At the initial meeting of the prospective BEQUEST partners (before the submission of the bid for EU funding), it was recognised that an inter-disciplinary approach for assessing SUD would be required that did not then exist (Cooper, 2002). A simple self-assessment technique, called PICABUE (see Figure 5.1), was used to gauge the prospective partners' individual and collective commitment to the principles underpinning sustainable development (Curwell *et al.*, 1998).

Following Elkins *et al.* (1991), these principles had previously been distilled by one of the BEQUEST partners (Mitchell *et al.*, 1995) from material flowing from the Earth Summit in Rio and its aftermath. Eclipse Research Consultants (1996) embedded these principles in a simple mapping technique so that partners could directly compare their own commitment with that of other members of the BEQUEST Network. Individually

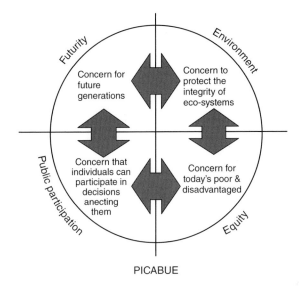

PICABUE

Figure 5.1 PICABUE's representation of the four principles underpinning sustainable development.

partners displayed very different levels of commitment to these principles in 1998 (see Figure 5.2; Cooper, 2002).

Jointly, in 1998, they were most committed to concern about future generations, and least committed to 'fair shares' for all (see left-hand side of Figure 5.3). Towards the end of the concerted action, partners' levels of commitment were again mapped (2001; see right hand side of Figure 5.3).

This second mapping shows that partners' aggregated commitments to the principles had barely changed over the life of the concerted action, except in relation to equity ('fair shares for all') which had increased significantly. One value of the mapping technique was that, during the life of the concerted action, it made explicit to partners that it was possible (indeed necessary) for them to continue to collaborate with each other without necessarily sharing the same levels of commitment to the principles underpinning sustainable development.

Another value of this mapping technique was later acknowledged by Fuller (2010); he identified it as a useful means of moving beyond treating sustainability as a cliché in tertiary education:

'The purpose of education is to teach students to think about sustainability and what it means. Furthermore, this task needs to be revisited urgently given the uncritical way that students are using the term. Students can decide for themselves if some action or system is sustainable but unless they have been alerted to the looseness of their thinking, they cannot do this effectively ... One model that has been found useful to introduce the concept of sustainable development to tertiary students is based on the principles distilled from a review of the sustainability literature .... The [PICABUE] model has proven useful because it is simple, yet conveys the essence of the issues and their interaction. Importantly, it is also visually easy to remember'.

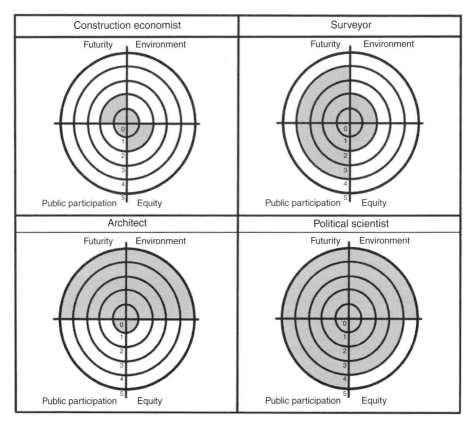

Figure 5.2   Individual BEQUEST member's commitment to sustainable development principles.

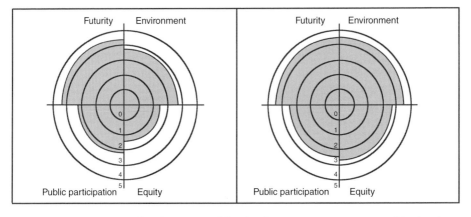

Figure 5.3   BEQUEST members' aggregated levels of commitment to sustainable development principles at the start and end of the concerted action.

5.4 *The legacy of BEQUEST*

The concerted action involved building consensus over the language and vision of SUD across a wide range of stakeholders involved in the production of the urban environment, as well as across a range of spatial and temporal scales, development activities, and environmental and social issues (Bentivegna *et al.*, 2002). The resulting vision of SUD produced was that of a relative, adaptive process in which the current urban fabric is gradually adapted over time to suit more sustainable lifestyles. A framework for structuring information on SUD was developed which provided what was then a unique, integrated representation of the scope and extent of the subject area that linked together socio-economic and technical dimensions as well as planning, property, design and construction interests, in time and space (see Figure 5.4).

This framework was accompanied by a BEQUEST Toolkit which set out the 'grid references' of an information system to support decisions taken about the evaluation of SUD (Vreeker *et al.*, 2009; see Figure 5.5).

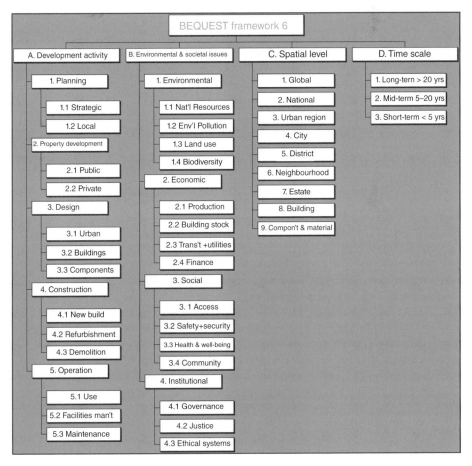

Figure 5.4   The BEQUEST Framework. Source: Stephen 2005. Reproduced with the permission of Taylor and Francis.

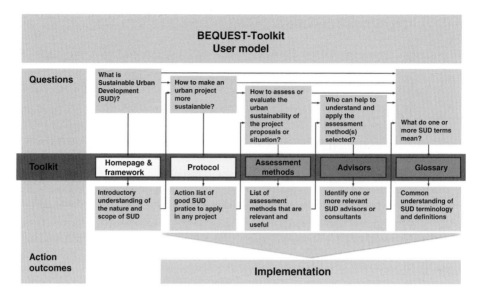

Figure 5.5   The BEQUEST Toolkit. Source: Stephen Curwell 2005. Reproduced with the permission of Taylor and Francis.

When the concerted action finished, a special issue of the International Journal of Building Research and Information was dedicated in 2002 to its outputs and their reception. Reviewing the relevance of BEQUEST, Kohler (2002) suggested that its principal merit was:

> '… to have imagined such a Toolkit and created a first prototype. This allows one to judge if and how this type of tool and above all this type of planning heuristics can address the needs of different actors in different situations. It further addresses which tools are needed, how they can be combined and how such tools [protocols and assessment methods] can be integrated in a larger participatory process at many different scales within the urban process'.

In other words, the BEQUEST Framework was welcomed as breaking new ground, as the first integrated, multi-scalar, decision-support mechanism for supporting the assessment of urban sustainability. This challenge has subsequently been taken up and significantly furthered by others, not least by the Japanese CASBEE City tool for the 'Comprehensive Assessment System for Built Environment Efficiency' (Murakami *et al.*, 2011).

The BEQUEST Toolkit also drew praise from outside the built environment domain – in the study of mathematical thinking (Solomon, 2008). Here it was selected as one of a number of tools that illustrated how to extend mathematical fluency and learning in specific professional and non-professional domains. It was commended here as a means by which stakeholders could identify the wide range of actions they needed to consider when pursuing SUD, along with a range of appropriate assessment methods and tools they could then employ when they did so.

Kohler (cited by Hamilton *et al.*, 2009) also concluded that the Toolkit was valuable for similar reasons because:

> 'As the concepts of participatory planning are becoming more firmly embedded with the planning system, the BEQUEST Toolkit becomes even more relevant. … For this reason [it] has also been found to offer educational benefits for those entering regeneration, planning, sustainable communities and the building professions …. It is current being used to support teaching a number of European universities, including Florence, Salford, Napier (Edinburgh) and Lusofona (Lisbon), and in the USA'.

And he noted that access to the Toolkit continued be maintained by popular request,

> 'On the rare occasions when the server is down at the University of Salford the author [Kohler] receives complaints from around the world and requests for the Toolkit to be restored!'

Unfortunately the web address cited as providing access to the BEQUEST Toolkit – http://www.research.scpm.salford.ac.uk/bqtoolkit/index.htm – is now defunct.

5.5 Defining SUD

In 1996, Wheeler published his 166-page monograph containing an analytical review of sustainable urban development. Based on this extensive review, he proposed as a definition of SUD:

> 'Sustainable urban development seeks to create cities and towns that improve the long term-health of the plan's human and ecological systems'.

This brief definition does have the merit of not being entirely human species-centric but it remains just an expression of aspirations. As if sensing this, Wheeler added, as a supplement:

> 'Means to achieve this objective include protecting and restoring natural ecosystems in urban areas, creating community environments that nurture human potential, using land and resources wisely, and facilitating human lifestyles that contribute to global stability'.

But this addendum simply extended the wish list of desires without offering any clue as to how these could be achieved.

Conversely, BEQUEST was more strongly focused on implementation: it failed to offer a concise or cogent definition of SUD. Apart from the meaning implied by the components listed in its Framework, none of the four Routledge volumes on SUD co-produced by members of the BEQUEST Network offered a formal definition of the term – perhaps unsurprising given the Network's focus on providing practical aids to support decision-making. Instead it was claimed, in volume 4, that SUD was 'a shared journey, a process, not a product or final destination' (Cooper and Symes, 2009). Kohler was cited in volume 3 (Hamilton *et al.*, 2009) as suggesting that BEQUEST's use of

PICABUE indicated a four-sided definition of SUD covering ecological integrity, equality, participation and futurity. In his earlier review of BEQUEST, Kohler (2002) had drawn attention to its vision and methodology as having broadened the scope of what was meant by SUD, by extending it beyond what was normally considered as being solely environmental to include economic and social dimensions. And he made a large claim about what he saw would be the resultant effect of this, stating that:

> '[This broader formulation of SUD] increasingly becomes a complete alternative to the actual development model of late modernisation (globalisation and the widening of social inequalities etc.). By enlarging the scope, the difficulties of finding aggregate models for the different components of SUD have led to the abandonment of classical optimisation models'.

In 1998, the year that the BEQUEST concerted action started, Campagni argued:

> 'The concept of sustainable development is steadily approaching recognition, if not full disciplinary autonomy, becoming the focus of new theoretical and normative reflection. However, the same cannot be said of a more specific field of application of that same concept – the urban environment. In our opinion, this has been hindered until recently by some unresolved problems – of definition, methodology and epistemology'.

And here, Campagni claimed, part of the problem was that definition of what was meant by 'urban' in this phrase SUD remained problematic, just as others had previously suggested for the term 'sustainable development' itself (Palmer *et al.*, 1997). Campagni offered his own definition of the phrase,

> 'Sustainable urban development may be defined as a process of synergetic integration and co-evolution among the great subsystems making up a city (economic, social, physical and environmental), which guarantees the local population a non-decreasing level of wellbeing in the long term, without compromising the possibilities of development of surrounding areas and contributing by this towards reducing the harmful effects of development on the biosphere'.

This broader definition of SUD also has merit, not least because of its prescient inclusion of the notion of 'well-being' – an issue that has become central to present day discussions, in planning circles, about the purpose of place-making (Husam *et al.*, 2015).

One year later, when Earthscan published its Reader in Sustainable Cities (Satterthwaite, 1999), it contained a whole section on 'Linking sustainable development and cities'. But the Reader did not include the term SUD in its index, though it did the use the phrase '(urban) development'. So, at the turn of the century, delineation of what SUD meant was still in its infancy. Yet lack of precise (let alone concise) definition has not hampered or deterred widespread use of the term 'sustainable urban development'. Employed as a search term in Google (July 2015), it produced more than 27 million results. Likewise entered into Google Scholar, it resulted in 1.8 million returns.

5.6 *The diffusion of SUD*

Over the past 20 years, the term has spread and steadily become internationally institutionalised. As early at 1998, the European Commission sought to promote action on SUD in the European Union (EC, 1998). In 2004, during the Dutch Presidency of the EU, the Rotterdam Urban Acquis proposed the adoption of the concept of what it called 'integrated sustainable urban development' (ISUD) as a means of addressing the EU's Lille Action Programme (FIRBUAD, 2015) By 2007, SUD had formally become part of UN policy through the establishment of its Sustainable Urban Development Network (SUD-Net; UN-HABITAT, 2007). By 2009, the European Commission had moved on to promoting the achievements of, and opportunities, for SUD as part of its Regional Policy (EC, 2009). The EC also produced 224 pages of consultative guidelines for how to co-operate with the Third World on SUD – guidelines it based on seven principles without offering a formal definition of the term (ALNAP, 2015). By the end of that decade, even the International Olympic Committee was requiring cities bidding for the Games to demonstrate their ability to address what it took to be the principles of SUD (Wiltschko, 2009). Such international institutionalisation of the term continues unabated. For example, the OECD has recently announced publication of its Sustainable Urban Development Policies in Ageing Cities (OECD, 2015). Nor has this uptake been confined to international organisations. The term has also been adopted at lower spatial scales, for instance by groupings of cities and by NGOs. For example, the C40 SUD Network is seeking to equip and empower municipal decision-makers to plan sustainably (C40 Cities, 2012). And the World Urban Campaign (2015) is seeking to promote dialogue about 'how to improve our urban future' through its SUD to 2050 initiative.

How robust are the empirical underpinnings for this multiplicity of policy imperatives, or for the guidance that has followed in their wake? This remains an open question. But scepticism seems in order here. There is a commonly observed distance between the high aspirations stated in policy imperatives for the built environment and their eventual outcomes (see Cooper and Foxell, 2015). This can be seen, to give just one example, in the United Kingdom (UK) government's promotion of eco-towns (Warwick, 2015). SUD is unlikely to be immune from this malaise. For, as Bianco and Giuliano (2011) concluded from their review of the work of Urban Sustainability Centres in the United States:

> 'Much of the argument in SUD is made by analogy (and/or by illegitimate borrowings) and is not evidence based'.

Surveying the progress of SUD across Europe 16 years ago for the United Nations-Economic Commission for Europe, Tsenkova (1999) concluded that urban development programmes were still aimed at economic growth as an over-riding goal. Six years later, Donovan *et al.* (2005) added a similar warning, drawn from their 'real time', on the ground investigation of urban regeneration in the UK. They identified a range of barriers that can prevent realisation of SUD, however broadly defined:

> 'Like many other studies that focus on the range of factors preventing sustainable development, [our] study indicates that the fundamental requirement for economic growth continues to drive key urban regeneration decisions, even when sustainability is generally upheld as a

laudable principle within that process. The economic imperative exacerbates the institutional and perceptual barriers to sustainability, as actors fall back into established ways of working and designing rather than trying to engage with the plethora of possibilities that sustainable development offers. On this understanding, sustainable urban development, according to the definitions provided by Brundtland ... will never be achieved'.

Rees (2012) offered a more principled objection to SUD, grounded in the laws of physics:

'Techno-industrial society and modern cities are inherently unsustainable. This conclusion flows from the energy and material dynamics of growing cities interpreted in light of the second law of thermodynamics. In second law terms, cities are self-organizing, far-from-equilibrium dissipative structures whose 'self- organization' is utterly dependent on access to abundant energy and material resources .... anthropogenic degradation now exceeds ecospheric regeneration and threatens to undermine the very urban civilization causing it. To achieve sustainability, global society must rebalance production and consumption, abandon the growth ethic, re-localize our economies and increase urban-regional self-reliance, all of which fly in the face of prevailing global development ideology'.

The limitations imposed on SUD by these energy and material flows have recently been examined for large cities (Kennedy *et al.*, 2015; Wei *et al.*, 2015).

5.7 The framing of and tools for SUD

The lack of a succinct but robust definition and the absence of a strongly grounded evidence base for what works have not stopped attempts to put SUD into practice. For example, the European Sustainable Development Network (ESDN) has sought to map urban sustainable development in Europe and beyond (Lepuschitz and Pisano, 2014). Taking 'the concept of urban SD as everything that is related to SD in an urban context', the ESDN argued (Lepuschitz *et al.*, 2014) that:

'... urban sustainable development needs to be seen as the sum of on-going transformative processes applied to help transitioning cities (or urban areas) to a more sustainable future. These processes that happen at the urban level will have effects not only on the city itself but 'outside' the city and, hence, have a more widespread effect – locally, regionally, nationally and globally – requiring, therefore, a multi-level governance approach'.

Following Kelvani (2010) and UN-DESA (2013), the ESDN portrayed its 'features of urban sustainable development in a radar graph illustrating "exemplary cities"' (see Figure 5.6).

Employing this approach, the ESDN suggested, requires taking into account six blocks of features:

1. A social perspective
2. An economic front
3. An environmental aspect
4. The viewpoint of access

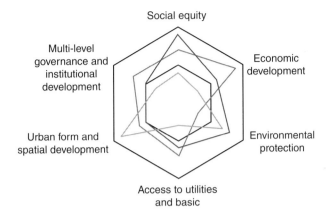

Figure 5.6   The ESDN radar graph for visualising sustainable urban development. Source: http://www.sd-network.eu/quarterly%20reports/report%20files/pdf/2014-January-Framing_Urban_Sustainable_Development.pdf.

5. The connections derived from urban form and spatial development
6. The attention of multi-level governance and institutional development.

There appears to be little agreement about which or how many issues attempts to implement SUD need to tackle. For instance, the Urban Development Institute of Australia (UDIA, 2009) mapped SUD, using four 'core areas', against 10 key themes, as captured in its Sustainable Urban Development Matrix (see Figure 5.7).

The UDIA established this matrix to promote better understanding of the range of aspects underpinning SUD. The matrix is accompanied by case studies and further information about state, national and international examples. The robustness of the evidence base employed for assembling the matrix was clearly a sensitive issue. For, as the Institute declared:

> 'The UDIA does not validate or endorse the contents of the case studies included in the matrix [although the]... case studies are subject to a peer review by the UDIA's SUD Committee and are provided for information. The accuracy of the content is the responsibility of the contributing author'.

More recently, the University of Westminster (Joss *et al.*, 2015) brought together an international team to examine the 'prospects for standardising sustainable urban development' through 'an empirical and conceptual overview of the current emerging field of eco-city frameworks'. The term 'eco-city' is used as an umbrella term here (Joss *et al.*, 2015) for:

> '... encapsulating a variety of concepts, models and practices which aim to further urban sustainability at neighbourhood, city or city-regional levels. These may be given various closely-related labels such as "sustainable city", "low carbon city", "resilient city", and "smart city", among others'.

Joss *et al.* (2015) identified what they called a 'proliferation' across a 'polycentric' international research community of 43 different 'replicable urban sustainability frameworks' in support of 'an exponential rise in urban sustainability initiatives ... since the early

CORE AREAS	CONSUMER (Awareness/Behaviour)	INFRASTRUCTURE	URBAN PLANNING	BUILDING DESIGN
ECOSYSTEMS	Valuing native and endemic flora and fauna as well as landscapes as part of a wider ecosystem	Efficient and sensitive services layout minimises impact on the ecosystem	Understanding and valuing ecosystem opportunities and constraints into integrated urban planning outcomes	Considered building designs that integrate and respect the natural environment
WASTE	Valuing waste as a resource and understanding the benefits of practicing waste management through avoiding, reducing, reusing, and recycling	Appropriate infrastructure systems provided to enhance, value and facilitate reducing, reusing and recycling waste	Urban design that considers opportunities to reduce waste sent to landfill	Built form outcomes that reduce waste sent to landfill
ENERGY & COMFORT	Understanding and valuing energy efficiencies and how it benefits our wellbeing and mitigates the impact of climate change	Structures that lead to energy efficiencies and reduce reliance on traditional supply	Urban planning that reduces the demand for non-renewable energy sources	Built form outcomes that reduce the demand for non-renewable energy sources
MATERIALS	Understanding and use of materials that reduce the impact on the environment and contribute to human wellbeing	Infrastructure solutions based on material synergies and choices that are more sustainable	Urban planning that promotes environmentally responsible material usage and synergies	Building design and built form outcomes that showcase environmentally responsible material use
WATER	Total water cycle management	Infrastructure solutions supportive of and based upon total water cycle management principles	Total water cycle management integrated into urban planning decisions	Buildings that are designed, built and landscaped to reduce the demand on potable water
COMMUNITY	Good community health and wellbeing can be obtained by engaging with the community to understand and achieve community aspirations, spirit and ownership	Early provision of hard and soft infrastructure to encourage and promote cohesive communities	Urban planning that promotes legible, well connected and accessible communities	Built form solutions and facilities that allow for diversity of demographic profiles, facilitatin community cohesion and intergenerational communities
ECONOMY	Valuing local economies and quantifying intangibles as part of the business case	Hard and soft infrastructure and facilities providing opportunities for economic development	Urban planning that is robust, flexible and able to respond to changing economic conditions	Initiatives that encourage robust and varied built form uses to stimulate economic prosperity
TRANSPORT	Encouraging public transport use and introducing mechanisms to reduce reliance on private cars as the primary mode of transport	Strategies that improve public transport and walking/cycling infrastructure	Providing a safe and attractive public realm for cyclists, pedestrians and public transport modes to reduce car dependency	Built form facilities and initiatives designed to promote walking and cycling
AFFORDABILITY	Promotion of initiatives that provide economic benefits at establishment and over their lifecycle whilst meeting expected functionality and design	Innovations in infrastructure design and use that reduce lifecycle costs while achieving necessary performance targets	Urban planning that provides a measurable net economic benefit for stakeholders relative to business as usual	Examples of building design elements that offer economic, environmental or socio-political benefits while being cost effective at establishment and over their lifecycle, relative to business as usual

Figure 5.7　The UDIA Sustainable Urban Development Matrix. Source: Robyn Ganzer 2009. Reproduced with the permission of UDIAWA.

2000s' Joss *et al.* (2015). These frameworks range alphabetically from the ASEAN Environmentally Sustainable Model Cities through to the Stockholm Environment Institute (2008) REAP for Local Authorities. Joss *et al.* (2015) noted that:

'… while sustainable urban development arguably always needs to be understood as locally contextualised, the "sustainable city" concept as concept, policy and practice has become increasingly globalised and ubiquitous'.

Once again, this raises the tension between local and global approaches to SUD (Cooper, 1999) and the plea, first made by made by Rees (1999), for assessment methods which contribute to delivering global, and not just local, improvements in sustainability. This issue – concern for the absolute global limits to sustainable urban development – was subsequently explored, if only in relation to energy, by Lowe (2006).

5.8　Expansion/dilution of SUD

As the Westminster review above makes clear, the term SUD now has a considerable number of challengers for space, time and attention in policy-making and implementation arenas. These include:

- *Positive development* – 'an innovative new paradigm in which the built environment provides greater life quality, health, amenity and safety for all without sacrificing resources or money' (Birkeland, 2008)

- *Regenerative design* – 'processes that restore, renew or revitalize their own sources of energy and materials, creating sustainable systems that integrate the needs of society with the integrity of nature' (Cole, 2012)
- *Resilience* – 'new mitigation and adaption methods, developing new standards for design, planning and products, new skills related programmes, test, trial, demonstrate and certify new innovations to future proof our built assets' (BRE, 2014)
- *Climate change* – 'understanding how climate change will affect the urban environment is crucial … this area includes urban climate, sustainable buildings, renewable energy in urban environments and the use of plants within the urban environment' (Walker Institute, 2015).

To this list must be added SUD's near and far synonyms: *sustainable urban planning, urban sustainability, sustainable communities, sustainable cities, eco-cities* and *smart cities*.

At the same time as the rise of all these rivals and synonyms, the term SUD is being expanded (and possibly diluted) by becoming an indiscriminate catch-all term for describing a host of issues relating to the built urban environment and beyond. For instance, the recent *Sustainable Development Reader* in Routledge's *Urban Reader Series* (Wheeler and Beatley, 2014) claimed that the dimensions of SUD now encompass:

- Climate change planning
- Land use and urban design
- Transportation
- Environmental planning and restoration
- Social equity and environmental justice
- Economic development
- Green architecture and building, as well as
- Food systems and health.

This increasingly wide compass of issues embraced can be traced back to the failure to establish a concise yet workable definition of the term SUD since its first coinage. Without such a definition, the term is, it would seem, almost infinitely expandable in terms of what it is taken to encompass – from (public) transport systems (Rabinovitch, 1992; Bannister, 2000), through crime prevention (Cozens, 2002), culture (UNESCO, 2015) and cultural heritage (Tweed and Sutherland, 2007), to social and institutional innovation (Mieg and Töpfer, 2013) and health and well-being (Siri and Capon, 2015).

5.9 *Elaborating, not extending, SUD*

Rather than extending the range of issues to be covered by SUD, research effort might be better focussed on providing further elaboration of how its implementation can be aligned with the principles underlying sustainable development. This is particularly so for the principle of 'futurity' – concern for future generations. Part of the lack of attention to this SD principle may be traced back the Earth Summit in Rio in 1992.

In its statement of principles, the Summit (UNEP, 1992) called, under Principle 21, for 'global partnership' in order 'to achieve sustainable development and ensure a better future for all' – but without setting in place institutional responsibilities, mechanisms or instructions for how this could be subsequently achieved. More conspicuous by its absence was the Summit's lack of attention to the past, to the cultural heritage bequeathed by previous generations: these concerns the Summit's summary document (Meakin, 1992) failed to mention.

Futurity was also one of the principles that was least developed by the BEQUEST Network. This is ironic since, as reported above, it was a principle to which members had suggested they were strongly committed. The BEQUEST Framework did offer a set of timescales for decision-making about SUD, set at short, medium and long. But these timescales only ranged forward for 20 years – shorter than the 40–50 lifetime that many individual buildings are amortised over (Australian Government, 2006). Brandon and Lombardi subsequently (2005) drew on Kohler's (2003) presentation to the EU-funded IntelCity Project to focus attention on what they saw as the importance of time in the evaluation of SUD (see Figure 5.8).

But, despite the continuing interest in applying 'futures' scenario methodologies to cities (Hunt *et al.*, 2012), Brandon (2015) suggested that elaboration of a more sophisticated treatment of time in SUD, in relation to inter-generational equity, remains 'the elephant in the room'.

Difficulty in tackling 'futurity' has not been restricted to SUD. Inter-generational decision-making has long been recognised as an endemic problem across sustainable development not least because it raises the issue of social justice. As Dobson (1999) asked in his edited book *Fairness and Futurity*, if future generations are indeed owed justice, 'what should we bequeath them?'. Such questions are difficult, as Honey-Rosés *et al.* (2013) observed, because:

'Seriously engaging with the needs, hardships, and aspirations of future generations is an emotional experience as much as an intellectual endeavour'.

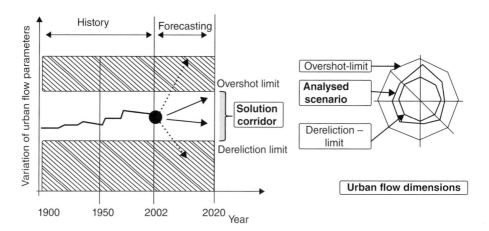

Figure 5.8   Kohler's Cycles of Transformation for the city and its culture.

Their exploration of futurity (through guided visualisation exercises) with participants led Honey-Rosés *et al.* (2013) to believe that:

> '… our most effective strategy for helping distant generations may be through our active support of near and overlapping generations to reorient them toward sustainability'.

Perhaps some of the difficulties encountered in tackling futurity could be alleviated by the simple expedient of adopting a 'five generation' framework for decision-making about SUD (Cooper, 2008). This could enable more balanced attention to be given past, present and future generations (see Figure 5.9).

Employing such a framework might also lead to engagement with a broader range of stakeholder 'voices' in decision-making about SUD, along with a more even-handed treatment of both the tangible and intangible components of cultural heritage. Doing so would require the SUD research community to develop methods for capturing and acting on information drawn from across this five-generation time-span. And, in turn, this would necessarily involve using data capture and engagement techniques (Abram, 2007; Platt and Cooper, 2005) that give commensurate attention to both professionals' understanding of SUD and to other (lay) stakeholders' lived experience (Van Manen, 1990) as legitimate currency when negotiating SUD decision-making.

5.10 Conclusions

Three questions were posed at the beginning of this chapter.

5.10.1 So what is meant now by the term SUD?

This remains a question that it is not simple to answer. For while the use of phrase is proving to be durable, it also turning out to be a highly elastic term. The lack of an agreed (let alone concise) definition for SUD means that, like sustainable development

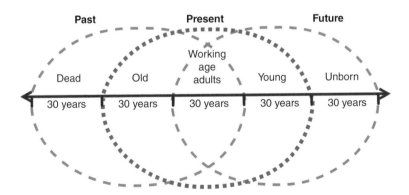

Figure 5.9 Five-generation decision-making: a framework for giving equal attention to the past, present and the future.

before it, it remains vague, contentious and hence difficult to implement. And, like sustainable development, the meanings attributed to it are highly political because they are values-based. SUD has become a catch-all portmanteau term. This has given the term flexibility, enabling it to retain relevance over a longer period of time without falling out of fashion because of its continual re-invention. Conversely, this also means that SUD is vulnerable to dilution (being drained of specific meaning) and so to being replaced by rival terms with a more 'single issue' focus (if not necessarily more precise definition). SUD has retained traction, especially amongst policy-makers in international organisations and amongst the international academic research community. But its take-up remains restricted. It hasn't become a generally used, widely publicly shared, term. This is signalled, for instance, by the lack of an SUD Wikipedia page unlike its near relatives – sustainable city, sustainable communities, smart cities or eco-cities.

5.10.2 What framings and tools are being offered for implementing SUD?

SUD is, Joss *et al.* (2015) suggested, close to being 'ubiquitous'. It is being strongly promoted, especially by international organisations that appear to see it as a useful vehicle for delivering their own organisational objectives; ranging from enabling third world co-operation and development, solving transport problems, to improving health and well-being. So there are now multiple framings of SUD on offer, each with extensive advice and guidance, accompanied by tools, on how to use SUD in support of such aims. Yet, despite growth in the international deployment of the term, it should not be assumed this means universal acceptance. In the United States, 'sustainability' may have become a 'mantra' guiding the policy decisions of public sector actors (Whittemore and Forgey, 2014). This is not the case, for instance, in the UK. The current (English) Conservative government (UK Government, 2015) has moved, in the archiving on the national government website of previous policy statements, to disassociate itself from the term 'sustainable communities' – the favoured form of words under the previous Labour Government for promoting SUD – and by extension from the 2007 Act of Parliament that underpins it. Such circumstances led Ellis (2015), the Research Director of the UK's Town and Country Planning Association, to conclude,

> 'In English local authorities, sustainable [urban] development is long dead and no longer on the agenda',

before adding defiantly,

> 'But this agenda isn't going to go away. Because it is right'.

5.10.3 And is SUD still relevant and useful as a focus for research in today's circumstances?

One answer to this question is given by the continued flow of publication of practice-orientated research on SUD. This is growing unabated, across a wide range of domains, communities of practice, and geographies (e.g. Jepson and Edwards, 2010; Freitag *et al.*,

2013; Holden *et al.*, 2014; Hornyanszky, 2014). Yet, despite a continued desire for stand-ardisation (e.g. Joss *et al.*, 2015), implementation of SUD stills lacks the agreed meth-ods, protocols and procedures that BEQUEST originally sought to establish. To these now need to be added the accompanying skill sets (Roberts, 2009) for implementing SUD's underlying goals. Given subsequent growth in understanding of the (environ-ment, participation and equity) principles of sustainable development, what we now know about these component parts needs clearer exposition so that they can be more robustly applied to confront continuing obstacles (e.g. lack of political will, finances and skills). And such attempts at application need to be effectively monitored and evaluated in order to provide a more robust evidence base for what does and does not work when implementing SUD.

The exception here is the principle of futurity – particularly as this relates to inter-generational equity. This remains largely unregarded by the SUD research community and so the meaning, significance and practical application of this principle await signifi-cant attention. As a research endeavour, this needs to be matched by an equal emphasis on how SUD can embrace sustaining 'the past' in the form of the tangible and intangible cultural heritage embedded in the built environment.

A clear research agenda is discernible from the arguments rehearsed in this chapter. Members of what Joss *et al.* (2015) called the 'polycentric' international SUD research community need to:

1. Move towards a shared, tighter and clearer definition of SUD
2. Specify an agreed set of minimum 'threshold' requirements that any urban develop-ment has to meet to qualify as 'globally sustainable'
3. Ensure that these requirements are encapsulated in an agreed set of processes that result in a balanced approach to each of the underlying principles of sustainable development
4. Apply these requirements consistently so that meaningful international compari-sons can be made, while allowing for necessary local, cultural and contextual differences, and
5. Build an openly shared, empirically robust, evidence base grounded in longitudinal monitoring and evaluation of what does and doesn't work.

in order to:

6. Express the results in forms that policy-makers, practitioners and lay community members can comfortably understand and apply.

Until this occurs, SUD will remain what it is now, despite two decades of constant research activity – an unproven aspiration whose effective long run implementation has yet to be demonstrated or evaluated. SUD has come a long way since 1991 in terms of its growing international acceptance as a policy imperative. But it still lacks a globally relevant yet locally grounded evidence base that illustrates its effective long-term imple-mentation. Till then, the ambition that drove the formation of the BEQUEST Network two decades ago – evaluation of the built environment based on a common interna-tional language and a shared platform for implementing SUD – remains unfulfilled.

This ambition looks all the more pressing given the new sustainable development goal (No. 11.3) that the UN (2015) has set for making cities more sustainable:

'By 2030, enhance inclusive and sustainable urbanization and capacity for participatory, integrated and sustainable human settlement planning and management in all countries'.

References

Abram, S. (2007) Living through regeneration – capturing multiple stakeholder perceptions to enrich the qualitative research methods curriculum, *CEBE Transactions* **4**(2), 67–84.

AlWaer, H., Fazey, I., Searle, B., Dawson, E., Cooper, I. (2015) *Enhancing Wellbeing: Inclusive, Community Collaborative Approaches to Place Making*, Symposium Report, Centre for Environmental Change and Human Resilience (CECHR) and The Geddes Institute for Urban Research, University of Dundee.

ALNAP (2015) *Towards sustainable urban development: a strategic approach*, Consultative Guidelines for Sustainable Urban Development Co-operation. Available at: http://www.alnap. org/resource/6678 (accessed 5 November 2015).

ASEAN (2015) *From islands of excellence to a sea change: the ASEAN ESC Model Cities Programme*. Available at: http://modelcities.hls-esc.org (accessed 9 November 2015).

Australian Government (2006) *Accounting Assets: depreciation and amortisation*. Available at: http://www.treasury.nt.gov.au/PMS/Publications/BudgetFinance/TreasDir/TD-A2.3.pdf (accessed 9 November 2015).

Bannister, D. (2000) Sustainable urban development and transport – a Eurovision for 2020, *Transport Review* **20**(1) 113–130.

Bentivegna, V., Curwell, S., Deakin, M., Lombardi, P., Mitchell, G., Nijkamp, P. (2002) A vision and methodology for integrated sustainable urban development: BEQUEST, *Building Research and Information* **30**(2), 83–94.

Bianco, H., Giuliano, G. (2011) *Towards evidence-based sustainable communities: Report on survey of Urban Sustainability Centers in US universities*, USC Centre for Sustainable Cities, University of Southern California.

Birkeland, J. (2008) *Positive Development: From Vicious Circles to Virtuous Cycles through Built Environment Design*, Earthscan, London.

Brandon, P. (2015) *Sustainable Futures: Intro, Presentation to the Future Challenges in Evaluating and Managing Sustainable Urban Development*, Knutsford, Cheshire.

Brandon, P., Lombardi, P., Bentivegna, V. (1997) *Evaluation of the Built Environment for Sustainability*, Spon, London.

Brandon, P., Lombardi, P. (2005) *Evaluating sustainable development*, Blackwell Publishing, Oxford.

BRE (2014) BRE seeks partners for new built environment resilience centre, *Press Release*, Building Research Establishment, Garston.

C40 Cities (2012) *Sustainable Communities Initiative: Sustainable Urban Development*, C40. Available at: http://www.c40.org/networks/sustainable_urban_development (accessed 11 November 2015).

Campagni, R. (1998) Sustainable urban development and reasons for a research programme, *International Journal of Environment and Pollution* **10**(1), 6–27.

Cole, R. (2012) Regenerative design and development: current theory and practice, *Building Research and Information* **40**(1), 1–6.

Cooper, I. (1999) Which focus for building assessment methods – environmental performance or sustainability? *Building Research and Information* **27**(4/5), 321–331.

Cooper, I. (2002) Transgressing discipline boundaries: is BEQUEST an example of 'the new production of knowledge'? *Building Research and Information* **30**(2), 116–129.

Cooper, I. (2008) *Workshop on the Role of Visioning in Urban Regeneration*, International Research Institute, Center for Technology in Government, University at Albany.

Cooper, I., Symes, M. (2009) *Sustainable Urban Development Volume 4: Changing Professional Practice*, Routledge, Abingdon.

Cooper, I., Foxell, S. (2015) Closing the policy gaps: from formulation to outcomes, Guest Editorial, *Building Research and Information* **43**(4), 399–406.

Cozens, P. (2002) Sustainable urban development and crime prevention: through environmental design for the British city, *Cities* **19**(2) 129–137.

Curwell, S., Hamilton, A., Cooper, I. (1998) The BEQUEST network: towards sustainable development. *Building Research and Information* **26**(1), 56–65.

Curwell, S., Deakin, M., Symes, M. (eds) (2005) *Sustainable Urban Development, Volume 1: The Framework and Protocols for Environmental Assessment*, Routledge, Abingdon.

Deakin, M., Mitchell, G., Nijkamp, P., Vreeker, R. (eds) (2009) *Sustainable Urban Development: Volume 2: The Environmental Assessment Methods*, Routledge, Abingdon.

Deakin, M., Vreeker, R., Curwell, S. (2009) Introduction. In: *Sustainable Urban Development, Volume 3: The Toolkit for Assessment* (eds Vreeker, R., Deakin, M., Curwell, S.), Routledge, Abingdon, pp. 1–14.

Dobson, A. (ed.) (1999) *Fairness and Futurity: Essays on Environmental Sustainability and Social Justice*, Oxford University Press, Oxford.

Donovan, R., Evans, J., Bryson, J., Porter, L., Hunt, D. (2005) *Large-scale Urban Regeneration and Sustainability: Reflections on the 'Barriers' Typology*, Working Paper 05/01, School of Geography, Earth and Environmental Sciences, University of Birmingham,.

Eclipse Research Consultants (1996) *PICABUE: Mapping Commitment to Sustainable Development – a Self-assessment Technique*, ERC, Cambridge.

Elkins, T., McClaren, D., Hillman, M. (1991) *Reviving the City: Towards Sustainable Urban Development*, Friends of the Earth, London.

Ellis, H. (2015) *Planning and Sustainable Energy, Joint Town and Country Planning Association and Sustainable Built Environment East Workshop*, Cambridge City Council, England.

EC (1998) *Sustainable Urban Development in the European Union: a Framework for Action*, Commission of the European Communities, Brussels.

EC (2009) *Promoting Sustainable Development in Europe: Achievements and Opportunities*, Commission of the European Communities, Brussels.

FIRBUAD (2015) *Cooperation of the EU Member States in the Field of Urban Development: Rotterdam Urban Acquis*. Available at: http://www.bbsr.bund.de/BBSR/EN/UrbanDevelopment/UrbanDevelopmentEurope/EuropeanUrbanPolicy/Projects/MemberStateCooperation/MemberStateCooperation.html (accessed 11 November 2015).

Freytag, T., Gössling, S., Mössner, S. (2014) Living the green city: Freiburg's Solarsiedlung between narratives and practices of sustainable urban development, *Local Environment* **19**(6), 644–659.

Fuller, R. (2010) Beyond cliché – reclaiming the concept of sustainability, *Australian Journal of Environmental Education* **26**, 1–12.

Hamilton, A., Curwell, S., Mitchell, G., James, P. (2009) Decision support for sustainable development: the origins and potential of the BEQUEST Toolkit. In: *Sustainable Urban Development, Volume 3: The Toolkit for Assessment* (eds Vreeker, R., Deakin, M., Curwell, S.), pp. 17–38, Routledge, Abingdon.

Holden, M., Esfahani, A., Scerri, A. (2014) Facilitated and emergent social learning in sustainable urban redevelopment: exposing a mismatch and moving towards convergence, *Urban Research and Practice* **7**(1), 1–19.

Honey-Rosés, J., Le Menestrel, J., Arenas, D., Rauschmayer, F., Rode, J. (2014) Enriching intergenerational decision-making with guided visualization exercises, *Journal of Business Ethics* **122**(4), 675–680.

Hornyanszky, E. (2014) Exchange of knowledge and expertise for sustainable urban development: experiences from cross-disciplinary and transnational cooperation between practitioners and researchers in the Öresund region, *Urban Research and Practice* **7**(1), 101–106.

Hunt, D.V.L., Lombardi, D.R., Atkinson, S., Barber, A., Barnes. M., Boyko, C.T., Brown, J. Bryson, J., Butler, D., Caputo, S., Caserio, M., Coles, R., Cooper, R., Farmani, R., Gaterell, M., Hale, J., Hales, C., Hewitt, C.N., Jankovic, L., Jefferson, I., Leach, J., MacKenzie, A.R., Memon, F., Pugh, T.A.M., Sadler, J.P., Weingaertner, C., Whyatt, J.D., Rogers, C.D.F. (2012) Using scenarios to explore urban UK futures: A review of the literature 1997 to 2011. In: *Designing Resilient Cities: A Guide to Good Practice* (eds Lombardi, D., Barnes. M., MacKenzie, A.R.), IHS BRE Press, Bracknell.

Jepson, E., Edwards, M. (2010) How possible is sustainable urban development? An analysis of planners' perceptions about new urbanism, smart growth and the ecological city, *Planning Practice and Research* **25**(4), 417–437.

Joss, S., Cowley, R., de Jong, M., Muller, B., Park, B., Rees, W., Roseland, M., Rydin, Y. (2015) *Tomorrow's city today: prospects for standardising sustainable urban development*, University of Westminster, London.

Kelvani, R. (2010) A review of the main challenges to urban sustainability, *International Journal of Urban Sustainable Development* **1**(1/2), 5–16.

Kennedy, C., Berger, G., Muller, B. (2015) Energy and material flows of megacities, *Proceedings of the National Academy of Sciences* **112**(19), 5985–5990.

Kohler, N (2002) The relevance of BEQUEST: an observer's perspective, *Building Research and Information* **30**(2), 130–138.

Kohler, N. (2003) *Cycles of Transformation for the City and its Culture*, Intelcity Workshop, University of Salford.

Lepuschitz, K., Pisano, U. (2014) *Mapping urban sustainable development in Europe and beyond*, ESDN Case Study No. 15, ESDN, Vienna.

Lepuschitz, K., Pisano, U., Berger, G. (2014) *Urban sustainable development approaches of three different cities: Copenhagen, Newcastle, Vienna*, ESDN Case Study No. 14, ESDN, Vienna.

Lowe, R. (2006) Defining absolute environmental limits for the built environment, *Building Research and Information* **34**(4), 405–415.

Meakin, S. (1992) *The Rio Earth Summit: Summary of the United Nations Conference on Environment and Development*, Science and Technology Division, UNEP.

Mieg, H., Töpfer. K. (eds.) (2013) *Institutional and Social Innovation for Sustainable Urban Development*, Routledge Studies in Sustainable Development, Routledge, Abingdon.

Mitchell, G., May, A., MacDonald, A. (1995) PICABUE: a methodological framework for the development of indicators of sustainable development, *International Journal of Sustainable Development and World Ecology* **2**, 104–123.

Mumford, L. (1921) *The Collapse of Tomorrow*, reprinted in Mumford, L. (1976) *Findings and Keepings: Analects for an Autobiography*, Secker and Warburg, London, pp. 61–67.

Murakami, S., Kawakubo, S., Asami, Y., Ikaga, T., Yamaguchi, N., Kaburagi, S. (2011) Development of a comprehensive city assessment tool: CASBEE-City, *Building Research and Information* **39**(3), 195–210.

OECD (2015) *Sustainable Urban Development Policies in Ageing Societies*, Organisation for Economic Co-operation and Development, Paris.

Palmer, J., Cooper, I., van der Vorst, R. (1997) Mapping out fuzzy buzzwords – who sits where on sustainability and sustainable development. *Sustainable Development* **5**, 87–93.

Platt, S., Cooper, I. (2005) *Urban Futures: Embracing Change, ResearchGate*. Available at: https://www.researchgate.net/publication/262611781_Urban_futures_-_embracing_change (accessed 11 November 2015).

Rabinovitch, J. (1992) Curitiba: towards sustainable urban development, *Environment and Urbanisation* **4**(2), 62–67.

Rees, W. (1999) The built environment and the eco-sphere: a global perspective, *Building Research and Information* **27**(45), 206–220.

Rees, W. (2012) Cities as dissipative structures: global change and the vulnerability of urban civilization. In: *Sustainability Science: the Emerging Paradigm and the Urban Environment* (eds Weinstein, M., Turner R.), Springer, New York, pp. 247–273.

Roberts, P. (2009) Sustainable communities: policy, practice and professional development. In: *Sustainable Urban Development, Volume 4: Changing Professional Practice* (eds Cooper, I., Symes, M.), Routledge Sustainable Urban Development Series, Routledge, Abingdon, pp. 127–145.

Satterthwaite, D. (1999) *The Earthscan Reader in Sustainable Cities*, Earthscan, London.

Solomon, Y. (2008) *Mathematical Literacy: Developing Identities of Inclusion*, Routledge, London.

Siri, J., Capon, A. (2015) *Health and wellbeing in sustainable urban development*, GDSR Brief 2015, International Institute for Global Health, United Nations University.

Stockholm Environment Institute (2008) *Resources and Energy Analysis Programme (REAP)*. Stockholm Environment Institute. Available at: www.sei-international.org/mediamanager/documents/Publications/Climate/reap.pdf (accessed 9 November 2015).

Tsenkova, S. (1999) Sustainable urban development in Europe: myth or reality?, *International Journal of Urban and Regional research* **23**(2), 361–364.

Tweed, C., Sutherland, M. (2007) Built cultural heritage and sustainable urban development, *Landscape and Urban Planning* **83**(1), 62–69.

UNEP (1992) *Rio Declaration on Environment and Development, United Nations Environment Programme*, UNEP. Available at: www.unep.org/Documents.Multilingual/Default.asp?documentid=78&articleid=1163 (accessed 9 November 2015).

UDIA (2009) *Sustainable Urban Development Matrix*, Urban Development Institute of Australia, Subiaco, Western Australia.

United Nations (2015) *Transforming Our World – the 2030 Agenda for Sustainable Development: Sustainable Development Goals*, Sustainable Development Knowledge platform, United Nations. Available at: https://sustainabledevelopment.un.org/?menu=1300 (accessed 1 January 2016).

UN-DESA (2013) *An integrated strategy for sustainable cities*, Policy Brief No. 40, UN-DESA, Rome.

UNESCO (2015) *Culture and sustainable urban development*, Concept Note, United Nations Educational, Scientific and Cultural Organisation. Available at: http://www.unesco.org/new/fileadmin/MULTIMEDIA/HQ/CLT/images/Concept_Note_Report_CultureandCities.pdf (accessed 10 November 2015).

UN-HABITAT (2007) *Sustainable Urban Development Network*. Available at: http://mirror.unhabitat.org/content.asp?typeid=19&catid=570&cid=5990 (accessed 11 November 2015).

UK Government (2015) *Sustainable Communities Act* UK Government. Available at: www.gov.uk/government/speeches/sustainable-communities-act (accessed 11 November 2015).

Vreeker, R., Deakin, M., Curwell, S. (eds) (2009) *Sustainable Urban Development: Volume 3 The Toolkit for Assessment*, Routledge, Abingdon.

Van Manen, M. (1990) *Researching lived experience*, State University of New York Press, Albany, NY.

Walker Institute (2015) *Impacts and Consequences of Climate Change – Built Environment* Walker Institute. Available at: www.walker-institute.ac.uk/research/impacts/built.htm (accessed 10 November 2015).

Warwick, E. (2015) Policy to reality: evaluating the evidence trajectory for English eco-towns, *Building Research and Information* **43**(4), 486–498.

Wei, Y., Huang, C., Lam, P., Sha, Y., Feng, Y. (2015) Using urban-carrying capacity as a benchmark for sustainable urban development: an empirical study of Beijing, *Sustainability* **7**, 3244–3268.

Wheeler S. (1996) *Sustainable Urban Development: a Literature Review and Analysis*, Monograph 51, Institute of Urban and Regional Development, University of California, Berkeley.

Wheeler, S., Beatley, T. (2014) *Sustainable Development Reader*, Routledge Urban Reader Series, Routledge, Abingdon.

Whittemore, A., Forgey, F. (2014) Where is what called Sustainability? A survey of policies ostensibly and explicitly linked to sustainability in the US, *Planning, Practice and Research* **29**(4), 405–425.

Wiltschko, G. (2009) *Principles of Sustainable Urban Development in the Bidding Process for the Olympic Games*, Masters thesis, Vienna University of Technology, Vienna.

World Urban Campaign (2015) *SUD to 2050*, World Urban Campaign. Available at: http://www.worldurbancampaign.org (accessed 11 November 2015).

Section 2
Design and Evaluation Tools and Technology

Chapter 6

Crowdsourcing Public Participation in Sustainable Built Environment Development: The Democratisation of Expertise

Sidney Newton
Faculty of Built Environment, The University of New South Wales, Sydney, NSW 2052, Australia

6.1 Introduction

'Three hundred miles and more from Chimborazo, one hundred from the snows of Cotopaxi, in the wildest wastes of Ecuador's Andes, there lies that mysterious mountain valley, cut off from the world of men, the Country of the Blind.' (Wells, 1911). Thus begins one of H.G. Wells' best known short stories, '*The Country of the Blind*'. In this short story a sighted intruder (a mountaineer named Nuñez) falls upon a remote and entirely blind community that has fully adapted to life without sight. The community has no concept of sight and Nuñez can do nothing to explain what it is that he sees or why his having a fifth sense might warrant the adulation and authority he expects. On the contrary, the would-be king is dismissed and derided because he does not understand the world he has encountered in a way that is meaningful to the blind inhabitants. So much for the proverb: 'In the land of the blind, the one-eyed man is king'.

In the context of sustainable built environment development, Nuñez and the one-eyed man might readily be taken as euphemisms for the planning and design experts generally charged with the management of sustainable development projects. In this sense, such experts are commonly held to exercise a special, more advanced level of knowledge and awareness than the lay person (Ericsson, 2014) This enables experts to 'see' things that the general community of non-experts cannot perceive without considerable effort and guidance, at best (Sternberg and Frensch, 1992). However, one of the problems with this notion of expertise as the harbinger of privileged insight (in any context but most especially where social complexity is manifest) is how it is used increasingly to fuel the rhetoric of control (Stirling, 2014).

The rhetoric of control now pervades the sustainable built environment development literature, even in the ostensibly hallowed corners of public participation. For example,

Future Challenges in Evaluating and Managing Sustainable Development in the Built Environment,
First Edition. Edited by Peter S. Brandon, Patrizia Lombardi and Geoffrey Q. Shen.
© 2017 John Wiley & Sons Ltd. Published 2017 by John Wiley & Sons Ltd.

the Planning Institute of Australia asserts that public participation in planning is necessary 'so that a proposal, policy or strategy may be shaped and influenced in response to community values and comment' (PIA, 2011). In other words, that public participation is necessary so that the experts can be better informed to tell the community what to do. 'Inviting people to gather in a room for a public hearing is the recognised format for engaging citizens, and has been since New England town hall meetings were implemented centuries ago' (Gordon *et al.*, 2011). Here, public participation is conceived as something to be provided to the lay community (and controlled) by the expert community. The expectation seems to be, in keeping with the proverb, that in the complex land of sustainable development, the expert is king.

What the tale of Nuñez suggests, however, is that the lay community of 'blind' public participants may have a propensity for dealing with sustainable built environment development that is entirely more meaningful (and realisable) for them as local stakeholders – despite the supposed advantage of expert insight. Like Nuñez, the sustainable development experts may believe themselves to have superior knowledge and skills (and by definition that would not be an unreasonable assumption) but find that the general community is actually far more capable of achieving an actual sustainable outcome in the context of their local situation. The role of expertise in sustainable built environment development warrants further consideration, and this chapter seeks to develop the argument that a more effective approach to sustainable development requires a more democratic and transformative approach to planning and design. Ultimately, it will be argued, it is the community that enables and takes transformative action in the context of sustainable development. In that regard, the study addresses the particular challenge set by Stirling (2014): to emancipate transformation-based action.

In order to demonstrate the viability of transformative action, the study considers a range of approaches available to enable and promote public participation in sustainable built environment development. The emphasis is on recent technology-enabled initiatives. The purpose of the review is to demonstrate that emerging digital technology is still broadly conceptualised and deployed as a supplement to the existing power dynamic, where experts manage public engagement and engagement is generally limited to knowledge exchange. However, entirely more disruptive technologies are also beginning to emerge. Particular attention is paid to virtual reality (VR) technologies, through which public participation in sustainable built environment development can be reconsidered and redesigned into a more effectively democratic governance structure. The aim of the study is to highlight the opportunity to crowdsource public participation in sustainable development planning, design, construction, operation and indeed the entire life-cycle of a built facility: to enable an effective democratic participation that places public and expert in a laterally mutual space of discourse.

6.2 The context of sustainable built environment development

Sustainable development in its broadest and simplest sense seeks to balance immediate needs with future needs (World Commission on Environment and Development, 1987). However, within this manifestly simple statement lies a myriad of complexities (Masnavi, 2013).

In the first instance, particular needs must be identified and prioritised in order to determine what actually has to be balanced. A value figure or some other metric must be estimated against each need, and future needs have to be forecast. Agreement on the needs to be considered and the values to be included have to be negotiated across the diverse, changing and generally conflicting interests of various stakeholder groups. It is in the nature of holistic sustainable development that external impacts across complex ecologies must also be recognised and incorporated. Often incommensurate social, environmental and economic considerations have to be balanced and traded in some way. The interactions of local versus global frameworks must be articulated and reconciled. Sustainable development is inherently complex. But complexity is often mere grist to the mill of modern science. Complexity is not especially problematic per se. The critical issue for sustainable development in the context of the built environment is that the inherent complexity is also fundamentally wicked (Rittel and Webber, 1973).

A wicked problem is generally distinguished by six key characteristics (Conklin, 2006):

1. There is no definitive statement of the problem, meaning each problem is an evolving set of interdependent issues and constraints.
2. There is no definitive solution, meaning each new solution reveals new problems that continue evolving as long as consideration is made.
3. There is no authoritative or objective measure of solution quality, as this is likely to depend on the various judgements of individual stakeholders acting on independent values and goals.
4. There is no other identical problem, with multiple interdependent factors operating in a dynamic context. There may be similar or equivalent problems but never identical.
5. Every attempt at a solution has lasting unintended consequences which are likely to spawn further (wicked) problems and irrevocably change the nature of the current problem.
6. There can be no given alternative solution, and it is a matter of creativity to devise candidate solutions and a matter of judgement to determine which are valid and have most utility.

Aligned to the wicked nature of sustainable development is the increasing social complexity presented by stakeholders of different gender, ethnicity, culture, age, education, discipline, community group and so on. Social complexity adds significantly to the potential for communication breakdown and only exacerbates the uncertainty and complexity that attends the sustainable development process. Uncertainty and poor communication can then lead to disengagement from and distrust of the development process by the very stakeholders most impacted by any development – the local community (Dalton, 2004). The prevalence of insecurity and sense of injustice that flows from public disengagement in sustainable development decision-making then prompts increasingly more radical proposals for governance reform. At the one extreme, there is a call to adopt the top rung of Arnstein's (1969) ladder of citizen participation and provide public stakeholders with unfettered decision-making rights over a development (Gordon *et al.*, 2011). At the other, there is a call for greater authoritarianism as perhaps the only means of breaking through the developing democratic impasse (Hickman, 2010).

In other words, that the raft of alternative views and additional bureaucratic hurdles ('red tape') associated with extensive public participation has become obstructive and counter-productive in and of its self. The radicalisation of opinion is increasingly characterised as a failure of public governance (Evans and Davies, 2015).

For many, the failure of governance stems directly from the impoverished democratic models on which current governance systems typically are based (Shearman and Smith, 2007). We will return to this issue in more detail later. Democratic models in any political context aim to enable a process where diverse stakeholders are able to contribute to a sustainable solution through respectful and well-informed consideration (Gastil, 2008). In that regard they directly parallel the intention of public participation in sustainable built environment development. In both contexts much is being made of the potential for new communication technologies to enable greater and more effective engagement of the public in decision-making processes (Krätzig and Warren-Kretzschmar, 2014). Sustainable built environment development is in many ways a pioneer in the use of new technology to improve public participation, and it is worth reviewing a range of those initiatives.

6.3 Background to technology-enabled public participation

To be most effective, sustainable built environment development needs to understand and accommodate the impact that a given development (and other options) might have on the local and the broader community. This calls for the constituents of each stakeholder community to engage with the development process at all stages and to participate directly in relevant deliberations. Public perceptions and attitudes are important to know (Gordon *et al.*, 2011). The problem with increased public participation is that it comes at a cost and can present a double-edged sword: there are unintended consequences. Broader participation generally means it is a more expensive process, takes longer, generates a broader range of increasingly more extreme and conflicting perspectives and can often be driven by ulterior motives (Stein, 2004). At the same time, when public concern is denied or dismissed, community tensions can be exacerbated and frustration can lead to conflict and confrontation (Hamilton *et al.*, 2001).

Communication is long held to be the key to resolving any such impasse (GTZ, 2006). All too often however a managerial approach to communication is favoured where the public are simply advised of a development in general terms and invited to provide very specific responses. This level of communication is inadequate, particularly in the case of sustainability where the key issues are often broad-ranging, context-dependent and highly technical (Al-Kodmany, 2000). Fortunately, new digital technologies are greatly expanding and improving the communication options (Krätzig and Warren-Kretzschmar, 2014).

The introduction of digital communications technologies to support urban planning has tended to build on conventional meetings and workshop formats – leveraging relatively recent technologies such as web-based surveys, digital document exchange, email and rudimentary visualisations to complement the face to face processes (Hague and Loader, 1999). More immediately, the power of digital social networks to facilitate collaboration has been used to shift entire communication processes online and enable more collective action outcomes (Shirky, 2008). Action outcomes are particularly important in the context of public participation in sustainable built environment development, where the focus needs to be on deliberation and those forms of communication which can progress beyond mere discussion to actual solutions or decisions that represent the best possible outcome for a given circumstance (Gordon and Manosevitch, 2010). Deliberation complicates communication as it demands both the rigorous rational analysis of an issue and the social framework that incorporates important underlying communication norms (respect, equality, ethics etc.; Gastil, 2008). So, to be effective, public participation requires the digital support of tools that are both analytical and social in nature and which work collectively rather than in isolation from each other (Hamilton *et al.*, 2001).

Early efforts to improve public participation in sustainable built environment development decision-making focussed on translating the otherwise relatively abstract and idiosyncratic representations associated with urban planning (architectural sketches, data-rich maps, planning scenarios etc.) into forms that the lay public could more readily comprehend (Rixon and Burn, 2008). But, at its best, deliberation requires all parties to contribute and share their ideas and understanding. Rendering the technical documents of experts more accessible to the lay public does little to enable the same public to express and contribute their own ideas in technical and spatial terms in return (Gordon and Manosevitch, 2010). The advent of interactive online technologies (such as Web 2.0 and multiplayer video games) provide a key platform for content generated by the public to be uploaded and presented alongside expert technical information. Social media also enables online special interest groups to leverage and develop more technical expertise in pursuit of their common goals (Kanter and Fine, 2010).

The appropriation of emerging digital technologies to support an improved democratic decision-making process may, however, hide a significantly more sinister intent. According to Stirling (2014), in the ostensible name of public participation and re-engagement, the imperative for instrumental action and social diversity is (ironically) used to conceal controlling interests and subjugate democratic discourse. In the context of a sustainability crisis, characterised as radicalisation and promoted by imperatives, the call is for greater trust in and dependency on domain experts (Beeson, 2010). This nurtured climate of authoritarianism constrains the very public discourse it is claimed to be facilitating. Various well-intentioned interventions have actually tended to polarise public opinion around particular apocalyptic assertions by ramping up the rhetoric on both sides of the debate. The negative character of polarised debate has, in its turn, suppressed more nuanced and democratic consideration of contending positive anticipation (Stirling, 2013). Thus, technology-enabled public participation in sustainable development has led to a very particular and rather fettered form of public participation: a form of public participation where control is exercised through a subtle confirmation of incumbent control structures (Leach *et al.*, 2012). Truly democratic public participation is being drowned in a mire of imperatives that demand action and determination when what is required is more reflective consideration and debate.

Stirling (2014) seeks to render more explicit the insidious tyranny of current sustainability policy and process by characterising two competing forms of democratic action.

On the one hand there is a top-down, transition-based action. Transition-based action leads to stepwise change within the existing framework of incumbent control structures. As such it appears less threatening, more familiar and ultimately more inevitable. Technological innovation is often characterised as a progressive and stepwise process (Venuvinod, 2011) and it is no accident that transition-based action is most often associated with and driven by technological innovations. On the other hand there is a bottom-up, transformation-based action that challenges and disrupts incumbent control structures. Transformation-based action leads to more fundamental shifts in knowledge and practice and is typically driven by emergent social and cultural innovation. In this sense, transformation-based action subscribes more to the unicorn model of innovation (Payne, 2014) where progress can be bold and rapid. Transformation-based action is driven by a plurality of knowledge and values and, according to Stirling (2014), an essential combination of both knowing and doing.

In keeping with transformation-based action, the appropriation of technology is best realised using the crowd as an open, unruly and agonistic contention (Boudreau and Lakhani, 2013). Such crowdsourcing is possible using various technology contexts, but nowhere is the phenomenon more prevalent or foundational than in VR gaming technologies (Edery and Mollick, 2009). VR is a broad-based technology, positioned as a future hub technology that is capable of marshalling a range of other technologies and delivering those functionalities through a hyper-immersive experience. Of course VR does have immediate relevance to transition-based action if it is employed merely to extend the incumbent framework of managed discourse. However, VR also establishes a propensity for direct public action by supporting and empowering individuals to contribute in a more direct and active manner.

6.4 The potential of virtual reality

Virtual reality (VR) has become increasingly difficult to define as it becomes increasingly more popular and widespread as an emerging technology and future potential. In basic terms, VR refers to a range of technologies that prompt a user to perceive that they are having a concrete experience of something without the actual thing being present (Ijsselsteijn, 2004). There is no particular requirement for the VR experience to replicate a real world experience (it can be unrealistic), but the obvious potential for VR in a sustainable built environment development context is in terms of real world possibilities. Most specifically, VR offers the opportunity for users to experience and create real world experiences that are otherwise not available to them.

VR technologies are also as varied and sometimes contentious as the range of definitions for VR. Fundamentally, VR requires the ability to render and display a scene so that it presents as if the user is able to view in any direction, move through the scene at will and interact with objects in the scene. The goal is to immerse the user in a scene and so, the higher the quality of rendering, the faster the frame-rate, the more stereoscopic, the more immediate the feedback to movement, the wider the field of view and so on, then the more authentic the VR experience. It is possible to deliver an acceptable level of visual immersion on a screen, but the bigger the screen the better; multiple wrap-around screens improve the experience further and head-mounted displays can completely immerse the user in a visual experience. But of course, concrete experience involves more sensory modalities than just visualisation. Concrete experience is egocentric in the sense that it generally involves looking, hearing, smelling, touching, interacting and moving from and with some virtual self-representation. Stereo and location-based sound, physical movement mirrored in the virtual environment, responsive environmental factors (temperature, precipitation, air movement etc.), haptic feedback, physical objects available to the user that correspond to VR objects and first-person viewpoints all add to the immersive qualities of the experience (van den Hoogen *et al.*, 2009). However, not all immersive technologies add equally to the experience, with stereo rendering, field of view and physical movement found to be of particular significance (Cummings and Bailenson, 2015).

VR immersion is the technological quality of the experience, but ultimately experience is a psychological phenomenon. The psychological counterpart to immersion is presence. Presence is a state of consciousness where the VR experience provides the sense of being in the concrete experience (Schubert *et al.*, 2001). Presence is generally thought of as an increasing function of immersion and can be considered in both subjective and objective terms: subjective because it is a state of mind about which the individual can express their perceptions, objective because it leads to responsive behaviours which can be observed (Slater *et al.*, 1998). Nevertheless, presence remains difficult to evaluate and quantify explicitly. As more is understood about cognition, more is also understood about how the process of being present must act on different cognitive levels and in different perceptual dimensions simultaneously (Wirth *et al.*, 2007). Significantly, presence is not merely a factor of the physical presence in space, as described above, but rather a composite of physical/spatial presence and social presence. Social presence brings into play the requirement that the intentions or affordances associated with a physical/spatial environment are realised or enacted in accordance with the pre-reflexive predictions (social expectations) of the agent (Riva, 2009). In other words, exposure to identical VR will produce different levels of presence and different experiences for different people, according to their various backgrounds, intentions and expectations.

From this perspective, VR is positioned as a spectrum of immersive technologies that create in varying degrees and in various ways a sense of being in (experience of) a fabricated situation. The most sophisticated interactive VR systems with practical application to sustainable built environment development currently are to be found in video game engines (the kernel of coding used to drive a collection of actual video game implementations). Of particular relevance is the recent emergence of hyper-immersive, first-person, multi-user video game engines made available on what is effectively an open-source basis (for examples, see www.unrealengine.com and unity3d.com). The most powerful video game engines are now free to acquire for a range of purposes, they allow third party modifications and they are supported online by a significant and committed community of users and developers. However, what is most striking about such VR game engines is the added capability they now provide to act as the hub technology for a broad spectrum of other digital systems and networked devices.

Sophisticated VR game engines are able to communicate with most common external data exchange standards and provide ready development solutions for more bespoke requirements. This means that VR game engines sit comfortably within the digital network of pervasive information and communication technologies referred to as the Internet of Things: things ranging from specific computing devices and applications to everyday things such as buildings, posters, pot plants and potentially every other object 'wired' into the digital world (Mattern and Floerkemeier, 2010). At the same time, there is a push to make more of the huge collection of data held by various government agencies more readily available and open to the public. This push is also part of the recent initiative to encourage technology-enhanced forms of participatory government and public service delivery (for examples, see data.gov.au and data.london.gov.uk). Open data is 'data that can be freely used, reused and redistributed by anyone – subject only, at most, to the requirement to attribute and share alike' (opendefinition.org). Of course the complement to this public data is the vast array of data routinely now being collected by individuals, private agencies and commercial organisations, both general business operations and specialist data service providers and analysts. There can be little doubt that the collection, storage and processing of data is increasing at a compounding rate (Hilbert and López, 2011).

The potential application of this vast data resource and increasing technological integration to the urban context is broad and substantial (Foth, 2009). In particular, rendition of the data is no longer restricted to output in the form of text on a screen or to interaction limited by a computer keyboard and mouse. Human experience of data, and in our context the public space to which such data refers, stands on the verge of a technical revolution: a technically driven revolution in how we emotionally and cognitively experience the built environment (Townsend, 2013). Traditional distinctions between the real and the virtual and between VR and augmented reality are being dissolved (Hughes, 2012). A critical consequence of this human-technological integration is how the further blending of real space with virtual space might impact our notions of location and self (Benyon, 2012). The effective design of future spatial realities (actual, digital and blended) will be contingent on these emerging concepts of location and self (McCreery *et al.*, 2013). It is a timely juncture to reformulate the framework within which location and self might usefully be considered in the development of digital systems that make sense of spatial data, particularly in the context of the emerging VR technologies that sit directly at the confluence of blended reality.

VR game engines are able to interact (read from and write to) this array of external data and processing capability. Each specific situation represented in the VR game engine can comprise: (i) certain environmental conditions, (ii) objects and their properties, (iii) actors and their behaviours and (iv) data input/output feeds. The VR environment can accurately represent a range of conditions such as: (i) the relative positioning of the sun for a specific location, date and time, (ii) the lighting effects of weather conditions and air pollution and (iii) the shadows cast by natural and artificial light-sources, ambient lighting and so on. Objects in the environment can include buildings, equipment, natural features such as rivers and trees, specific materials such as glass and moving objects such as vehicles. All objects can be assigned dimensions, mass, articulation points, movement restrictions, strength and consequential actions specific to circumstances. Actors or avatars can be scripted to behave in certain ways in response to specific criteria, such as the proximity of other actors or objects, and can interact with users based on sophisticated artificial intelligence programming. The VR environment can also interact with (read and write) a multitude of external data feeds, including web browsers, video streams, motion capture, other software and the Internet of Things more generally. All of these conditions, properties, behaviours and feeds are processed in parallel, using very capable rendering and physics processors to determine the frame by frame resolution of the VR environment over time and with imperceptible lag.

VR in the form of a video game environment is not the future however. Recent high-profile acquisitions of VR technologies by the likes of Facebook, Google, HTC and Apple give a strong indication that the future use of VR will be far more pervasive than just for simulation and entertainment. VR is being lauded as the future interface to everything and more of a medium than a device (The Verge, 2015). In that context the potential application of VR to public participation in sustainable built environment development is an open, blue-sky thinking exercise. The purpose of this study, however, is to demonstrate the more immediate potential of VR. It will do that by describing a crowdsourcing approach to public participation in sustainable built environment development that is already active. The potential of such an approach more generally is to democratise expertise and challenge the incumbent power relationship in sustainable built environment development to be more in favour of the general public.

6.5 Using virtual reality as a crowdsourcing approach to public participation in urban planning

To illustrate the potential of VR to support public participation at the planning stage of a sustainable built environment development, the focus is on VR as a creative visualisation tool. This is not to suggest that visualisation is only applicable to the planning stage, nor is it that visualisation is the only aspect of VR that is applicable at the planning stage. Rather, VR as a creative visualisation tool is used merely to demonstrate one key aspect of VR at one particular stage in a project life cycle.

Public participation is a critical consideration for almost every planning process of any scale. The application of visualisation to support the process of public participation has a long tradition (Forester, 1999), and the use of three-dimensional (3D) visualisation is a well-established method of representing spatial data in a readily communicable form (Hamilton *et al.*, 2001). Despite the enthusiastic uptake, however, a comprehensive evaluation of the impact and effectiveness of the many and varied forms of 3D visualisation in this context is yet to be established (Salter *et al.*, 2009). What is known is that, to be effective, public participation requires a combination of essential components that includes 3D visualisation (Appleton and Lovett, 2005).

A critical limitation of current 3D visualisation technologies is generally expressed in terms of the perceived trade-off between realism (the level of detail and rendering quality) and the substantial resources required to produce and access such a rendition (Lai *et al.*, 2010). The more realistic the model, so the argument goes, the more effort it requires to produce the model; the larger the files, the more problematic the file exchange; the more powerful the display technology required, the more elaborate the user interface has to be; and the more expertise is required to make changes to the model, the more the technology excludes effective user participation (Gordon *et al.*, 2011). Emerging VR technologies begin to uncouple the realism of a 3D visualisation from the resourcing spiral. For example, laser scanning technology is developing rapidly, providing automatic and immediate processing of massive point-clouds into 3D polygonal and surface models that can be used directly in 3D visualisations (Chen *et al.*, 2013). Video game technology is also being enhanced to enable the creation of viable urban environments, geometries and object representations within a visualisation, on the fly and with minimal technical training (Moloney, 2015).

The accelerating pace of technology development that is enabling more direct input and manipulation of virtual worlds is being complemented with novel forms of virtual experience. Whether the experience is of an entirely virtual world that is made to look and perform like an actual real world situation or a virtual enhancement of an actual real world situation, VR technology offers a level of immersion and presence that previous 3D visualisation could not provide. For example, rather than reinforce the largely false and often prescribed civic scale of a project using the birds-eye view of a conventional visualisation fly-through, the first-person VR system is able to present a fully immersive and interactive pedestrian experience at the more human scale of the street level. Indeed, the first-person perspective has been shown to promote presence without the need for high-fidelity visualisations: models need not be photo-realistic if they are well situated (Moere and Hill, 2012).

The scope for public participation in the planning and design of sustainable built environment developments is broadening and deepening and signals new possibilities to crowdsource development proposals and modifications from the lay community. By way of one example, the visualisation platform developed and managed by Urban Circus (2015) has the capacity to accurately model urban landscapes and for users to quickly and easily experience and modify a variety of project proposals. Urban Circus is only one of several commercial services available internationally that has been built using video game technology. It has been applied to a variety of projects for a range of purposes. A useful case study in the context of this study is the particular application of Urban Circus to support the Victorian Government Department of Transport, Planning and Local Infrastructure (Crisafi and Guy, 2013) to develop a virtual 3D model of central Melbourne, Australia.

According to Crisafi and Guy (2013), the traditional reliance on architectural drawings and physical 3D models as the basis for visualisation and development assessment is costly to produce, difficult to update and relatively immobile. An original virtual model of Melbourne city was generated in Urban Circus from terrain, aerial cadastral and building information databases. The video game technology on which Urban Circus is built provides for direct and rapid manipulation of building envelopes so that proposed or possible changes in developments and planning policy can be considered against the changed dimensions, floor areas, heights, site-lines, statutory compliance, shadows and other implications specific to particular locations. Changes can be proposed with minimal instruction in the modelling software itself (making it accessible to lay people). Implications can be expressed in technical and economic terms measured automatically from the revised model and/or as a first-person VR experience within a simulated situation under various environmental conditions.

The current Melbourne model in Urban Circus is used primarily to assist in the assessment of major development proposals across the cumulative impact of multiple proposals within a rapidly changing city rather than any single possibility in isolation. Crisafi and Guy (2013) claim that it also enables improved understanding and provides for better consensus building and evidence-based integrated decision-making. Furthermore, the interactive model is provided across Government and made available to the public. In this way, the input and consideration of any development proposal is genuinely more open to the crowdsourcing of ideas and opinions – moving to a greater democratisation of what is traditionally an expert-centric decision-making process.

However, as Creighton (2005) points out, public participation partakes of intense human interaction and remains largely a craft rather than a science. In other words, trying to legislate for increased public participation may be as fraught as trying to legislate for democracy – perhaps people, like horses, will only do what they have a mind to do. An important driver in this regard is whether the democratisation of expertise will be mutually beneficial to all stakeholders – which, manifestly, it will not be. This means that any attempt to disempower experts will be challenged. For example, there is a strongly promoted sense that providing lay people with advanced planning and design tools will merely produce better informed bad planning and design (Healey, 1998) – that expertise is an essential requirement. Certainly where such perceptions are prevalent public participation is likely to remain nominal (Voinov and Bousquet, 2010), and this will apply regardless of the enabling technology.

In contrast, there is growing recognition that expertise itself has limitations, most especially where expert opinion is applied to forecasting the future (Buchanan, 2013). Krueger *et al.* (2012) argue for a paradigm shift from traditional ideals of unbiased and impartial experts towards unbiased processes of expert contestation and a plurality of expertise. Whilst somewhat idealistic in its own right, given that all human opinion is biased (Kahneman, 2011), the open process of expert contestation is exactly what systems such as Urban Circus have the potential to help promote. To reference back to the case made by Stirling (2014), sustainability itself was only realised through democratic struggle in the face of the concentrated power and fallacies of, so-called, expert control. A process of orderly technical transition to sustainable built environment development might remain inherent within any systemic solution, the likes of Urban Circus included. However, within the framework of potential control and nominal public participation to which any enabling democratic technology might succumb, there lies within VR technology an innate, almost primordial genealogy for disruption and unruly democratisation that will be difficult to suppress. This is where the greatest potential for video game technologies such as Urban Circus actually resides.

6.6 Summary

The VR platform developed and managed by Urban Circus is only one of a number of such services currently available. The example is intended to demonstrate that video game technology is already being adopted and used in established planning processes. However, the capacity for such technologies to enable a lay community to contribute direct modifications to a project proposal, evaluate outcomes and input alternatives moves conventional 3D visualisation to an enabling technology for public participation. Multiple stakeholders will be able to amend and propose sustainable built environment developments, much akin to the Wiki model of open database editing.

The issue of course is that, without expertise in urban planning, design, construction and operation of the built environment, there is a high risk of impractical, unviable and non-compliant proposals being generated. Such 'noise' has the potential to drown-out feasible solutions. This is where VR as a hub technology has a role to play in providing access to relevant data, calculations, regulations and rudimentary analysis specific to any proposal. That is certainly not to suggest that all planning, design, construction and operational expertise can or should be automated. However, the rapidly improving capacity for automated systems to translate naïve expressions of built form into rich representations of viable development solutions does point to a significant improvement in the potential for creative input by otherwise lay public.

The fundamental argument of this paper is that this emerging functionality will enable public stakeholders to shape and incorporate viable solutions to sustainable built environment development situations. On that basis, the power relationship of expert to non-expert might largely be dissolved and public participation in sustainable development projects will be transformed. More significantly, in the future, ongoing transformation will become the norm. Somewhat perversely, given the duality articulated by Stirling (2014), the move from transition to transformation will be instigated by the very incumbent power frameworks that seek to deny the radical technological, political, economic and cultural changes required to enable sustainable development and emancipate understandings of transformation itself.

References

Al-Kodmany, K. (2000) Public participation: technology and democracy. *Journal of Architectural Education* **53**, 220–228.

Appleton, K., Lovett, A. (2005) GIS-based visualisation of development proposals: reactions from planning and related professionals. *Computers, Environment and Urban Systems* **29**, 386–395.

Arnstein, S.R. (1969) A ladder of citizen participation. *Journal of the American Planning Association* **35**, 4, 216–224.

Beeson, M. (2012) The coming of environmental authoritarianism. *Environmental Politics* **19**, 2, 276–294.

Benyon, D. (2012) Presence in blended spaces. *Interacting with Computers* **24**, 219–226.

Boudreau, K.J., Lakhani, K.R. (2013) Using the crowd as an innovation partner. *Harvard Business Review* **91**, 4, 61–69.

Buchanan, M. (2013) Forecast: What Physics, Meteorology and the Natural Sciences Can Teach Us About Economics. Bloomsbury Publishing, London.

Chen, J., Wua, X., Wang, M.Y., Li, X. (2013) 3D shape modelling using a self-developed hand-held 3D laser scanner and an efficient HT-ICP point cloud registration algorithm. *Optics and Laser Technology* **45**, 414–423.

Conklin, J. (2006) Dialogue Mapping: Building Shared Understanding of Wicked Problems. John Wiley & Sons, Ltd, Chichester.

Creighton, J.L. (2005) The Public Participation Handbook: Making Better Decisions Through Citizen Involvement. Jossey-Bass, San Francisco.

Crisafi, T., Guy, B. (2013) Planning Melbourne with 3D virtual environments. *International Urban Design Conference, Melbourne*, pp. 1–7.

Cummings, J.J., Bailenson, J.N. (2015) How immersive is enough? A meta-analysis of the effect of immersive technology on user presence. *Media Psychology* **2015**, 1–38.

Dalton, R. (2004) Democratic Challenges, Democratic Choices: The Erosion of Political Support in Advanced Industrial Democracies. Oxford University Press, Oxford.

Edery, D., Mollick, E. (2009) Changing the Game: How Video Games are Transforming the Future of Business. FT Press, New Jersey.

Ericsson, K.A. (2014) Expertise. *Current Biology* **24**(11), 508–510.

Evans, J.W. Davies, R. (eds) (2015) Too Global to Fail: The World Bank at the Intersection of National and Global Public Policy in 2025. Directions in Development, World Bank, Washington, D.C.

Forester, J. (1999) The Deliberative Practitioner: Encouraging Participatory Planning Processes. MIT Press, Cambridge, Mass.

Foth, M. (ed) (2009) Handbook of Research on Urban Informatics: The Practice and Promise of the Real-Time City. Information Science Reference, IGI Global, Hershey.

Gastil, J. (2008) Political Communication and Deliberation. Sage, Thousand Oaks.

Gordon, E., Manosevitch, E. (2010) Augmented deliberation: Merging physical and virtual interaction to engage communities in urban planning. *New Media and Society* **13**(1), 75–95.

Gordon, E., Schirra, S., Hollander, J. (2011) Immersive planning: a conceptual model for designing public participation with new technologies. *Environment and Planning B: Planning and Design* **38**, 505–519.

GTZ (2006) Strategic Communication for Sustainable Development: A Conceptual Overview. GTZ Rioplus, Bonn.

Hague, B.N., Loader, B.D. (eds) (1999) Digital Democracy: Discourse and Decision Making in the Information Age. Routledge, London.

Hamilton, A., Trodd, N., Zhang, X., Fernando, T., Watson, K. (2001) Learning through visual systems to enhance the urban planning process. *Environment and Planning B: Planning and Design* **28**, 833–845.

Healey, P. (1998) Collaborative planning in a stakeholder society. *The Town Planning Review* **69**(1), 1–21.

Hickman, L. (2010) James Lovelock: humans are too stupid to prevent climate change. *Guardian*, 29 March, pp. 2–5.

Hilbert, M., López, P. (2011) The world's technological capacity to store, communicate, and compute information. *Science* **332**(6025), 60–65.

van den Hoogen, W.M., Ijsselsteijn, W.A., de Kort, Y.A.W. (2009) Effects of sensory immersion on behavioural indicators of player experience: movement synchrony and controller pressure. In: Breaking New Ground: Innovation in Games, Play, Practice and Theory (eds B. Atkins, H. Kennedy), DiGRA 2009 Proceedings, London, pp. 1–4.

Hughes, I. (2012) Virtual worlds, augmented reality, blended reality. *Computer Networks: The International Journal of Computer and Telecommunications Networking* **56** (18), 3879–3885.

Ijsselsteijn, W.A. (2004) Presence in Depth. PhD thesis, Eindhoven University of Technology, Eindhoven.

Kahneman, D. (2011) Thinking, Fast and Slow. Penguin Books, London.

Kanter, B., Fine, A.H. (2010) The Networked Nonprofit: Connecting with Social Media to Drive Change. Jossey-Bass, San Francisco.

Krätzig, S., Warren-Kretzschmar, B. (2014) Using interactive web tools in environmental planning to improve communication about sustainable development. *Sustainability* **6**, 236–250.

Krueger, T., Page, T., Hubacek, C., Smith, L., Hiscock, K. (2012) The role of expert opinion in environmental modelling. *Environmental Modelling and Software* **36**, 4–18.

Lai, P.C., Kwong, K-H., Mak, A.S.H. (2010) Assessing the applicability and effectiveness of 3D visualisation in environmental impact assessment. *Environment and Planning B: Planning and Design* **37**, 221–233.

Leach, M., Rockström, J. Raskin, P., Scoones, I., Stirling, A.C., Smith, A., Thompson, J., Millstone, E., Ely, A., Arond, E., Folke, C., Olsson, P. (2012) Transforming innovation for sustainability. *Ecology and Society* **17** (2), 11.

Moloney, J. (2015) Videogame technology re-purposed: towards interdisciplinary design environments for engineering and architecture. *Procedia Technology* **20**, 212–218.

Masnavi, M.R. (2013) Environmental sustainability and ecological complexity: developing an integrated approach to analyse the environment and landscape potentials to promote sustainable development. *International Journal of Environmental Research* **7** (4), 995–1006.

Mattern, F., Floerkemeier, C. (2010) From the Internet of Computers to the Internet of Things. Institute for Pervasive Computing, ETH Zurich, Zurich.

McCreery, M.P., Schrader, P.G., Krach, S.K., Boone, R. (2013) A sense of self: the role of presence in virtual environments. *Computers in Human Behavior* **29**, 1635–1640.

Moere, A.V., Hill, D. (2012) Designing for the situated and public visualization of urban data. *Journal of Urban Technology* **19** (2), 25–46.

Payne, M. (2014) How to Kill a Unicorn: How the World's Hottest Innovation Factory Builds Bild Ideas That Make it to Market. Crown Publishing Group, New York.

PIA (2011) Public Participation. Planning Institute Australia, Kingston.

Rittel, H.W.J., Webber, M.M. (1973) Dilemmas in a general theory of planning. *Policy Sciences* **4**, 155–169.

Riva, G. (2009) Is presence a technology issue? Some insights from cognitive sciences. *Virtual Reality* **13**, 159–169.

Rixon, A., Burn, S. (2008) Visualization techniques for facilitating stakeholder decision making in urban planning. *E-Government and Community Informatics* **4**, 2.

Salter, J.D., Campbell, C., Journeay, M., Sheppard, S.R.J. (2009) The digital workshop: exploring the use of interactive and immersive visualisation tools in participatory planning. *Journal of Environmental Management* **90**, 2090–2101.

Schubert, T., Friedmann, F., Regenbrecht, H. (2001) The experience of presence: factor analytic insights. *Presence-Teleoperators and Virtual Environments* **10** (3), 266–281.

Shearman, D., Smith, J.W. (2007) Challenge and the Failure of Democracy. Praeger, Wesport.

Shirky, C. (2008) Here Comes Everybody: The Power of Organizing Without Organizations. Penguin, New York.

Slater, M., Steed, A., McCarthy, J., Marinelli, F. (1998) The influence of body movement on presence in virtual environments. *Human Factors: The Journal of the Human Factors and Ergonomics Society* **40** (3), 469–477.

Stein, J.M. (2004) Classic Readings in Urban Planning. APA Planners, Chicago.

Sternberg, R.J., Frensch, P.A. (1992) On being an expert: a cost–benefit analysis. In: The Psychology of Expertise: Cognitive Research and Empirical AI (ed. R.R. Hoffman). Springer, New York, pp. 191–203.

Stirling, A. (2013) Pluralising progress: from integrative transitions to transformative diversity. *Environmental Innovation and Societal Transitions* **1**, 82–88.

Stirling, A. (2014) Emancipating transformations: from controlling 'the transition' to culturing plural radical progress. STEPS Working Paper 64, STEPS Centre, Brighton.

The Verge (2015) *Virtual Reality*. Available at: www.theverge.com/a/virtual-reality (accessed 12 December 2015).

Townsend, A.M. (2013) Smart Cities: Big Data, Civic Hackers, and the Quest for a New Utopia. W.W. Norton and Company, New York.

Urban Circus (2015) *Visualisation Platform*. Available at: www.urbancircus.com.au (accessed 12 December 2015).

Venuvinod, P.K. (2011) Technology Innovation and Entrepreneurship: Part 1 My World, My Nation. Kluwer Academic, the Netherlands.

Voinov, A., Bousquet, F. (2010) Modelling with stakeholders. *Environmental Modelling and Software* **25**, 1268–1281.

Wells, H.G. (1911) The Country of the Blind and Other Stories. Thomas Nelson and Sons, London.

Wirth, W., Hartmann, T., Böcking, S., Vorderer, P., Klimmt, C., Schramm, H., Saari, T., Laarni, J., Ravaja, N., Gouveia, F.R., Biocca, F., Sacau, A., Jäncke, L., Baumgartner, T., Jäncke, P. (2007) A process model of the formation of spatial presence experiences. *Media Psychology* **9**, 493–525.

World Commission on Environment and Development (1987) Our Common Future. Oxford University Press, Oxford.

Chapter 7
2050 – The Invisible Future

Sara Biscaya[1] and Ghassan Aouad[2]
[1] *School of the Built Environment, University of Salford, Salford, M5 4WT, UK*
[2] *Applied Science University, East Al-Ekir, Bahrain*

7.1 The future

When Marco Polo told the emperor of the Tartans, Kublai Khan (Calvino, 1974), tales of the cities he had visited during his expeditions, he never envisioned a future city developed through City/Building Information Modelling (CIM/BIM).

The world is and has always been in constant change: our time is no different. We face important challenges that will have an impact on future generations. Whether we like it or not, whether we are ready or not, the world as we know it will no longer exist in 2050.

7.1.1 Worst case scenario

The world population is expected to see significant growth in future years of 30% (WBCSD, 2010). The trend is for populations to migrate to cities and by 2050 it is expected that 70% of the world population will be living in cities (WBCSD, 2010; HM Government, 2013; Dixon and Cohen, 2015). This suggests a significant transformation in the design and development of our cities.

This presents a problem as natural resources have been shrinking given our patterns of consumption, wasteful life-style (WBCSD, 2010; HM Government, 2013) and climate changes along with inadequate governance and policy responses necessary to manage the balance hindering sustainability.

Population growth is predicted to have a higher impact on urban development than previously (HM Government, 2013; Dixon, 2015). Cities need to be reconceptualised and redesigned, which presents new work opportunities in different industries and sectors. New homes, vehicles and infrastructures will be needed, but they need a major cultural shift in the way they are designed.

Cities are also predicted to grow at a faster pace for the next 35 years and so require planning now to prove sustainable in the future.

Future Challenges in Evaluating and Managing Sustainable Development in the Built Environment,
First Edition. Edited by Peter S. Brandon, Patrizia Lombardi and Geoffrey Q. Shen.
© 2017 John Wiley & Sons Ltd. Published 2017 by John Wiley & Sons Ltd.

The global economic and environmental crises at the end of the 2000s shook people's faith, proving that we need more than a short-term strategy for our economy and for our planet. The continued use of fossil fuel-based energy and the accelerated use of natural resources are affecting and damaging key ecosystems services, endangering our supplies of food, clean water and fish (WBCSD, 2010; HM Government, 2013). The impact on the climate is increasing at a fast rate: more and more weather disasters, scarcities and famines are having a disastrous impact on communities around the world.

We have been using more resources than our planet provides: we use and waste water, we have been deforesting the planet at great speed, we have polluted the air with carbon emissions and we have been contaminating soils to produce more in less time.

If we continue this behaviour, world poverty will increase and the natural resources will be extinguished within the next century.

Is that what we really want for our future generations?

7.2 What future?

The challenges identified above are global and provide new opportunities in the built environment but they also present greater responsibilities in their delivery.

A wrong move might cause irreversible damage but continuing on this path, or inertia, can be just as destructive a process. It is time to be audacious but not thoughtless.

This brings us to the built environment and the challenges it faces. We are looking into an unpredictable future, yet never have we been more aware of the consequences of our actions. The future needs to be planned and safeguarded. So why not think of technology as one of the means to achieve a more sustainable built environment?

The development of a digital economy and its widespread growth in a number of sectors such as education, government, leisure and entertainment has created numerous market possibilities. The digital economy is supported by the fast growing impact of new technologies on different facets of community life, cultural experiences, future society and the economy.

The digital economy aims at a more sustainable society, communities and culture, with new economic models that perceive information technology as a utility.

The built environment is known for its traditional processes, methods and software applications. This is particularly the case in the construction industry, an industry known for its traditional and 'old fashioned' ways (Latham, 1994; Egan, 1998). This does not relate just to the adoption of software, which has been available for quite some time; it is also the processes and the stakeholders' behaviour that enable the necessary changes to take place.

Is it really like this?

New improved technologies have the power to change that.

Digital technology is not the only driver for change. It is not possible to think of how technologies can assist in shaping the future of the built environment without relating them to the challenges we face.

Figure 7.1   Future model: people and creativity.

Whilst a major factor is the growth of population resulting in city growth, a related factor of that population growth is the increase of the ageing population. This requires planning when not only building and transforming cities but also infrastructures, livelihoods and lifestyles, which in turn create business opportunities.

According to various surveys the future will require a high degree of experiment and creativity (Figure 7.1) in all sectors transforming people's values, human development, economy, agriculture, forest, energy, buildings, mobility and materials (WBCSD, 2010; IBM, 2012; HM Government, 2103). In 2050 these sectors will have undergone profound changes, thus embracing a more sustainable vision.

7.2.1 People

People are at the forefront of these challenges. New technologies and processes will require more qualified people who are willing to work hard and make changes. As the future will see an almost unprecedented level of change, one of the most important skills to have will be adaptability (HM Government, 2013). The construction industry needs new young people who have actually lived their whole life surrounded by technology, making it natural to them. Such a change might alter the conservative construction industry mind set, enabling it to move forward.

Younger generations are equally more aware of the impact of their actions on the planet. The same youth that we wish to see engaging with the construction industry will shape it for the future (HM Government, 2012; ARUP, 2013). They will use technology with more precision and ease than any other generation up to now. For them, information is available with a finger swipe or keyboard press: new worlds, universes, places and people. They relate to what they have known since they were born: they think tri-dimensionally, they move through spaces that relate to different dimensions and so it is only natural that they use technology to represent the world as they 'see it' whilst embracing Information Technology (IT).

7.2.2 Smart technologies and CIM/BIM

This leads us to new developing technologies. These are in constant mutation and development. The construction industry is no stranger to these by now but the implications they have for future development are still far from what they may become in helping to shape the future.

Technologies such as CIM and BIM and smart cities development are key elements in shaping the future of the built environment (Worthington, 2012; HM Government, 2013; Philip, 2013).

CIM and BIM processes and technologies enable practitioners and stakeholders to understand and test the design and construction beforehand. If 2015 was acknowledged as bringing many benefits for the construction industry, such as tracking the impact of design changes on operating costs and real time walkthrough of the modified design by clients (ARUP 2013; Philip 2013; Raja, 2015), in 2050 the benefits will have excelled all expectations. Smart cities development has begun to change the way citizens inhabit their cities and the way planners acknowledge and address their needs. This is the beginning of a major shift in the way we think about our cities.

7.2.3 Environmental challenges

Dominating all the challenges are the environmental considerations that transform what we build, what we build with and how we build (HM Government, 2013).

It is not just the evident climate changes but also the acknowledgement of our impact on those changes. The construction industry urgently requires an intervention on its carbon footprint (Hammond and Jones, 2008; Hertwich and Peters, 2009; SKANSKA, 2010; HM Government, 2013) and in understanding and identifying the future work opportunities that sustainable construction brings.

7.3 The present and the future

Changes will have to take place in two stages: the awareness and wake up stage and the implementation stage. No changes can be achieved without careful consideration of the recent past, analysis of the present and a vision for a possible future. It is very difficult to predict the future but it is of utmost necessity to provide a vision for such a future so as to face its challenges.

Currently the built environment is engaging in a transformation process that will change the way we design and construct. Smart technologies have provided the major driver for those changes but how should they be applied to provide for a better future?

As mentioned, the major challenge in the built environment is building and transforming cities, infrastructures, livelihoods and life styles (UKaid, 2010; WBCSD, 2010) while reducing the waste of natural resources and guaranteeing a secure economy. To build and transform cities it is essential to identify the key elements in city development: buildings, mobility and materials.

7.4 Future city in 2050

City development is local and will require a careful identification of deeper local and environmental understanding (WBCSD, 2010; HM Government, 2013; Dixon, 2015).

There will be two different streams of city development: existing cities and new settlements (WBCSD, 2010; Dixon, 2015; Dixon and Cohen, 2015), implying either the adaption of existing infrastructures or building them from scratch.

To engage the people with these new developments it is imperative to consider people's values, life styles and behaviour through an understanding and integration of local environments, conditions and aspirations in the process.

In 2050 cities will have developed into megacities grown out of existing ones or will be designed from scratch due to population growth and migration, subsequently concentrating in urban areas (WBCSD, 2010; Dixon *et al.*, 2015). The problem of shrinkage of resources will be accentuated and will require different approaches designed to minimise waste in all forms, encouraging biodiversity and ecosystems to develop peoples' sense of wellbeing in a resourceful and energy efficient way.

The core of this urban rethinking will be the design and management of buildings, spaces and infrastructures. This thinking is not a 'one size fits all' as different cities and local environments will not be uniform (UKaid, 2010; Dixon, 2015). Different needs and opportunities will have to be assessed separately.

In the future design of cities, the Building Architect by 2050 will play an important role, comprising that of designer, urban planner and energy expert, to make the best use of new technologies that capture natural heating, cooling and lighting to achieve zero waste and zero carbon emissions. CIM and BIM will play a crucial part in this process, as they will allow for the design and reconceptualisation of different scale environments and flexible spaces to use and adapt in the future.

The different models created for existing cities and buildings and for new cities and buildings, along with their infrastructures, will allow stakeholders to test and predict future behaviours, preventing some problems that would otherwise arise (ARUP, 2013).

Integration, innovation and collaboration (UKaid, 2010; HM Government, 2012, 2013; Dixon *et al.*, 2015) are key words in this decade. Cities will need to develop an integrated approach to smart technologies and sustainable practices. Urban innovation will be at the core of city progress, enabling the quality of life of its inhabitants by supporting decision-making through the provision of better information. Collaboration and interdisciplinary thinking will provide solutions to urban challenges through emerging partnerships between society, academia and business.

Cities will have become part of an extensive net by 2050. Everything will be connected via Information Communication Technology (ICT). With city development there will be new and unknown social challenges that will require solutions whilst providing new opportunities.

Between 2017 and 2050 a mind shift will take place as our and younger generations will be faced with the irrefutable truth that continuing on this path will lead us to our own destruction. Some will embrace this truth better than others. As always some may accept this whilst others will seek to intervene.

Those at the vanguard of this transformation will be faced with many challenges, the first being their own development and the second the way the economy is thought of.

Human development will be a major driver for change in 2050 (WBCSD, 2010: ARUP, 2015). Part of this will be:

- Improvements in legislation and governance regarding intellectual property systems to encourage collaboration and integration;
- Investment to improve infrastructures in poorer countries to provide access to water, sanitation, energy, education, jobs, healthcare and mobility;
- Improvement of the business of caring for the ageing population; new approaches to urban design and management;
- Focus on local knowledge and strengths.

Following the most recent recession the necessity to rebuild trust among different countries and their economies was overcome by a more prominent issue – the need for a greener growth to improve the living conditions of existing and growing populations while providing for a more sustainable future.

Globalisation also contributed to this approach. Global companies required a stable environment to operate and expand and, at the local level, work mobility presented more opportunities for individuals to progress and experiment while gaining experience. New technologies and globalisation demanded an improved and more efficient global economy, more transparently, reflecting true-value pricing and tax alterations to encourage business growth and behaviour. The development of new technologies also needed a more effective economy to disseminate them. Changes in the way we think about business due to the development of e-commerce, renewable energies, sustainable infrastructure development and technology deployment require a more creative and smarter economy based on transparent collaboration between countries and public–private partnerships.

In 2050 the economic model will need to be productive and innovative (HM Government, 2013), resource-efficient and providing for sufficient and more inclusive jobs. The growth of the population, the revolution in human values and the resultant economy change drive the evolution of urban areas. Different cities will require different approaches to their design and development.

In an existing city with a historical context the aim will be to provide for new construction – expansion – and retrofit of the existing built environment to meet basic requirements, such as minimising waste and increasing recycling. The application of cleaner energies will also be at the forefront of the changes. This will probably take longer than designing a new city as a clear understanding and surveying of existing building conditions and infrastructures will be necessary and will take some time to assess.

The case of cities that stand in areas prone to environmental disasters such as floods or earthquakes will require a different approach. These will need a more rapid response to address economic and demographic growth, as most of the existing buildings and infrastructures are not adequate to the challenges they face. An ecological approach based on resilience and access to low-cost, low-carbon infrastructures and implementing reliable energy are probably the best solutions.

With almost the same profile as these are cities in risk locations such as those located in areas at risk of rising seas. Although they present different challenges these will definitely be derived from climate, allowing for more innovative design solutions that adapt and integrate climate change.

There will also be cities that are designed from scratch to address the influx of population and these are probably the easiest to develop. Their development will be looking into optimised design for sustainability in every aspect. More innovative and holistic solutions may possibly be applied as they provide for a clean slate in terms of design development. The energy systems applied can all be based on clean energies and resources. A closed loop design (WBCSD, 2010) is more likely to be applied, reducing waste and energy consumption while raising the economy.

This proves that different cities will require different solutions that will need to be carefully thought through in light of their implications. Culture, environment, precedence, economy and geographic context need to be carefully analysed and understood to provide for a more holistic solution. Whilst considering the environment, deforestation and agriculture also need to be taken into account.

Being concentrated in expanding cities, how will we provide for food and clean air? Agriculture and forests within our city design development are one possible solution. This will require urban planners and designers to provide forward thinking in terms of infrastructures to support and include these ideas.

New opportunities will arise from farming in poorer parts of the globe. Developing countries invest in research to provide for a more efficient and sustainable way of farming in under-developed countries. These in turn will bring benefits for them through profits and learning new methods of provision.

At an individual level we will be encouraged to produce part of our food supply in our own space within the city. Co-operative production is a possible solution: neighbourhoods develop their own schemes for farming and exchange different produce with other neighbourhoods.

Clean air will be a major consideration in future cities. The deforestation of most of the world's major forests has had a huge impact on the environment, increasing carbon emissions and extinguishing biodiversity and water. The extraction of wood and the use of forests as farmland or biomass will have ceased by 2050. Some forests should have begun to expand in 2050, recognising the importance of forestation in maintaining the climate equilibrium.

Urban forests are included in the design of cities, providing for clean air and shade in countries that require it. The planting of trees and other vegetation within cities offers natural areas that are both economic and environmental assets by absorbing carbon and giving wind protection whilst also providing recreational and social features.

Renewable and clean energies will also play an important role in the sustainable development and maintenance of cities. Wind and solar photovoltaic energies are applied due to their increased support by government authorities and technology development that guarantees their cost-efficient application, making them cheaper than gas or oil.

New cities will demand a sustainable maintenance that can only be achieved through the application of new and smart technologies. This is not simply a matter of design and retrofit but a guarantee of their maintenance and monitoring.

ICT is applied in city development and monitoring, allowing for a more effective control of energy efficiency and waste.

7.4.1 Buildings

Buildings and spaces are part of the making of cities. In 2050 new and retrofitted buildings should be able to achieve a zero net energy. This integrates building design considerations, affordability and high-performance materials. Legislation policies and incentives will be in place to ensure that buildings meet the established standard requirements. This is cross-sectional and worldwide.

BIM will allow for this to be easier and more effective while less time-consuming. In 2013 the construction industry had a huge impact on the greenhouse effect and carbon emissions (HM Government, 2013).

In 2050 different types of information regarding different design aspects, from materials to wind forces or even water pressure in plumbing systems, will be accessible to the design team through BIM models, enabling a better understanding of the implications of their choices, constraints and opportunities (Eastman *et al.*, 2011; ARUP, 2013) which include reducing CO_2 emissions (Kensek and Noble, 2014).

In 2050 the design of buildings will provide a completely different set of job opportunities that were not even considered in 2015. Practitioners and stakeholders are far more efficient and productive, as real skill and talent are required to create and design buildings that deliver a sustainable performance in all their components. Also the intensive day to day BIM environment operation requires a more skilful workforce.

Energy efficiency will no longer be a concern for its impact on the environment and on economics. Government costs and incentives drive the change, enforcing transparency of energy efficiency in buildings. Sustainable buildings will present more value for buyers. This will engage stakeholders in enforcing the effective application of standards and legislation that comply with energy efficiency codes and practices (WBCSD, 2010; HM Government, 2013).

All parties are involved in the process from inception to demise of project planning and sharing risks. Through BIM, all stakeholders are able to access information and work on the different models that build up the overall model (Eastman *et al.*, 2011). The problem of ownership of the model has been overcome through the application of co-creation, open sources and different types of intellectual property regimes. BIM allows for an integrated design approach but also for the maintenance and monitoring of building resources from inception to demise. The construction process is now a truly integrated process (Eastman *et al.*, 2011; Crotty, 2012) and no longer do designers engage in the building design process in an autocratic way. Everyone should be on board: sharing information, ownership and, ultimately, risks. This creates a more integrated sector by reducing conflict and making for a more efficient construction industry.

Integrated retrofit in buildings also provides for new opportunities while decreasing costs. Owners will increasingly demand BIM models by the end of each project for further use and application not only in Facilities Management (FM) but also to use when changes to their building use are required – as so often happens. Versatile and adaptable functionality is far easier to achieve if your model is accurate. Within a city context this is an even more relevant contribution to the whole of the city modelling, testing and monitoring process.

BIM monitoring at different scales of building and different building levels will be achieved through the use of metering controls and information flow between services and appliances and the produced models.

Governments and corporations take the lead and showcase the application of energy efficiency monitoring and reflective response through CIM and BIM applications, providing for not only best practices but also to set an example and educate the public.

Energy efficiency in building will only be achieved in 2050 thanks to the creation and implementation of international codes and tax incentives for building. Governments subsidise the building investments and make regular audits of energy performance. If it is found that they have not performed well or that they have wasted excessive amounts of energy they may well face mandatory renovation.

The integration of teams at the early stages of the design process providing for new contractual terms was also a driver for building efficiency to be carefully considered in the design process (Eastman *et al.*, 2011: Crotty, 2012).

And of course there are also the consumers. These can be monitored regarding their energy consumption attitudes and end performance. By 2030 continuous campaigns to increase awareness of energy use could be set in place and, by 2050, could be included in education and civic behaviour.

Energy efficient buildings require a more integrated design approach that will necessarily have to be included at an early stage of the design, involving architects and structural, mechanical and electrical engineers. This is not problematic since BIM is the process and provides the software that builds all the models not only of one building but also of all the buildings within a city along with its infrastructures. BIM is now used as a powerful tool that integrates other more diverse smart city technologies to provide for a holistic idea of a city. An information model that integrates all the different models that relate to the design of buildings, spaces and infrastructures within a city will be a reality in 2050.

BIM will be used to achieve a high energy efficiency performance to meet the new standard codes (Crotty, 2012; Kensek and Noble, 2014). These will need to be strictly enforced. Different buildings with different uses, either new or refurbished, will be designed to use information and communication technology as sensors to improve the buildings' level of energy use.

Everything can be envisioned before it happens. Endless solutions to problems are available as BIM is an intelligent project model in which information is embedded so it can be shared between stakeholders throughout the whole process (Eastman *et al.*, 2011; Philip, 2013; ARUP, 2015). The BIM process has transformed the way that we design cities, buildings and systems to perform throughout their entire life cycle (Crotty, 2012; ARUP, 2013; Kensek and Noble, 2014). Process management is now effective and ends in a more high-quality outcome. You can control not only the design process but also the construction and facility management of every element of the built environment (Eastman *et al.*, 2011; Crotty, 2012; Kensek and Noble, 2014).

Everything will be possible, everything is digital, model-based, allowing for informed judgments resulting in improved solutions to existing or occurring problems.

The construction sector will be based on intensive knowledge which means that industry, academia and the civic society are required to work intensively and interdisciplinarily (Dixon *et al.*, 2015) to deliver a better end product.

7.4.2 Mobility

Infrastructure and mobility are directly related with economic growth and city development. They are also related with carbon emissions and energy consumption. This is one area of sustainable development that will have endured a difficult process but by 2050 will be delivering amazing results.

With the increase of population, transport volumes will also rise but can be stabilised through the application of ICT reducing the number of transport deaths close to zero and reducing CO_2 emissions.

Electric vehicles are already a reality in 2017 but by 2050 they will have become mainstream and 'ride along' vehicles designed for one to pick up and leave in any area within the city limits. They will use sustainable biofuel and hydrogen reducing the CO_2 emissions drastically. Fuel alternatives are thus the key research topic to develop.

The integration and collaboration between industry and academia will result in high technology developments to enhance the public and private transportation net while achieving energy-efficient levels never thought to be possible.

Aircraft will be highly fuel-efficient, based on light materials, aerodynamics and technological engine efficiencies, while biofuel is being tested for its application in aviation. Planes will be made of new composite materials, making them cheaper and more suitable for mass production. Air travel is currently increasing with globalisation and will continue to do so in such an exponential manner that air traffic management insists on developing and improving aircraft capabilities, data precision and communications to reduce fuel waste.

Interdisciplinary collaboration between decision makers, planners and industries will revolutionise the transportation infrastructure. ICT deployment of information routes will keep people aware of their transport possibilities/alternatives in real time, allowing them to make informed decisions on which means of transport to use depending on the time/place/availability and commodity. Smart technologies provide for real-time information flow on transport availability and commodity but they will also play a relevant role in integrated urban planning of fast-growing cities. In this future, Intelligent Transportation Systems (ITS) connect vehicles to each other and vehicles to infrastructures. International standards will be applied in possible fuel materials, vehicle design and engineering development.

Vehicles will be equipped with the safest sensors developed to date. Vehicle interconnection and connection with the infrastructure will decrease deaths from accidents but they will also provide for controlling traffic jams and for individuals to evaluate if going from A to B in your own vehicle is the most energy efficient and quickest solution. People that live outside the cities will also have access to different transportation, including low-cost, sustainable powered vehicles using low-cost cleaner energy. There will be a new net for these new energy vehicles spread through the whole transportation infrastructure.

Railroads and marine infrastructure also present a more holistic solution to integration of use via the application of ICT but also through the integration of different countries within one system. Shipping also engages in the use of bio-fuels as these will have increasingly become more competitive. The proposed changes to this sector can only become truly energy efficient through planning and routine changes along with engine development (HM Government, 2013).

All these improvements need to be considered by manufacturers, suppliers, fuel industry infrastructure providers, planners, urban developers and public transportation providers in city design and development.

The connectivity and deployment of ICT in transportation and mobility is guaranteed through CIM and BIM application. Countries develop their own models of their cities and infrastructures, which in turn are connected across different countries, providing for a massive mapping, overlapping and linkage of models.

7.4.3 Materials

In 2050 waste will have become unacceptable, driving the focus on closed-loop recycling. The construction industry is well known for its poor carbon footprint and considerable waste disposal problems (Latham, 1994; Egan, 1998; HM Government, 2013). All this will have changed in the next three decades with the development and application of tighter standards and codes enforced by policy makers and government authorities.

Materials are re-engineered to be applied and used again in different contexts and for multiple purposes or even be reduced to raw materials in order to manufacture other products. This means that the whole approach to materials and products has been rethought in the light of new construction technologies and materials application.

Different materials with high-efficiency performance will be developed in all kinds of sectors. This will translate not only into high efficiency in their development but also in their application, for example in lightweight transport and renewable energies. 2050 envisages the end of greenhouse gas emissions and the waste of energy and water in materials development and production. Wastewater is considered a resource for manufacturing purposes, bringing a whole different vision to the use of wastewater even in domestic environments.

It is definitely the beginning of a new way of understanding and relating to materials and resources.

Materials applied that are exhaustively used in the construction industry suffer a major change in their production, guaranteeing an improved energy efficiency e.g. cement and steel (SKANSKA, 2010). The built environment will be more efficient than ever. Designers will think of materials in such a way that these are recycled time and again or transformed to create different materials that last longer. End products are made with less material under different processes and ultimately last longer. It is a greater power for us and a win situation for the planet: landfills cease to exist, as they will no longer be necessary and mining exists to recycle materials perceived as new business opportunities.

Sustainable materials development does not rely solely on design but is intertwined with a different model of business innovation and the implementation of new processes. No longer is a material's waste related only with its manufacturing and life cycle process but also with the end consumer. This plays a significant part in materials recycling and transformation into different ones. This will require a closer relationship between material manufacturers and their consumers. Understanding their needs and behaviour while also trying to change the way they approach closed-loop recycling is at the head of this change (WBCSD, 2010).

Consumers will play a different role in this process. They will be more involved with material reuse and will find different uses for different materials at different scales and levels of their daily life. Recycling will be perceived as not only a civic duty but as quite an enjoyable mission that enhances creativity and strengthens relations between different types of consumers.

Creativity will be used for material development and application in the construction industry. In 2050 we will witness a transforming holistic approach to energy efficiency in the construction industry: from the city scale, with the use of smart technologies to assist in more informed sustainable solutions and decisions in the way we live in our cities, to buildings designed to comply with the energy codes while still providing for the needs of their occupants, ending in the development and deployment of high-performance materials that guarantee a closed-loop recycle system.

Material production will become part of an integrated process that involves the co-operation of industry, governments, manufacturers and suppliers to develop more synchronised processes and regulations.

These new businesses models will also entail the logistics process to dismantle existing materials and structures for recycling. Everything, from processes to transformation, presents a potential opportunity for development and growth.

Policy makers and governments will reward companies that effectively implement processes of materials manufacturing, through the reduction of energy production costs, emissions costs and tax penalties. Nothing will be left to chance and all the developments and solutions presented will have been carefully thought through in terms of their impact on the planet and its population.

7.4.4 BIM role and impact

Building Information Modelling plays an important role in the future changes that take place between 2017 and 2050.

The development of a model that comprises the whole life cycle of a building facility will have taken such a leap that it is now applied in city development, urban planning, space and infrastructure management, buildings design and materials deployment to attain sustainability within the built environment.

As with the different specialties models, the holistic BIM approach to urban development is based on different models overlapping and connecting with each other. This will provide the built environment with a powerful tool that detects issues not only at a micro scale, like buildings, but also at a macro scale, like an entire city. Urban planning will have the potential to experiment and create possible solutions to environmental challenges in different urban regions, addressing each as an individual identity that requires attention and creative solutions to overcome its weaknesses.

Infrastructures within these urban centres will be tested and predictions can be made regarding their behaviour with different layouts, materials and different days and times of the day. Cross-referencing different existing industries within a city and the implications for traffic is a reality that allows for the maintenance of a sustainable environment.

Energy efficient vehicles with sensors that are connected to smart city technologies and models will have lowered to zero the number of human lives lost in car accidents on the roads. Vehicles will be sensitive to people's moods, smell and physiognomy providing for mechanisms that overcome these in any eventuality.

Alongside this, people will have developed their own networks to share vehicles or use community vehicles that will be more efficient and use clean energies.

At the beginning and end of this chain of users, roads will have become lanes of information interconnected with all the different urban infrastructures and buildings. With this amount of information, it is only natural that the talking point of 2015, 'Big Data', is in 2050 debated not only for the huge amount of information to be shared: huge volume, high resolution, diverse, varied and rapidly growing/changing (Dixon *et al.*, 2015) but also due to the resulting privacy and security issues that it presents. This will have been overcome through the use of open data databases and co-creation of information between different stakeholders.

CIM and BIM will no longer be about a city or building's life cycle but about the whole built environment development and monitoring to achieve and maintain high sustainable performance at all scales and levels.

7.5 Invisible BIM 2050

Collaborative work envisioned by Kiviniemi *et al.* (2005) is a new reality and has spread to different industries and sectors (Figure 7.2).

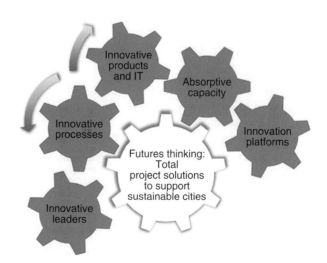

Figure 7.2   The future.

The designers' biggest dream has always been to be able to project their concepts, to develop them and to build them without restrictions. Restrictions imposed were merely due to the incapacity of others to perceive the world as they did: to develop spaces in such a way that everything is possible. All sensations are present to its occupant. While space is only visual and sensed through the body, now all senses are involved in the experience. What was termed immersive design in 2015 will be a reality by 2050 enabled by BIM, recreating our imaginary spaces in models that are buildable in all possible dimensions.

The insurance industry will have had to change its methods to accommodate this new reality. Insurance will need to cover all stages of the design and construction process based on collaborative work: shared model, shared information, shared issues and responsibilities.

In the automobile industry, vehicles will be developed to be informed of the driver's requirements and to comply accordingly. Vehicles will be connected to each other through ICT. They will be developed in such a way that the engine informs the driver of any malfunction and provides information regarding the intended destination from their database to calculate the best route. Accidents will be minimal as vehicles have sensors that allow detours and identification of basic forthcoming dangers to avoid.

Necessarily the food industry will have embraced BIM and developed a system that derives from it called Harvest Information Modelling (HIM) and all farmers will apply it in the harvest. It will be amazing how effective it will be in tracking information on the weather, the growth of produce and the right time to harvest.

Distributers and suppliers will be able to develop a coordinated system that acknowledges immediately the harvest is ready and the best way to commercialise it.

In education the Education Information Modelling (EIM) will allow all possibilities in regards to different pedagogic methods at different levels but will also identify special needs that students might have, allowing for better decisions from the educators/tutors.

BIM has allowed us to use information in new fields and at different levels with all the benefits and constraints that this entails. In 2050 it will also allow us to imagine new possibilities for information application and use.

This could include sensors that connect to brainwaves and, when connected to BIM software, allow all stakeholders to project their model in a collaborative environment. It will be amazing what they project and how the built environment will be created through the connections established. No longer will there be problems or misunderstanding within disciplines and between different specialties. CIM and BIM will have become Built Environment Information Modelling (BEIM). Only one single model comprising everything, no more the different models for different specialities that may or may not be integrated. The level of design and construction sophistication can have developed beyond all expectations.

Design knows no limits and so buildings in different shapes with materials never before seen can be produced by these means: based on nature but without damaging nature – biomaterials. The shapes are unprecedented, allowing spatial experiences that impact on more than one of our senses. Buildings will be able to be more like organic systems that change according to their occupants' needs through changes applied to the original model.

The streets of 2050 will be information routes that allow pedestrians and vehicles to not interfere with each other. There will be no traffic jams, as the models will provide information to the vehicles to prevent it. Whilst still called Smart Cities they are now real. They will have become centres of information and models of the different layouts of the city: buildings, public and private spaces, streets, different means of transportation, people and their needs and requirements.

Designers will be able to test their designs to optimise their performance. Contractors will then use the model to 'rehearse' construction, coordinate drawings and prepare shop and fabrication drawings.

BIM enables collaboration among designers, constructors and owners in ways the construction industry has never known before. While in the beginning there were several models exchanged between teams in 2050 there will be only one for everything. It is a true 'spider's web' of information where nothing is missed or disregarded.

Whilst it will use the same terminology and standards that enable the effective production of all the information, users will also know exactly what each other is referring to, even if they do not speak the same language.

Using digitised versions of paper drawings from the architects and Computer Aided Design (CAD) drawings to produce cost estimations will be a thing of the past. The new models will be produced by such high-quality software that they will allow for a high level of consistency between design and estimation. The odds of errors will be significantly reduced. The software will have become so intelligent that it can speculate numerous possible changes from one actual change done on the design. Designers and cost estimators will therefore be able to communicate from the early stages of design, making the whole process smooth. The only thing that might work against the cost estimation is the changes that the model allows for.

Costs associated with training will no longer exist, as children are educated within the BEIM subsystem, i.e. the EIM system. CIM and BIM are the processes that started this change and met the challenges. Sustainable processes, materials and life-style depend on people's behavioural changes but they also rely on how its success in different aspects can be measured and amended; and BIM provides for just that.

Marco Polo might not have been able to predict a city developed through CIM/BIM but, if he had, Kublai Khan would have bought the idea and developed it in his own city.

7.6 Constraints to the vision

The truth is that now in 2017 we are at a crossroads where everything can go wrong if we do not start having a more conscientious attitude towards the planet and population. Especially us: stakeholders and key players in the built environment industry have a huge responsibility on our shoulders.

What can go wrong? Everything.

What can we do? Everything.

There is a need for an urgent, more integrated, interdisciplinary and creative approach to sustainability issues in all sectors of the built environment. The planet has limited resources that need to be well managed and protected. If there is no mind-shift and we do not find a way to agree in key areas that need to be addressed, if the global and local economies do not find a more creative and innovative way of making it work and regain people's trust while rethinking the environmental identified issues, there is a serious possibility that we will cause irreparable damage to the planet. This ultimately will increase the levels of poverty, hindering future development.

Natural resources need urgent attention: clean water has implications for food security. Deforestation needs to be stopped and reforestation must take place to guarantee air quality.

Energy resources and renewable energies are to take a more prominent role if we intend to promote and guarantee a healthy living for populations in the long run.

Buildings and infrastructures also require attention so as to not continue on the same path, ending with cities that are impossible to live in and buildings that can kill us through their design, materials and energy use.

Everything can go wrong and unfortunately everything is connected in a way that has cause–effect reactions in all sectors. Shifting efforts requires a change in peoples' values; but also governmental and policy makers are required to take action and promote sustainable livelihoods and life styles in an expanding population.

We have presented what some might call a utopian vision of the future but such a vision is necessary to face the challenges ahead while providing for possible solutions to overcome them.

What we do know is: the world does not allow for any more environmental mistakes, growth population is happening now, concentration of populations in urban areas is the present and the future. Consequently the built environment will be faced with many challenges that have a high risk of irreversible damage for future generations. Interdisciplinary work between academia, industry and governments is key in answering the challenges ahead.

What we can aspire to provide is a vision that presents possible solutions for the different identified problems, making us hope for a better future in which we play a significant and positive role.

References

ARUP (2013) *Building Information Modeling: The Future Today? Intelligent Modeling Is Gaining Ground.* Available at: http://www.ecmag.com/section/systems/building-information-modeling-future-today (accessed 15 June 2015).

ARUP (2015) *Drivers for Change: What Will our World be Like in 2050?* Available at: www.arup.com/Publications/Drivers_of_change.aspx (accessed 28 June 2015).

Calvino, I. (1974) *Invisible Cities* (English translation), Harcourt Brace, San Diego.

Crotty, R. (2012) *The Impact of Building Information Modeling: Transforming Construction.* Spon, Oxford.

Dixon, T. (2015) Future cities: urbanization and the impact on the construction and property sector. In: *Building Better, Recommendations for a More Sustainable UK Construction Sector,* Westminster Sustainable Business Forum, London, pp. 23–25.

Dixon, T., Cohen, K. (2015) Towards a smart and sustainable reading 2050 vision. *Town and Country Planning,* January, pp. 26–33. Available at: http://www.tcpa.org.uk/data/files/Journal_Blurb__Sample_Articles/Jan_2015_Sample.pdf (accessed 15 June 2015).

Dixon, T., Barlow, J., Grimmond, S., Blower, J. (2015) *Smart and Sustainable, Using Big Data to Improve People's Lives in Cities*. University of Reading, Reading.

Dixon, T., Farrelly, L., Pain, K. (2015) A smart and sustainable urban future. *Estates Gazette*, 21 March 2015, pp. 100–102.

Eastman, C., Teicholz., P., Sacks, R., Liston, K. (2011) *BIM Handbook: A Guide to Building Information Modeling for Owners, Managers, Designers, Engineers and Contractors*, 2nd edn, John Wiley & Sons, Inc. Hoboken.

Egan, J. (1998) *Rethinking Construction. Report from the Construction Task Force*, Department of the Environment, Transport and Regions, London.

Hammond, G.P., Jones, C.I. (2008) Embodied energy and carbon in construction materials, *Proceedings of the Institution of Civil Engineers, Energy* **161**(2), 87–98.

Hertwich, E.G., Peters, G.P. (2009) Carbon footprint of nations: a global, trade-linked analysis, *Environmental Science Technology* **43**, 6414–6420.

HM Government (2012) *Industrial Strategy: Government and Industry in Partnership: Building Information Modelling*. Available at: https://www.gov.uk/government/uploads/system/uploads/attachment_data/file/34710/12-1327-building-information-modelling.pdf (accessed 28 June 2015).

HM Government (2013) *Industrial Strategy: Government and Industry Partnership, Construction 2025*. Available at: https://www.gov.uk/government/uploads/system/uploads/attachment_data/file/210099/bis-13-955-construction-2025-industrial-strategy.pdf (accessed 28 June 2015).

IBM (2012) *Smarter Cities for Smarter Growth: How Cities can Optimize their Systems for the Talent Based Economy*. Available at: http://www.zurich.ibm.com/pdf/isl/infoportal/IBV_SC3_report_GBE03348USEN.pdf (accessed 28 June 2015).

Latham, M. (1994) *Constructing the Team: Joint Review of Procurement and Contractual Arrangements in the UK Construction Industry*. Department of the Environment, London.

Kensek, K., Noble, D. (2014) *Building Information Modeling: BIM in Current and Future Practice*, John Wiley & Sons, Inc., Hoboken.

Kiviniemi, A., Fischer, M., Bazjanac, V. (2005) Integration of multiple product models: IFC model servers as a potential solution. In: *Proceedings of the 22nd CIB W78 Conference on Information Technology in Construction, Dresden*, CIB Publications, London, p. 304.

Philip, D. (2013) *CIC BIM 2050 Group*. Available at: http://www.bimtaskgroup.org/bim2050-group/(accessed 10 May 2015).

Raja, K. (2015) *How the Futuristic Building Information Modeling Would be Like?*. Available at: http://www.wamda.com/updatednews/2015/02/how-the-futuristic-building-information-modeling-would-be-like (accessed 10 May 2015).

SKANSKA (2010) *Carbon Footprint in Construction Examples from Finland, Norway, Sweden, UK and US*. Available at: http://www.skanska-sustainability-case-studies.com/index.php/latest-case-studies/item/140-carbon-footprinting-in-construction (accessed 10 May 2015).

UKaid (2010) *Cities: the New Frontier*, Department of International Development, London. Available at: https://www.gov.uk/government/uploads/system/uploads/attachment_data/file/67689/cities-new-frontier.pdf (accessed 10 May 2015).

WBCSD (2010) *Vision 2050, The New Agenda for Business*, World Business Council for Sustainable Development, New York. Available at: http://www.wbcsd.org/WEB/PROJECTS/BZROLE/VISION2050-FULLREPORT_FINAL.PDF (accessed 10 May 2015).

Worthington, J. (2012) *Re-Engineering the City 2020–2050*, EPSRC Position Paper in *Retrofit 2050*. Available at: http://www.edgedebate.com/wp-content/uploads/2013/01/130101_john-worthington-position-paper-design-agency-1.pdf (accessed 18 June 2015).

Chapter 8
The Role of Carbon in Sustainable Development

Srinath Perera[1] and Michele Florencia Victoria[2]
[1] *School of Computing Engineering & Mathematics, Western Sydney University, Penrith, NSW 2751, Australia*
[2] *Department of Architecture and Built Environment, Northumbria University, Newcastle upon Tyne, NE1 8ST, UK*

8.1 Introduction

Energy and emissions issues have become one of the most significant topics discussed and debated over the past two decades. The issue surrounding the impacts of greenhouse gas (GHG) emissions on the environment was contested and global agreements seem difficult to implement. The situation is changing rapidly within a global context with the United States recently declaring this as one of the fundamental global threats the mankind is currently facing (Obama, 2015). The work of the Intergovernmental Panel on Climate Change (IPCC) and their reports along with the global climate change lobby have been crucial in awakening the world to this reality. Figure 8.1 illustrates the statistics on global (2010) and the UK (2014) emissions by sector. Accordingly, all sectors are contributing equally towards total emissions in the UK while power, agriculture and industry sectors are predominant in the global context. Given that, the global construction industry is responsible for 30–40% of energy consumption and 30% GHG (UK-GBC, 2013). The importance in regulating carbon emissions in the construction industry becomes paramount in achieving global emission reduction targets. Forecasts indicate that the global construction market is to grow over 70% by 2025 (HM Treasury, 2013a). Therefore, there is a clear need to cut down energy demand and emissions. However, curtailing construction activity is not a solution since most types of developments involve construction and global economy highly depend on construction outputs where it acts as an economic growth regulator. Hence, the problem appears to be much complex and requires multiple strategies in achieving the emission reduction targets.

Therefore, this chapter highlights the need for managing carbon in the construction industry, which takes mainly two forms, namely, Operational Carbon (OC) and Embodied Carbon (EC). Measurement of OC and EC has a similar underlying concept though the process is distinctly different. Therefore, this chapter unveils the underlying methodologies of measuring OC and EC and discusses them in detail, giving more

Future Challenges in Evaluating and Managing Sustainable Development in the Built Environment,
First Edition. Edited by Peter S. Brandon, Patrizia Lombardi and Geoffrey Q. Shen.
© 2017 John Wiley & Sons Ltd. Published 2017 by John Wiley & Sons Ltd.

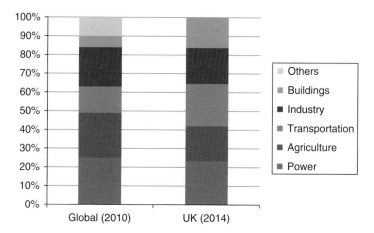

Figure 8.1   Emission by sector – Global and the UK. After: Committee on Climate Change (2015) and Intergovernmental Panel on Climate Change (2014).

attention to EC due to the changing focus from OC to EC. In addition, measurement of OC is standardised in most developed countries while EC measurement is still developing and, thus, suffers due to lack of a standard method of measurement, lack of rich data sources, problems in accuracy of estimating and the like. Further, EC measurement plays a vital role in dual currency approach, where cost and carbon are evaluated in parallel to optimise design solutions.

In summary, this chapter introduces OC and EC in construction as the two main types of carbon emissions from construction outputs and explains the measurement process, tools and sources available for estimating. The chapter also discusses the significance of system boundary in life cycle assessment of buildings and issues pertinent to it. A discussion on carbon hotspots is presented by drawing evidence from the literature and comparing literature findings with the case studies presented in this chapter. The shifting of focus from OC to EC is explained and the significance of EC reduction in low carbon trajectory is highlighted. Further, the dual currency approach in construction is discussed by emphasising the significance of EC measurement to dual currency evaluation. In addition, a discussion about drivers and barriers of carbon management is also presented. Finally, future trends and challenges for the construction industry in terms of carbon estimating are identified and the need for standardised approaches to carbon estimating is reiterated.

8.2 Operational and embodied carbon in construction

The GHG from the construction industry can be categorised primarily as OC and EC (also known as capital carbon). OC includes the emissions resulting from the operation of buildings (heating, lighting and air-conditioning are often referred to as regulated emissions) and EC includes all the emissions during the life of a building, except operational emissions. EC is the emissions that occur during the production of building materials, components, associated transport and assembly or construction (includes raw

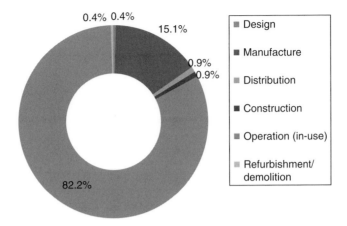

Figure 8.2 Emissions from construction industry. After: HM Government (2010).

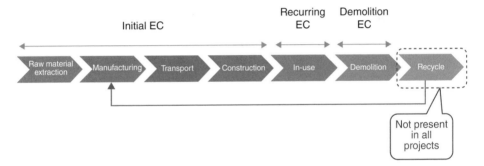

Figure 8.3 The scope of EC in the life cycle of a building.

material extraction, manufacturing, transport, construction, alteration, repair, replacement, demolition, recycle/reuse; Hammond and Jones, 2011; Ibn-Mohammed *et al.*, 2013; RICS, 2014). Figure 8.2 illustrates the proportion of emissions at various phases of building construction. As indicated in Figure 8.2, more than three-quarters of the emissions occur during the operation phase of a building, which includes both OC (emissions resulting from energy consumption for heating, cooling, air-conditioning and lighting) and EC (emissions resulting from repairs, maintenance and replacement). All other emissions indicated in Figure 8.2 are part of EC emissions. The scope of EC is illustrated in Figure 8.3. Further, a few scholars (Chen, Burnett, and Chau, 2001; Ramesh, Prakash, and Shukla, 2010) categorise EC into three types, such as Initial EC (raw material extraction, manufacturing, transport and construction), Recurring EC (in-use EC, such as repair, maintenance and replacement) and Demolition EC (EC during demolition). Where EC can be saved due to efforts to recycle scrap materials or products after demolition, it will be accounted in the footprint of the project; however, not all projects have this phase. Even though EC covers a wider scope in the building life cycle, generally the magnitude of the OC appears to be much higher than the EC, as indicated in

Table 8.1   OC and EC (and energy) relationship from various studies.

Building type	Life cycle of analysis (years)	Operational carbon (%)	Embodied carbon (%)	Country	Source
Office	30	65	35	UK	RICS (2014)
	60	61	39		Skanska (2010)
	25	33 (Energy)	67 (Energy)		Yohanis and
	50	66 (Energy)	34 (Energy)		Norton (2002)
	100	83 (Energy)	17 (Energy)		
	60	80	20	US	Ayaz and Yang (2009)
Semi-detached house	30	63	37	UK	RICS (2014)
Detached house	100	69 (Energy)	31 (Energy)	Australia	Fay, Treloar, and Iyer-Raniga (2000)
Apartment housing 1	50	55 (Energy)	45 (Energy)	Sweden	Thormark (2002)
Apartment housing 2	50	40 (Energy)	60 (Energy)	Israel	Huberman and Pearlmutter (2008)
Supermarket	30	80	20	UK	RICS (2014)
Warehouse	30	24	76	UK	RICS (2014)

Figure 8.2. However, the contributions vary significantly for different building types in different locations, as indicated in Table 8.1.

Table 8.1 and Figure 8.4 present a comparison of EC and OC and energy data from various studies in various countries (the number within the brackets in the *x*-axis of the graph indicates the assumed duration of the building life cycle). It is obvious from Table 8.1 and Figure 8.4 that, generally, OC contributes more towards emissions from buildings, except in low energy intensive buildings like warehouses. It is also interesting to note that, when the period of analysis is shorter, the impact of EC/energy is much higher than OC/energy, accounting up to 67%. Therefore, the life of the building also plays an important role in determining the impact of EC, which cannot be ignored. This is clear in Figure 8.4 where EC proportion reduces with the increase in life span of office buildings from 25 to 100 years.

In understanding the concept of EC one has to first understand the concept of Embodied Energy (EE). EE is the sum of all types of energy used in the production of a material or component. In principal, it is a form of accounting technique. Since production of energy results in some form of carbon emissions there is a close relationship between EE and EC. Therefore, EC is the total amount of carbon emitted in the production of a material or component (note: carbon emitted during the production of the energy required to produce the material or component is included herein).

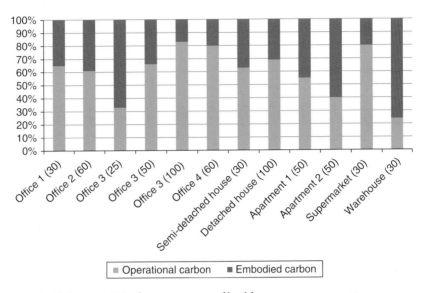

Figure 8.4 OC versus EC of various types of buildings.

However, embodied energy cannot be directly interpreted as EC in some instances (Brandt, 2008; Lélé, 1991). This is because OC is roughly proportional to the operational energy and the magnitude depends on the type of energy (or fuel) used whereas EC cannot be directly related at all the times as material production process emit or sequester carbon (Hammond and Jones, 2011). Ayaz and Yang (2009) draw the examples of EC in cement and timber to better illustrate this scenario (i.e. cement emits about half of its EC during the chemical process and the timber sequesters carbon during its growth). Therefore, it is important that a clear distinction is maintained when attempting to interchange carbon in the place of energy.

8.3 Estimating OC and EC

8.3.1 System boundaries

Knowledge on system boundary is fundamental to estimate OC and EC. In fact, system boundary is a key decision to be made before estimating. A system boundary simply means the stages considered in the measurement of carbon emissions of a construction project. In other words, from which stage to which stage the carbon emissions are to be accounted. There are five commonly used system boundaries based on which a life cycle assessment of a building is made. These are:

- Cradle to Gate: emissions released from raw material extraction until the product leaves the manufacturing factory gate;
- Cradle to Site: emissions released until the delivery to construction site;

- Cradle to Construction: emission released until the end of construction;
- Cradle to Grave: emission released until the demolition and disposal of the building;
- Cradle to Cradle: net emissions released until the recycling of any scrap material after demolition.

These boundaries are mapped against the TC350, EN 15978 standard methodology for the assessment of building Life Cycle Assessment (LCA) depicted in Figure 8.5. As the boundary becomes wider, the accounting process becomes more complicated and tedious, because there is a need to obtain project-specific data and respective data sources such as conversion factors. However, the Cradle to Grave boundary will provide a holistic account of building carbon footprint than the Cradle to Gate boundary. Nevertheless, the Cradle to Gate boundary is preferred in many reported studies due to the fact that most available databases are based on the cradle to gate system boundary (Hammond and Jones, 2011; Sansom and Pope, 2012) as other boundaries are project-specific and depends on material supply chains. Therefore, the same building with different system boundary analyses will yield different results. This makes a system boundary one important dimension of carbon estimating which should not be ignored when comparing studies.

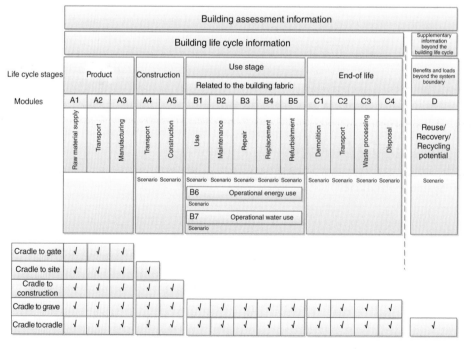

Figure 8.5   System boundaries mapped onto TC350, EN 15978:2011 standard methodology for the assessment of a building life cycle (Adopted from: British Standards Institution, 2011).

8.3.2 Estimating OC

The OC of a proposed building in the UK is estimated using the Standards Assessment Procedure (SAP – for domestic buildings), the Simplified Building Energy Model (SBEM – for non-domestic buildings) or other approved software tools. The software calculates the monthly building energy consumption and the carbon emissions for given inputs. Inputs include general information about the building, description of the building geometry, construction, use, HVAC and lighting equipment, as illustrated in Figure 8.6 (Building Research Establishment, 2014). Accordingly, the Building CO_2 Emission Rate (BER) should be less than the Target CO_2 Emission Rate (TER) to approve the building design (as per the Part L of the Building Regulations compliance). Operational emissions are expressed in mass of CO_2 emitted per year per square metre of the usable floor area of the building ($kg/m^2/year$). As discussed earlier, OC is proportional to operational energy; thus, OC is based on the energy consumption of the building. Further to Part L of the Building Regulations (in the UK), OC estimating is compulsory and is straightforward.

Further, OC estimating forms an important part of Cradle to Grave and Cradle to Cradle LCA of buildings. As presented in Figure 8.5, the main energy consumption of in-use stage is the operation of the buildings (HVAC and lighting). Hence, OC is calculated by estimating the annual energy consumption of the building and converting it using carbon conversion factors for fuels, available at Department for Environment Food and Rural Affairs (2015) for the UK reporting.

While the OC of a proposed building is calculated using modelling software, the actual OC (from actual operational energy consumption) can be calculated from a meter reading during the use of the building (Ekundayo *et al.*, 2012). A few studies (Pan and

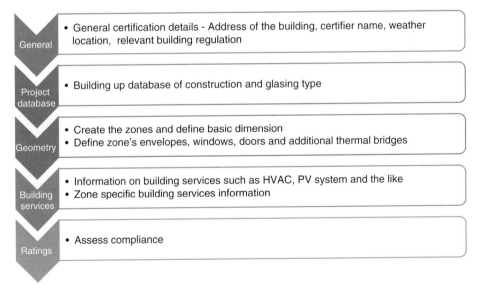

Figure 8.6 Order of data entry into iSBEM to calculate the BER for a proposed (non-domestic) building. Modified from: Building Research Establishment (2014).

Garmston, 2012; UK-GBC, 2008, 2014) have pointed out that there is a gap between the predicted and the actual performances of buildings and stress the importance of attending to this issue. As a result, CIBSE developed a platform named CarbonBuzz to manage the gap between the predicted and actual performances. This emphasises the importance of harmonising predicted and actual emissions in reaching a zero carbon target.

8.3.3 Estimating EC

Estimating EC follows a completely different process to that of OC. Measurement of EC has evolved during the recent past. Initially, the Inventory of Carbon and Energy (ICE) of Hammond and Jones (2008, 2011) became the fundamental source of reference for EC estimating (cradle to gate) which is composed of a dataset of mass CO_2 emissions per mass of a set of materials. Hence, the mass of materials that constitute a building needs to be quantified to estimate the amount of EC of a building. RICS (2014) guidance notes clearly set out the steps in estimating EC based on a bottom-up approach – deconstructing a building element up until the material, labour and plant components and applying ICE EC factors to arrive at the total amount of EC of the building. This is a tedious task as a building constitutes numerous items, which needed to be decomposed to follow this method. In addition to that, RICS (2014) also suggests ways of estimating EC during earlier stages of a building's life (see Table 8.2) which are given less thought by many researchers due to lack of EC data and difficulty in obtaining project data. (Refer to Ashworth and Perera (2015) for a detailed account of measuring EC.)

Table 8.2 The RICS guidance on measuring EC during various life cycle stages of a building (After: Victoria *et al.*, 2015).

Stages	System boundary	Estimating method	Data source
Product stage	Cradle to gate	Σ Mass of material (kg) × EC conversion factor (Kg CO_2/kg)	Inventory of Carbon and Energy (UK), Hammond and Jones (2011), SimaPro, GaBi
Construction process stage	Gate to construction	Σ Fuel consumed × EC conversion factor for the respective fuel	DEFRA Greenhouse Gas Conversion Factor Repository, GHG Protocol calculation tools
Use stage	Construction to grave	Σ Number of replacements × quantity of material × EC conversion factor	BCIS Life Expectancy of Building Components (BCIS, 2006) + product stage sources
End of life stage		Σ Fuel consumed × EC conversion factor for the respective fuel	Construction stage sources

The process can be somewhat simplified using the itemised EC dataset for standard building items (Franklin and Andrews, 2011) that is in accordance with the Standard Method of Measurements (SMM6). This is commonly referred to as the UK Building Blackbook for estimating the EC of buildings and structures and is presented in a similar form to building price books used for cost estimating. It is presented in a dual currency format of EC and cost.

The carbon reduction potential of buildings is higher during the early stages of a design than in the detail stages. The reason being that the development of design carries a further commitment to the specification of the building. Changes at the latter stages of design are more expensive as the cost of redesign increases with the further commitment to designs. Therefore, when cost and carbon are committed, the ability to change the design diminishes and, thus, the reduction potential decreases. This implies that there is a greater carbon reduction potential during the early stages of design. Hence, there is a huge need for early stage carbon estimating. However, estimating carbon during the early stages of design is not an easy task and calls for robust databases, heuristic approaches and mathematical models.

There are various web-based tools which are freely accessible and make EC measurements less tedious. However, each tool has its limitations. Table 8.3 review some of the freely available tools to gain insights into EC estimating. Table 8.3 indicates the increasing popularity of EC measurements from a simple 'early stage tool' like the Construction Carbon Calculator to a more advanced 'detail design stage tool' like iCIM. From the table, it is clear that the scope and limitations of each tool vary significantly, which demonstrates the need for standardised tools, rules and regulations for EC measurement similar to OC measurement. Further, Figure 8.7 maps the identified tools based on their applicability in different design stages. Accordingly, there is a number of tools that exist to aid design decision-making during either the early stages or the detail stages of design and none seems to be applicable to both stages. Further, there is only a limited number of early design stage tools available compared to detailed stage tools. This is mainly due to a lack of understanding of design and carbon relationships and limitations in datasets for early stage EC estimating. Furthermore, an important missing phenomenon in the above tools is the cost indication also called the 'dual currency of construction' (discussed later in this chapter). Nevertheless, iCIM claims to provide cost estimates along with carbon when integrated within a BIM platform (see also Section 24.26 in Ashworth and Perera, 2015). Furthermore, a range of tools available in other countries such as Elodie in France, thinkstep's GaBi Build-it in Germany, Tally® in the United States and a number of tools in the Netherlands (see Anderson, 2015).

8.3.4 Accuracy of EC estimating

A major concern in carbon estimating is the accuracy of estimates. It is not surprising to find variations in the estimates produced for the same building by different estimators (Clark, 2013). A few scholars (Clark, 2013; Dixit *et al.*, 2010; Ekundayo *et al.*, 2012)

Table 8.3 An overview of the identified EC estimating tools.

Tool name	System boundary	Inputs	Output	Limitations
Construction Carbon Calculator (Web-based tool) (Build Carbon Neutral, 2007)	Cradle to construction	Floor area, number of floors above ground and below ground, primary structural system, eco region, vegetation and landscape	Tonnes CO_2	Applicable to US context and commercial or multi-family projects
Embodied CO_2 Estimator (Web-based tool) (Phlorum, 2011)	Cradle to construction (excluding transport)	Floor areas, number of floors, building perimeter, glazing ratio and brief elemental specifications	Tonnes CO_2	Not for very early stage, requires information on the likely specification
Steel Construction Embodied Carbon Tool (Computer based tool) (TATA Steel, 2014)	Not clear	upper floor areas, number of storeys, upper floor construction type, structural grid size (primary span and secondary span), roof structure, fire protection columns, upper floor concrete type, vertical bracing, voids in upper floors, % of void in upper floors and void walls	Total EC – CO_2 figure; EC per one unit floor area – CO_2/m^2	Only for superstructure of steel buildings
Green Footstep (Web-based tool) (Rocky Mountain Institute 2009)	Not clear	Location, size of site, building type, floor are, expected life, project completion year	Site carbon storage – tonnes CO_2, construction emissions – tonnes CO_2, operational emissions – tonnes CO_2/year	Data sources of the tool are US-based; output graphs seems less user friendly, hence difficult to interpret the results

Tool	System boundary	Coverage / inputs	Output	Notes
Building Carbon Calculator (Excel-based tool) (University of Minnesota, 2014)	User can determine the system boundary	Predictions of operating energy, potable water, wastewater, solid waste, materials, transportation, soils, vegetation	Immediate construction impact – CO_2, recurring annual impact – CO_2/year and total over building life cycle – CO_2	Minnesota context, requires users to input EC impact, more focused on OC, depends on lots of predictions for energy usage and the like
Carbon calculator for construction projects (Environment Agency, 2012)	Cradle to construction+OC	Material quantity (mass) and fuel quantity	tonnes CO_2	Mass of all material and fuel usage needed to be input by the users
Interoperable Carbon Information Modelling (iCIM) (BIM-based tool)	Cradle to construction	Integrated in BIM platform; thus, when designs are drawn/uploaded in the platform EC measurement is automated	tonnes CO_2	Only for detailed design stage

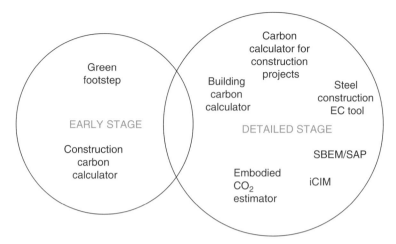

Figure 8.7   Mapping the identified carbon-estimating tools according to their application during different design stages.

identified that variations in EC measurements are due to several factors, such as system boundary, method of estimating, assumptions, data sources used and element classification, which are discussed below.

System boundary

EC estimate can be based upon five system boundaries, as discussed in Section 8.3.1. Therefore, an estimate with a cradle to grave boundary will have higher figures than an estimate with a cradle to gate boundary. Therefore, a system boundary is one factor to be considered when comparing studies and using data from other studies for analysis purposes.

Method of estimating

There can possibly be two main methods in carbon estimating:

- Manual estimating: this can be either a bottom-up approach of estimating using ICE data source and other relevant sources or itemised estimating approach using Blackbook or other similar published data source. Even though Blackbook is primarily based on ICE data, it is not the exclusively source and Blackbook team has sourced new data to develop their dataset. Therefore, there are possibilities of variations. Furthermore, missing data in ICE and Blackbook need to be sourced from local manufacturers, suppliers or contractors, which can vary from project to project.
- Automated estimating: automated systems have a unique in-built program for extracting quantities and retrieving carbon data. Hence, different standards and algorithms adopted by the system for measurement will result in variations. In addition, most

softwares use the ecoinvent database (Victoria *et al.*, 2015) which is updated from time to time. These can lead to results which vary from manual measurements.

Assumptions

Assumptions are an important cause of variations. Due to the fact that EC estimates are mainly produced from detailed cost plans or BOQ, if an item description is imprecise then assumptions have to be made to proceed with the estimate. For instance, a concrete staircase measured in 'Nr' has to be broken into concrete, formwork, reinforcement, balustrades and finishes to get the carbon estimate of that element. In this case, assumptions play a major role in the carbon estimate. Further, assumptions vary from person to person, project to project and cannot be standardised. Therefore, this is a major obstacle towards improving the accuracy of EC estimating.

Data sources

As explained under the method of measurement, data sources other than ICE and Blackbook might vary from study to study due to differences in manufacturers, suppliers, contractors, the age of data source and the like. This will result in differing EC estimates.

Element classification

Element classification is a common variation among studies. Different studies (Clark, 2013; Halcrow Yolles, 2010a, b; Sturgis Associates, 2010) adopt different element classifications such as NRM, SMM/BCIS – older version, British Council of Offices 2011, bespoke in-house standards; and some studies did not follow any standard. This makes the cross-comparison of findings difficult.

8.3.5 Carbon hotspots

The concept of carbon hotspots has been devised to identify elements that have a greater proportion of EC. These are also referred to as carbon critical elements. The EC estimating process is aided by the creation of heuristics-based rules relating to carbon hotspots. When considering the Pareto 80:20 rule, 20% of the building elements are responsible for 80% of the emissions, these are known as carbon hotspots. RICS (2014) defines 'Carbon hotspots' as the carbon significant aspect of the project, which can be building elements or other aspects of a project as a whole, such as procurement and transport. Further, carbon hotspot does not necessarily mean the most carbon-intensive elements but can also include elements where EC measurement data is easily available and/or elements with the greatest carbon reduction potential. Therefore, the total EC of a building can be estimated as follows:

$$C_E = EUQ_{sub} \cdot CF_{sub} + EUQ_{frame} \cdot CF_{frame} + EUQ_{floor} \cdot CF_{floor} + \ldots + EUQ_n \cdot CF_n + k$$

where C_E refers to the total EC of the building, EUQ refers to the element unit quantity of each carbon hotspot, CF refers to the carbon factor of each element and *k* refers to a constant with minor EC components. However, to apply this technique two types of data are required:

1. Carbon hotspots;
2. Carbon factors of building elements.

These carbon hotspots may vary from project to project depending on the type of the building. Generally, foundations, frame, roof, walls and floors are the most common carbon hotspot elements. Furthermore, the complex nature of measuring services in the early stage and their low reduction potential compared to other elements make services a less significant carbon hotspot even though they might contribute 10–25% of the total EC (Hitchin, 2013; RICS, 2014). Another study found that cladding finishes and services are the biggest elements of recurring carbon emissions (repair, maintenance and replacement) for an office building (Cole and Kernan, 1996). Hence, taking account of the services and finishes elements during initial design decision-making can make a significant difference in managing EC.

There are a few published studies on the EC analysis of office buildings in the UK (see Table 8.4). The first four case studies are based on primary data analysis carried out by the authors. Findings of other studies are aligned to a standard format to present it in a consistent way (NRM compliant element classification). Accordingly, substructure and superstructure together contribute to more than 80% of EC in office buildings in the UK. In particular, substructure, frame, upper floors and external wall are identified as 'carbon hotspots' in case study buildings (see Figure 8.8). This is in line with the findings of most of the studies. The services element demonstrates a huge variation among presented studies ranging from 0.93–25%. This is mostly due to differences in the scope of analysis of the services element and the methodology employed. However, case study findings and the findings of Halcrow Yolles (2010b) are mostly consistent. The case studies have limitations in EC quantification of major services, like electrical installations, gas installations, communication installations, fire and lighting protection installation and various other specialist installations, primarily due to lack of EC data. As a result, the EC of building services of the case studies are comparatively low. Furthermore, many studies do not clarify what constitutes the services element in their analysis, which becomes a drawback for comparisons. Moreover, when the EC of building services items are closely analysed it appears to be very small, resulting in a low contribution. Further, RICS (2014) claims that the EC reduction potential of the services element is very low. Hence, services could be excluded from carbon hotspots. However, the authors do not draw any conclusions regarding the EC of building services, as the findings are based on only a few studies and this is a potential area for further research.

Analysing further, it is clear that lack of EC benchmarks is also a significant drawback for early stage EC estimating. Therefore, the authors highlight the need to develop elemental EC benchmarks, which is another potential area of research. Nevertheless, the WRAP Embodied Carbon Database is an initiative by WRAP and UK Green Building Council (2014) towards EC database development. Over time, this could be an important source for EC datasets and information.

Table 8.4 Embodied carbon analysis of office buildings (After: Victoria *et al.*, 2015).

	Case study 1	Case study 2	Case study 3	Case study 4	Published studies			
					Halcrow and Yolles (average of three case studies)	Sturgis Associates	WRAP	Davis Langdon (30 case studies) from Clark (2013)
Substructure	43.79%	32.6%	33.84%	48.27%	89% (some elements are combined)	25%	18.3%	Structure 45–85%;
Superstructure	54.66%	62.66%	61.69%	49.17%		56%	58.24%	Facade 5–25%
Internal finishes	0.57%	2.09%	3.12%	0.91%	Not given	Fit-out (shell and core) 8%; Fit-out (Cat B) 8%	8.619%	4–25% (internal walls included)
Fittings and furnishings	0.05%	0.05%	Excluded	0.002%			Not given	
Services	0.93%	2.59%	1.35%	1.64%	3%	4% (waste)	11.96%	2–25%
Others					8% (external works)		2.9% (external works)	

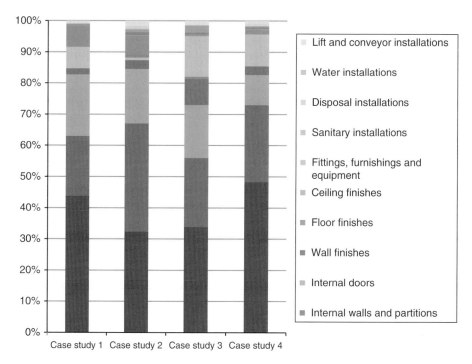

Figure 8.8   The EC elemental profile of case study buildings.

8.4 Shifting of focus

8.4.1 Zero carbon policy

The Code for Sustainable Homes (CSH) by BREEAM paved the way for a zero carbon policy in 2006 which was withdrawn by the Government in March 2015 except for legacy cases (see Department for Communities and Local Government, 2015). However, a zero carbon policy remains in effect. The zero carbon policy for homes simply means that all emissions arising as a result of the operational emissions of a building on a site should be offset by possible means, referred to as Allowable Solutions (Zero Carbon Hub, 2014). Figure 8.9 illustrates the concept more clearly. According to Figure 8.9, a zero carbon home needs to meet three criteria. First, energy efficiency should be achieved at the minimum specified standard (Fabric Energy Efficiency Standard; FEES) through fabric performance; second, the remaining carbon emissions should not exceed the carbon compliance level set in Part L; finally, after meeting the first two requirements (i.e. carbon compliance), the remaining emissions should be offset to reach the zero carbon policy (Zero Carbon Hub, 2014).

On the other hand, Osmani and O'Reilly (2009) identified several barriers in achieving the 2016 zero carbon homes target. That includes legislative barriers (lack of clarity in requirement and expected outcomes in the policy), cultural barriers (lack of customer demand), financial barriers (lack of data on the cost of achieving zero carbon homes)

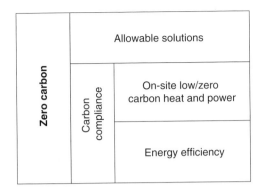

Figure 8.9   The zero carbon definition. Modified from: Zero Carbon Hub (2014).

and technical barriers (moving from conventional design and technology, though it was considered the least significant barrier). Further, Osmani and O'Reilly (2009) pointed out that, even though the zero carbon homes target of 2016 seems technically feasible, it requires proper strategies and plans and effective implementation.

While there is no firm definition or policy for zero carbon non-domestic buildings due to varying energy usage pattern for different types of buildings (especially unregulated), the UK government has stated in a consultation report (Department for Communities and Local Government, 2008) that the minimum compliance for non-domestic buildings will be to achieve zero levels for all regulated emissions. This was then followed by the phase three final report on zero carbon non-domestic buildings, which reviewed the scope of the energy efficiency standard and re-calculated achievable carbon compliance target levels (Communities and Local Government, 2011).

Ultimately, the scope of zero carbon buildings totally focuses on the OC of the buildings. Yet, HM Government (2010) reported that around 10% of UK emissions are to be embodied emissions and it is expected to account for over 5.5 years of additional total UK emission by 2050 if no change is made. As a result, a few studies and consultation reports have reviewed existing definitions (Marszal *et al.*, 2011; McLeod *et al.*, 2012; UK-GBC, 2008) and proposed a new definition to incorporate embodied impacts into zero carbon policy (Hernandez and Kenny, 2010; Lützkendorf *et al.*, 2014; McLeod *et al.*, 2012; UK-GBC, 2014). Furthermore, Embodied Carbon Industry Task Force (2014) foresee that EC could be considered as an 'Allowable Solution' in the near future.

There should be a section indicating the shifting of focus from OC to EC due to zero carbon buildings dealing with the OC component of carbon emissions.

8.4.2 The dual currency approach

One often criticised fact about low and zero carbon building is the cost of achieving it. Initially, developing a zero carbon design was a bottleneck to designers due to advanced technologies and high capital cost involvement compared to conventional designs (Catto, 2008). However, now designers are handling this challenge wisely and designing passive designs with active solutions to address climate change; and it is believed and proved that low and zero carbon buildings are attainable at an efficient cost similar to conventional buildings (Sturgis and Roberts, 2010; Target zero, 2012) or at a little higher cost. A recent study by the Sweett group (Zero Carbon Hub and Sweett, 2014) validates the above claim by modelling different house types. The findings suggest that zero carbon homes can be achieved at an additional cost of between £ 34/m² and £ 53/m² in 2020. Moreover, a recent case study on a commercial building (Torcellini *et al.*, 2014) proved that zero energy building can be attained at no additional cost when best cost controlling practices are implemented. Therefore, the cost of construction can no longer be a barrier to the development of zero carbon buildings.

However, it is not easy to attain the desired level of carbon emissions at an efficient cost. It demands expertise knowledge and wise decision-making. For instance, selection of a carbon efficient material might add to the cost significantly while not bringing huge savings in EC. The decision to go ahead with such a material would not provide the desired value for money. Therefore, design decision-making requires a high amount of knowledge and information. Ibn-Mohammed *et al.* (2013) explain this issue through a marginal abatement cost curve. Accordingly, costs tend to increase as reduction measures are applied to minimise emissions. However, the relationship between cost and carbon is not well grounded yet and only a few studies have dealt briefly with this side of the discussion in the zero carbon buildings debate. Further, the relationship might differ depending on the type of buildings. Therefore, it is important that this knowledge is captured and made transparent so that developers, clients and building professionals can make the right decision from alternative design solutions.

Moreover, cost and carbon are now often treated as dual currency for construction projects. Most construction clients, who are concerned about sustainability, are also conscious about the cost of the development. Therefore, there is a huge need to achieve the right balance between cost and carbon (see Figure 8.10). Now, the focus is shifting towards achieving the optimum balance between carbon and cost in designs. This in the future may expand into multiple currencies/dimensions like waste, time and the like.

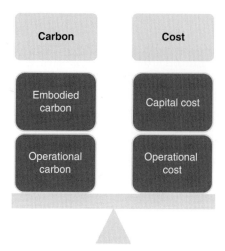

Figure 8.10   The dual currency of construction projects.

Next, it is important to look beyond zero carbon targets to understand the long-term role of carbon in the built environment.

8.4.3 Low carbon trajectory in built environment towards 2050 goal

The Kyoto Protocol 2050 target aims at 80% reduction in emission levels from 1990 levels, with sub-targets assigned to all signatories. The UK, as one of the signatories, is leading the way forward by ambitious targets through the Climate Change Act 2008, setting its own targets for the country. Accordingly, 2016 is the first and often criticised milestone dealing with zero-carbon homes. All new homes should be zero-carbon from 2016 in the UK. However, the inclusion of existing stock for the target remains undecided. Further, there are many carbon reduction incentives that operate in the UK. ECO and green deal are two such schemes that were introduced to improve the energy efficiency of existing housing stock. The next target is the 2019 zero carbon buildings. Improvements made to the Part L of the Building Regulations lead towards the achievement of the 2016 and 2019 targets. The Low Carbon Routemap for the Built Environment in the UK sets 34% reduction by 2020, followed by 50% and 80% reductions in 2025 and 2050, respectively. However, Kyoto set the 2020 target as 18% reduction globally, in which the UK is committed to reduce 30–40%. Furthermore, the routemap demands 21% reduction across the EC by 2022 and a 39% reduction by 2050 (The Green Construction Board, 2013).

Figure 8.11 clearly indicates the increasing significance of EC management in the built environment. The fact that zero carbon necessarily means not only zero OC but also zero EC is gaining paramount importance within the industry. However, along with so many drivers, there are also several barriers for carbon management in the built environment.

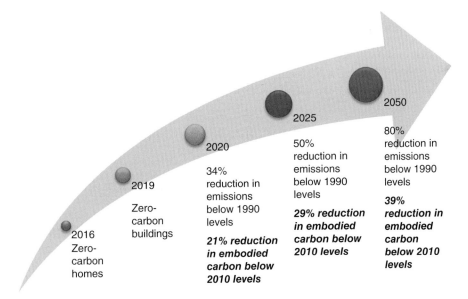

Figure 8.11   2050 low carbon trajectory – the UK.

8.5 Drivers and barriers in managing carbon emissions in construction

Carbon emissions are influenced by a number of factors, including consumption, international trade, population growth, economic growth, structural change to a service economy, energy consumption and energy intensity of the economy (Blanco *et al.*, 2014; Pielke Jr, 2009). Out of these, some are less likely to be controlled by the government (like population growth); and some could not be controlled as it might affect the wellbeing of the country (like economic growth). This indicates the complexity of the problem. Nevertheless, government bodies are taking several initiatives to drive carbon management in the construction industry as illustrated in Figure 8.12. On the other hand, there are several barriers in reaching the goal (as indicated in Figure 8.12). It is interesting to note that some issues that are identified as barriers by Osmani and O'Reilly (2009) are evolving as potential drivers.

These are further analysed in the following section.

8.5.1 Drivers for managing carbon emissions

Kyoto protocol
The first international treaty to come into force in 1997, which set emission reduction targets to the developed nations to be achieved by 2050. While this is seen as a driver, scholars also pointed out some major shortfalls, like prominent GHG-emitting countries such as the United States and Canada stepping back from the protocol and the non-inclusion of major developing nations (like India and China due to their lower per capita emissions) which are now becoming leading emitters in the world (Gunawansa, 2010). Nevertheless, the Kyoto protocol drives the vision of a fossil-free economy (Oberthür and Ott, 1999) by bringing nations together towards a common goal.

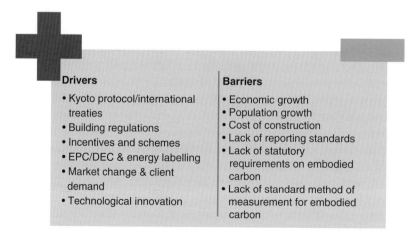

Figure 8.12   Drivers and barriers for carbon management in construction.

Building regulations

As per Part L of the UK Building Regulations for new buildings, the CO_2 emission per annum of a building, referred to as the Building Emission Rate (BER), should not exceed the Target Emission Rate (TER) in order to get approval (UK Building Regulations, 2013). This imposes a constraint on the OC in buildings due to the fact that the OC contributes nearly 70–80% of total emissions. Further, emissions cuts were introduced since 2002 through to 2019 to achieve a zero OC building (UK-GBC, 2014). Therefore, clearly Building Regulations Part L drives carbon management. However, there are missing components like unregulated emissions (cooking, IT appliances) and EC which are not covered under the Building Regulations. Furthermore, it was also reported that there exists a huge gap between predicted and actual emissions (Pan and Garmston, 2012; UK-GBC, 2008, 2014) which is again a serious issue; and initiatives like the CarbonBuzz platform developed by CIBSE help to manage the gap between the designed and the actual performance.

Incentives and schemes

'Green Deal' allows consumers (domestic and non-domestic) to obtain finance from accredited providers to improve the energy efficiency of their building at no upfront cost, where the cost is paid back through utility bills; Energy Company Obligation (ECO) requires energy suppliers to improve the energy efficiency of domestic consumers. However, the Guardian reported that the above twin schemes of the UK government to cut energy wastage tend to fail due to high interest rates (Harvey, 2014). Furthermore, the ambition of the ECO was under achieved in 2013 where a 70% fall in the cavity wall insulation was reported in comparison to 2012 rate compared to 2012; and a need for improvement in the scheme was highlighted (Committee on Climate Change, 2014a). Therefore, the UK government needs to react immediately on these issues for green deal and ECO to continue to be drivers of carbon management.

Further, the CRC energy efficiency scheme requires large private and public sector organisations to monitor energy use and report emissions. Allowances have to be purchased at a cost of £ 16 per tonne of CO_2. However, this policy is considered to be complex and the Committee on Climate Change (2014a) articulates that it should be re-designed.

Renewable Heat Incentive (RHI) is a financial support programme for renewable heat. RHI pays participants of the scheme to generate and use renewable energy to heat their buildings, both domestic and non-domestic (Department of Energy and Climate Change, 2012).

Energy performance certificate/display energy certificate

An Energy Performance Certificate (EPC) has to be provided whenever a building is constructed, sold or rented. On the other hand, large public buildings require a Display Energy Certificate (DEC). EPC classifies buildings on a banded scale from A (best) to G (worst). This band also provides a numerical indication of SAP rating (energy consumption per unit floor area) for dwellings and the annual CO_2 emission per floor area for other buildings. Earlier an EPC conveyed only the energy performance of the building (Anderson, 2006). However, government subsequently decided to incorporate cost estimates for improvements in energy usage which will communicate effective information to the building owner. Recently, a few changes to EPC and DEC came into force which require commercial and public buildings (exceeding a floor area of 500 m^2) that are frequently visited by the public to display EPC and DEC at a prominent place in the building, showcasing the rising concern on energy and environmental performance of buildings and creating public awareness (GVA, 2013). Similarly, energy labelling indicates appliance energy efficiency. Appliances with a higher energy rating save more energy, reducing utility bills. Further, 80% or more savings are reported to be achieved with energy efficient appliances (Committee on Climate Change, 2014a). These labelling and declaration systems raise public awareness and drive carbon management.

Market change

In a world of competition, businesses that do not adapt to market change are unlikely to reap competitive benefits. Generally, none of the leading companies would want to be affected due to inaction to market changes (Okereke, 2007). Therefore, change in the construction market drives low carbon developments.

Technological innovation

Technological innovation is clearly a driver for a low carbon built environment. Manufacturing companies exploring alternatives to production processes and supply chain management leads to low carbon options. For instance, the cement and concrete industry is reported to be continuously reducing emissions by increasing their use of bio-fuels and alternative raw materials and introducing modified low-energy clinker types and cement with reduced clinker content (Damtoft *et al.*, 2008).

8.5.2 Barriers for managing carbon emissions

Economic growth

A positive correlation was noticed between per capita emissions and per capita income/GDP (economic indicator) in the fifth assessment report of the IPCC (Blanco *et al.*, 2014). The report further observed high economic growth in the recent past in Asia compared to other regions. As a result, per capita emissions are said to have declined in all regions except in Asia. Apparently, the output of the construction industry correlates with economic output, hence, governments manipulate the output of the construction industry to trigger economic growth. Therefore, economic growth has a huge impact on carbon management in the construction industry. That implies higher economic growth, most likely leading to higher emissions, which remains as a barrier. However, increasing sustainable developments will help lower this effect.

Population growth

Undoubtedly, each new person added to the world population increases GHG emissions. Blanco *et al.* (2014) noted that most studies reported that an increase in population stimulates more than a proportional increase of emissions. Furthermore, population is one of the major factors altering construction demand (Bee-Hua, 2000; Department for Business Innovation and Skills, 2013; Tang *et al.*, 1990). Therefore, population growth tends to increase construction demand, resulting in increased emissions.

Cost of construction

Initially, cost was considered to be a huge barrier for zero carbon buildings compared to conventional designs (Catto, 2008). However, it is believed and proved that low and zero carbon buildings are attainable at an efficient cost similar to conventional buildings (Sturgis and Roberts, 2010; Target Zero, 2012) or at a little higher cost. A recent study by the Sweett group (Zero Carbon Hub and Sweett, 2014) validates the above claim by modelling different house types; and the findings suggest that zero carbon homes can be achieved at an additional cost of between £ 2900 and £ 6300 in 2020. Moreover, a recent case study on a commercial building (Torcellini *et al.*, 2014) proved that zero energy building can be attained at no additional cost when best cost-controlling practices are implemented. Yet, cost is considered as a barrier with minimal potential to hinder sustainable development.

Lack of reporting standards

There is no formal reporting procedure yet on the carbon accountability of businesses (Embodied Carbon Industry Task Force, 2014). Having one will help manage emissions and help the government to audit emissions and revise action plans towards the 2050 goal. Failing might lead to a gap between the predicted and actual emissions, resulting in missed targets.

Lack of statutory requirements on EC

As discussed earlier, Building Regulations Part L regulates OC. However, EC has not been part of any regulations yet. This is a huge drawback to achieving a fossil-free economy by 2050, as it is reported that EC can contribute up to 70% of total emissions from buildings (Embodied Carbon Industry Task Force, 2014). Nevertheless, proposals are made by task groups to incorporate EC as an Allowable Solution in the zero carbon definition. But the likeliness to incorporate seems to be very low, as the current zero carbon definition itself receives numerous criticisms; and the findings of Osmani and O'Reilly (2009) on the achievability of 2016 zero homes target are said to be ambitious, with the current definition. Therefore, a lack of stringent statutory requirements on EC is and will continue to be a huge barrier to achieving the 2050 target.

Lack of standard method of measurement and benchmarks on EC

Even though there are no regulations to control EC, the construction industry has taken initiatives and is on board with measuring EC in projects. One recent initiative in the UK is the WRAP EC database (WRAP and UK Green Building Council, 2014). However, lack of a robust method and procedures to estimate carbon in a consistent way has become a bottleneck (Dixit *et al.*, 2010, 2012; HM Government, 2010). Scholars noticed variations in EC measurements due to various factors, like system boundary, method of estimating, assumption, data sources and element classification, as discussed in Section 8.3.4 (Clark, 2013; Dixit *et al.*, 2010; Ekundayo *et al.*, 2012). Not all factors identified can be standardised, though the system boundary, the method of measurement and the element classification can be standardised. Lack of any such standardised method is a barrier for EC management.

8.6 *Need for carbon estimating in construction*

Among the barriers discussed in the previous section, the government can easily over-come the lack of reporting standards, the lack of statutory requirements on EC and the lack of a standard method of measurements and benchmarks on EC. Especially, carbon estimating is crucial for a fossil-free economy. Lord Kelvin, a mathematical physicist, said '*If you cannot measure it, you cannot improve it*'. Hence, carbon estimating is impor-tant to reduce it and improve the environmental performance of the design. In addition to that, the dual currency approach is gaining popularity. Therefore, government and professional bodies are responsible for developing practices and standards that facilitate dual currency assessment of construction projects and create awareness in the industry.

What are the benefits?
Carbon management can result in many benefits as illustrated in Figure 8.13. Accordingly, the benefits are multi-faceted and shared by many. Key benefits can be summarised as follows (HM Treasury, 2013b):

- Reduces costs.
- Unlocks innovation and drives better solutions.
- Drives resource efficiency.
- Provides competitive advantage and export potential.
- Contributes to climate change mitigation.

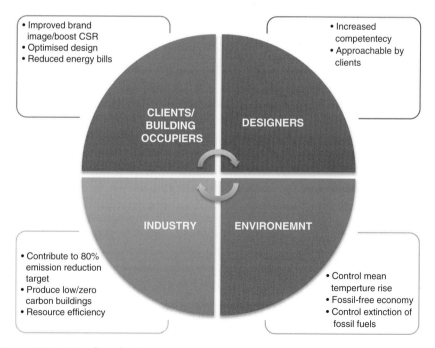

Figure 8.13   Benefits of carbon management.

Table 8.5 Carbon and cost plans during design developments (Source: Victoria *et al.*, 2015. Reproduced with permission of BSI).

RIBA stages	Cost plan	Carbon plan	Technique
1 Preparation and brief	Order of cost estimate	Order of carbon estimate	Single rate estimating – unit, superficial area
2 Concept design	Formal cost plan 1	Formal carbon plan 1	Single rate estimating – unit, superficial area, cube
3 Developed design	Formal cost plan 2	Formal carbon plan 2	Elemental estimate
4 Technical design	Formal cost plan 3	Formal carbon plan 3	Approximate quantities
	Pre-tender estimate	Pre-tender carbon estimate	Bill of quantities
	Post-tender estimate	Post-tender carbon estimate	Adjusted bill of quantities

Who can do it?

Undoubtedly, a Quantity Surveyor (QS) is the ideal project team member to conduct carbon estimating. Cost estimating being a core competency of the QS, estimating carbon ideally fits with the same skill set. Also, dual currency approach again affirms that QS is the ideal person to deal with it, as both cost and carbon plans can be produced in parallel using the same techniques (but different data sources; e.g. in-house data sources, Price book for cost, UK Building Blackbook for carbon and costs) as explained in Table 8.5. However, measurement of carbon is only one aspect of the carbon emissions management process. Hence, the design team in general and project managers in particular have a greater role in managing carbon emissions and achieving greater levels of sustainability in construction projects and developments.

Unfortunately, carbon estimating lacks a robust data set to facilitate estimating during design development. Therefore, it is important that QS or cost and project management practices produce carbon analysis similar to cost analysis at the end of the pre-contract stage or at the end of a project. Further, organisations such as BCIS should also take an initiative in producing publicly available carbon analysis along with cost analysis. To this extent WRAP has taken steps in the right direction. This will encourage industry practitioners to treat carbon the same as cost throughout the project, establishing a dual currency approach. Ultimately, a dual currency approach is the way forward for managing carbon emissions in achieving a sustainable construction industry.

8.7 Future trends

Based on the above discussions, this paper foresees the following trends in the construction industry in the future:

- Construction business plans will include low carbon transition strategies (HM Government, 2010).

- Zero carbon buildings could be achieved at zero additional cost (Torcellini *et al.*, 2014).
- EC to be included as an 'Allowable Solution' in zero carbon policy (Embodied Carbon Industry Task Force, 2014).
- Tendency of mandating EC emissions as part of Part L of Building Regulations.
- Mandatory reporting of project carbon in WRAP Embodied Carbon database, so that it can lead to benchmark development and creating of better data set for EC.
- Development of a UK wide materials database for EC (Embodied Carbon Industry Task Force, 2014).
- BCIS to produce carbon plans along with cost plans that will facilitate cost and carbon planning and controlling during design development.
- New and innovative technologies will indicate their EC or embodied energy usage in the production of new material and components.
- EC or embodied energy data for all building material and components will become a standard in product literature and marketing. This might extend a dual currency approach to marketing products.
- Roles of project cost managers will include 'dual currency management' approaches.

8.8 Conclusions

The global construction industry is responsible for 3040% of energy consumption and 30% GHG emissions and forecasts indicate that the global construction market will grow more than 70% by 2025. Although issues and doubts about the causes of climate change are becoming increasingly clear, there are many global obstacles to overcome in providing a global response to managing emissions. Therefore, carbon management has gained significant attention in sustainable development, as it can result in severe and adverse consequences if not managed. Especially, OC happened to be in the spotlight until recently due to its overwhelming contribution in total emissions. However, Studies have now also pointed out the EC can account up to 70% of total emissions. Most developed countries are taking steps (such as after the zero carbon policy) towards managing OC and aiming to achieve zero carbon levels. This again brings into focus the need to manage the EC component in buildings. Therefore, EC started gaining importance and the focus is gradually shifting from OC to EC. Out of 80% total emissions reductions to be achieved by 2050, 39% of reductions are attributed to EC. This highlights the significance of EC in sustainable development. However, to reduce emissions it needs to be measured first. While OC measurement is standardised, EC measurement is still developing and there are no standard methods of estimating EC. The datasets available for EC estimating are very limited and in some cases questionable. Issues related to system boundaries are not yet resolved. There are several estimating tools available on the web to aid EC estimating but these are based on different underlying methods and system boundaries. Among these, early stage estimating tools are limited. Another important dimension of appraisal, cost indication, is missing in the identified tools. Nevertheless, the future of the construction industry is expected to rely on dual currency appraisal that can enlighten construction clients and investors. It calls for tools that combine both carbon and cost assessment of alternative designs. In addition to that, it is important that this information can be generated starting from early stages of design and during design development. However, estimating carbon during the early stages is still in its infancy and a robust dataset and carbon hotspots are yet to be grounded to facilitate early stage EC estimating.

The main issues in estimating and managing carbon revolve around achieving global agreements in reducing emissions. The question arises as to how long it will take the world to come together in agreeing on measures for reducing carbon emissions. Then by that time will it to be too late, will our actions in the present day compromise the life of future generations? Can the global construction industry achieve carbon neutral or broadly zero carbon construction, balancing development needs with environmental impacts? These are questions that remain at large and can only be resolved by consensus, greater awareness and research and technological development.

Acknowledgements

The authors would like to acknowledge Northumbria University for funding the research project and E.C. Harris for supporting the project by providing required data.

References

Anderson, J. (2015) *Embodied Carbon and EPDs*. Available at: http://www.greenspec.co.uk/building-design/embodied-energy/ (accessed 7 August 2015).

Ashworth, A. and Perera, S. (2015) *Cost Studies of Buildings*. Routledge, Oxford.

Ayaz, E., Yang, F. (2009) *Zero Carbon isn't Really Zero: Why Embodied Carbon in Materials Can't be Ignored*. Available at: http://www.di.net/articles/zero_carbon/(accessed 30 April 2015).

BCIS (2006) *BCIS Life Expectancy of Building Components*. BCIS, London.

Bee-Hua, G. (2000) Evaluating the performance of combining neural networks and genetic algorithms to forecast construction demand: the case of the Singapore residential sector. *Construction Management and Economics* **18**(2), 209–217.

Blanco G., Gerlagh, R., Suh, S., Barrett, J., de Coninck, H.C., Diaz Morejon, C.F., Zhou, P. (2014) Drivers, trends and mitigation. In: *Climate Change 2014: Mitigation of Climate Change*. Contribution of Working Group III to the Fifth Assessment Report of the Intergovernmental Panel on Climate Change (eds O. Edenhofer, R. Pichs-Madruga, Y. Sokona, E. Farahani, S. Kadner, K. Seyboth, A. Adler, I. Baum, S. Brunner, P. Eickemeier, B. Kriemann, J. Savolainen, S. Schlömer, C. von Stechow, J.C. Minx). Cambridge University Press, Cambridge, pp. 10–19.

Brandt, A.R. (2008) Converting oil shale to liquid fuels: energy inputs and greenhouse gas emissions of the shell in situ conversion process. *Environmental Science and Technology* **42**(19), 7489–7495.

British Standards Institution (2011) BS EN 15978:2011 *Sustainability of construction works. Assessment of environmental performance of buildings. Calculation method*. BSI, London.

Build Carbon Neutral (2007) *Construction Carbon Calculator*. Build Carbon Neutral, London.

Building Research Establishment (2014) *iSBEM: An Interface for SBEM (Simplified Building Energy Model). User guide*. Communities and Local Government, UK.

Catto, I. (2008) Carbon zero homes UK style. *Renewable Energy Focus* **9**(1), 28–29.

Chen, T.Y., Burnett, J., Chau, C.K. (2001) Analysis of embodied energy use in the residential building of Hong Kong. *Energy* **20**(4), 323–340.

Clark, D.H. (2013) *What Colour is your Building?: Measuring and Reducing the Energy and Carbon Footprint of Buildings*. RIBA Enterprises Limited, London.

Cole, R.J., Kernan, P.C. (1996) Life-cycle energy use in office buildings. *Building and Environment* **31**(4), 307–317.

Committee on Climate Change (2014a) *Factsheet: Buildings*. Available at: http://www.theccc.org.uk/wp-content/uploads/2014/08/Fact-sheet-buildings2014_Final1.pdf (accessed 17 March 2016).

Committee on Climate Change (2014b) *UK Emissions by Sector* Available at: http://www.theccc.org.uk/charts-data/ukemissions-by-sector/(accessed 29 April 2015).

Committee on Climate Change (2015) *Meeting Carbon Budgets – Progress in Reducing the UK's Emissions. 2015 Report to Parliament*. Committee on Climate Change, London.

Communities and Local Government (2011) *Zero Carbon Non-domestic Buildings Phase 3 Final Report*. Stationery Office, London.

Damtoft, J.S., Lukasik, J., Herfort, D., Sorrentino, D., Gartner, E.M. (2008) Sustainable development and climate change initiatives. *Cement and Concrete Research* **38**(2), 115–127.

Department for Business Innovation and Skills (2013) *UK Construction – an Economic Analysis of the Sector*. Department for Communities and Local Government, London.

Department for Communities and Local Government (2008) *Definition of Zero Carbon Homes and Non-domestic Buildings – Consultation*. Department for Communities and Local Government, London.

Department for Communities and Local Government (2015) *Policy Paper – 2010 to 2015 Government Policy: Energy Efficiency in Buildings*. Available at: https://www.gov.uk/government/publications/2010-to-2015-government-policy-energy-efficiency-in-buildings/2010-to-2015-government-policy-energy-efficiency-in-buildings#appendix-7-code-for-sustainable-homes (accessed 17 March 2016).

Department for Environment Food and Rural Affairs (2015) *Greenhouse Gas Conversion Factor Repository*. Available: http://www.ukconversionfactorscarbonsmart.co.uk/ (accessed 23 July 2015).

Department of Energy and Climate Change (2012) *Low Carbon Technologies*. Available at: https://www.gov.uk/government/policies/increasing-the-use-of-low-carbon-technologies/supporting-pages/renewable-heat-incentive-rhi (accessed 4 May 2015).

Dixit, M.K., Fernández-Solís, J.L., Lavy, S., Culp, C.H. (2010) Identification of parameters for embodied energy measurement: a literature review. *Energy and Buildings* **42**(8), 1238–1247.

Dixit, M.K., Fernández-Solís, J.L., Lavy, S., Culp, C.H. (2012) Need for an embodied energy measurement protocol for buildings: a review paper. *Renewable and Sustainable Energy Reviews* **16**(6), 3730–3743.

Ekundayo, D., Perera, S., Udeaja, C., Zhou, L. (2012) *Carbon Review and Qualitative Comparison of Selected Carbon Counting Tools*. Paper presented at The Construction, Building and Real Estate Research Conference of the Royal Institution of Chartered Surveyors, Las Vegas, Nevada, pp. 36–43.

Embodied Carbon Industry Task Force (2014) *Embodied Carbon Industry Task Force Recommendations – Proposals for Standardised Measurement Method and Recommendations for Zero Carbon Building Regulations and Allowable Solutions: The Alliance of Sustainable Building Products*. Available at: http://www.asbp.org.uk/uploads/documents/resources/Embodied%20Carbon%20Indusrty%20Task%20Force%20Proposals_June%202014_Final[1].pdf (accessed 17 March 2016).

Fay, R., Treloar, G., Iyer-Raniga, U. (2000) Life-cycle energy analysis of buildings: a case study. *Building Research and Information*, **28**(1), 31–41.

Franklin and Andrews (2011) *UK Building Blackbook: The Cost and Carbon Guide: Hutchins' 2011: Small and Major Works*. Franklin and Andrews, Croydon, UK.

Gunawansa, A. (2010) The Kyoto Protocol and beyond: a south asian perspective. In: *Crucial issues in climate change and the kyoto protocol asia and the world* (eds K.-L. Koh, L.-H. Lye, J. Lin), World Scientific Publishing, Singapore, pp. 473–503.

GVA (2013) *EPC and DEC Requirements*. GVA, London.

Halcrow Yolles (2010a) *Embodied Carbon Sustainable Offices: a Supplementary Report*. South West Regional Development Agency, Plymouth.

Halcrow Yolles (2010b) *Sustainable Offices – Embodied Carbon*. South West Regional Development Agency, Plymouth.

Hammond, G., Jones, C. (2008) *Inventory of Carbon Energy (ICE)*. University of Bath, Bath.

Hammond, G., Jones, C. (2011) *A BSRIA Guide: Embodied Carbon. The Inventory of Carbon and Energy (ICE)*. BSRIA, London.

Harvey, F. (2014) UK on track to miss carbon targets, climate change advisers warn, *The Guardian*. Available at: http://www.theguardian.com/environment/2014/jul/15/uk-miss-carbon-targets-climate-change-advisers (accessed 17 March 2016).

Hernandez, P., Kenny, P. (2010) From net energy to zero energy buildings: defining life cycle zero energy buildings (LC-ZEB). *Energy and Buildings* 42(6), 815–821.

Hitchin, R. (2013) *CIBSE Research Report 9: Embodied Carbon and Building Services*. CIBSE, London.

HM Government (2010) *Low Carbon Construction – Innovation and Growth Team Final Report*. HM Government, London.

HM Treasury (2013a) *Construction 2025 – Industrial Strategy: Government and Industry in Partnership*. HM Treasury, London.

HM Treasury (2013b) *Infrastructure Carbon Review*. HM Treasury, London.

Huberman, N., Pearlmutter, D. (2008) A life-cycle energy analysis of building materials in the Negev desert. *Energy and Buildings*, 40(5), 837–848.

Ibn-Mohammed, T., Greenough, R., Taylor, S., Ozawa-Meida, L., Acquaye, A. (2013) Operational vs. embodied emissions in buildings – a review of current trends. *Energy and Buildings* 66, 232–245.

Intergovernmental Panel on Climate Change (2014) *Climate Change 2014 Mitigation of Climate Change: Working Group III Contribution to the Fifth Assessment Report of the Intergovernmental Panel on Climate Change*. Committee on Climate Change, Cambridge.

Lélé, S.M. (1991) Sustainable development: a critical review. *World Development* 19(6), 607–621.

Lützkendorf, T., Foliente, G., Balouktsi, M., Wiberg, A.H. (2014) Net-zero buildings: incorporating embodied impacts. *Building Research and Information* 43(1), 62–81.

Marszal, A.J., Heiselberg, P., Bourrelle, J.S., Musall, E., Voss, K., Sartori, I., Napolitano, A. (2011) Zero energy building – a review of definitions and calculation methodologies. *Energy and Buildings* 43(4), 971–979.

McLeod, R.S., Hopfe, C.J., Rezgui, Y. (2012) An investigation into recent proposals for a revised definition of zero carbon homes in the UK. *Energy Policy* 46, 25–35.

Obama, B. (2015) *Clean Power Plan*. Available at: https://www.whitehouse.gov/the-press-office/2015/08/03/remarks-president-announcing-clean-power-plan (accessed 7 August 2015).

Oberthür, S., Ott, H. (1999) *The Kyoto Protocol: international climate policy for the 21st century*. Springer, New York.

Okereke, C. (2007) An exploration of motivations, drivers and barriers to carbon management: the UK FTSE 100. *European Management Journal* 25(6), 475–486.

Osmani, M., O'Reilly, A. (2009) Feasibility of zero carbon homes in England by 2016: a house builder's perspective. *Building and Environment* 44(9), 1917–1924.

Pan, W., Garmston, H. (2012) Building regulations in energy efficiency: compliance in England and Wales. *Energy Policy* 45, 594–605.

Phlorum (2011) *Embodied CO_2 Estimator*. Phlorum, New York.

Pielke Jr, R.A. (2009) The British Climate Change Act: a critical evaluation and proposed alternative approach. *Environmental Research Letters* 4(2), 024010.

Ramesh, T., Prakash, R., Shukla, K.K. (2010) Life cycle energy analysis of buildings: An overview. *Energy and Buildings* 42(10), 1592–1600.

RICS (2014) *Methodology to Calculate Embodied Carbon*, 1st edn. RICS, London.

Rocky Mountain Institute (2009) *Green Footstep*. Rocky Mountain Institute, Denver.

Sansom, M., Pope, R.J. (2012) A comparative embodied carbon assessment of commercial buildings. *The Structural Engineer*, **2012**, October, 38–49.

Skanska (2010). *Carbon footprinting in construction – examples from Finland, Norway, Sweden, UK and US*. Available at: http://www.skanska-sustainability-case-studies.com/index.php/latest-case-studies/item/140-carbon-footprinting-in-construction (accessed 3 January 2016).

Sturgis Associates (2010) *Carbon Profile: Ropermark Place*. Sturgis Carbon Profiling, Cambridge.

Sturgis, S., Roberts, G. (2010) *Redefining Zero: Carbon Profiling as a Solution to Whole Life Carbon Emission Measurement in Buildings*. RICS, London.

Tang, J.C.S., Karasudhi, P., Tachopiyagoon, P. (1990) Thai construction industry: demand and projection. *Construction Management and Economics* **8**(3), 249–257.

Target Zero (2012) *Guidance on the design and construction of sustainable, low carbon office buildings*. Target Zero, Oxford.

TATA Steel (2014) *Steel Construction Embodied Carbon Tool*. TATA Steel, London.

The Green Construction Board (2013) *Low Carbon Routemap for the UK Built Environment*. The Green Construction Board/WRAP/The Climate Centre/ARUP, London.

Thormark, C. (2002) A low energy building in a life cycle – its embodied energy, energy need for operation and recycling potential. *Building and Environment*, **37**(4), 429–435.

Torcellini, P., Pless, S., Leach, M. (2014) A pathway for net-zero energy buildings: creating a case for zero cost increase. *Building Research and Information* **43**(1), 25–33.

UK-GBC (2008) *The Definition of Zero Carbon*. UK-GBC, London.

UK-GBC (2013) *UK-GBC Statistics*. Available: http://www.ukgbc.org/content/key-statistics-0 (accessed 18 December 2013).

UK-GBC (2014) *Building Zero Carbon – The Case for Action Examining the Case for Action on Zero Carbon Non Domestic Buildings*. UK-GBC, London.

UK Building Regulations (2013) UK Building Regulations Approved Document (Part L1A), UK Government, London.

University of Minnesota (2014) *Building Carbon Calculator*. University of Minnesota, Minnesota.

Victoria, M., Perera, S., Davies, A. (2015) Developing an early design stage embodied carbon prediction model: a case study, *Annual ARCOM Conference*, **31**, 7–9.

WRAP and UK Green Building Council (2014) *Embodied Carbon Database*. Available at: http://www.wrap.org.uk/content/embodied-carbon-database (accessed 17 March 2016).

Yohanis, Y. G., Norton, B. (2002) Life-cycle operational and embodied energy for a generic single-storey office building in the UK. *Energy*, **27**(1), 77–92.

Zero Carbon Hub (2014) *Zero Carbon Policy*. Available at: http://www.zerocarbonhub.org/zero-carbon-policy/zero-carbon-policy (accessed 12 August 2014).

Zero Carbon Hub and Sweett (2014) *Cost Analysis: Meeting the Zero Carbon Standard*. Zero Carbon Hub, London.

Chapter 9
Supporting Risk Assessment in Building Resilient Cities

Terrence Fernando and Matar Alzahmi

Thinklab, University of Salford, Salford, M5 4WT, UK

9.1 Introduction

There is significant evidence of the growth of natural disasters on a global level. For instance, in the years 1900 to 1909 natural disasters occurred 73 times, whereas from 2000 to 2005 this number increased to 2788 (Kusumasari *et al.*, 2010). As stated by Guha-Sapir *et al.* (2011), the number of victims increased to 232 million in the period 2001–2010, with most of the incidents caused by hydrological disasters. Therefore, building resilience in cities to natural disasters should be considered as an important factor in sustainability.

Scientific research has shown that disaster risks not only exist because of the presence of a physical hazard, they are compounded by the presence of vulnerability (Aldunce and León, 2007). Therefore, there is an urgent need to shift our focus from emergency response and recovery towards a sustainable disaster mitigation framework (McEntire, 2004; Pearce, 2003) that focuses on building resilience within a disaster prone area, involving public agencies and the local community to reduce the impact of a hazard (Trim, 2004). Carpenter *et al.* (2001) emphasised that resilience has the characteristics of: (i) the amount of change a system can undergo whilst retaining the same structure and function, (ii) the degree to which a system is capable of self-organisation and (iii) the degree to which a system can build the capacity to learn and adapt. Within this context, the focus of disaster management needs to change as follows (Pearce, 2003): from hazard to vulnerability reduction, from reactive to proactive, from single agency to partnerships, from response management to risk management, from planning for communities to planning with communities. However, these changes require new partnership models, an emphasis on the early stages of the disaster management cycle and novel technological solutions that can promote collaborative risk assessment involving a range of stakeholders (Aldunce and León, 2007). These changes could be supported by a technology platform that can map vulnerabilities (social, infrastructure, economic, natural) for a single or multiple hazards as well as their cascading effects on society and the economy. Such a

Future Challenges in Evaluating and Managing Sustainable Development in the Built Environment,
First Edition. Edited by Peter S. Brandon, Patrizia Lombardi and Geoffrey Q. Shen.
© 2017 John Wiley & Sons Ltd. Published 2017 by John Wiley & Sons Ltd.

platform could potentially allow multi-agencies to establish a common understanding of vulnerabilities, explore 'what-if' scenarios, identify the impact of various hazards on society and the economy in different local contexts, implement mitigation measures and answer the challenging question of 'Are we prepared for disasters?'. This chapter presents the challenges that should be addressed for strengthening local risk assessment in order to reduce the vulnerability of a place.

9.2 Theoretical framework for capturing the degree of vulnerability of a place

Disaster risk has been expressed as a function of a hazard (its magnitude and effects), the vulnerability of a community and the exposure of an area to a specific disaster. This has been further detailed and broadened by Cutter (1996) with her vulnerability of place model. Cutter argued that hazard potential is determined by the risk and the mitigation related to a specific geographic context and the social fabric that brings about a specific vulnerability of a place.

Increasingly, the environment and society are characterised by densely populated urban areas (Lall and Deichmann, 2011). As a result, the overall vulnerability (of people, infrastructure, environment and the economy) has increased as they have been exposed to the new risk situations of a place. As a result, a hazard could have profound effects on the sustainability of cities. For example, prolonged infrastructure failures will cause losses to businesses due to the employees' problems of access to work, the customers' problems of access to business premises, the effects on distribution and supply channels and, hence, negative effects on local economies in cities. Cities in which these infrastructures are located do not operate as closed systems. They are interdependent on many other systems for their smooth operation and, if not properly coordinated, this will result in cascading impacts that can cause both social and economic vulnerability which is 'place' dependent.

Therefore, building on our current understanding, further work is required to develop a comprehensive theoretical framework that can be used to capture local vulnerability, the level of vulnerability (low, medium, high) and measures for reducing the vulnerability.

9.3 Local risk assessment process

As described in the United Kingdom (UK) Emergency Preparedness Report (*Guidance on Part 1 of the Civil Contingency Act 2004*) from the Cabinet Office (2013), Integrated Emergency Management offers a comprehensive approach to the prevention and management of emergencies. It has six steps: *Emergency Preparedness* relates to the first four steps which are anticipation, assessment, prevention and preparation, while *Emergency Response and Recovery* covers the final two steps. The Emergency Preparedness Report from the Cabinet Office (2013) also suggests that risk assessment should form the foundation for emergency planning and business continuity plans which can then be tested by detailed appraisals and exercises. Risk assessment helps multi-agency planners decide

Figure 9.1   The six-step risk assessment process.

what resource requirements they need and what multi-agency activities need to be planned collaboratively in order to prepare for disaster. In the United States (US), the US Department of Health and Human Services (2002) suggests, if a risk assessment is to be successful, then it must be understood and communicated appropriately to everyone concerned.

The risk assessment process itself consists of multiple steps. The six-step risk assessment process deployed in Australia and New Zealand is widely recognised as being good practice (Australia/New Zealand Standards Committee, 2009) and is now used in the UK. These steps are Contextualisation, Hazard Review, Risk Analysis, Risk Evaluation, Risk Treatment and Monitoring and Reviewing (Figure 9.1).

The first step of this risk assessment process is contextualisation which is vital for the entire risk assessment process. It is important to establish an accurate representation of the characteristics of a local area and the local risks, such as an overview contextualisation of social intelligence (e.g. the demographic, ethnic and social composition of the community), geographical distributions, the identification of vulnerable groups, the level of community resilience, the local environment and an understanding of local vulnerabilities, the characteristics of space (urban, rural, mixed), scientific sites, the local infrastructure (transport, utilities, business), the critical supply network and critical services (telecommunication hubs, health, finance etc.) and an overview of potentially hazardous sites (and their relationships with communities) or sensitive environmental sites (FEMA, 2010). This type of information can help the various agencies establish a collective understanding of the local risks and vulnerabilities.

Furthermore, the dependencies of these aspects should also be considered in developing the local risk context. City infrastructure managers and emergency planners require a more holistic approach in order to understand the complex make-up and the cascading impacts and consequences of networked infrastructure systems rather than considering them as individual systems. Furthermore, infrastructure facilities such as transportation, telecommunications, healthcare, water supply and electricity supply are deeply embedded within social systems in cities and are indicative of some of the latent social effects that take place within a city's system. For example, as presented by Hogan (2014), a failure of an electrical sub-station can have a cascading effect on water supply, healthcare, transport, telecoms, businesses and so on. Some of these cascading effects can propagate and grow over time, leading to fatalities, social unrest, public disorder incidents, environmental damage and so on. Therefore, in order to have a deeper understanding of the local risk context, there is an urgent need for further research to model the complex inter-connections among infrastructures, social systems and the economy, requiring multi-simulation models. Some of the modelling techniques that can be used in modelling cascading effects are system dynamics, Bayesian belief networks and multi-agent based approaches.

9.4 Multi-agency collaboration and community engagement

Multi-agency collaboration is important in the risk assessment process to allow agencies to move towards a common understanding of the local risks and develop a common risk mitigation plan. Emergency management calls for the completion of dynamic, ever-changing tasks (Mendonça *et al.*, 2007; Salas *et al.*, 2008). It has been suggested that the scale of disasters in recent years has made it important to move away from traditional, centralised disaster management activities (Aldunate *et al.*, 2005; Bier, 2006; Perrow, 1984). In light of this fact, collaboration between multiple agencies is now seen as vital in disaster management (Waugh and Streib, 2006; Eide *et al.*, 2012). Collaboration is simply when representatives of different organisations combine their efforts, resources and knowledge to make decisions and produce things for which they share responsibility (Kamensky *et al.*, 2004). While the necessity for collaboration has been established, the challenges relating to it are considerable. A lack of effective collaboration between different agencies is commonly cited in reports in disasters (see, e.g., Norges Offentlige Utredninger, 2012).

Kapucu and Garayev (2011) suggested that weaknesses in multi-agency collaboration led to numerous recent failures in emergency management. In the United States, they point to the terrorist attacks on 11 September 2001 (9/11) and Hurricane Katrina as events in which effective collaboration between agencies was not put into practice. In the case of 9/11, there was a failure in collaboration between intelligence agencies before the event, while in the case of Hurricane Katrina there was a lack of coordination between responders after the event. In both cases, an overall lack of organisation and preparedness is cited as the reason for failures in response to these events; and it is suggested that an increased focus on collaboration is required (Kapucu and Van Wart, 2006).

One challenge relating to collaboration is that it is a relatively new concept for many managers and leaders (Kapucu and Garayev, 2011). Moreover, effective collaboration requires that issues concerning communication within, and between, response organi-sations are addressed. These issues can relate to resources and to organisational and decision-making processes. Decision-making forms the foundation of emergency man-agement and is a problem in emergency situations for many reasons. First, the need to make immediate or quick decisions has been found to affect the quality of decision-making (Buchanan and O'Connell, 2006; Flueler, 2006). Second, emergency situations naturally cause significant stress among decision-makers (Paton, 2003). Third, the level of past experience of similar situations is an influence (Moynihan, 2008). Fourth, there is often a limit to the amount of information available. All these factors are found to be made more complicated by the need for multiple agencies to collaborate their response (Bigley and Roberts, 2001; Carley and Lin, 1997; Sellnow *et al.*, 2002). In short, the more agencies that are involved, the more complicated the decision-making is. Although research into decision-making is widespread, it tends to focus on decision-making at an individual level, team or organisational level. There is a lack of research into decision-making that occurs between organisations.

Collaboration presents challenges beyond decision-making. For instance, repre-sentatives of many agencies need to have a clear grasp of their role, what they are responsible for and what tasks they have to carry out. Moreover, knowledge of an emergency situation needs to be shared and accessible to all responders from the dif-ferent agencies. Furthermore, communication needs to be efficient and the agencies involved in collaboration have to understand how the other agencies are structured (Eide *et al.*, 2012).

In summary, multi-agency collaboration is increasingly seen as vital in emergency management but it presents a range of challenges relating to decision-making, commu-nication, the sharing of knowledge and the understanding of the structure, roles and responsibilities of the agencies involved. Therefore, further research is required in stud-ying the nature of collaboration and the tools and methods for enhancing multi-agency collaboration. Generic collaboration models such as the one developed by Patel *et al.* (2012) and activity models (Mishra *et al.*, 2011) could offer a sound theoretical foundation for investigating the collaboration challenges in multi-agency collaboration in disaster management.

9.5 *Technology platforms for interactive risk assessment*

It is vital that risk assessment is understood and communicated in an appropriate way (US Department of Health and Human Services, 2002). The need for a technology platform that can enhance collaboration and collaborative decision-making concerning risk assessment has been argued for in the literature (Van Westen, 2013). Furthermore, studies have shown that the presentation of hazards, vulnerability, coping capacity and risk in the form of digital maps has a higher impact than traditional information repre-sentations (Martin and Higgs, 1997; Husdal, 2001). As a result, with the increasing use of digital maps by disaster managers, it is expected that visualisation, provided in a proper way, has the potential to be a highly effective communication tool (Kolbe *et al.*, 2005; Marincioni, 2007; Raper, 1989; Zlatanova *et al.*, 2002).

However, little research is evident on the exploration of the nature of such a collaborative platform (Van Westen, 2013) based on interactive risk visualisation maps. Many researchers (Kraak, 2006) have argued that interactive risk visualisation in the risk assessment process can help agencies explore high-risk areas, assess the location of vulnerable people and vulnerable areas and view the capacities and resources available for those at risk in order to lessen their vulnerability. Furthermore, the creation of different visual scenarios can improve agencies' collective understanding of risk levels and of their capacities.

Interactive hazard maps provide an effective medium for visualising risk information and bridging communication barriers among varying stakeholders. Moreover, these maps aid in the assessment, analysis and mitigation of risks (Dransch *et al.*, 2005). When fabricating a hazard map, one must keep in mind the purpose of the map, the intended audience, how data will be displayed and where it will be used (Friedmannova *et al.*, 2007). Also the creation of effective interactive hazard maps takes into consideration community knowledge through the utilisation of participatory mapping methods. These methods aim to involve locals in the mapping process, to reflect local views in governmental policy and to develop a mutual understanding of surrounding risks (Institute for Ocean Management, 2007). If constructed appropriately, community-based hazard maps can help bridge the knowledge gap between community members, local government, non-governmental organisations and members of the international disaster response and risk reduction community. As a result, efforts should continue to educate local communities in the utilisation of hazard maps in order to identify vulnerabilities and increase communication among stakeholders.

An obvious area of interest for multi-agency disaster management teams is mapping. Mapping has become the keystone for risk assessment and communication. Indeed, it has been shown that how a map is presented and, therefore, visualised has an important effect on how the user is able to communicate the information presented by the map (Alphen *et al.*, 2009). Although computers can create photo-realistic three-dimensional models (Kot *et al.*, 2005), what is most important is the user's ability to manipulate maps to highlight and emphasise the most relevant information for their purpose (MacEachren and Ganter, 1990).

Basically, there are two ways of approaching mapping which can be used as part of a platform for multi-agency emergency planning. First, the 'communication approach' stresses the need for maps to accurately represent and display the reality of an area. On the other hand, the 'visualisation approach' suggests that maps can also be used to predict and simulate hypothetical events (MacEachren and Ganter, 1990). The main concept in the first approach is to transfer what is known about an area or situation. However, mapping can also be used to encourage users of visual thinking about a problem in a new, visual way (DiBiase *et al.*, 1992) and, therefore, possibly come up with new solutions to a problem. It has been suggested that interactivity, an effective user interface and visualisation tools can encourage users to be more flexible in their approaches to problems (McCarthy *et al.*, 2007). Underlying this is the view that the user of a mapping programme should be thought of as an active participant and not just as a passive receiver of information (Morss *et al.*, 2005) especially given that multi-agency decision-making is an active, dynamic process.

9.6 Conclusion

This chapter has argued the importance of focusing on risk assessment with a view to building resilience and hence contributing to the creation of sustainable environments. The key challenges presented in this chapter are: the creation of a comprehensive theoretical framework that can be used to capture local vulnerability, the implementation of an information platform that can help multi-agencies to establish a collective understanding of the local risks and vulnerabilities, a multi-simulation framework that can capture cascading effects on physical infrastructure, social and economic sustainability, multi-agency collaboration models that can promote greater team work and technology platforms that can bring risk data on to an interactive visual form to support comprehension and sound decision making. Advances in these areas could help to reduce local vulnerability, hence increasing the resilience and sustainability of our environments.

References

Aldunate, R.G., Pena-Mora, F., Robinson, G.E. (2005) Distributed decision making for large scale disaster relief operations: drawing analogies from robust natural systems. *Complexity* **11**(2), 28–38.

Aldunce, P., León, A. (2007) Opportunities for improving disaster management in Chile: a case study. *Disaster Prevention and Management: An International Journal* **16**(1), 33–41.

Alphen, J.V., Martini, F., Loat, R., Slomp, R., Passchier, R. (2009) Flood risk mapping in Europe, experiences and best practices. *Journal of Flood Risk Management* **2**(4), 285–292.

Australia/New Zealand Standards Committee (2009) *Risk Management – Principles and Guidelines*, AS/NZS ISO 31000, November 2009.

Bier, V.M. (2006) Hurricane Katrina as a bureaucratic nightmare. In: *On risk and disaster: Lessons from Hurricane Katrina* (eds R.J. Daniels, D.F. Kettl, H. Kunreuther). University of Pennsylvania Press, Philadelphia, pp. 243–254.

Bigley, G.A., Roberts, K.H. (2001) The incident command system: high reliability organizations for complex and volatile task environments. *Academy of Management Journal* **44**(6), 1281–1299.

Buchanan, L., O'Connell, A. (2006) A brief history of decision-making. *Harvard Business Review* **84**(1) 32–41.

Cabinet Office (2013) *Emergency Preparedness Non Statutory Guidance Accompanying the Civil Contingencies Act 2004: A Reference Document*. Available at: https://www.gov.uk/government/publications/emergency-preparedness (accessed 4 April 2016).

Carpenter, S.R., Walker, B., Anderies, J.M., Abel, N. (2001) From metaphor to measurement: resilience of what to what? *Ecosystems* **4**, 765–781.

Carley, K.M., Lin, Z. (1997) A theoretical study of organizational performance under information distortion. *Management Science* **43**(7), 976–999.

Cutter, S.L. (1996) Vulnerability to environmental hazards. *Progress in Human Geography* **20**(4), 529–539.

DiBiase, D.A.M., MacEachren, A.M., Krygier, J.B., Reeves, C. (1992) Animation and the role of map design in scientific visualisation. *Cartography and Geographic Information Systems* **19**, 201–214.

Dransch, D., Etter, J., Walz, U. (2005) Maps for natural risk management. *International Cartographic Conference (La Coruna, Spain 2005)*. Available at: http://www2.ioer.de/recherche/pdf/2005_walz_dransch_etter_icc2005.pdf (accessed 4 April 2016).

Eide, A.W., Halvorsrud, R., Haugstveit, I.M., Skjetne, J.H., Stiso, M. (2012) Key challenges in multiagency collaboration during large-scale emergency management. In: *AMI for Crisis management, International Joint Conference on Ambient Intelligence, Pisa, Italy*, pp. 21–24.

FEMA (2010) *Publication 1*, Federal Emergency Management Agency, Washington, D.C.

Flueler, T. (2006) *Decision-making for complex socio-technical systems: robustness from lessons learned in long-term radioactive waste governance.* Springer, Dordrecht.

Friedmannova, L., Konecny, M., Stanek, K. (2007) An adaptive cartographic visualization for support of the crisis management. In: *XXIII International Cartographic Conference – Cartography for Everyone and for You, Moscow, 2007*, pp. 1–9. Available at: geogr.data.quonia.cz/lgc/optimalizovane/Adaptive-cartography-for-CM_Friedmannova-Konecny-Stanek_Autocarto_2006-1.pdf (accessed 4 April 2016).

Guha-Sapir, D., Vos, F., Below, R., Ponserre, S. (2011) *Annual Disaster Statistical Review 2010.* Centre for Research on the Epidemiology of Disasters, Luovain.

Hogan, M. (2014) *Anytown: A Practitioner-led Exploration of Interdependency and Complexity*, UEL Sandcastle Event, Chicago.

Husdal, J. (2001). *Can it Really be that Dangerous? Issues in Visualization of Risk and Vulnerability.* University of Utah, Salt Lake City. Available at: http://www.husdal.com/2001/10/31/can-it-really-be-that-dangerous-issues-in-visualization-of-risk-and-vulnerability/ (accessed 4 April 2016).

Institute for Ocean Management (2007) *Training the trainers on community based hazard map development*, Anna University, Chennai. Available at: http://www.adrc.asia/events/Chennai/Presentation/Final%20Report%20Tentative.pdf (accessed 4 April 2016).

Kamensky, J.M., Burlin, T.J., Abramson, M.A. (2004) Networks and partnerships: collaborating to achieve results no one can achieve alone. In: *Collaboration using Networks and Partnerships* (eds J.M. Kamensky, T.J. Burlin), Rowman and Littlefield Publishers, Lanham, pp. 3–20.

Kapucu, N. Van Wart, M. (2006) The emerging role of the public sector in managing extreme events: lessons learned. *Administration and Society*, **38**(3), 279–308.

Kapucu, N., Garayev, V. (2011) Collaborative decision-making in emergency and disaster management. *International Journal of Public Administration* **34**(6), 366–375.

Kolbe, T.H., Gröger G., Plümer L. (2005) CityGML: interoperable access to 3D city models. In: *Geo-information for Disaster Management* (eds P.J.M. van Oosterom, S. Zlatanova, E.M. Fendel), Proceedings of the International Symposium on Geo-information for Disaster Management, Delft, 21–23 March 2005, Springer, Heidelberg.

Kot, B., Wuensche, B., Grundy, J., Hosking, J. (2005) Information visualisation using 3D computer game engines case study: a source code comprehension tool. *CHINZ 2005 Proceedings of the Sixth ACM SIGCHI New Zealand Chapter's International Conference on Computer–Human Interaction: Making CHI natural*, pp. 53–60.

Kraak M.J. (2006) Why maps matter in GIScience. *The Cartographic Journal* **43**(1), 82–89.

Kusumasari, B., Alam, Q., Siddiqui, K. (2010) Resource capability for local government in managing disasters. *Disaster Prevention and Management* **19**(4), 438–451.

Lall, S., Deichmann U. (2011) Density and disasters: economics of urban hazard risk. *The World Bank Research Observer Advanced Access*, July 7.

MacEachren, A.M., Ganter, J.H. (1990) A pattern identification approach to cartographic visualisation. *Cartographica* **27**(2), 64–68.

Marincioni, F. (2007) Information technologies and the sharing of disaster knowledge: the critical role of professional culture. *Disasters* **31**(4), 459–476.

Martin, D., Higgs, G. (1997) The visualization of socio-economic GIS data using virtual reality tools. *Transactions in GIS* **1**(4), 255.

McCarthy, S., Tunstall, S., Parker, D., Faulkner, H., Howe, J. (2007) Risk communication in emergency response to extreme floods. *Environmental Hazards* **7**(3), 179–192.

McEntire, D. (2004) Development, disasters and vulnerability: a discussion of divergent theories and the need for their integration. *Disaster Prevention and Management* **13**, 193–198.

Mendonça, D., Jefferson, T., Harrald, J. (2007) Collaborative adhocracies and mix-and-match technologies in emergency management. *Communications of the ACM* **50**(3), 44–49.

Mishra, J.L., Allen, D.K., Pearman, A.D. (2011) Activity theory as a methodological and analytical framework for information practices in emergency management. In: *Proceedings of the Eighth International Conference on Information Systems for Crisis Response and Management* (eds M.A. Santos, L. Sousa, E. Portela), Lisbon, Portugal, May 2011.

Morss, R.E., Wilhelmi, O.A., Downton, M.W., Gruntfest, E. (2005) Flood risk, uncertainty and scientific information for decision making: lessons from an interdisciplinary project. *Bulletin of the American Meteorological Society* **86**(11), 1593–1601.

Moynihan, D.P. (2008) Learning under uncertainty: networks in crisis management. *Public Administration Review* **68**(2), 350–365.

Norges Offentlige Utredninger (2012) Report NOU 2012: 14. Rapport fra 22. juli-kommisjonen. Available at: http://www.regjeringen.no/nb/dep/smk/dok/nou-er/2012/nou-2012-14. html?id=697260 (accessed 25 October 2012).

Patel, H. Pettitt, M., Wilson J.R. (2012) Factors of collaborative working: a framework for a collaboration model. *Applied Ergonomics* **43**(1), 1–26.

Paton, D. (2003) Stress in disaster response: a risk management approach. *Disaster Prevention and Management* **12**(3), 203–209.

Pearce, L. (2003) Disaster management and community planning, and public participation: how to achieve sustainable hazard mitigation. *Natural Hazards* **28**, 211–228.

Perrow, C. (1984) *Normal Accidents: Living with High-risk Technologies.* Basic Books, New York.

Raper, J.F. (1989) The 3D geoscientific mapping and modeling system: a conceptual design. In: *Three Dimensional Applications in Geographical Information Systems* (ed. J.F. Raper). Taylor and Francis, London, pp. 11–20.

Salas, E., Cooke, N.J., Rosen, M.A. (2008) On teams, teamwork, and team performance: discoveries and developments. *Human Factors: The Journal of the Human Factors and Ergonomics Society* **50**(3), 540–547.

Sellnow, T.L., Seeger, M.W., Ulmer, R.R. (2002) Chaos theory, informational needs, and natural disasters. *Journal of Applied Communication Research* **30**(4), 269–292.

Trim, P. (2004) An integrative approach to disaster management and planning. *Disaster Prevention and Management* **13**, 218–225.

US Department of Health and Human Services (2002) *Communicating in a Crisis: Risk Communication Guidelines for Public Officials.* Department of Health and Human Services, Washington, D.C.

Van Westen, C.J. (2013) Remote sensing and GIS for natural hazards assessment and disaster risk management. *Remote Sensing, GIScience and Geomorphology* **17**(3), 259–298.

Waugh, W.L., Streib, G. (2006) Collaboration and leadership for effective emergency management. *Public Administration Review* **66**(s1), 131–140.

Zlatanova, S., Rahman, A.A., Pilouk, M. (2002) 3D GIS: current status and perspectives. In: *Proceedings of the Joint Conference on Geo-spatial Theory, Processing and Applications*, 8–12 July, Ottawa, Canada, 6 pp. CDROM.

Chapter 10
Towards an Intelligent Digital Ecosystem – Sustainable Data-driven Design Futures

Tuba Kocaturk

Department of Architecture, University of Liverpool, Liverpool, L69 7ZN, UK

10.1 Introduction

'The best way to predict the future is to invent it' (Alan Kay).

As data-driven and intelligent design is introducing and establishing a new set of economic, social and cultural values, we have started to question some of our age old assumptions and conceptions about our built habitat. This chapter will focus on the role of 'design' in tackling challenges for a sustainable future, raise questions and provoke a debate about *data-driven and computational design innovation* and its position in the current debate of sustainable development. The motivation is to reconfigure and challenge our 'business as usual' mode of thinking for more agile and adaptive solutions for the future, through design innovation, and explore the role *informatics* can potentially play in discovering new modes of imagining, creating and operating for a socially inclusive, economically and environmentally viable future.

Today, the requirement to achieve sustainability places new demands on human societies to do three things differently than the (pre)industrial period: to *produce*, *consume* and *organise* sustainably by increasing efficiency, by reducing the ecological footprint of consumption patterns while enabling real improvements in the quality of life and by engaging and encouraging participation (Souter, 2012). A recent report by Arup (Stewart *et al.*, 2014) refers to four *megatrends* as the game-changing forces that will shape the world in the future and present more challenges and opportunities as they transform the way society and markets function: global urban population growth, demographic and socio-economic shifts, increase in the frequency and intensity of extreme weather events and the exponential advances in technology converging nano-technology, bio-technology, information technology and cognitive science; all of which will contribute to changing the ways in which we work, live, build and communicate.

Future Challenges in Evaluating and Managing Sustainable Development in the Built Environment,
First Edition. Edited by Peter S. Brandon, Patrizia Lombardi and Geoffrey Q. Shen.
© 2017 John Wiley & Sons Ltd. Published 2017 by John Wiley & Sons Ltd.

10.2 Changing role of 'design' for sustainable futures

In July 2013, the United Kingdom (UK) Government published the Industrial Strategy Report for Construction, which introduced (i) smart *construction and digital design* and (ii) *low carbon and sustainable construction* among the top strategic priorities underpinning sustained growth across the economy and an improved quality of life for citizens (Construction 2025, 2013). Until recently, sustainability in architectural and urban design domains had a special focus and emphasis on 'environment' and 'energy' concerns including minimising waste, responding to existing needs and making the most efficient use of our existing resources. However, there is a growing tendency, in recent years, that associates sustainable design with *design innovation* through propositions that promote new behaviours, new life styles and new ways of playing, working, consuming and producing in and for the future. This opens up a whole new set of discussions regarding the role 'design' and 'architects' can and will play for the development of a sustainable future, not only to serve 'environmental sustainability', but also with a highlighted emphasis on economic and social sustainability. This raises a series of questions such as: *How can design and operation of buildings contribute to the economic, social and environmental sustainability*? *What is the scale and level of intervention this contribution could be achieved and sustained*? The answers to these questions are not simple but point towards the two crucial and transforming dimensions of sustainable development: one is the technological and the other is the political dimension. While technology will act as a catalyst to drive design innovation, the political dimension will have a profound effect on shaping the means, actors and scales of 'designer' interventions and thereby can help enhance, stabilise or diminish possible, probable or desirable scenarios proposed for the future.

Although it is difficult to isolate the technological dimension from the political and policy dimensions, in the following sections I will explore the potential of technology in driving design innovation and potentials for embedding computation, big data, artificial intelligence and real-time connectivity into the conception and realisation of a sustainable built habitat. This discussion will lay the foundation of a data-driven model of a future *digital ecosystem* as a distributed, adaptive and socio-technical system. The chapter will provide alternative scenarios whereby the conceptual development, design, construction and operation of buildings could be intricately linked to past or instantaneous data in a continuous loop where buildings themselves could become active data generators and, as such, contribute to the continuity of a sustainable and integrated *digital ecosystem* for the built environment.

10.3 Emerging concepts, challenges and trends

10.3.1 Transformational potential of technology

Technology is having a transformational effect on Architectural Design. At the heart of the technological change lies the transformation of the Architecture, Engineering and Construction (AEC) industry from a document-based to an information-based business.

Digital modelling, data-driven design and computational design technologies are offering architects, engineers and other building professionals the means to explore vastly complex building forms and systems very quickly and to digitise, store and compare information that can be used to create highly intelligent, highly efficient buildings in ways that were simply not possible previously. Similarly, analysis software makes it possible to model complex building behaviour, including environmental and structural performance, pedestrian flow, code compliance and other systems and to open up unprecedented possibilities in embedding intelligence into the conception and realisation of buildings. Much criticism is placed on the 'waste' and the way our industry operates. The current discussion of Building Information Modelling (BIM) focuses precisely on this aspect and on the necessity to reduce inefficiencies through: (i) promoting greater transparency and collaboration and (ii) enabling intelligent decisions about greater energy efficiency leading to carbon reductions and a critical focus on the whole life performance of facilities (UK Government, 2012).

A similar shift of emphasis is also present at the urban realm where urban designers and planners are frequently adopting new set of tools to shape design decisions and to create opportunities to tackle higher order urban issues and develop transferrable design codes. Design codes, in this context, can be defined as certain rules or principles, as key components of good urban design (e.g. ease of movement, continuity, enclosure, adaptability) that can be applied to the process of making a place and then captured in written and drawn form for reuse. The process of creating these codes helps to align interests between key stakeholders at early stages, including the creative architect, the developer and the planner (Walt *et al.*, 2014).

Technology and digital media/tools, however, cannot be considered as the only force that is currently re-shaping architectural industry. Through the use of diverse media and technologies, new networks, collaboration styles and work practices have also emerged and in turn have facilitated the development of new methods to deal with the emerging knowledge and complexity affecting the ways in which the technology is applied and used (Kocaturk and Codinhoto, 2009). Maybe one of the most important consequences of the on-going technological debate is the renewed position and changing perception of the role *design* and *designers* play for the society and the economy. According to recent research by the Design Council, the contribution of *design* to the UK economy alone is £71.7 billion in value, equivalent to 7.2% of total GVA (Design Council, 2015).

Michael Speaks (2011) pointed out the crucial distinction between *design as a product* and *design as a creative process* in order to fully recognise and appreciate the value it generates through innovation:

> '… debate over the value of architecture is now focused less on style and the exquisite, designed object, and more on the economic and societal value added by design. … The most promising development, in this regard, and one that affects architecture and design practice as well as design education, is the growing recognition that design is not only a product—a table, building, plan or landscape—but also a creative process and a powerful engine of innovation. Design, as we all know, has become an important feature of our increasingly innovation driven economy' (Speaks, 2011).

Technology plays a crucial role in this on-going exploration of the new values that design can offer and in understanding the potential contribution of architectural design to the emerging understanding of 'sustainable development'. In this regard, technology can be recognised primarily as an *enabler* and, at best, as an *innovation infrastructure*: (i) for the design and production of better performing buildings (*product level*), (ii) for better informed, collaborative and more efficient design to production processes (*process level*) and (iii) for better control, maintenance and management of building operations (*operational level*).

10.4 The rise of big data

Using data in the AEC industry is not new. Data is fundamental to architectural design and production, where both architects and engineers continuously create, modify, share and simulate data in an organised way. Data, which is embedded in our drawings, three-dimensional (3D) models and contracts are translated into 'architectural spaces', and building operators use data from architects and users to operate and manage buildings. However, historically, the collection of data has been difficult and expensive. Its format and structure did not allow ease of use, which often required manual transfer from paper records into digital systems. Therefore, data applications were usually restricted to specific technical functions instead of aiding high-level decision making (Construction Industry Knowledge Base, 2015).

Data already underlies much of modern Architecture, Engineering, Construction and Operations; nonetheless, what is new to the industry is the amount of data that is currently available to us and our improved capacity to share, capture, measure, compile, process and translate data into meaningful and actionable information through smart technologies, enhanced data standards and visualisation techniques (Barista, 2014). Although the potentials are vast, Architectural practice and Construction sector (at large) are slow to adopt data-driven approaches. A recent publication by Deutsch (2015) identifies two immediate problems that concern the adoption of data tools within architectural design firms: first is the translation and systematisation of very large and unknown data sets for efficient use; and second is the lack of knowledgeable data experts within design firms who can intelligibly curate diverse data sources and tools according to the project needs. This has led to a growing number of data analysis and software programming experts making their way into the AEC field in recent years to meet the growing demand. A small number of firms offer sophisticated data analytics services to deduce insights from large unstructured datasets, some of which have been translated into commercial products by App developers (e.g. CityMapper, OpenStreetMap) and used by designers in innovative and compelling ways (Walt *et al.*, 2014). A recent report on top technology tools and trends for AEC professionals (Barista, 2014) summarises two of the most common data application areas in the sector as: (i) the development of analytic dashboards that summarise large data sets (e.g. space/energy usage, energy requirements) to help decision-making and quickly compare design options and (ii) data-mining of BIM models to help identify common patterns across designs that can be reused on future projects. The same report also outlines four ways design teams benefit from data-driven design (Barista, 2014):

1. *Enhance iterative design* – through the improved ability of designers to capture and analyse key performance metrics during conceptual design, which can then be used to optimise early prototypes.
2. *Re-use project data* – through collection of data on different projects which can then be applied in future projects
3. *Track occupant behaviour* – through tracking the behaviours and movements of people within buildings/spaces, designers can test early design intents against actual use of spaces.
4. *Automate the planning process* – through the application of algorithm-based approaches to improve the traditional project planning process.

The transition to a digital economy is indeed central in enabling the design and construction industry to meet its ambitions and to adapt to the fundamental changes in our everyday lives. Both the impact and scale of this transition will become more dramatic with the increase in global data traffic, two-thirds of which is predicted to move on to cloud computing systems by 2016 (Cisco, 2016). This implies the introduction of even more complex and diverse interactions (e.g. through the Internet of Things) between buildings, infrastructures and humans. Such developments have already made a significant impact in other industries and are likely to be a step change in how we build and operate in the near future. The report also argues that real-time data feedback will give us a better understanding of building performance, resulting in smarter designs, requiring less material and reducing the overall carbon footprint.

10.5 From green to smart: New focus/new metrics

Big Data's impact on design has often been used alongside a highly popular term: *Smart (or Intelligent) Design*. A recently published report by Arup in collaboration with the Royal Institute of British Architects (RIBA) addresses the radical transformation in the design of buildings and cities through data-driven approaches and methods (RIBA, 2013). One of the repercussions of these new approaches is the transformation of our perception as to what counts as a 'sustainable' design solution. Sustainable design solutions are now expected not only to be 'green', but also smart, intelligent and interconnected. The recurring themes of responsiveness, adaptability and flexibility in various publications (Cook and Das, 2007; Wang *et al.*, 2012) are considered to be key areas in which smart buildings differentiate from 'conventional' buildings and are often referred to as 'automated' or 'intelligent' buildings, which incorporate smart and interconnected technologies to make their operations more intelligent and responsive, ultimately improving their performance. Furthermore, smart buildings are considered as a vital part of the next generation building industry (Wang *et al.*, 2012) in the sense that they address sustainability issues through the utilisation of computation and intelligence to achieve the optimal combinations of overall comfort level and energy consumption.

In this regard, the shift of emphasis from 'green design' to 'smart design' has brought into the picture considerations of operational sustainability, thereby introducing new 'economic' and 'social' performance indicators. In other words, instead of designing a building that solely promises to be environmentally efficient, we now focus equally on the design of buildings that predict, adapt and respond to changing scenarios (e.g. user behaviour) through the use of intelligent systems. In this revised, improved, user-/context-sensitive approach to 'building design', much of our earlier metrics, values and assumptions are being challenged. For example; in building construction, the life-cycle cost of a building is usually associated with two key cost indicators: *capital* and *operational*. These are associated with separate, distinct stages: *capital costs* are assessed during acquisition, design and construction; *operational costs* of the completed development are calculated for the building's entire operational life. This metrics has been challenged already back in 1998 by a ground-breaking and controversial paper (Evans *et al.*, 1998) published by the Royal Academy of Engineering, which brought into perspective a third (hidden) cost indicator in addition to the capital and operational costs: *the cost of the people who use the building*, referring to their salary costs and productivity. This third indicator is crucial in order to understand the real economic impact of a building (in addition to social and environmental) where the relative cost across the three indicators has often been explained with the 1:5:200 rule; 1 refers to the capital cost, 5 refers to the cost to maintain the building over its life and 200 refers to the cost of the people using the building. Although very frequently quoted, there is no actual research which verifies this ratio and obviously a more realistic ratio would depend on a large number of variables, as well as the 'lifetime' years of the building in question. This has been challenged by various researchers, such as Hughes *et al.* (2004), where the authors proposed 1:0.4:12 as a more realistic ratio, based on the evaluation of three office buildings. Although there is considerable variation in the different ratios proposed by different researchers for different building types, what is common to all these propositions is the fact that the third indicator outweighs the capital and operational costs, combined, over the lifetime of a building. In other sectors, this disproportionately high hidden value is frequently quoted and coined with the term 'iceberg principle', meaning that much of the focus is on the little that can be seen rather than the disproportionate costs hidden below the water level. This also implies that designing intelligently in the early stages of development can lead to an exponential improvement of the overall life-cycle costs and performance of a building as well as the productivity and wellbeing of its users.

10.6 *Predicted versus actual performance*

One of the highly acknowledged contributions of effective integration of big data into the discussion of sustainable building design is the revelation of the 'gap' in energy efficiency between the predicted (energy efficiency of a building during its design) and the actual (energy efficiency once the building is in use). This means that a majority of our buildings are not performing as well as planned or expected (Bordass *et al.*, 2001; Demanuele *et al.*, 2010). Various initiatives such as PROBE and CarbonBuzz have been instrumental in the identification of this *Performance Gap* through the review and evaluation of existing buildings. Post-occupancy evaluation (POE) involves the systematic evaluation of (existing) buildings in use by assessing how well buildings match users' needs and aims at improving building design and performance. This is achieved through systematic data collection, analysis and comparison of predicted and actual performances against pre-identified criteria and provides designers with valuable information regarding the in-use performance of their designs (Preiser *et al.*, 1987). The PROBE studies (*Post-occupancy Review of Buildings and their Engineering*), which ran from 1995 to 2002, highlighted the lack in feedback regarding the actual performance of buildings through POE and suggested that actual energy consumption in buildings will usually be twice as much as predicted (Bordass *et al.*, 2001). In 2008, RIBA and the Chartered Institution of Building Services Engineers launched CarbonBuzz, a free online platform for benchmarking and tracking energy use in projects from design to operation, through which practices can share and publish building energy consumption data anonymously. CarbonBuzz allows users to track, review and compare energy records and contributing factors and generate reports on their data for external use. This allows design firms to go beyond compliance of mandatory Building Regulations calculations, to compare design energy use (predicted) with actual energy use side by side, and to refine their estimates in order to close the performance gap. Figure 10.1 is generated from data obtained from the CarbonBuzz website and illustrates the comparative evaluation of the predicted and actual CO_2 emissions of three different building types (distinguished by sectors of use: education, health and offices). As shown, the actual CO_2 emissions are approximately 46% higher than predicted in the office buildings, 90% higher than predicted in the education buildings and over 138% higher than predicted in the health buildings.

According to a recent paper by Menezes *et al.* (2011), who investigated the gap between the predicted and actual energy performance of non-domestic buildings, the underlying causes of discrepancies between detailed energy modelling predictions and in-use performance of occupied buildings relate to the use of unrealistic input parameters (assumptions), inefficient and superficial use of the modelling/simulation technologies (tools), unpredictable occupancy behaviours and inefficiencies in facility management (Figure 10.2).

Initiatives as described earlier in generating and sharing data concerning the actual energy performance of our existing building stock will certainly help bridge the gap

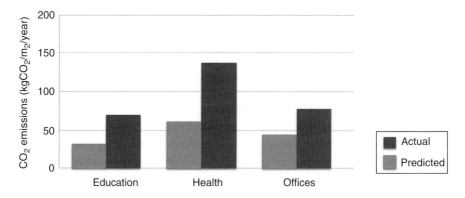

Figure 10.1   Comparison of median CO_2 emissions between actual and predicted performances of buildings across three sectors (data obtained from CarbonBuzz).

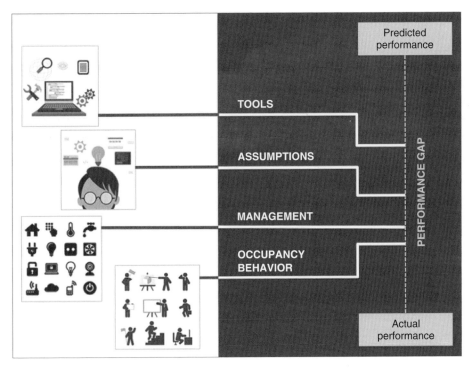

Figure 10.2   Four major factors contributing to the gap between the predicted and the actual performance of a non-domestic building.

between theory and practice to achieve strategic goals. However data alone, most certainly, will not be adequate to address the issue at hand as we will also need to have the right tools, processes and mindset in place to interpret and make sense of the data in order to develop an efficient and timely response. The efficiency of such a response has been closely linked to a 'digital maturity level' in a recent report by the BIM2050 work group (Built Environment 2050, 2014). The report identifies and describes four distinct and progressive waves (Figure 10.3), each referring to an improved degree of maturity of our digital state in the coming 30–40 years. The waves correspond to the lag of information exchange between formal transactions, using available technology and processes, where progression is coined with a reduction of the difference between the information required and the actual information available to make an efficient decision, in order to minimise the margin of error (e.g. performance gap). Moving through to wave 4 will imply that transactions will be almost instantaneous and computing power will enable vast simulation options (Built Environment 2050, 2014).

According to this feedback cycle wave analysis, the report places our present state in the AEC within the first wave, defined as *Analogue Decisions*. Although the design, simulation and modelling tools available in the market today allow the creation of various digital assets (e.g. 3D models, simulations), these tools do not all talk to one another and the processes and products are usually disconnected. This indicates reliance on 'highly

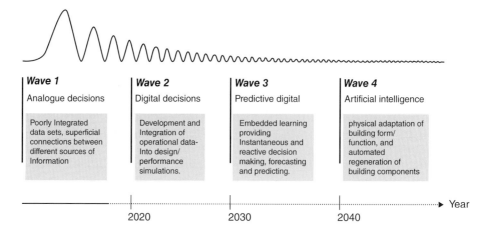

Figure 10.3   Feedback cycle waves in relation to states of digital maturity (Source: Built Environment 2050, 2014; © Philp, Thompson).

engineered digital processes to control poorly integrated data sets' (Built Environment 2050, 2014) and the application of superficial connections between different sources of information. The next wave, *Digital Decisions (2020–2030)*, is identified with an improved state of integrated processes and technology platforms that can allow the efficient collation of design, construction and operational data. This will then enable the progressive development of data sets from real-time building use and allow other technologies to integrate these data sets more readily for more efficient and accurate decision making. The third wave, *Predictive Digital (2030–2040)*, is identified with further improvements in 'learning' derived from real-time building use that can lead to opportunities to develop almost instantaneous reactive decision-making, forecasting and predicting requirements for intervention. This will result in buildings being more self-sustaining, efficient and responsive to the occupants and external environment with which they interact. The fourth wave, *Artificial Intelligence (2040+)*, is identified with designing buildings that are more self-sustaining, efficient, interactive and responsive to the occupants and to the external environment. It is predicted that the developments in material and biological sciences will offer even greater efficiencies through physical adaptations (of building form and function) and automated regeneration of building components.

Whether the predicted digital transformation, in this or in similar reports, will be achieved within the predicted timelines is of less importance compared to the combined socio-technical and organisational change this transformation will eventually create (Kocaturk, 2013). There are already various experimental yet disparate applications in current practice, albeit limited in number and scale. As the industry is going through one of the largest and most disruptive transformations in history, the more important question to raise is how architecture, as a discipline and as an industry, will manage to capitalise on these developments to drive innovation.

10.7 *Towards a digital ecosystem – Scenarios for implementation*

Amplified intelligence is a relatively new term which implies the front-line delivery, discovery, scenario planning and modelling to the early stages of the creative process, thereby informing the design and realisation by contextual information and real-time intent (Danson *et al.*, 2015).

This description provides a very accurate revelation of the true value of technology adoption in (sustainable) design through computation, big data, artificial intelligence, real time connectivity and predictive simulations in the design process. Through such amplification, intelligence is put to use in real time which promises an enormous shift that creates less dependency on personal, theoretical and historical assumptions but more emphasis on fact-based decision-making informed by actual data (Figure 10.4). This requires sophisticated data analytics services to deduce insights from large unstructured datasets. Data analytics means turning data into contextual and actionable information. (e.g. user behaviour, real-time intent). These insights will then lead to various models (2D, 3D, parametric, BIM) built according to possible future scenarios that would then need to be simulated and analysed to understand potential consequences and checked against various performance criteria (e.g. pedestrian flow, code compliance etc.) to open up unprecedented possibilities to develop the necessary digital and physical solutions in the actual realisation of the buildings (Figure 10.4).

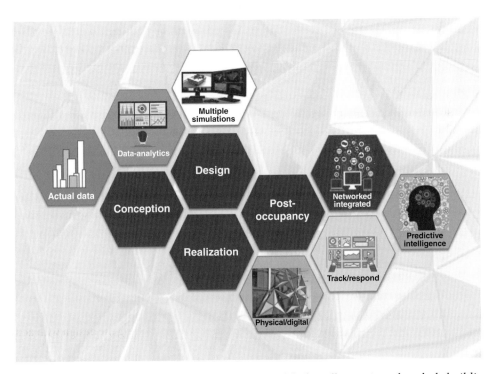

Figure 10.4 A possible scenario for embedding *Amplified Intelligence* into the whole building life-cycle, from conception through to design, realisation and post-occupancy.

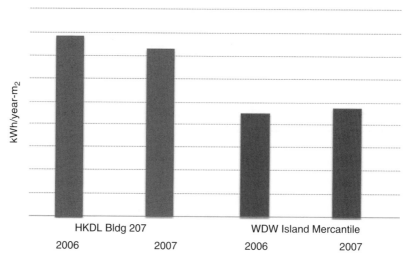

Figure 10.5 Comparison of energy Intensity per floor area between two Walt Disney buildings, HKDL in Hong Kong, WDW in Orlando (Source: Ben Schwegler).

A recent keynote speech by Ben Schwegler, Senior Vice President/Chief Scientist at World Disney Imagineering, provided anecdotal evidence to support the claim that data analytics has the potential to give us radically new insights that challenge our 'business as usual' mode of thinking. In this presentation, Ben Schwegler (pers. comm.) gave a comparative evaluation of energy consumption patterns between the two Walt Disney Parks (one in Hong Kong, China, and one in Orlando, USA) in two consecutive years. Figure 10.5 shows a typical comparative evaluation of the energy consumption values of the main building by using conventional 'consumption per floor area' metrics, where the main building in Hong Kong had been observed to use almost double the energy used by the building in Orlando. However, a thorough analysis, which took into account the building function and context revealed that the perceived difference was not to be interpreted merely as an inefficacy of the building in Hong Kong but that it was closely related with the local customs and cultural behaviour. The shop doors in Hong Kong were always kept open due to local cultural perception that closed doors would indicate a closed shop, causing energy loss but at the same time increasing the number of transactions. Therefore, a change in the metrics of evaluation from 'per floor area' to 'per transaction' instead indicated (Figure 10.6) that Hong Kong was actually using much less energy than used in Orlando to generate the same amount of transactions. This is a text book example of how 'isolated' data analysis (as used in the majority of cases in common practice) which excludes 'people', 'context' and 'practices' can be very misleading.

In the sections above, I emphasise the process of front-loading the design with actual data generated earlier to inform new design processes. This presents one of the most intrinsic dilemmas in our sector: that we base the majority of our decisions on 'past' information. In other words, the information we use during design is not instantaneous. Although this approach is often seen as being practical and justifiable for the

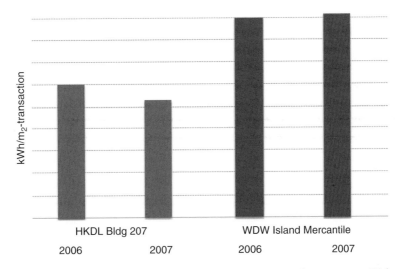

Figure 10.6 Comparison of energy Intensity per transaction between two Walt Disney buildings, HKDL in Hong Kong, WDW in Orlando (Source: Ben Schwegler).

design stage, it becomes less relevant and less reliable to base our choices, during post-occupancy, solely on information that is actually out of date. This is indicated as one of the reasons why construction is risky and requires large organisations to manage risk and uncertainty, according to a recent report (Built Environment 2050, 2014). An alternative and possible future scenario would be for buildings to be equipped with smart sensors, social media and mobile phones, to track and capture real-time information (e.g. from its users) in order to reduce the information lag to a point where we only deal with *converging and emerging information* (referring to waves 2 and 3 in Figure 10.3). This would imply a systemic shift from the reactive 'sense and respond' approach to more predictive and proactive approaches and solutions (Danson *et al.*, 2015). For example, in large commercial buildings, the heating and air-conditioning often function 'just in case'. Some of the more advanced systems use CO_2 sensors to indicate the real use. Thus instead of running these systems all the time, sensors can activate these systems as and when they are needed, which can bring significant savings. However, such systems cannot predict changing behaviours and uses, so they only start reacting when the air quality gets worse. By combining several data sources such as mobile phones and different sensors, we could predict the use of the buildings on a very detailed level and start adjustments, not only in the technical systems, but also in different services to improve the quality of end-user experience and building efficiency. Though it is important to note that such proactive solutions would only work efficiently if integrated with other systems within the building in a networked manner, because responding to localised information could create confusion in other functions of the building and, more importantly, networked information can help clarify the often blurry line between correlation and causation and generate more accurate insights. Similarly, individual buildings can be aggregated to each other, connecting their information and operation in a networked manner. Such integration could be implemented on a larger scale, by co-monitoring and linking data (e.g. energy use) across buildings, for example, in a university campus. Space arrangements can then be linked to energy consumption patterns for more efficient interventions, and recommendations can be made such as for the arrangement of venues for different lectures and other activities within the campus.

10.8 Conclusions: Future value propositions

The scenarios described in the previous section are not too far from realisation whereby the design, construction and operation of buildings would be intricately linked to past or instantaneous data in a continuous loop where buildings themselves would become active data generators and, as such, contribute to the continuity of a sustainable and integrated built ecosystem.

The opportunity to embed intelligence into any component of our individual buildings and connect them in real time, merging the physical world of objects and humans, resonates with Mitchell's (2006) prediction of our cities transforming into artificial ecosystems of interconnected, interdependent, intelligent digital organisms. He defined this new condition of built environment as 'programmable' and emphasised that the design of its software became as crucial — socially, economically and culturally — as that of their hardware. Mitchell's analogy gives crucial hints for answering the questions this chapter initially posed and explored: *how can the design and operation of buildings contribute to the economic, social and environmental sustainability?* and *what is the scale and level of intervention this contribution could be achieved and sustained?*. As an attempt to answer these questions, the chapter explored the potential of technology in driving design innovation and the transformational power of embedding computation, big data, artificial intelligence and real-time connectivity into the conception and realisation of buildings for a sustainable built habitat. The chapter identified the crucial role technology plays in the emergence of new values, both for the architectural profession and for a revised understanding of 'sustainability' in the context of built environment. Through various best practice examples and future-oriented scenarios, this chapter identified technology as an enabler and provider of the necessary infrastructure to drive design innovation at three levels: *product, process and operational* – through the design of better performing, better informed and better managed buildings within a connected *digital ecosystem*. This proposition lays the foundation for an expanded understanding of 'sustainable design' that is not limited merely to 'environmental' concerns, but also takes into account the wider economic and social considerations. This is a radical departure from the earlier practices and understanding of sustainability in architecture, which not only empowers diverse actors and stakeholders (including end users) but also challenges the established notions of ownership and agency in the process of deploying technology in our everyday life.

We are witnessing a strong shift of emphasis from 'energy efficient design' to 'context and user aware design' and from 'creating static objects' (buildings) to 'designing interactive systems' with long-term building performance in mind. Simpson (2013) refers to this shift by reviewing possible future value propositions, new commissioning and fee structures, as well as disruptive business models as likely to emerge from it for the architectural profession and for the industry at large:

'... It changes the value proposition for designers from creating static objects (buildings) to designing interactive systems, taking into account the true ownership cost over the useful life of the structure. Under this new paradigm, the designer's value proposition for clients shifts from the short-term (design fees paid up front before the building actually opens) to long-term (designing with long-term building performance in mind, producing direct benefits that accrue over decades). Paying for design services over the life of a structure greatly reduces the up-front financial burden on the client while at the same time providing a long-term income stream for the architect – essentially an annuity as long as the building performs according to the predicted metrics. It also radically changes the nature of decision-making' (Simpson, 2013).

The challenges that lie ahead for sustainable development are highly complex and multi-dimensional and will require innovation at many levels across many disciplines (including architects, designers and technology developers) and the long-term solutions will re-establish the underlying parameters of economic, social and environmental policies. The potentials that real-time data, connectivity and predictive intelligence have will undoubtedly alter the traditional relationship between humans and their environments. We need to develop a deep multidisciplinary understanding of the problems and opportunities to discover how *information* can be linked to *performance* and what this can imply for society, the environment, the economy and the practice of design.

References

Barista, D. (2014) The big data revolution: how data-driven design is transforming project planning, published as part of the Technology Report 2014: *Top tech tools and trends for AEC professionals*. In: *Building Design and Construction Online*. Available at: http://www.bdcnetwork.com/big-data-revolution-how-data-driven-design-transforming-project-planning (accessed 10 February 2016).

Bordass, B., Cohen, R., Standeven, M., Leaman, A. (2001) Assessing building performance in use: energy performance of probe buildings. *Building Research and Information* **29**(2), 114–128.

Built Environment 2050 (2014) *A Report on Our Digital Future*. CIC BIM2050 Group. Available at: http://www.cic.org.uk/download.php?f=be2050-cic-bim2050-2014-1.pdf (accessed 10 February 2016).

Cisco (2016) *Global Cisco Global Cloud Index: Forecast and Methodology 2011–2016*. Available at: http://www.cisco.com/cisco/web/UK/tomorrow-starts-here/files/global_index_whitepages.pdf (accessed 10 February 2016).

Construction 2025 (2013). Industrial Strategy: Government and Industry in Partnership. Available at: https://www.gov.uk/government/uploads/system/uploads/attachment_data/file/210099/bis-13-955-construction-2025-industrial-strategy.pdf (accessed 10 February 2016).

Construction Industry Knowledge Base (2015) *Big Data for Buildings*. Available at: http://www.designingbuildings.co.uk/wiki/Big_data_for_buildings (accessed 10 February 2016).

Cook, D.J., Das, S.K. (2007), How smart are our environments? An updated look at the state of the art. *Pervasive and Mobile Computing* **3**(2), 53–73.

Danson, F., Pierce, D., Shilling, M. (2015) *Amplified Intelligence*, Deloitte University Press. Available at: http://dupress.com/articles/tech-trends-2015-amplified-intelligence/(accessed 10 February 2016).

Demanuele, C., Tweddell, T., Davies, M. (2010) Bridging the gap between predicted and actual energy performance in schools. *Proceedings of World Renewable Energy Congress* **9**, 25–30.

RIBA (2013) *Designing with Data: Shaping our Future Cities*. Available at: http://www.architecture. com/TheRIBA/AboutUs/InfluencingPolicy/Designingwithdata (accessed 10 February 2016).

Deutsch, R. (2015) *Data-Driven Design and Construction: 25 Strategies for Capturing, Analyzing and Applying Building Data*, John Wiley & Sons, Inc., Hoboken.

Evans, R., Haryott, R., Haste, N., Jones, A. (1998) *The Long Term Costs of Owning and Using Buildings*, Royal Academy of Engineering, London.

Hughes, W.P., Ancell, D., Gruneberg, S., Hirst, L. (2004) Exposing the myth of the 1:5:200 ratio relating initial cost, maintenance and staffing costs of office buildings. *Proceedings of the Annual ARCOM Conference* **20**, 373–381.

Kocaturk, T. (2013) Emerging socio-technical networks of innovation in architectural practice. *International Journal of Architectural Computing* **11**(1), 21–36.

Kocaturk, T., Codinhoto, R. (2009) Dynamic coordination of distributed intelligence in design. *Proceedings of the eCAADe Conference* **27**, 61–68.

Menezes, A.C., Cripps, A., Bouchlaghem, D., Buswell, R. (2011) Predicted vs. actual energy performance of non-domestic buildings: using post-occupancy evaluation data to reduce the performance gap. *Applied Energy* **97**, 355–364.

Mitchell, W.J. (2006) Smart city 2020. *Metropolis*. Available at: http://www.metropolismag.com/ April-2006/Smart-City-2020/(accessed 10 February 2016).

Preiser, W., Rabinowitz, H., White, E. (1987) *Post-occupancy Evaluation*. Van Nostrand Reinhold, New York.

Simpson, S. (2013) The power of big data/big design. *Design Intelligence*. Available at: http://www. di.net/articles/the-power-of-big-data-big-design/(accessed 10 February 2016).

Souter, D. (2012). *ICTs, the Internet, and Sustainability: A Discussion Paper*. International Institute for Sustainable Development. Available at: https://www.iisd.org/pdf/2012/changing_our_ zunderstanding_of_sustainability (accessed 10 February 2016).

Speaks, M. (2011) New values of new design, *Proceedings of the Annual Conference of the Association for Computer Aided Design in Architecture* **31**, 60–63.

Stewart, C., Luebkeman, C., Morrell M., Lynne, G. (2014) *Future of Rail 2050*. Arup Rail Business and Arup Foresight + Research + Innovation Think Tank. Available at: http://publications.arup. com/Publications/F/Future_of_Rail_2050.aspx (accessed 10 February 2016).

Design Council (2015) *The Design Economy*. A report on the value of design to the UK economy. Available: http://www.designcouncil.org.uk/sites/default/files/asset/document/The%20Design% 20Economy%20executive%20summary_0.pdf (accessed 10 February 2016).

UK Government (2012) *Industrial Strategy: Government and Industry in Partnership*. UK Government Report on Building Information Modelling. Available at: https://www.gov.uk/ government/uploads/system/uploads/attachment_data/file/34710/12-1327-building-information-modelling.pdf (accessed 10 February 2016).

Walt, N., Doody, L., Baker, K., Cain, S. (2014) *Future Cities: UK Capabilities for Urban Innovation*. Report Published by Future Cities Catapult, 17 pp. Available at: http://publications.arup.com/ Publications/F/Future_Cities_UK_Capabilities_For_Urban_Innovation.aspx (accessed 10 February 2016).

Wang, Z., Wang, L., Dounis, A.I., Yang, R. (2012), Integration of plug-in hybrid electric vehicles into energy and comfort management for smart building. *Energy and Buildings* **47**, 260–266.

Chapter 11
Smart Cities Case Study – The Nottingham Experience

Marjan Sarshar[1], Anton Ianakiev[1] and Alison Stacey[2]
[1] *School of Architecture, Design and the Built Environment, Nottingham Trent University, Nottingham, NG1 4FQ, UK*
[2] *Economic Development, Nottingham City Council, Nottingham, NG2 3NG, UK*

11.1 Background

European Union (EU) cities are facing significant challenges as the population grows. The impact of climate change places visible constraints on city systems and infrastructures. Many cities still grapple with the effects of the economic crisis as the gap between the rich and the poor increases. The EU Commission (2012) has published some key data for why it is necessary to scale-up smart cities funding and accelerated learning between the cities:

- Cities create 80% of the EU's gross domestic product (GDP) with their concentration of trade, business and 'people expertise'. Cities are a driving force in generating Europe's economic growth.
- They will become even more important as the proportion of Europeans living in urban areas grows from just over two-thirds today to a forecast 85% by 2050.
- 68% of the EU population lives in urban areas, which consume 70% of energy. This accounts for 75% of the EU's total greenhouse gas emissions.
- Urban transport is responsible for one-quarter of all the emissions from road transport.

Many cities are experiencing tensions on their current infrastructure systems. Roadways, power grids, telecommunications lines and public transportation have to handle increasing demand and prepare for more extreme climate conditions. The aging population places additional pressures on city resources. In response to these challenges cities must innovate. New generations of technologies are emerging, however many cities face innovation barriers to the adoption of advanced technologies and new working

Future Challenges in Evaluating and Managing Sustainable Development in the Built Environment,
First Edition. Edited by Peter S. Brandon, Patrizia Lombardi and Geoffrey Q. Shen.
© 2017 John Wiley & Sons Ltd. Published 2017 by John Wiley & Sons Ltd.

methods. The organisational systems and procedures in many local authorities remain traditional, unable to accommodate significant change.

In tough economic times, businesses are reluctant to scale-up and rapidly deploy innovative technologies despite potential cost savings and longer-term emissions reductions.

The EU Commission is faced with the task of facilitating innovation in cities and businesses. In Horizon 2020 (EU Commission, 2012), the EU has decided to concentrate its funding on a limited number of city demonstration projects with high impact. The idea is that industry tests technology in a given city to show that the technology it developed works on the ground and can be implemented for *reasonable costs* and *has advantages for citizens* and the whole community. Substantial funding has been allocated to 'Light House City' projects, to lead the way and demonstrate not only the new technologies, but also the management and governance methods of large-scale change and innovations. These projects therefore are partnerships between industry and local authorities to demonstrate the uptake of new technologies – so that other cities may follow. In the first round of Light House City funding in 2014, EU funded three consortia, each composed of three core cities (i.e. a total of nine cities). Remourban was one of these consortia projects (Remourban Project, 2014) and includes the cities of Nottingham (United Kingdom; UK), Valladolid (Spain) and Tepebassi (Turkey). Each of these cities has a population of around 300,000 and provides a demonstrator for medium-sized cities.

11.2   Remourban

The Remourban consortium is composed of 22 partners across seven different countries; five cities, three research institutions, five large industries and 9 SMEs (small and medium-sized enterprises), with a funding of 25 million Euros.

As well as the three core cities of Nottingham, Valladolid and Tepebassi, there are two follower cities, Seraing (Belgium) and Miskolc (Hungary), which will demonstrate how to replicate and learn from the project findings.

11.2.1   Objective

The main objective of Remourban is to develop a model that leverages the convergence of: (i) sustainable districts and built environment, (ii) sustainable urban mobility and (iii) integration of city infrastructures and processes to achieve carbon reductions, improve the quality of life for the citizens and regenerate the economy. This will be facilitated through management and governance systems, financial models and evaluation frameworks to achieve this convergence (as shown in Figure 11.1).

The project will run for five years (2015–2020) starting by obtaining city audits, to ascertain the current situation and understand the level of achievements at the end of the project. It then aims to design innovative solutions and implements them. Finally, it will assess the results and fine-tune the interventions (Figure 11.1).

Each city has identified which areas of intervention and improvement are needed, based on its individual characteristics. Much of the efforts in Valladolid and Tapebessi is

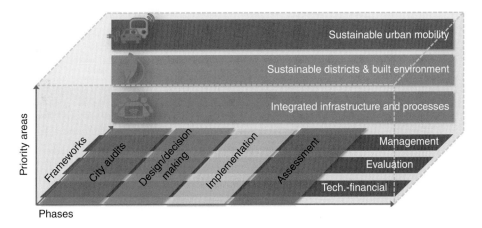

Figure 11.1   Multi-dimensional urban regeneration model.

focused on improved mobility, while Nottingham has placed more emphasis on sustainable built environment.

As well as improving the three light house cities and the two follower cities, the project is tasked with: (i) developing a model of how cities can replicate and learn from each other and (ii) developing and implementing citizen engagement models which place the citizens at the heart of transformations in cities.

11.2.2 Replication and city learning

The innovations and learning in Remourban have to scale-up and be replicable across EU cities which are seeking similar solutions. There are different levels of learning, as shown in Figure 11.2. While the 'follower' cities (Seriang and Miskolch) directly participate in the project and replicate relevant areas, the project actively seeks 'interested cities' and 'cities with high potential for implementation'.

This has opened substantial research questions and lines of enquiry around: How do cities learn? and What is a 'learning city'? This is a new area of investigation which will have substantial impact on EU cities. At present, this model seems to suggest that learning is hierarchical, which is highly debatable.

The experience of Remourban cities seems to demonstrate that learning is bi-directional and it is more about how cities learn from each other, rather than how do cities follow light house cities. However, the funding for light house cities allows them to spend more effort and resources on city learning.

11.3 Nottingham case study

This section examines the role of Nottingham in the Remourban Project (2014) and some of the current challenges.

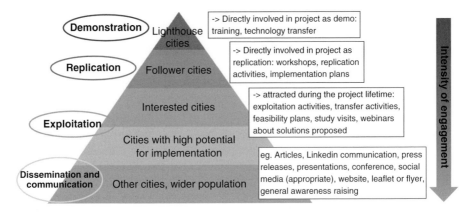

Figure 11.2 Replication of findings across EU cities.

11.3.1 The city

Nottingham is one of the major cities in East Midlands in the UK and has official population of 305 750. The wider city urban area has a population of 729 977. Nottingham City Council (NCC) and the County have developed local strategic plans for EU investment 2014–2019 (Circa £100 million with around £40 million private leveraged match expected) (NCC, 2010), with three focal areas:

- Smart Energy Communities – focussing on retrofit and district heating;
- Low carbon transport technologies;
- Support for low carbon SMEs – focussing on innovation.

Over the last three years, public and private capital investment have been steered according to the strategy, resulting in energy-saving retrofit investment into around 12 000 of Nottingham's homes (1 in 10) and 3500 (1 in 35) homes with PV systems (NCC, 2010). The city is now looking to steer investment into harder to treat areas such as solid wall insulation. Nottingham has one of the UK's largest district heating networks and significant expansion to this heating network is planned.

Nottingham City developed a City 2020 Energy (and Carbon) strategy in 2010, which was adopted with cross-party consensus. The strategy covers domestic, commercial, public and industrial infrastructure, energy saving, energy generation and transport.

The city and the surrounding regions have a full Sustainable Energy Action Plan (SEAP) for the EU Covenant of Mayors (2015) that details and provides costs for the specific investments required to achieve the plan.

Nottingham's successful public transport network now carries around 75 million passengers a year. Since 2003, the number of passengers has increased significantly and, unlike most other English cities, Nottingham has experienced a renaissance in bus use, reflecting the high standards of quality whilst Nottingham's tram network has been heralded as the most successful light rail project in the country. The city has a fleet of 45 electric buses, making it the largest fleet in Europe in 2014. In addition, the city's tram network is undergoing substantial extension. Over half of Nottingham's residents have no access to a car.

For the Remourban project, the city dedicated a deprived district of the city (Sneinton) as the demonstration site for smart city innovations.

11.3.2 The demonstration site

The area around Sneinton Road, Sneinton, in Nottingham (Figure 11.3) has been allocated as the Remourban demonstration site. The site has over 450 homes, the majority of which (65%) is social housing belonging to Nottingham City Council (NCC) and managed on their behalf by Nottingham City Homes. The area is very close to the existing district heating network. The housing stock needs upgrading to a much more energy efficient state. Close to the site is one of the city's famous landmarks – George Green's Windmill and science centre (Figure 11.4).

The project is focused on seven property typologies in Nottingham within the Sneinton area, ranging from one-bedroom flats to three-bedroom terraced houses and, in age, from 1900 to the 1970s. The energy efficiency retrofit work will be open to all tenures within the defined streets and property types so that households, regardless of ownership, will benefit from the project.

The Remourban innovations are focused around:

1. Built environment;
2. Mobility;
3. Integration of infrastructures, enabled by information and communication technologies (ICT).

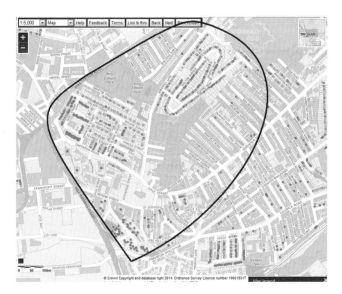

Figure 11.3   Sneinton demonstration site.

Figure 11.4 Green's windmill.

11.3.3 Built environment innovations

Built environment will focus upon:

- Low-energy retrofitting of the housing stock;
- Low-temperature district heating systems;
- Passive house (EnerPHit) retrofitting.

Figure 11.5   450 houses will be retrofitted for 50% energy efficiency.

Low energy retrofitting

The 450 housing stock in Sneinton will be retrofitted through a number of measures, in particular; solid wall insulation, better heat distribution, intelligent controls and solar panels (Figure 11.5).

Despite the variations in age and construction type, the common characteristic of most of the selected properties in the area is *the lack of insulation in the walls*, whether these are constructed from solid brick, solid concrete or various types of infill cladding on timber studs between solid cross-walls. The city has insulated most of the cavity walls, as these solutions are cheaper and better understood. In Remourban, the project will focus on innovations in solid wall insulation to reduce heat loss through the walls by 80%.

The current heating distribution system of standard radiators will be replaced with a new Skirting Heating system. The skirting heating provides several advantages over standard radiators; providing even room temperature and warming room surfaces. This can allow the room temperature to be lowered in relation to a standard radiator system. Warming of the room surfaces helps prevent the formation of mould and condensation. Thermostats and zoning will allow each room to be individually controlled, further reducing energy usage.

The intelligent control system will be configured to provide billing for energy supplied from the District Heating scheme as well as energy consumed within each individual property. At present, all district heating customers pay a standard tariff, thereby there is no incentive to reduce consumption. The system will provide dual streams of information; one for the energy provider in order to improve billing accuracy and one for the consumer. The consumers will be able to assess their own energy usage within the property and will be able to adjust their energy use on a room by room basis.

The scheme of four blocks is proposed to be fitted with a large Solar Thermal System and potentially a Photovoltaic (PV) Array. The energy from the solar thermal system will be distributed directly to the individual buffer vessels to be consumed within the properties.

The south facing roofs of the remaining blocks will be fitted with photovoltaic systems to give a total array size in the region of 75 kWp. This system would generate electricity that could be provided to each property or could be configured as a standalone system to provide power to the grid. The exact configuration would depend on the ownership of the system and the complexity of the connections.

The Nottingham district energy network

This district heating network is comprised of 68 km of insulated pipework carrying pressurised hot water around Nottingham City Centre to the north of the city, making it one the UK's largest networks. This is used to satisfy the heating and hot water requirements of 4700 dwellings and over 100 commercial premises, including the city's two main shopping centres, the National Ice Centre/Nottingham Arena, Nottingham Trent University (NTU), large office developments, theatres and various other large local developments.

The heat energy mainly comes from the annual incineration of municipal waste at Eastcroft incinerator, which is used to create a supply of high-pressure steam, pumped directly into the heat station. Back-up is provided by gas boilers, ensuring a reliable supply; however these are only operational 5–10% of the time. As this is a Combined Heat and Power (CHP) plant, the steam is also run through generating turbines to produce 60 GWh of electricity annually. This is supplied to large commercial customers through a private wire network, with the excess spilled to the UK National Grid.

Currently the temperature of the water in the pipes is at 90 °C and the heat from the return pipes (70 °C) is wasted. Much of the excess heat is dumped in the local river. The city would benefit from innovative heat storage systems and the use of low-temperature return pipes. There is evidence in Scandinavian countries that water at even 60 °C can be effectively circulated in the pipes.

The Remourban project intends to introduce low-temperature district heating to the city. This will be the first of its kind in the UK. The process has to initially learn from the experience of other countries, Denmark in particular. How local authorities can learn from other cities and countries is one of the key transformations in the smart city's journey.

The project initially created technical and health and safety credibility for this initiative. Nottingham Trent University (NTU), which is a key partner in the Remourban project, organised a workshop for key stakeholders, inviting professors from Denmark to present the technical case for this innovation. The workshop was very well received by the delegates, who were primarily operational and middle managers. The next phase is to get the commitment of senior managers. A senior management trip to Copenhagen was organised in 2015 to visit their low temperature networks, where the senior decision makers can see the system in operation and assess the impact on people's lives and ask questions about public accountability aspects. If successful, the senior managers will sponsor the upgrade to low-temperature district heating, aiming to create a best practice example in the UK.

Passive house retrofitting

One of Remourban's contributions will be passive house retrofitting, for the first time internationally. In general passive house standards are applied to new homes and there is very little retrofitting experience of existing housing stock. Within the Sneinton area, a block of nine three-bedroom houses have been selected to be retrofitted as closely as possible to the Passivhaus standard for refurbishment (known as EnerPHit). These nine houses were constructed with a concrete cross-wall type construction (William Moss design), probably in the 1960s. Most of the houses are owned by the City Council and managed by Nottingham City Homes. The housing is generally occupied by council tenants, typically families. Currently, the houses are uninsulated and built with a combination of concrete cavity walls (unfilled) and timber panelling (typical untreated U-value of $2.1 \, W/m^2K$ or worse). The houses are an unusual design with an exposed space at ground floor, behind the entrance door. A second door leads to a central staircase, with two storeys to the front and rear offset such that the roof is higher at the rear. The rear section effectively includes three storeys, with an unheated garage at the base. The windows are mainly double-glazed (installed pre-2002). Heating is by gas for both space and hot water (supplied by mains gas). Heating systems generally have a relatively new boiler, rated C or above with in-room thermostat, programmer and thermostatic radiator valves.

This unusual construction presents an interesting challenge for a deep retrofit project and will provide some excellent learning experiences for Passivhaus installations.

The project is currently in the phase of designing the passive house solutions which will be implemented during 2016. As part of the design phase, a design competition was organised for the students at NTU, where many new imaginative ideas emerged.

11.3.4 Mobility action

The mobility interventions focus on the following schemes: (i) a last mile delivery system, (ii) a car club and (iii) increasing the electric vehicle charging points.

Nottingham leads the way in sustainable transport. It is the first city in the UK to have a stringent environmental standard for all buses entering the City Centre. The 45 electric buses already make a significant contribution (Figure 11.6). They are much more efficient than diesel or diesel/electric hybrid buses, in terms of primary energy and much less polluting. They are also much quieter in operation and induce less ground-borne vibration. Consequently, the bus market could contribute a significant amount to the UK's 2020 carbon goal and Nottingham's Strategic Sustainability Target to reduce the city's carbon emissions by 26% of 2005 levels by 2020.

Figure 11.6   Nottingham enjoys 45 fully electric buses.

11.3.5 Last mile delivery system – local hub collection and delivery

This innovation significantly reduces the necessity for heavy goods vehicles (HGV) to enter the city for the final delivery of the goods. It is an interesting example of how cities can partner with local businesses for carbon reduction, improved environment for the citizens and growth of local business.

The HGVs will deliver their goods to a depot outside the motorway. A local SME (To-You) will organise the final delivery of the goods to the businesses and households via electric vehicles. This improves the city's air quality and reduces congestion. The delivery of the goods will normally be organised outside the rush hour traffic. There will be a network of local depots to assist the operations.

The solution is scalable, cost-effective and makes more effective use of existing infrastructures. The SME has segmented the customer market to meet the demands of the different market segments effectively, to tackle the exponential growth in urban deliveries, demands for click and collect, returns and same day delivery.

The proposed solution will not require substantial local authority investments; however collaboration with the SME in areas of planning, restrictive traffic access legislation, priority use of bus lanes and other existing municipal infrastructures will assist with the commercialisation process.

The Remourban project will focus on the development of one local depot in the Sneinton area – a small urban consolidation centre (SUCC). The SUCC will be where deliveries come in and electric vehicles go out. It will include charging facilities and cold storage for food distribution. The initial focus of the UCC will be to serve the homes and businesses in and near the project area to reduce fossil fuel vehicle movements for internet shopping and local goods deliveries.

The aim is to grow this service from this initial phase of work in the Sneinton area to cover the whole city.

11.3.6 City Car Club Nottingham

The City Car Club Nottingham is a national organisation (www.citycarclub.co.uk) that the NCC is using to provide a car hire service. You can hire vehicles by the hour that are electric or hybrid. There will be eight vehicles at eight sites in Nottingham, for businesses and for individuals. City Car Club enables you to hire vehicles 24 hours a day, 7 days a week. You can hire one for as little as half an hour, an hour, a day or as long as you need – you only pay for the time you use. And to make life easy, the vehicles are accessed with a smart-enabled membership card. Once registered, the user can reserve a car online or by phone, day or night and even last minute.

11.3.7 Electric vehicle charging points

The city will use joint regional funding and Remourban funding to increase the electric vehicle (EV) charging points across the city.

11.4 Integrated infrastructures

The Remourban project aims to create integrated infrastructures, enabled by ICT which empowers the end user to make informed decisions in real time. It focuses on three key city simulation models: (i) ICT for City Architecture Infrastructure, (ii) ICT for Energy Consumption Infrastructure and (iii) ICT for Transport Infrastructure and Buildings.

The system aims to provide real time data for each one of the models by deploying the necessary monitoring devices to create online links between the models and to collect data in real time. This will be used by local authorities and will also enable *citizens' engagement and empowerment* through the provision of open, consistent data.

This poses serious technical challenges, however; most importantly each city needs to understand why it requires the data and how the data will influence decision making and quality of life. Requirements capture is a critical part of effective integration. During the first few months of the project, an audit was conducted of all the relevant city services as a base line measure for future improvements. During this exercise, some potential areas for integration were identified. These include:

- An integrated transport management system, which would make the position of the buses visible, show the traffic flow across the city, show the availability of car parking spaces, show the availability of EV charging points and so on.
- A waste collection system that alerts householders with expected time of bin lorry arrival and could help alert householders and organisations to help reduce the need to keep bins in the street for longer than is necessary and reduce missed collections.

- Citizen reward systems, which would reward sustainable behavior and life style choices, for example intelligent parking charges can be according to the vehicle emissions, people who reduce energy consumption in the homes can be rewarded and so on.
- Street lighting poles can be upgraded to improve wireless 4G connectivity. The installation will be of microcell transmitters to augment the macro cell installations. Free Wi-Fi can be provided in the Sneinton demonstration area.
- Sewage and foul drainage – there is the potential to integrate heat reclaim from waste water to support passive house standard retrofit. There may need to be communication with the water company (Seven Trent Water) about the maximum amount of heat that can be extracted from waste water if the process is to be replicable, to ensure there is no fat build-up in sewage pipes.
- Renewable energy generation and distribution data from solar panels, wind turbines and other sources should be available. This data can support community energy schemes, removing the barriers for distributed and local generation.

Areas where data collection and integration will be more difficult would include:

- Electric grid – the vast majority of the grid is managed and owned by a private Distribution Network Operator (Western Power Distribution Ltd). It is also unlikely that grid quality or transformer level data will be available to a live data feed. National grid data systems tend to be highly controlled and with restricted access to prevent malicious interference.
- Gas grid – there is little or no opportunity for integration of the gas grid into the project as it is owned by the National Grid. However, data on decreased gas demand as homes move over to district heating through the grid will be available from nationally published annual data sets.

11.5 Discussion on added value

Is 'Smart Cities' a fad or a genuine contribution to progress through innovation? The term was initially branded through ICT companies, trying to generate new business from the cities. However, in recent years, the agenda has been supported by the EU and the UK government and the amount of funding, resource allocation and thinking space is beginning to make a difference (Europa, 2015). Benefiting from this agenda requires strong city leadership.

In Nottingham, the funding is supporting a process of innovation and discovery. The city had benefited from strong leadership in advance of the project. The provision of 45 electric buses, the district heating network and the tram system are testimony to this leadership. The Remourban project is facilitating and accelerating this agenda. For the first time the NCC has a role of 'Head of Smart Cities', where much of the role is to understand the governance, legislative and communication barriers to innovation and facilitate the removal of barriers. There is strong support from the city's senior management for this role.

The project has enhanced the partnership between NCC and NTU, for co-creation. The university supports the city in, for example, the approval and implementation of low temperature district heating systems, examining and strengthening the citizen engagement agendas and so on. There are well organised communication links between the two organisations, at an academic, middle management (implementing the innovations) and senior management level (developing and resourcing strategies).

Similar co-creation platforms must develop between NCC and the citizens. The city is at the early stages of examining and evaluating the current practices and developing a strategy for transforming these relationships. In the Sneinton area, most of the housing stock belong to NCC and this has simplified the decision-making process on retrofitting options. In Valladolid (Spain) where the demonstrator area has been privately owned, it has proved difficult to obtain house owners' permissions for deep retrofitting.

NCC is considering how to roll out the learning from the demonstration site to the rest of the city through concentrating and aligning its resources. This will eventually lead to the strengthening of the low carbon retrofitting supply chain in the city, opening new business opportunities within the city.

Therefore, the Remourban project has accelerated the change process which had already begun. Designating an area within the city as a demonstration site has proved valuable for the innovative businesses who need to pilot new technologies in a real world setting. The city receives requests from companies with research and development (R & D) funding from EU and UK to pilot their novel technologies, or help develop cases for use and so on. Thereby, the area is beginning to become an innovation magnet. However, at present, there is little funding to support this by-product of the Remourban project.

Some of the emerging questions from this case study include:

- How can you improve and expand the citizen engagement strategies?
- How can Local Authorities accelerate low carbon distributed energy, through scaling-up community energy agendas?
- How do cities learn and how can you develop a generic framework for accelerating cross-city learning?
- Which are the priority areas of city infrastructure integration, and what are the business models to support this integration?

References

EU Commission (2012) *Smart Cities and Communities Communication*, Brussels, 10 July 2012. Available at: http://europa.eu/rapid/press-release_MEMO-12-538_en.htm (accessed 1 October 2015).

EU Covenant of Mayors (2015) *EU Covenant of Mayors for Climate and Energy*. Available at: http://helpdesk.eumayors.eu/docs/seap/341_320_1305035896.pdf (accessed 18 March 2016).

Europa (2015) Smart Cities and Communities. Available at: http://ec.europa.eu/eip/smartcities/about-partnership/how-does-it-work/index_en.htm (accessed 18 March 2016).

NCC (2010) *Energy Strategy 2010–2020*. Nottingham City Council. Available at: http://www.nottinghamcity.gov.uk/CHttpHandler.ashx?id=19119&p=0 (accessed 18 March 2016).

Remourban Project (2014) *Remourban Project*. Available at: http://www.remourban.eu/(accessed 18 March 2016).

Section 3
Engaging with Practice, Stakeholders and Management

Chapter 12
Value-oriented Stakeholder Engagement in Sustainable Development: A Conceptual Framework

Margaret K.Y. Mok and Geoffrey Q. Shen
Department of Building and Real Estate, The Hong Kong Polytechnic University, Hong Kong, China

12.1 Stakeholder engagement in sustainable development

12.1.1 Definition of sustainable development

The origin of 'sustainable development' can be traced back to the 1970s (Zheng *et al.*, 2014). However, it did not receive public attention until the United Nations World Commission on Environment and Development (WCED) remarked on this concept in its report, *Our Common Future*, during the late 1980s (Brundtlandt, 1987). Sustainable development is such a broad and complex notion that there appears to be no universal definition (Zheng *et al.*, 2014). Sage (1999) conceptualised it as a tool to satisfy human needs 'through simultaneous socioeconomic and technological progress and conservation of the earth's natural systems'. Manoliadis *et al.* (2006) described it as an approach to strive for an increased quality of life and wellbeing by utilising the scarce resources of the society in an effective and ecologically responsible manner. In the aforementioned WCED's report, sustainable development was defined as 'development which meets the needs of the present without compromising the ability of future generations to meet their own needs' (Brundtlandt, 1987). The definition by WCED was a commonly referred one which has been cited in many publications across various disciplines (Manoliadis *et al.*, 2006; Mather *et al.*, 2008; Priemus, 2005; Steurer, 2005; Willers, 1994). Looking through these various interpretations, the main features of sustainable development can be summarised. First, it contains three core dimensions of 'social', 'economic' and 'environmental' (Department of the Environment, 1994; Sage, 1999; United Nations, 2014). Second, this concept not only focuses on the current impacts brought by construction activities, but also emphasises the needs of and the potential threats to future generations. Third, sustainable development is a continuous process of enhancement instead of being a one-off activity (Meadowcraft, 2000).

Future Challenges in Evaluating and Managing Sustainable Development in the Built Environment,
First Edition. Edited by Peter S. Brandon, Patrizia Lombardi and Geoffrey Q. Shen.
© 2017 John Wiley & Sons Ltd. Published 2017 by John Wiley & Sons Ltd.

12.1.2 The needs and challenges of engaging stakeholders in sustainable development

Sustainable development involves a wide range of stakeholders with different backgrounds and conflicting interests, where stakeholders in the context of sustainability are defined as 'any entity, group or individual who can affect or is affected by the activities around and achievements of a defined issue, past, present and future' (Feige *et al.*, 2011). The successful planning, development and implementation of sustainable development necessitate a comprehensive inclusion and effective engagement of all stakeholders. However, challenges in motivating and engaging stakeholders in the pursuance of sustainable development have been reported by many practitioners. For instance, the identification of stakeholders is often incomplete where the concerns and controversies of hidden stakeholders are often overlooked. There lacks a systematic and rigorous approach to recognise and analyse all needs of stakeholders and their priorities, leading to an inappropriate mediation and balance between these conflicting values. Furthermore, the engagement process of many large public developments has been criticised as one-sided, in which only a few major players are involved in the project decision-making; without adequate consultation with the external stakeholder groups regarding their prioritisations of social, economic and ecological concerns towards sustainability goals (Li *et al.*, 2012). This chapter proposes a value-oriented stakeholder engagement approach for sustainable development, by integrating stakeholder theory, value management (VM) methodology and social network analysis (SNA). This approach can help project teams to address complex stakeholder issues, model intricate stakeholder relationships, encourage the dialogues between stakeholders and ultimately achieve stakeholder-oriented value creation.

12.2 *Approaches to stakeholder engagement*

12.2.1 Definition

Stakeholder engagement is a structured process with the use of strategic methods to involve, communicate and build robust relationships with both internal and external stakeholders in the entire project lifecycle (Leung *et al.*, 2014a; Mok *et al.*, 2015). According to a literature review by Reed (2008), the stakeholder engagement concept was realised in the late 1960s and it has been considered as an essential element to pursue sustainable development since the 1990s.

Theories to conceptualise and classify stakeholder engagement have evolved progressively during the past decades. Mather *et al.* (2008) proposed three perspectives to conceptualise stakeholder engagement:

1. A *strategic management tool* to resolve conflicts, apprehend knowledge from stakeholders, and increase stakeholders' commitment and their sense of ownership in the project;
2. An *ethical need* to increase social equity and fairness by involving all parties who have democratic rights to express their views in the decision-making process;

3. A *social learning platform* that stakeholders can understand each other's needs and views, and build a common language and shared objectives for the ongoing development phase.

Mather *et al.* (2008) also pointed out that, in order to achieve sustainability goals, stakeholder engagement should be considered from a combination of these three perspectives. Another four ways was proposed by Reed (2008) to classify stakeholder engagement:

1. The required levels of stakeholder involvement;
2. The essence of engagement itself with regards to the directions of communications;
3. Theoretical foundation (e.g. normative versus pragmatic);
4. The purposes and objectives of the engagement process.

Effective engagement in sustainable development should involve both internal and external stakeholders. Normally, internal stakeholders are influential and play strategic roles in project decision-making, including clients, designers, contractors and consultants; in contrast, external stakeholders are the project-affected groups and are therefore the normative ones, for example, the media, pressure groups, green groups, local communities, the general public and future generations (Fang *et al.*, 2012; Leung *et al.*, 2014a). Engaging external stakeholders is particularly crucial in sustainable development projects because it expands the spectrum of stakeholder issues from mainly institutional and economic concerns towards including social and environmental responsibilities with a more global vision (Feige *et al.*, 2011).

12.2.2 Stakeholder engagement methods

Various engagement methods are available to involve stakeholders where different approaches serve different degrees of engagement. Stakeholder engagement contains five levels, namely: informing, consultation, involvement, collaboration and empowerment (Victorian Government Department of Sustainability and Environment, 2005). Based on this ladder of engagement, Yang *et al.* (2011) identified a typology of existing operational engagement methods; for example, bulletin boards and newsletter serve the purpose of informing, interviews and focus groups serve the purpose of consultation, while stakeholder circle can achieve a level of collaboration. The choices of engagement approaches are context specific; depending on the engagement objectives, required degree of involvement and the composition of stakeholder representatives (Reed, 2008). In fact, no single method is the best because different methods have their own strengths and limitations. Yang *et al.* (2011) also suggested that, depending on the situation, components of different approaches can be combined to develop a suitable engagement means. Irrespective of the methods used, the stakeholder engagement process should be taken into account as early as possible and throughout the whole project lifecycle. Reed (2008) suggested that stakeholder engagement should start right from the project identification stage and feasibility study and be maintained even in the evaluation of project outcomes after the construction is completed. Earlier phases give higher flexibility to incorporate stakeholder opinions into the project design. It is vital to engage stakeholders early, otherwise they may perceive the design proposal as finalised and become unmotivated to speak out in the engagement process.

12.3 *Value-oriented approach of stakeholder engagement in sustainable development*

This section introduces a value-oriented approach of stakeholder engagement for sustainable development, as shown in Figure 12.1. The proposed approach is based on stakeholder theory, with the integration of VM methodology and SNA.

12.3.1 Stakeholder theory

A sustainable development project often involves many stakeholders of discrete backgrounds and diverse claims in the project. The project teams often face challenges in completely identifying stakeholders and striking a reasonable balance between conflicting stakeholder needs, leading to trade-off among stakeholders and failures to achieve sustainability goals. The application of *stakeholder theory* is a potential method to address these problems.

The stakeholder theory was introduced by Freeman (1984) in his renowned publication '*Strategic Management: A Stakeholder Approach*' where stakeholders are defined as groups or individuals who contribute in the 'human process of joint value creation' (Freeman, 1994). This theory seeks to improve values and morale in organisational

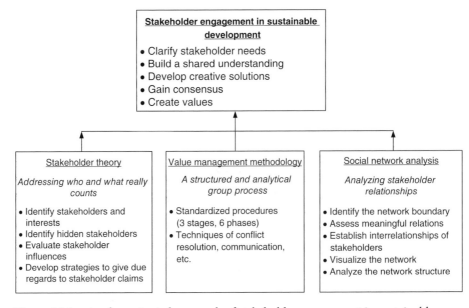

Figure 12.1   A value-oriented approach of stakeholder engagement in sustainable development.

management. It also answers the question of 'who or what really counts' by identifying the stakeholders of an organisation, modelling their relations, predicting their likely behaviours and impacts and developing strategic approaches to give due regards to their claims. In the past two decades, stakeholder theory has been applied in the construction industry to manage the numerous project stakeholders, where project stakeholders are defined as 'individuals and organisations who are actively involved in the project, or whose interests may be positively or negatively affected as a result of project execution or successful project completion' (Project Management Institute, 1996).

According to '*Sustainable Regeneration: Good Practice Guide*' developed by the British government (Department of the Environment, Transport and the Regions, 1998), there are eight sustainability indicators for sustainable urban development projects, including: (i) building and land use, (ii) community participation, (iii) economy and work, (iv) energy, (v) pollution, (vi) transport, (vii) waste and resources, (viii) wildlife and open space. Regarding community participation, a sustainable development project should start engaging the local community when establishing the development proposal, should involve them in the action and decision-making process and should take into consideration the peripheral stakeholders (Couch and Dennemann, 2000). That is to say, a successful sustainable development project requires an effective engagement of stakeholders and a proper balance between their interests (Karlsen, 2002). Negative attitudes, conflicts and controversies of stakeholders can hinder project implementation, giving rise to substandard works and overruns in cost and time (Olander and Landin, 2005). A rigorous and systematic approach is needed to identify and evaluate the needs and influences of stakeholders in project planning and implementation and to identify the hidden stakeholders and agendas (Jergeas *et al.*, 2000). Early and active involvement of stakeholders in the planning and design stages can prevent or alleviate many potential problems and obstacles.

The integration of stakeholder theory and VM methodology provides the project teams with qualitative and quantitative data to address complex and diverse stakeholder issues, with a focus on stakeholder value creation taking into account the characteristics of sustainable development projects. Applying stakeholder theory in our value-oriented approach can serve the following purposes:

1. Identifying the nature and strength of stakeholder impacts;
2. Recognising the invisible stakeholders;
3. Building a shared understanding on the interests of various stakeholders;
4. Developing innovative solutions;
5. Reducing potential problems and controversies in project implementation;
6. Enhancing stakeholder engagement and communication in sustainable development projects.

12.3.2 Value methodology

Value methodology (VM) is an organised and systematic group decision-making process, involving stakeholders from multi-disciplines, which aims to improve the value of projects, services or products by providing the necessary functions at the lowest possible overall cost without sacrificing the expected performance (Leung and Yu, 2014). In the past decades, the definitions and techniques of VM have been advancing to achieve sustainable development within the built environment. In earlier years, value was simply related to cost and functions, whereas VM refers to a systematic and strategic group process aiming to attain value for money by fulfilling all required functions with the lowest cost, without compromising the quality and performance levels (Australian/ New Zealand Standard, 1994). Nowadays, the definition of value has shifted towards sustainable goals. According to Australian Standard (2007), VM is a structured process that seeks to achieve the best value for money by following a prescribed job plan. In addition, value is defined as achieving social justice and the highest satisfaction of stakeholder needs at the least utilisation of resources and the minimum level of environmental impacts.

VM provides a platform for key stakeholders to formally take part in project briefing and design, to elucidate their expectations and needs, to understand the interests of other stakeholders, to establish a shared understanding of the project, to create possible alternative solutions and to gain consensus on the project missions and requirements (Kelly and Durek, 2002). Applying VM in our value-oriented approach can improve stakeholders' understanding of the perspectives of others, build a shared language among stakeholders to collaborate towards sustainability goals and ultimately achieve the best value outcome of the project (Kirk and Spreckelmeyer, 1988; Shen, 1993).

12.3.3 Social network analysis

Building upon the social network theory, social network analysis (SNA) is a methodology which combines mathematical and computational tools to visualise social interactions and analyse their relational structures (Solis *et al.*, 2013). According to the social network theory, the behaviours and roles of a social actor are readily affected by other actors who connect to it within the same system environment; and the way these actors connect is influential to the robustness and performance of the entire system (Wasserman and Faust, 1994). Based on this network perspective, since stakeholders in sustainable development are interconnected by many kinds of social interactions, stakeholders' expectations and behaviours in project decision-making can be directly or indirectly affected by their neighbours in the relationship networks. Applying SNA to analyse stakeholder interactions is therefore useful as it helps to predict stakeholder behaviours and impacts, enhance stakeholder collaborations and ultimately improve stakeholder engagement in sustainable development.

Originating from the sociometry field in the 1960s, SNA has been widely used in construction management research (Moreno, 1960). For instance, Lin (2015) adopted SNA to investigate the job-site management structures and identify potential problems by investigating three social networks of site engineers: command management, technical consultation and interpersonal relations. Dogan *et al.* (2015) developed a social network approach to evaluate the coordination performance of construction project participants by deciphering their email communication networks. In the context of sustainable development,

Meese and McMahon (2012) used SNA to study the knowledge- and information-sharing structures of organisational members within an engineering consultancy in tackling sustainable development-related issues.

In our value-oriented stakeholder engagement approach, the application of SNA can achieve four main purposes:

1. Identifying key stakeholders who play important roles in determining project missions and requirements;
2. Developing a right list of stakeholders to be engaged in VM workshops;
3. Predicting the behaviours and impacts of key stakeholders by analysing their relationships and social structures;
4. Developing strategies to facilitate stakeholder communication and coordination towards sustainability goals.

There are five main steps in the general process of SNA: (i) setting up the network boundary (i.e. which stakeholders to be counted), (ii) establishing and assessing meaningful social interactions of stakeholders, (iii) visualising the relationship networks, (iv) investigating the network structures by mathematical means and (v) presenting the network analysis results (Yang and Zou, 2014). The formation of stakeholder communities and their social interactions are dynamic throughout the project lifecycle, however what SNA captures is only a snapshot of the network. Therefore, the SNA results should be continuously monitored and updated during the entire process of the value-oriented approach. For instance, SNA can be conducted once during each of the following milestones to update the stakeholder relationship analysis: pre-workshop stage, information phase, function analysis phase, creativity phase and evaluation phase of the workshop stage.

12.4 Process of the value-oriented stakeholder engagement approach

Following the Value Methodology Standard of SAVE International (2015), our proposed value-oriented stakeholder engagement approach for sustainable development comprises a systematic three-stage and six-phase process.

12.4.1 Pre-workshop stage

Active participation and satisfaction of VM workshops require pre-workshop preparation. The VM facilitator performs three main tasks in this stage: (i) *selecting key stakeholders* to be engaged in VM workshops, these may include stakeholders of different backgrounds and interests, (ii) *designing a seating plan* in the workshop to ensure each table contains an even distribution of participants with different stakes and expertise and (iii) *setting an overall workshop program* to ensure effective implementation and time control (Leung *et al.*, 2014b).

12.4.2 Workshop stage

This stage follows a sequential six-phase job plan, as identified in SAVE International's (2015) standard, to analyse functions of a project and improve value.

The *information phase* provides an opportunity for stakeholders to share information, make clear their needs and objectives, identify key issues and project constraints, grasp a whole picture of the project's current situation and set common goals (Leung and Yu, 2014; Mesmer-Magnus and DeChurch, 2009). This stage builds a shared understanding among stakeholders for group discussion and decision-making in the following phases.

In the *function analysis phase*, disparate views of stakeholders are systematically examined using a series of structured analysis tools (e.g. the Function Analysis Systematic Technique diagram). The main purposes of this step are twofold: (i) to determine the project objectives and functions and (ii) to review and fine-tune these functions for meeting the project's sustainability goals (SAVE International, 2015).

The creativity phase is a crucial step of the VM process where stakeholders generate alternative project solutions that are innovative and simultaneously fulfilling the previously established project missions and functions (SAVE International, 2015).

In the *evaluation phase*, stakeholders apply suitable evaluation tools to appraise the ideas produced in the creativity phase, discard the infeasible ones, rank the remaining ideas, and finally shortlist some potential ideas for further investigation (Male *et al.*, 1998). Pairwise comparisons are commonly used evaluation methods.

In the *development phase*, the VM team extends the shortlisted ideas into detailed proposals (SAVE International, 2015). Based on these proposals, the project team can determine whether to implement the alternatives or to initiate further discussions and refine the proposals.

In the *presentation phase*, a presentation and a report which record the proposed alternative solutions and their potential for value improvement will be prepared for the client's reference (SAVE International, 2015).

12.4.3 Post-workshop stage

In the post-workshop stage, the VM facilitator submits a formal final report to the client; then the core project team studies the report and decides whether to implement the value engineering alternatives (SAVE International, 2015).

12.5 *Using SNA to analyse stakeholder interrelationships*

Practitioners have been facing challenges in identifying the key stakeholders and engaging the right persons effectively in VM workshops towards sustainability goals in building projects. SNA is a potential method to overcome these difficulties by visualising the 'hidden stakeholders', identifying stakeholder relationships and analysing their structures and predicting the likely impacts of stakeholders through these relationship networks. This section introduces how SNA can be applied in the value-oriented stakeholder engagement approach.

12.5.1 Identifying the boundary of social networks

This step defines the network boundary, that is, project stakeholders involving in the relationship networks. Two methods can be used for stakeholder identification: the empirical knowledge-based method and the snowball sampling method (Yang and Zou, 2014).

In the *empirical knowledge-based method*, the project team and some major stakeholders are brought together via interviews and focus groups. Based on their experience and knowledge, these parties are invited to build up a list of stakeholders who should be engaged in VM workshops. This method is time-efficient since consensus on the stakeholder list can be easily gained when the core people meet and discuss (Yang and Zou, 2014). Although this method may not be able to yield a complete stakeholder list (i.e. including both internal and external stakeholder groups), the outcome might still be considered sufficient. This is because many politically sensitive issues are often involved in the feasibility study and project briefing stages, which may not yet be a proper timing for public disclosure before project missions, functions and core requirements are well developed by the core stakeholders.

Snowball sampling is widely applied in qualitative research for obtaining 'a study sample through referrals made among people who share or know of others who possess some characteristics that are of research interest' (Biernacki and Waldorf, 1981). This method is able to yield a complete network boundary by approaching external stakeholders through internal stakeholders. Also, it is suitable for studies aiming their attention on sensitive issues (Biernacki and Waldorf, 1981). However, this method takes a long time and may face ethical difficulties in the information collection process (Yang and Zou, 2014).

12.5.2 Assessing meaningful and actionable stakeholder relationships

Stakeholders in sustainable development are linked by many kinds of formal (e.g. contractual, hierarchical) and informal (e.g. trust, friendship, emotional support) relationships. This step is to determine the kinds of stakeholder relationships which are meaningful and actionable to be examined using SNA. Core stakeholders' opinions regarding the meaningful relationship types can be collected through interviews and focus groups in the network boundary identification process.

Our value-oriented approach focuses on the social interactions of project stakeholders, so as to achieve the ultimate goal of improving stakeholder engagement in sustainable development. Among various kinds of social interactions, information exchange and knowledge exchange are two meaningful stakeholder relationships to be analysed. According to Chinowsky *et al.* (2008), *information exchange* focuses on the provision or receipt of information, which necessitates the implementation of required tasks and accomplishment of individual goals, while *knowledge exchange* emphasises the sharing of skills or expertise regarding 'why tasks are being done in specific ways and how the tasks can be improved for mutual benefit'. For both relationships, there are two directions: *providing* and *receiving* (Chinowsky *et al.*, 2008) and three types: *independent*, *dependent* and *interdependent* (Thompson, 1967).

12.5.3 Establishing the interrelationships between stakeholders

Relationships can be *binary* (where '1' denotes existing and '0' denotes absence) or *valued* (where the value represents the tie strength) and *undirected* or *directed* (Meese and McMahon, 2012). Our valued-oriented approach investigates directed and valued stakeholder interrelationships. Therefore, by means of surveys or interviews, this step is to invite project stakeholders who are identified in the first step (i.e. those involving in the relationship networks) to complete two tasks: (i) determining the existing information sharing (or knowledge exchange) relationships between stakeholders and (ii) evaluating the directions and strengths of ties based on three tie attributes: frequency, access and quality. *Frequency* describes how often a stakeholder exchanges information (or knowledge) with other project stakeholders for simple task completion (or facilitating the tasks for mutual benefits). *Access* refers to the extent that a stakeholder exchanges information (or knowledge) with others in a timely manner. *Quality* refers to the quality of the information (or knowledge) being exchanged, for example, its accuracy, completeness and comprehensibility. When a tie exists, the respondent should be invited to rate these three tie attributes separately using a five-point scale, where '1' denotes the lowest level (i.e. the least frequent, the least timely access, and the lowest quality respectively) and '5' denotes the highest level (i.e. the most frequent, the most timely access and the highest quality respectively). A value indicating the tie strength can be obtained by multiplying the three scores of frequency, access and quality.

The collected relational data are often stored in matrix format (Meese and McMahon, 2012). An *adjacency matrix* should be built for this purpose. Table 12.1 shows an example of this matrix. The first row and column represent project stakeholders existing in the relationship network, as identified in the first step. The cells of the matrix denote the strength of relationships between each particular stakeholder pair. It should be noted that cells on the diagonal are zero since there should be no information or knowledge exchange within the same stakeholder group.

12.5.4 Visualising the social networks of stakeholders

This step uses SNA software to create and visualise the social networks of stakeholders. There are many SNA software packages available for network visualisation and investigation, for example, NetMiner, UNICET, Pajek, StOCNET, STRUCTURE and MultiNet

Table 12.1 An example of the adjacency matrix.

	S1	S2	S3	S4	S5
S1		6	2		
S2				20	
S3					12
S4	20				3
S5					

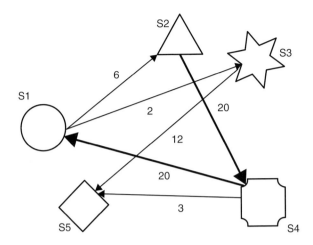

Figure 12.2 The concept map of project stakeholders.

(Huisman and Van Duijn, 2005). According to Furht (2010) and Newman (2010), if the network size is huge (i.e. composed of stakeholders and interactions), NetMiner can be a suitable choice of software due to its high abilities in processing huge data sets and exploring the networks interactively. For more details about NetMiner the reader is referred to Cyram (2014). The adjacency matrix and the node and link profiles are the basic input data required for network visualisation and investigation. Figure 12.2 presents a conceptual network map of the project stakeholders. Stakeholders and their interactions are indicated by the nodes and edges respectively. Node shapes denote different stakeholder categories. The numbers above and the thicknesses of the edges reflect the strengths of relationships.

12.5.5 Analysing the network data

Examining stakeholder relationship networks by mathematical means can yield more accurate results (Wambeke *et al.*, 2012). Eight SNA metrics can be calculated in this step.

Density and cohesion are two SNA metrics at the network level. *Network density* is defined as the proportion of real ties in the network to the greatest likely number of links when all nodes are attached together (Parise, 2007). This indicator reflects the network's connectivity and its range is from zero to one. A higher density implies more social interactions existing between the stakeholders. *Network cohesion* is the number of links or the length of a link required to access other network actors, where geodesic distance is the basis of calculation (Yang and Zou, 2014). This indicator shows the overall complexity of a network.

Degree centrality, betweenness centrality, status centrality and brokerage are four metrics at the node/link level. *Degree centrality* is defined as the number of relationships emitted from (specified as 'out degree') or entering (specified as 'in degree') a node in the network (Parise, 2007). Degree difference can be obtained by deducting the in degree from the out degree value, this metric can therefore reflect the immediate impact of a stakeholder on its network neighbours in communication activities. In addition, based on the results of degree centrality, nodes can be further categorised into five types (i.e. isolate, transmitter, receiver, carrier, ordinary; Yang and Zou, 2014). The number of isolated nodes identifies the project stakeholders who are peripheral members in the relationship networks. *Betweenness centrality* measures how frequently a node (or link) lays down between other node (or link) pairs based on geodesic distance (Kim *et al.*, 2011). This indicator recognises nodes (or links) which act as go-betweens in the network. Therefore, a node (or link) of high betweenness centrality is the information broker among stakeholders in communication activities. *Status centrality* measures the number of a node's direct neighbours, plus the number of indirect neighbours which connect the focal node through its direct neighbours (Katz, 1953). Similar to degree centrality, this indicator can be categorised into in status and out status based on the directions of links. This metric captures the overall influence of a stakeholder in communication activities. *Brokerage* measures how often a node plays the role of coordinator, itinerant, gatekeeper, liaison or representative in hooking up different subgroups in a network (Meese and McMahon, 2012). A partition vector should be set to calculate this metric, and stakeholder category can be considered as the vector. Project teams should pay greater alert to the nodes of high brokerage because they have largely contributed to the propagating impacts of the network.

Local and global interfaces are two SNA indicators at the subgroup level. *Local interface* measures the number of direct links connecting different pairs of subgroups under a selected node partition (Fang *et al.*, 2012). In contrast, *global interface* calculates the total number of direct and indirect links bridging different pairs of subgroups under the same selected node partition (Fang *et al.*, 2012). These two metrics tell us which pairs of stakeholder groups are more closely related and therefore require higher collaboration.

12.5.6 SNA application for stakeholder analysis in mega projects

Given its analytical strength in deciphering relational structures, SNA is a rigorous stakeholder analysis method with high potential for application in mega and complex developments. Mega construction projects take place in a complex, non-linear and dynamic environment underlying the cross impacts between social, economic, environmental and technological factors (Cicmil and Marshall, 2005). In addition, a mega project often involves numerous stakeholders with different levels and kinds of investments and concerns in the project. Evaluating the issues and influences of stakeholders, maintaining a proper balance between their interests and attaining alignment between project goals and stakeholder expectations have therefore become essential, yet challenging steps, of successful mega project delivery (Cleland, 1999; Karlsen, 2002). In the past decades, there has been an unsatisfactory record of stakeholder management in mega projects. Despite a rapid growth of stakeholder analysis and engagement methods, project teams still confront difficulties in completely identifying stakeholders and accurately assessing their relationships and influences. These obstacles may be attributed to the weaknesses of the current stakeholder analysis practice. In existing practice, project teams perform stakeholder classification and prioritisation by evaluating individual stakeholder attributes based on the empirical knowledge of team members. The drawbacks are threefold. First, 'invisible' stakeholders who give little apparent impact may be missed out in the stakeholder identification process due to the cognitive limitation of project teams. Second, the assessment is subjective; its accuracy may be limited in large and complex developments. Third, the basis of evaluation relies heavily on the dyadic relationships between stakeholders and core project players, overlooking the actual interrelationships among stakeholders themselves. In reality, stakeholders of a mega project are interconnected by many kinds of relationships across functional and organisational borders and are therefore embedded in various social networks (Meese and McMahon, 2012). The salience and influences of stakeholders are subject to their network roles and positions, also the propagating effects produced by network structures. A rigorous method building upon the social network perspective is required for stakeholder analysis in mega projects.

SNA is a well-established structural analysis method to map stakeholder relationships and interactions in complex project environment. This approach shows a big step forward from traditional stakeholder analysis approaches. Instead of only focusing on core project players, SNA recognises almost all stakeholders, even the 'hidden' ones, by using a snowball rolling technique in the stakeholder identification process (Biernacki and Waldorf, 1981). A complete network boundary so defined enables the project team to make informed decisions which can reveal the actual relationship situations among stakeholders. Provided that the whole set of stakeholder relationships is determined, SNA uncovers the positions and roles of stakeholders in networks (e.g. central connector, peripheral actor, boundary spanner, information broker) by deciphering the relational structures (Meese and McMahon, 2012). Under the social network perspective, the traits and behaviours of stakeholders emanate from their interactions and social structural environment; also, stakeholders' impacts can circulate through the network and alter other members' attitudes (Rowley, 1997; Wasserman and Faust, 1994). By emphasising interactions rather than individuals, SNA enables project team to evaluate the behaviours and influences of stakeholders based on their relationship patterns and structures and to reach more sound project decisions that respond to these influences. To cope with the dynamics in a mega project, the application of SNA for stakeholder analysis can be prolonged longitudinally (Yang and Zou, 2014). In different project milestones, a project team can update the network boundary and re-measure the stakeholder relationships, so as to monitor the structural changes and adjust the stakeholder engagement strategies accordingly.

Sustainable development projects involve numerous stakeholders with distinct backgrounds and discrete interests. Many of these projects have been increasing in scale and complexity. The complex nature of these developments calls for a rigorous stakeholder analysis method to overcome the confrontations between stakeholders and to create the best stakeholder-oriented value which accommodates social, economic and environmental concerns. Applying SNA to stakeholder analysis in these projects can unlock the causes and consequences of stakeholder behaviours according to the interactions and social structures of stakeholders; this eventually derives a well-informed rationale for forming stakeholder engagement strategies and improves project decision-making.

12.6   *The conceptual framework and its potential applications*

Figure 12.3 presents a conceptual framework of the value-oriented stakeholder engagement approach in sustainable development. This framework integrates stakeholder theory, VM and SNA. Its application is project-based. It aims to answer the question of 'who and what really counts' and address complex stakeholder issues in mega construction projects to achieve sustainability.

In this approach, VM is used to engage stakeholders since it offers a platform to understand stakeholder needs, build a shared understanding, gain consensus and create values. The VM process here follows the standardised three-stage and six-phase procedures, including: pre-workshop stage, workshop stage (information, function analysis, creativity, evaluation, development and presentation phases) and post-workshop stage. At the start of each stage and phase, project managers should first identify which stakeholders to be involved by using empirical knowledge-based method or snowball sampling method. During each stage/phase in the VM process, stakeholders communicate and exchange lots of information which relates to their stakes in the project or achieving sustainability. These communication and information exchange relationships between stakeholders are identified and assessed based on three attributes: frequency, timely access and quality. By computing SNA metrics at the network, node/link and subgroup levels, the structural characteristics of the stakeholder communication and information exchange networks are analysed to understand the stakeholder roles and evaluate their impact levels. By doing so, project managers can conduct stakeholder prioritisation and determine a list of key stakeholders at every stage/phase in the VM process. Accordingly, the core project team can develop appropriate strategies to better engage all stakeholders, in particular those who play important roles in communication and information exchange to achieve sustainability. This approach (including the integrated process of VM and SNA) should be applied from the early project stages (e.g. preliminary design) as it accommodates greater flexibility. To cope with the dynamics of stakeholder community and relationships in sustainable development, the whole process of this approach should be run again periodically at different milestone stages of the project; that is, the network analysis results, stakeholder priority list and the engagement strategies should be continuously monitored and also updated.

12.7   *Conclusions*

Sustainable urban developments are complex, dynamic and unique in nature. These projects often comprise multiple stakeholders from different backgrounds with diverse expectations and interests in the project. It becomes crucial to establish a common ground for multiple stakeholders to build a shared understanding and work collaboratively. Ineffective engagement of and value creation for stakeholders may bring about bitter controversies and social conflicts. Effectiveness in assessing stakeholder interests and creating stakeholder-oriented value has become a major determinant for the success of sustainable development. To cope with these challenges, this chapter introduces a value-oriented stakeholder engagement approach for sustainable urban development,

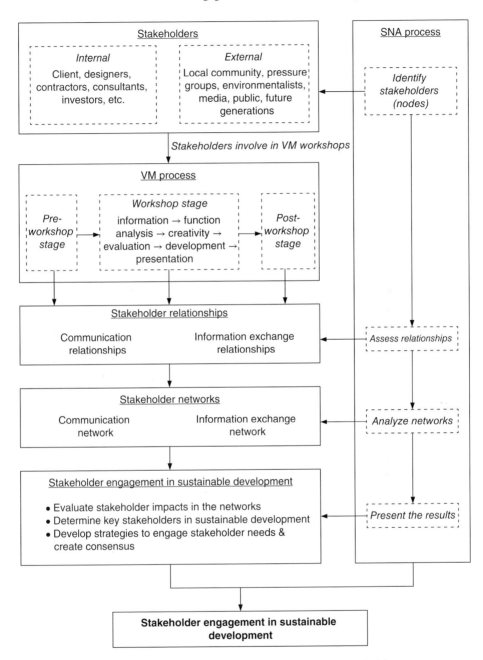

Figure 12.3 A conceptual framework of the value-oriented stakeholder engagement approach in sustainable development.

which is built upon stakeholders theory, VM and SNA. This chapter begins with a historical background of sustainable development and the needs of engaging stakeholders in these complex project environment, which is followed by a theoretical foundation of and current approaches to stakeholder engagement. A conceptual framework of the value-oriented stakeholder engagement approach for sustainable urban development is then introduced. The three-stage and six-phase process of the proposed approach is explained in detail, followed by a thorough illustration of the application of SNA for analysing stakeholder interrelationships in sustainable development. This approach enables project team to identify completely the stakeholders of urban development and to model their interactions, which ultimately provides a rationale to address the complicated issues of stakeholder involvement and to foster value creation for stakeholders.

Acknowledgements

The authors wish to express their sincere gratitude to the Research Grants Council of the Hong Kong Special Administrative Region, China (PolyU5246/12E), the national Natural Science Foundation of China (NSFC) China (Project No. 71671156), and the Hong Kong Polytechnic University for funding support to the research projects on which this paper is based.

References

Australian Standard (2007) *Value management.* AS 4183-2007, Australian Standards, Canberra.
Australian/New Zealand Standard (1994) *Value management.* AS/NZS 4183-1994, Australia and New Zealand Standards, Canberra.
Biernacki, P., Waldorf, D. (1981) Snowball sampling: problems and techniques of chain referral sampling. *Sociological Methods and Research* **10**, 141–163.
Brundtlandt, G.M. (1987) *Our Common Future: World Commission on Economic Development.* Oxford University Press, Oxford.
Chinowsky, P., Diekmann, J., Galotti, V. (2008) Social network model of construction. *Journal of Construction Engineering and Management* **10**, 804–812.
Cicmil, S., Marshall, D. (2005) Insights into collaboration at the project level: complexity, social interactions and procurement mechanisms. *Building Research and Information* **33**, 523–535.
Cleland, D.I. (1999) *Project Management Strategic Design and Implementation.* McGraw-Hill, New York.
Couch, C., Dennemann, A. (2000) Urban regeneration and sustainable development in Britain. *Cities* **17**, 137–147.
Cyram (2014) *Using NetMiner.* Cyram Inc., Seoul.
Department of the Environment (1994) *Sustainable Development: the UK Strategy.* HMSO, London.
Department of the Environment, Transport and the Regions (1998) *Sustainable Regeneration: Good Practice Guide.* The Stationary Office, London.
Dogan, S.Z., Arditi, D., Gunhan, S., Erbasaranoglu, B. (2015) Assessing coordination performance based on centrality in an e-mail communication network. *Journal of Management in Engineering* **31**, 04014047.
Fang, C., Marle, F., Zio, E., Bocquet, J. C. (2012) Network theory-based analysis of risk interactions in large engineering projects. *Reliability Engineering and System Safety* **106**, 1–10.
Feige, A., Wallbaum, H., Krank, S. (2011) Harnessing stakeholder motivation: towards a Swiss sustainable building sector. *Building Research and Information* **39**, 504–517.

Freeman, R.E. (1984) *Strategic Management: a Stakeholder Approach*. Pitman, Boston.

Freeman, R.E. (1994) The politics of stakeholder theory: some future directions. *Business Ethics Quarterly* **4**, 409–421.

Furht, B. (2010) *Handbook of Social Network Technologies and Applications*. Springer, Heidelberg.

Huisman, M., Van Duijn, M.A.J. (2005) Software for social network analysis. In: *Models and Methods in Social Network Analysis* (eds P.J. Carrington, J. Scott, S. Wasserman), Cambridge University Press, New York, p. 311.

Jergeas, G.F., Eng, P., Williamson, E., Skulmoski, G.J., Thomas, J.L. (2000) Stakeholder management on construction projects. *AACE International Transaction* **2000**, 12.11–12.16.

Karlsen, J.T. (2002) Project stakeholder management. *Engineering Management Journal* **14**, 19–24.

Katz, L. (1953) A new status index derived from sociometric data analysis. *Psychometrika* **18**, 34–43.

Kelly, J., Duerk, D. (2002) Construction project briefing/architectural programming. In: *Best Value in Construction* (eds J. Kelly, R. Morledge, S.J. Wilkinson), Wiley-Blackwell, London, pp. 38–58.

Kim, Y., Choi, T.Y., Yan, T., Dooley, K. (2011) Structural investigation of supply networks: a social network analysis approach. *Journal of Operations Management* **29**, 194–211.

Kirk, S.J., Spreckelmeyer, K.F. (1988) *Creative design decisions: a systematic approach to problem solving in architecture*. Van Nostrand Reinhold Company, New York.

Leung, M.Y., Yu, J. (2014) Value methodology in public engagement for construction development projects. *Built Environment Project and Asset Management* **4**, 55–70.

Leung, M.Y., Yu, J., Chan, Y.S. (2014a) Focus group study to explore critical factors of public engagement process for mega development projects. *Journal of Construction Engineering and Management* **140**, 04013061.

Leung, M.Y., Yu, J., Liang, Q. (2014b) Analysis of the relationships between value management tecniques, conflict management, and workshop satisfaction of construction participants. *Journal of Management in Engineering* **30**, 04014004.

Li, T.H.Y., Ng, S.T., Skitmore, M. (2012) Conflict or consensus: an investigation of stakeholder concerns during the participation process of major infrastructure and construction projects in Hong Kong. *Habitat International* **36**, 333–342.

Lin, S.C. (2015) An analysis for construction engineering networks. *Journal of Construction Engineering and Management* **141**, 04014096.

Male, S., Kelly, J., Fernie, S., Gronqvist, M., Bowles, G. (1998) *Value Management: the Value Management Benchmark: a Good Practice Framework for Clients and Practitioners*. Thomas Telford, London.

Manoliadis, O., Tsolas, I., Nakou, A. (2006) Sustainable construction and drivers of change in Greece: a Delphi study. *Construction Management and Economics* **24**, 113–120.

Mather, V.N., Price, A.D.F., Austin, S. (2008) Conceptualizing stakeholder engagement in the context of sustainability and its assessment. *Construction Management and Economics* **26**, 601–609.

Meadowcraft, J. (2000) Sustainable development: a new(ish) idea for a new century? *Political Studies* **48**, 370–387.

Meese, N., McMahon, C. (2012) Analysing sustainable development social structures in an international civil engineering consultancy. *Journal of Cleaner Production* **23**, 175–185.

Mesmer-Magnus, J.R., DeChurch, L.A. (2009) Information sharing and team performance: a meta-analysis. *Journal of Applied Psychology* **94**, 535–546.

Mok, K.Y., Shen, G.Q., Yang, J. (2015) Stakeholder management studies in mega construction projects: a review and future directions. *International Journal of Project Management* **33**, 446–457.

Moreno, J.L. (1960) *The Sociometry Reader*. Free Press, Glencoe.

Newman, M. (2010) *Networks: an Introduction*. Oxford University Press, Oxford.

Olander, S., Landin, A. (2005) Evaluation of stakeholder influence in the implementation of construction projects. *International Journal of Project Management* **23**, 321–328.

Parise, S. (2007) Knowledge management and human resource development: an application in social network analysis methods. *Advances in Developing Human Resources* **9**, 359–383.

Priemus, H. (2005) How to make housing sustainable? The Dutch experience. *Environment and Planning B: Planning and Design* **32**, 5–19.

Project Management Institute (1996) *Project management body of knowledge.* Project Management Institute, Newtown Square.

Reed, M.S. (2008) Stakeholder participation for environmental management: a literature review. *Biological Conservation* **141**, 2417–2431.

Rowley, T.J. (1997) Moving beyond dyadic ties: a network theory of stakeholder influences. *Academy of Management Review* **22**, 887–910.

Sage, A. (1999) Sustainable development: issues in information, knowledge, and systems management. *Information, Knowledge, Systems Management* **1**, 185–223.

SAVE International (2015) *Value Methodology Standard.* Available at: http://www.value-eng.org/value_engineering_vm_standard.php (accessed 13 November 2015).

Shen, Q.P. (1993) *A Knowledge-based Structure for Implementing Value Management in the Design of Office Buildings.* PhD thesis, The University of Salford, Salford.

Solis, F., Sinfield, J.V., Abraham, D.M. (2013) Hybrid approach to the study of inter-organization high performance teams. *Journal of Construction Engineering and Management* **139**(4), 379–392.

Steurer, R. (2005) Corporations, stakeholders and sustainable development I: a theoretical exploration of business–society relations. *Journal of Business Ethics* **61**, 263–281.

Thompson, J.D. (1967) *Organizations in action: social science bases of administrative theory.* McGraw-Hill, New York.

United Nations (2014) *Prototype Global Sustainable Development Report.* United Nations Department of Economic and Social Affairs, Division for Sustainable Development, New York.

Victorian Government Department of Sustainability and Environment (2005) *Effective engagement: building relationships with community and other stakeholders.* The Community Engagement Network, Resource and Regional Services Division, Melbourne.

Wambeke, B.W., Liu, M., Hsiang, S.M. (2012) Using Pajek and centrality analysis to identify a social network of construction trades. *Journal of Construction Engineering and Management* **138**(10), 1192–1201.

Wasserman, S., Faust, K. (1994) *Social network analysis: methods and applications.* Cambridge University Press, New York.

Willers, B. (1994) Sustainable development: a new world deception. *Conservation Biology*, **1994** 1146–1148.

Yang, J., Shen, G.Q.P., Bourne, L., Ho, C.M.F., Xue, X. (2011) A typology of operational approaches for stakeholder analysis and engagement. *Construction Management and Economics* **29**, 145–162.

Yang, R.J., Zou, P.X.W. (2014) Stakeholder-associated risks and their interactions in complex green building projects: a social network model. *Building and Environment* **73**, 208–222.

Zheng, H.W., Shen, G.Q., Wang, H. (2014) A review of recent studies on sustainable urban renewal. *Habitat International*, **41**, 272–279.

Chapter 13
Sustainability in Practice in the United Kingdom – A Reflective Analysis

Trevor Mole

Property Tectonics, Manchester, M27 8UX, UK

13.1 Introduction

The debate about what universities and their staff should and should not be doing and what constitutes scholarship has been a topic of discussion for a long time and has never really gone away. For example, how important or otherwise is 'teaching' and what some universities call 'enterprise' activity within the mix, particularly as individual contributions in these areas form the basis for reward and career progression? What is missed, undervalued or unrecognised in the mix is both the 'scholarship of teaching' and the 'scholarship of application', as Boyer describes them (Boyer, 1990)[1]. It is readily appreciated in universities that theory leads to practice, but how many appreciate that practice also leads to theory?

When it comes to energy, environment and sustainability, there is an abject lack of understanding on the ground within organisations and stakeholders trying to make sense of a complex, multidimensional and dynamic business model, lacking maturity or conventional wisdom. This is not helped by the narrow interpretation of scholarship as conventional or basic research in universities being viewed as Boyer suggests

---

[1] It gives the author great pleasure to participate in the workshop on sustainable development in honour of Professor Peter Brandon, whom he has known and worked with for over 30 years since he first arrived at Salford University. Peter became head of the Division of Building and Surveying within the Department of Civil Engineering at Salford in 1985 when the author was a lecturer and course tutor in Building Surveying. At that time the research activity in building and surveying was very small and did not measure up in scholarship terms to the rest of the department, which made a significant academic contribution in civil engineering. Peter grew the size and reputation of the Building and Surveying Division across the board, especially in research and scholarship, eventually creating at Salford University one of the largest, most successful and most highly rated academic centres of excellence in the built environment in the world. The author considers Professor Peter Brandon an academic giant in the built environment and his contribution to construction and property in the UK and abroad is, in his view, unprecedented and unmatched to this day.

Future Challenges in Evaluating and Managing Sustainable Development in the Built Environment,
First Edition. Edited by Peter S. Brandon, Patrizia Lombardi and Geoffrey Q. Shen.
© 2017 John Wiley & Sons Ltd. Published 2017 by John Wiley & Sons Ltd.

'*as the primary and most essential form of scholarly activity with other aspects flowing from it*' (Boyer, 1990), a sort of top down model. Such a model in itself does not deliver all that is needed and therefore society does not achieve the important sustainability objectives, particularly in providing energy efficiencies and greener ways of producing and consuming energy. Maybe the world would benefit from academics recognising that '*scholarship in earlier times referred to a variety of creative work carried out in a variety of places and that its integrity can be measured by the ability to think, communicate and learn*' (Boyer, 1990). '*New intellectual understandings can arise* and may only arise *out of the very act of application where theory and practice vitally interact and one renews the other*' (Boyer, 1990).

Working in the laboratory of application, in practice, is a seat of learning and scholarship par excellence. This is particularly true working in a business like Property Tectonics, which is innovative and creative and has to be, because it can seldom compete as a small to medium sized enterprise (SME) in commoditised services with the larger organisations that are so good at this type of work. Property Tectonics has been in business for over 28 years and has developed many new and innovative products and services, especially in IT and energy efficiency. However, the shape and nature of the business has changed beyond recognition over the last five years or so and, if there is one factor that is responsible for this, it is the company's journey into sustainability which means professional services and products in energy conservation, waste recycling and microgeneration. This is not an easy business to be in because on the whole it is over-regulated, constantly changing, politically sensitive, multi-dimensional, complex, and fraught with risk and long lead-in times.

The decision to move the business into new areas including sustainability, energy efficiency and so on was based on a combination of rational decision making, intuition, a desire to build on strengths and the need to extend the culture and values of the company. An inherent wish to innovate and to be creative has made the company responsive to market demands for new products and services whilst harvesting some well-established commoditised services provided by the business, some of which were originally innovative. The company has always dedicated a lot of time and effort to establishing and reviewing its corporate vision, strategy and tactics. It is a journey and the way has to be simple, easily understood and bought into by every member of the team. Whilst the shape of the business has changed, the company knows where its roots lie, for example in building performance and evaluation; the company's leaders, human resources, investments and strategies follow the vision. New initiatives and new ventures initiated by the directors and senior managers must pass the first test. Will they delight customers? Will they make money? Will they enhance our company values in being good citizens? Customer relationships and experiences are fundamentally an extension of what we do internally and much of our innovation – certainly our move into energy and sustainable development – was based on what our customers, including new customers, wanted; our customers invariably make the journey with us. However, before we embark, much rational decision making and considerable risk management takes place across the business because there are no certainties or guarantees of a positive outcome. For all the objectivity, there is no substitute for entrepreneurship and the biggest problem we face is deciding what not to do.

13.2 Method

Knowledge capital is extremely important to professional practices but capturing knowledge is complex, especially in an SME such as Property Tectonics which is heavily engaged in innovation and new opportunities. Here, there is a need to support '*the development of new frameworks and tools which emphasise the overtly social nature of innovation in small construction professional practices: it is not a mechanistic, linear process; rather a fluid process where knowledge-based innovation flows from context-specific "one-off" encounters between knowledge workers and clients at the project level of resolution.*' (Shu-ling and Sexton, 2009).

Knowledge in practice is also inextricably linked to one's own field of knowledge and expertise and flows from professional activity. It is serious and demanding and has all the discipline and rigour associated with any research activity. However, capturing knowledge in practice using empirical research methodologies presents its own challenges because experience alone does not always lead to learning and knowledge; careful and structured reflection on experience is crucial. '*Reflective Practice is the capacity to reflect on action so as to engage in a process of continuous learning*' (Schon, 1983). There are various models of reflective practice that generally follow a similar cycle of reflecting on experience, learning from it and then testing what has been learned in a new situation towards continuous improvement. Gary Rolfe's reflective model in nursing asks three basic and useful questions: *What, So What and Now What?*

Reflective research is conducted on at least two levels, *careful interpretation* and *reflection* (Alvesson and Skoldberg, 2000) and in this chapter the author is looking at Property Tectonics' work in energy efficiency and sustainable development from his own perspectives, interpreting his own assumptions from those of other people and then subjecting his own assumptions to critical review. The author has adopted a further level by having his work scrutinised by other leaders (directors) in the business to valorise the results of his reflective analysis. This chapter is written in a narrative style to hopefully engage the reader in the language and context of the practitioner.

13.3 Reflective analysis

This reflective analysis is sectionalised to help the reader understand the different parts of the Property Tectonics' business being reviewed, followed in each case by the writer's reflective analysis of the work being undertaken.

13.4 Property Tectonics

Property Tectonics started in 1987 and provides multidisciplinary professional consultancy services in construction and property to customers in most sectors, including health, housing, commercial, retail, local authorities, schools and universities.

The company is currently working in many areas of interest in the sustainability field, much of which is pioneering and innovative. This includes energy assessment and asset management software under its Lifespan™ brand (see section 13.8), and design and procurement services across a range of multi-million pound projects, including large commercial biomass boilers and energy roof installations, waste recycling plants, energy efficiency measures in social housing and general energy assessment and advice. In most cases Property Tectonics acts as the lead consultants, which means pulling together or delivering expertise across a whole range of legal, financial, technical and business areas and in some cases being involved potentially directly in the business by way of shareholding in an Energy Services Company (ESCO) or Special Purpose Vehicles (SPVs) needed to deliver and operate specific projects.

Property Tectonics is also a major investor and shareholder in corporate approved inspector Property Tectonics Building Standards Limited which is authorised under the Building Act 1984 to carry out building control work in England and Wales. The company is also the major shareholder in Energy Tectonics Limited (ETL) which acts in effect as the retailer, designing and distributing energy products, including the application of the ZEDroof™ developed by conservation architect Bill Dunster OBE (ZED Factory) and one of the world's largest solar manufacturers based in Himin, China. This is a solar photovoltaic roofing system (not on roof) and ETL provides a design and build solution under an exclusivity distribution agreement with HiminZED for the United Kingdom (UK) retrofit market. ETL has also recently signed a distribution contract with Virtual Power Solutions Ltd which manufactures and supplies water, gas and electricity measurement and control equipment manufactured in Portugal, branded as Cloogy™ and Kisense™. Property Tectonics has an exclusivity contract with ETL to provide all professional and lead consultant services to the company.

Most of the work undertaken by Property Tectonics is cutting edge, applying and developing knowledge across several disciplines and perhaps most challenging is the need to provide integration which Boyer describes as '*making connections across disciplines, placing the specialties in larger context, illuminating data in a revealing way, often educating non-specialists, too*' (Boyer, 1990). Sustainability at any level requires a multidisciplinary approach and what staff in Property Tectonics often describe as 'connecting the dots', otherwise it will fail. It is also often an inescapable race against time because the whole landscape is changing so rapidly that plans created today, which may have been a long time in the making, have to be jettisoned tomorrow because the critical success factors are no longer valid. Change is inevitable but too much creates uncertainty and chaos, and there is no doubt that the changing policies of successive UK governments have caused mayhem and inhibited progress. Repeated governments have 'U'-turned on a number of issues, most recently the slashing of subsidies for biomass, anaerobic digestion, solar, wind and biogas as well as effectively ending the green deal, selling off the Green Bank and giving up on zero carbon homes. The effect that this will have on carbon reduction in the UK and the businesses and the people employed by them is yet to be fully assessed, but there is little doubt that subsidies are being curtailed and the present UK government's environmental policies could slow down the move towards more sustainable development in the UK.

13.5 Economics, investment and finance

Despite the uncertainty, the market appears to be improving, business interest in sustainability is increasing and, regardless of indecision by policy makers, the quest to save energy and to produce it from more sustainable sources is being recognised as a solid basis for investment. In the past this has probably been driven more by ethical considerations and kept to the margins of the money markets. Now the financial sector is recognising the rewards green finance can provide. For most organisations access to lable to solid and sustainable businesses is the major consideration and the decision whether to go for on or off balance sheet finance is a challenging one. On balance sheet options are only available to solid and sustainable businesses that can provide the required funding themselves or can provide the requisite security for investors through financing options such as debt funding, hire purchase and finance lease agreement. Balance sheet capital purchasing for energy conservation measures has to compete with other potential business projects which often have a higher priority and quicker payback than infrastructure projects.

Within current Property Tectonics projects, particularly in energy generation, most are favouring off balance sheet strategies. Customers are looking for a 'turnkey' arrangement with equipment suppliers, ESCOs or SPVs whereby they divest themselves of the risks and responsibility for implementing and operating the equipment and simply purchase the energy at competitive rates and this is where the savings are made. The viability of such a venture is dependent to a large extent on demand. If there is sufficient capacity in the plant to deliver customer demand and provide additional opportunity to export power to other users. then profit sharing increases the viability of the project for all the stakeholders.

There are many different scenarios but the company is working as lead consultant on a couple of large biomass, combined heat and power (CHP) solutions. For example, one is for a partly developed large brown field industrial site. The owner of the site is willing to lease land to the client, an SPV created to deliver the project and which will probably look to sell it on completion to an ESCO or similar to operate the completed plant. What the landlord gets out of the deal is rental on the land and an opportunity to receive additional income from the heat and electricity sold to other businesses across the estate. This is also a similar model to a number of ETL large roof replacements using the ZEDroof system, which is provided either as a separate project or combined with other energy generating plant. For example, company staff are working on a project in the east of England which will provide 3.2 megawatts of solar energy from the main buildings and boiler house and so on, and 10 megawatts and heat from a CHP biomass plant. The intention is that this will be funded using an off balance sheet option. Providing the energy roof (ZEDroof) to any plant housing or boiler house is becoming a standard design solution; it is aesthetically pleasing, functionally sound and combined with its energy producing capability makes it a desirable choice.

The economics attached to off-grid electricity generation is complex, mainly due to the array of incentives provided by government, but the underlying principle is relatively simple. Maximum returns are delivered when all the power can be used as it is generated without the need to put any unused energy back into the grid. This applies to both domestic and commercial installations. The business model and commercial viability of off-grid generation are significantly improved in situations where there is no reliance on income from exporting to grid nor, in fact, any reliance on grant and subsidies, which at present is difficult to achieve. However, given the government's desire to see less green subsidies and ensure new technologies pay their way, one wonders how long these tariffs and incentives will be around, and the looming end of term deadlines, for example, feed-in tariffs in 2016– create uncertainty and time pressures.

13.6 *National grid pressures*

The UK government managed to keep the lights on throughout last winter but, as the House of Lords Science and Technology Committee declared in its March 2015 report (House of Lords, 2015), the government should not be congratulated for it. The report stresses that this has been achieved at a cost to the taxpayer, by an over-reliance on fossil fuel generation and using measures which are in conflict with the government's wider aims to decarbonise electricity generation. It is acknowledged in the report that the UK's electricity system and requirements are undergoing considerable change and it is clear that demand and prices are going to increase over the coming years before the resilience of its electricity system improves.

Lack of continuous generation in many of the off-grid renewable energy supplies places them at some disadvantage. For example, using solar energy when it is at its peak during the day can in many instances mean that surpluses have to be fed back into the grid rather than used economically on site. However, battery technology is improving at a pace and even now is a viable option (even factoring in the cost of the batteries) in some situations and opens up opportunities to use power whenever it is required and irrespective of when it is produced, for example, solar energy produced during the day being used at night. This is also useful if the grid connection is less than the peak installed capacity. As storage becomes more viable and more widespread, then trading and brokering in stored power becomes a real possibility, making money by buying energy at one price and selling it for more money at peak times. This of course requires good metering and measurement and Property Tectonics is working with business partners to run a pilot scheme in south Wales.

Power-hungry industries, including areas of the public sector which can mop up cheaper and more reliable sources of power without reliance on the National Grid, all have a keen interest in off-grid generation. The company is working on a number of data centre projects where the ZEDroof provides a good investment opportunity. Data centres demand power and lots of it and therefore the ZEDroof solution with other off-grid generation fits the business model perfectly. However, grid resilience is also of concern to many heavy engineering industries as well as hospitals, universities and other public sector organisations. An ideal solution is to use the energy roof as an 'over roof' solution, providing more reliable pitch roof designs to existing flat roofs. In these cases – for example, nurses' and doctors' accommodation operating 24/7 and schools and so on – it is useful to exchange problematic flat roofs for pitch roofs. Additional insulation is simply laid on top of the existing roof surface; and generating much needed and cheaper power throughout the day makes it a very attractive option. These buildings are also improved aesthetically.

13.7 Waste recycling

Property Tectonics is involved, acting as lead consultant, on exciting waste recycling projects and these present interesting challenges. Anything to do with waste heightens the sensitivity of local town planners, the environment agency and the local community. Quite rightly, the environmental advantages and disadvantages have to be carefully considered equally, but moving into this territory is not for the faint hearted and requires enormous staying power. Often the technology being employed is state of the art and is imported from abroad; it is pioneering and, coupled with a backcloth of uncertainty, it presents considerable financial risk and emotional heartache to the customer/adventurer who is usually an early adopter of new technology. Property Tectonics has recently obtained planning permission for a road sweeper waste recycling plant 12 months after the application was submitted. This was made more complex because the site was quite near to a residential area and the upfront work, and cost of consultant fees and specialist advice, and the associated risks have been huge. These client entrepreneurs need to be celebrated; without them many of these important sustainability projects and technologies would not move forward.

Property Tectonics is about to embark on another project recycling rubber tyres, which will cost around £24 million and uses equipment imported from China. It can be imagined that such a project will need to be managed sensitively and handling the pre-planning process and managing public perception is of the utmost importance. The plant operates using a process of pyrolysis but the immediate public perception is that the tyres are being burnt when this is not the case. The plant and equipment operate at around 450 °C, which is a relatively low temperature and separates tyre shred into oil and carbon black. The process itself re-uses any waste gases by generating its own energy, using turbines, providing a very sustainable waste recycling facility. This is an excellent way of making use of end of life car and truck tyres that previously went to landfill.

The stakeholders are encouraged by the support of the local council, the county council, the UK Department of Trade and Industry and the Environment Agency, that have not, to date, objected to any part of the 'proposal in principle'. They have confirmed, as part of a pre-application planning meeting, that the customer should make a full planning application. The support is driven to some extent by the prospect of 104 low to medium skilled jobs at the plant in an area of traditional high unemployment. Despite the support of the council and the planners and all the statutory and performance safeguards, such as the Wrap Around Guarantee (WAG, see section 13.11), which have to be put in place, the project will hit barriers if objections are made by anyone formally residing in the UK. It is important that people do have a say in these matters and if too many (over five) objections are received then the issue has to go to full committee and the decision-making process may become extremely expensive and time-consuming and in the end could stop the project going ahead. This is after a substantial investment will have already been made making the application. This is a major fear for organisations looking to invest in the UK and they are potentially dissuaded by the high risk in time and expense associated with getting projects of this nature through the planning process.

13.8 Lifespan software

Property Tectonics has been involved in providing a number of related professional services to the social housing sector since the business started in 1987. Whilst the company has been and still is involved in delivering the traditional consultant contract procurement services, its main contribution in this sector as a business has always been at the strategic level: helping customers to produce asset management plans and delivering best value. All this has developed at a pace as Property Tectonics' knowledge capital has grown alongside the developments in information technology. This has sped the business along with a great deal of excitement to where it is today. It has undertaken condition surveys of tens of thousands of homes and been involved in some of the biggest housing stock transfers from local authorities to other private and arms-length organisations. The practice is used to doing large stock condition surveys and its biggest condition survey contract was to survey 13,500 homes. This work was provided because Property Tectonics had the software tools to collect and analyse the data and had developed its own software from the late 1980s, which is now sold under its Lifespan™ brand. The company could quite easily provide images from its archive to demonstrate the 'evolution of software' by showing pictures of its mobile technology used over the years: from machines and battery packs strapped on surveyors to the robust Psion machines, then a variety of smaller gadgets and to the tablets used today. Lifespan products have now developed into many areas relating to asset management and energy services and are undoubtedly among the market leaders.

Property Tectonics is probably unique in developing its own software solutions as the requirements have grown, using its own IT specialists to work in teams with its built environment professionals. This strategy led to the development of Lifespan energy software and, when the then Department of the Environment introduced its Standards Assessment Procedure (SAP) in 1992, the company produced mobile collection software which fully integrated the asset data within Lifespan Housing. A 'reduced' SAP methodology was also created called Lifespan Cut Down SAP soon afterwards so residential social landlord (RSL) customers could use this to collect generic energy data at low cost, providing valuable stock-wide analysis using the SAP methodology. Later, much later, in 2005 the government introduced a Reduced Data SAP methodology known as RdSAP which was adopted – as Lifespan RdSAP – as the energy efficiency analysis tool for its asset management software and to produce Energy Performance Certificates (EPCs) following the introduction of European Union legislation, 'the Energy Performance of Buildings Directive (EPBD)' in January 2003.

Lifespan RdSAP energy software is used by the company's housing clients and by independent energy assessors providing EPCs for buildings, which are required under European legislation. Most Lifespan users were chartered surveyors, because the company made its software available to the Royal Institution of Chartered Surveyors (RICS) and operated its Energy Assessor Accreditation Scheme under a partnership agreement. The RICS decided in November 2012 that it no longer wished to operate an energy accreditation scheme. It is understood that this was because it considered that the UK government was over-regulating matters and making the whole process too bureaucratic. Property Tectonics then created a partnership with

Sterling Accreditation Limited and most of the RICS members, who were practically all Lifespan RdSAP and commercial version Simplified Building Energy Model (SBEM) users, moved across to Sterling Accreditation.

Property Tectonics' focus has always been the data and, when the government was driven by the need to produce an EPC, Property Tectonics staff saw the value in the data which produced them. The constant updates and rewrites to SBEM, Display Energy Certificates (DEC) and especially RdSAP has created huge problems for the industry. It has stabilised a little but there is a pre-occupation with updating that places a huge burden on the energy business, which is already squeezed from all sides in the hard economic times. The low prices being paid for energy assessments (EPCs) is unsustainable and, until there is more opportunity in the market, better policing of compliance (see section 13.11) and more use of the valuable data to reduce energy consumption, the anticipated benefits from the EPBD legislation will not be achieved.

13.9 Energy management in social housing

Most Lifespan Housing customers have improved their housing stock significantly, including the energy efficiency aspects of their homes. This was one of the requirements of the Decent Homes Programme brought in by the Blair–Brown government in 2000 which aimed to provide a minimum standard of housing conditions for all those housed in public sector dwellings (council housing and housing associations), by a target date of 2010. This requirement reinforced the need for organisations (most were doing it anyway) to understand the condition of their stock and to monitor condition. The business has a huge amount of data collected over almost 30 years; it has been standard practice for it to collect energy data using the RdSAP methodology as part of the condition surveys for the past 10 years. Condition surveys are carried out on a regular basis and most customers have information now on *all* (100%) of their stock.

Property Tectonics' customers represent some of the most go-ahead organisations in the sector and are generally early adopters of new ideas and technologies; they are also keen to help educate their tenants about how to use their homes efficiently. Generally, across the RSL sector, most have embarked on replacing boilers, have improved levels of insulation and adopted sensible fabric first strategies to improve the energy efficiency of their stock. The company has not been involved directly with other measures such as CHP plants (applied to houses), district heating systems, heat pumps and so on, but again most have piloted alternative approaches depending on applicability to their estate. Property Tectonics has an interest in applying ETL's new energy roof product and staff are in discussions with a number of our RSL customers about piloting the ZEDroof within their estates. The application of the ZEDroof as a retrofit application in housing is not as straightforward as it is on larger-scale commercial applications and needs care before deciding on this option.

The uptake of solar panels by RSLs has been quite extensive and the vast majority have piloted the concept, while others have made quite a commitment by employing a variety of funding methods including the 'rent a roof' method. As outlined in section 13.5, there are a number of on and off balance sheet arrangements and renting the roof ostensibly to an

ESCO in return for cheaper electricity is one of them. Installation and maintenance are paid for from subsidies described as a feed-in tariff generation payment and a feed-in tariff export payment. The feed-in tariffs (FIT) designed by government to encourage homeowners to invest in cleaner technologies have been slashed over the years (see Table 13.1). It could be argued that the subsidy should come down, given that the cost of photovoltaic systems (pv) have reduced and the saving improves as the electricity prices increase. However, despite the recent dip in energy costs, prices are certain to rise in the UK (some believe substantially) during the next decade but reducing FIT is not encouraging householders and landlords to adopt cleaner and more sustainable forms of energy, which was the original objective. In any analysis all these factors have to be built in and there is uncertainty over how much of the power can be used when it is available, that is during daylight hours. Standard analysis assumes 50%, but is it? In reality the landlord does not know because it is not metered. Assuming 50% usage, a pv system will not have a payback of less than 10 years, unless it is being purchased without the need to borrow and for most the payback is between 11 and 14 years, which is quite good when one considers reasonable performance from the system for at least 20 years.

For the RSL community a big issue is who should get the benefit of the energy being generated: the householder or the RSL? If it is the householder, then this creates an imbalance in rents and who should be benefitting from what. Property Tectonics should be addressing some of these issues, especially as it is looking to provide a new solar product (ZEDroof) as an alternative replacement for existing worn-out roofs with a system which will generate up to twice the energy generally available from on-roof solar. It is important that the income and the power from the energy roof can be distributed within the RSL business to improve economic viability. This is a difficult argument when the landlord can replace more than two roofs for the price of one ZEDroof. The answer lies in providing ways for the landlord to meter usage, pool the benefit and provide reduced tariffs to a number of households and not just the ones with the roof. The other major consideration is, to maximise returns, the power must be used when it is available and several customers are looking at community energy solutions and using storage to that end. Tenant behaviour is also very important but it is also necessary to assist where possible, for example, by introducing additional electrical controls to support changes in behaviour by ensuring power is used at the right time or rather by applying appropriate demand management: a sort of white meter mentality which provides cheaper off-peak electricity, but in this case not during the night but during the day. That is where Cloogy and other devices and sensors come in. Cloogy products are manufactured in Portugal where they have been used quite extensively and they are now being distributed by ETL in the UK; these are innovative complementary product to the work Property Tectonics and ETL are delivering to their customers.

The term asset management systems no longer describes fully what asset management is about as traditional asset and energy data explodes beyond recognition. New and comprehensive digital information is coming through from the production of new buildings created in building information modelling and asset information is now being authenticated with real data on costs and performance as maintenance and improvement works are implemented. Traditional asset information systems and software tools are no longer sufficient as 'live data' enriches traditional data from an

Table 13.1 UK domestic feed-in tariffs (FIT).

Feed-in tariffs	FIT Year 1				FIT Year 2				FIT Year 3				FIT Year 4				FIT Year 5				FIT Year 6							
	2010				2011				2012				2013				2014				2015				2016			
	1	2	3	4	1	2	3	4	1	2	3	4	1	2	3	4	1	2	3	4	1	2	3	4	1	2	3	4
Generation	48.84	48.84	48.84	48.84	48.84	48.84	48.84	48.84	22.59	17.22	17.22	16.11	16.11	15.54	15.54	15.54	15.54	14.61	14.61	14.61	13.88	13.39	12.92	12.47	4.39	4.32	4.25	4.18
Export	3.44	3.44	3.44	3.44	3.44	3.44	3.44	3.44	4.85	4.85	4.85	4.85	4.85	4.85	4.85	4.85	4.85	4.85	4.85	4.85	4.85	4.85	4.85	4.85	4.91	4.91	4.91	4.91

increasing number of sensors and devices, providing building performance data in housing as never before; for the first time hard meaningful data on the behaviour and needs of tenants and occupiers can be gathered. Most are familiar with what building management systems can provide in controlling and monitoring a building's mechanical and electrical equipment, such as ventilation, lighting, power, fire and security systems. However, could the current possibilities have envisaged where this level of control can be afforded in every dwelling in the land as home automation takes on an entirely new and expanding meaning.

The impact of digital sensors and devices is creating new opportunities to collect and exchange data and integrate the physical world with computer-based systems to improve efficiency, accuracy and economic benefit. This 'Internet of Things' (IoT) as Kevin Ashton describes it (Ashton, 2015) will be disruptive as well as opportunistic, as sensors control the machines in peoples' lives such as the cars they drive and when central heating systems, lights and washing machines should come on. Automation is being taken to new levels, especially as systems learn from people behaviour, changing the way people live. Landlords therefore must change the way they manage their physical assets and the support they provide to the people who live in them. For Property Tectonics it is no longer about Lifespan Asset Management but about Lifespan Intelligent Homes.

One of the greatest impacts of these changes is that the industry has to embrace big data. Current software solutions operate using traditional relationship databases but data growth is coming from data sets from the IoT that are too unstructured or too big for traditional relationship data management systems. A new breed of companies is emerging to capture and analyse these new data sets and Property Tectonics has entered into partnership with SmartGateways to work on Lifespan Intelligent Homes. Firms such as Google, eBay, LinkedIn and Facebook have arguably been built around big data from the beginning, therefore unlike most other established companies, they did not have to integrate big data with more traditional sources. Big data together with its analytics can stand alone but, for established businesses and organisations such as the RSLs, big data must be integrated with other types of data needed to operate the business. This is particularly true in the transformation of asset management systems into the new concept of intelligent homes through the IoT and big data.

The opportunities are almost limitless but for example:

- Remote management of electronic devices from anywhere, anytime (lights, washing machine, oven and so on).
- Monitoring of temperature, fire, carbon monoxide and security sensors and even video information.
- Analysis of energy consumption and behaviour creating opportunities to offer guidance on reducing energy usage.
- Provide energy matching between homes and energy trading solutions.
- Better healthcare support for the elderly by monitoring their movements, warmth and alignment with the caring professions.
- Customised interfaces with washing machines, fridges and TVs for elderly and those with disabilities.

- Encouraging lifestyle changes for healthier living and improving energy efficiency.
- Better information to help in targeting fuel poverty and supporting individual households within their own communities.
- Energy management strategies have to factor in behavioural changes because at least one-third of the target carbon savings in the residential sector has to come from behavioural changes. The new digital revolution will empower householders with the information they need to make decisions and reduce emissions. This was recognised in a previous government's energy white paper in 2007 which required electricity monitors to be put into every home if requested. Households should be encouraged to have gas, electricity and water monitors and this is now relatively easy and cheap to achieve.
- Of course individual confidentiality will have to be maintained and arrangements on what information is shared with the landlord and what is not, have to be worked out but Property Tectonics and its partners, SmartGateways, will deliver an interoperable IoT system, big data management and analytics to provide a range of inter-connected services within Lifespan Intelligent Homes.

The role of the IoT and big data in Intelligent Homes becomes much more exciting at the neighbourhood level where a variety of data can be used, mined and analysed to inform and educate. By providing a hub that connects a variety of data and allows interoperability within the ecosystem, it will enable housing associations and other RSLs to engage in multi-agency collaboration, creating sustainable communities through IoT and big data. It will provide information on the energy performance of their homes in a holistic manner across a particular neighbourhood, weighing behavioural and physical (asset) criteria, creating opportunities to explore energy efficient neighbourhoods through energy trading, community energy schemes and energy matching. Data from homes can be integrated and analysed with other agencies (health, crime, antisocial behaviour and more) to create sustainable and secure neighbourhoods. Data analytics will help multi-agencies to deploy evidence-based interventions across the community.

The world is on the cusp of a data-sharing revolution with the IoT and big data presenting opportunities for organisations and the people they serve to seek answers and support from different communities, for example, using crowd sourcing to solicit contributions from large groups of people online rather than from traditional sources, including their existing landlords. The role of RSLs in this data-sharing revolution must be worked out and form part of their own digital agendas and, of course, the journey is littered with questions. It cannot be that everything is shared with everyone, so what data should be collected and shared, from whom and with whom and for what purpose? What are the risks and how do we protect individual confidentiality and anonymity whilst allowing the information to be useful and meaningful? How should the information be presented and what user interfaces are required? The risks are obvious and any solutions worked out will need to be pragmatic and secure, but the underlying philosophy of data integration, system interoperability and data sharing are fundamental challenges for the housing sector.

13.10 Energy Company Obligation

Energy Company Obligation (ECO) is a government scheme that requires the larger energy companies to deliver energy efficiency measures to domestic premises in Britain. ECO has recently been extended (delayed) and will run for two years until 31 March 2017. ECO has its critics who argue it is expensive, inefficient and is not helping the people it is aimed at. However, Property Tectonics is delighted to be involved in an ECO-funded works which form part of Arbed 2, which is a European Regional Development Fund and flagship Welsh government project aimed at tackling fuel poverty. Housing association and long-time Lifespan Housing customer, Melin Homes, is the scheme manager for the £27 million Welsh government initiative. Property Tectonics is providing software, project management support, technical monitoring and mandatory chartered surveyor reports, along with consultant advice on hard to treat properties. The hard to treat properties are having external wall insulation installed with support finance being provided by one of the UK's leading power and gas companies, E.ON, under the ECO scheme.

ECO is delivered by energy companies under the UK's independent regulator, the Office of Gas and Electricity Markets (Ofgem), that monitors the process very carefully, applying strict quality assurance procedures. The whole process is highly document-controlled, with safeguards to protect and advance the interests of consumers. Failure to comply results in fines and loss of finance; Property Tectonics's role is to basically support the Melin team, work closely with E.ON staff and fully exploit the advantages of Lifespan Project Management and Lifespan Housing within the team.

13.11 Compliance and warranties

Availability of government subsidy is a complex business, made more complex by the level of compliance controls being applied. Compliance, quality assurance and warranties are inextricably linked and there is now an almost entirely separate but parallel industry in these related areas.

Many of the energy compliance requirements in the UK have been driven by the EPBD legislation that came into force on 4th January 2003 and had to be implemented by 4th January 2006. The directive was recast in May 2010 in order to strengthen the energy performance requirements of buildings. The EPBD and the 2012 Energy Efficiency Directive, designed to remove barriers in the energy market and overcome market failures that impede efficiency in the supply and use of energy, are the two main pieces of legislation aimed at reducing the energy consumption of buildings. The Department of Communities and Local Government (DCLG) is the government department responsible for implementing the EPBD and the latest was implemented by the Energy Performance of Buildings (England and Wales) Regulations 2012. In short, this requires the production of EPCs for domestic and non-domestic buildings constructed, sold or let, Display Energy Certificates (DECs) and advisory reports for all large public buildings, air conditioning inspections of buildings and guidance on enforcement by the local weights and measures authority (trading standards).

The latest impact of the Energy Efficiency Directive is the 2014 Energy Savings Opportunity Scheme (ESOS) Regulations which provide a mandatory requirement for large companies (over 250 employees and £40 million turnover) to audit the energy used by their buildings, industrial processes and transport to identify cost-effective energy saving measures by 15th December 2015 and every four years afterwards. This is the responsibility of the Department of Energy and Climate Change (DECC) which means that two government departments, DECC and DCLG have to get their act together and ESOS is being monitored by the Environment Agency which many argue will be much more proactive in ensuring compliance than the overstretched local authority trading standards have been in ensuring compliance with EPBD.

As described above, Property Tectonics' EPC work extends to providing government-approved energy assessment software and lodgement facilities to produce domestic, non-domestic and display EPCs; in fact Property Tectonics was the first to have a fully web-based online system. The company has trained and accredited staff to undertake all different types of energy assessments, including air conditioning inspections. However, this is a very competitive, highly regulated market and Property Tectonics does not compete for EPC work but rather provides energy assessments and inspections for its own RSL customers (as outlined in section 13.8) and for commercial customers as part of a larger commission. EPCs are also used in the scheme of things outside constructing, selling and renting homes; for example, it is a requirement before ECO funding is provided and it is a pre-requisite for the application of solar in domestic applications where a 'D' energy rating must be achieved.

Property Tectonics recently developed new energy assessment software called Lifespan e-Count that is specifically designed to provide energy data analysis across multiple properties. It is an innovative web-based tool that can provide building users with a snapshot on how efficiently they operate their building. This is achieved by guiding users through a visual journey of energy reduction and carbon emissions. The software is based on tried and tested government-approved software and is particularly helpful in analysing DEC data and in addressing the requirements of ESOS. The system has also been white labelled for use by one of the biggest facilities/building contractors in the UK that is using the system across a number of large organisations. The e-Count software is available for any DEC qualified energy assessor registered with the Chartered Institute of Building Services or Sterling Accreditation. It is also possible to lodge an e-Count display certificate with Sterling Accreditation and the output from the system can be used by any lead ESOS assessor needing to analyse multi-site energy consumption.

Whatever Property Tectonics does, it is hyper-sensitive about ensuring that all the necessary quality assurances and product warranties are in place and that everything is done to the highest professional standards and, whilst government interventions can be over-bureaucratic, they do provide additional layers of protection. Staff in the business learned a great deal bringing the ZEDroof to market, having to put in place all the requisite design, product and installer quality requirements, which meant dealing with a considerable number of organisations, including insurance companies, accreditation schemes, independent specialists to guarantee calculations, along with the usual multi-disciplinary construction and engineering specialists. Property Tectonics' subsidiary and independent building control company, corporate approved inspector, Property Tectonics Building Standards Limited, has been heavily involved to ensure compliance throughout.

It is essential in the case of larger engineering projects, either in waste or energy generation and so on, that an engineering procurement and construction (EPC) contractor is appointed to act as a single point of contact, taking responsibility under a relevant contract for project risk, including its design, installation and performance. The contractor will usually also provide what is probably the most important legal document, providing protection for investors and the project company by way of a 'wrapper' or more accurately the WAG. The contractor will work with other members of the team and may well subcontract most of the practical work to others, but the WAG prevents uncertainty and legal confusion as it allocates unambiguous responsibility directly on the warrantor for any non-performance, inadequate performance, or delay in performance of any of the other contractors under their respective contracts.

CHP projects are encouraged with incentives to apply for a Combined Heat and Power Quality Assurance which is a voluntary scheme operated by DECC and is used to define, assess and monitor CHP schemes along with their energy efficiency and environmental performance. Certification under the scheme is used as principal evidence for determining eligibility for various benefits available to good quality CHP. These benefits, including climate change levy exemption, capital allowances and exemption from business rating, are designed to encourage the installation and operation of improved quality CHP schemes.

Large commercial generation projects involving solar, biomass or wind turbine must go through a rather complicated application process for a Renewables Obligation Certificate (ROC). The certificate is issued to an accredited generator for eligible renewable electricity generated and supplied to customers by a licensed electricity supplier. Ofgem is required to assess and accredit the generating station. After accreditation, Ofgem issues the ROC to the power generation businesses that operate renewable power generation systems. The ROC is a digital certificate which hold details of exactly how a unit of renewable electricity is produced, who produces it and who is buying the electricity. ROCs are available to new entrants until March 2017.

A new scheme was introduced in 2014 called Contract for Difference (CfD), which provides an alternative to ROCs. The CfD is basically a private law contract between a low carbon electricity generator and the low carbon contracts company which is a not for profit organisation with one shareholder – DECC's secretary of state. The current form of the CfD is based on a competitive tender which allows the market to purchase low carbon electricity at the best possible price for the consumer, which in turn means that incentives to invest in these technologies are reduced. This leads us into a whole new world of electricity market reforms designed to support low carbon generation by giving eligible generators a fixed price for the low carbon electricity they produce and sell to the market, thereby increasing their price certainty and investor comfort and confidence. However, the delays and uncertainties in the process and the future availability of both CfDs and ROCs has generally had the opposite effect. This is in turn linked to power purchase agreements and energy markets which fall outside the scope of this paper but the underlying message is that government incentives and tariffs available are complex and not straightforward. It is therefore important that low carbon electricity generators understand the complexities and the risks, which are invariably time-sensitive in terms of application, opportunity and availability.

13.12 Conclusion

Energy conservation, recycling, micro-generation, waste to energy and whatever else is developed by Property Tectonics that '... *meets the needs of the present, without compromising the ability of future generations to meet their own needs.*' (World Commission on Environment and Development, 1987) is done with an immense commitment to collaborative working and innovation which creates a real sense of satisfaction.

Sustainability is definitely an area of Property Tectonics' business which stretches the team's ability to think, communicate and learn. There are no manuals or standardised ways of doing things, practically every project is unique, the solution has to be worked out and the intellectual capital sends the business moving away from its competitors, differentiating the business in the market place. This is a strategy adopted by Property Tectonics from the very beginning, the leadership team being inspired emotionally by reading Tom Peters' book *In Search of Excellence* (Peters and Waterman, 1984) and then channelled strategically by adopting Michael Porter's competitive advantage model (Porter, 1985).

Sustainability is now connecting much of the company's previous innovative and pioneering work and knowledge capital, some of which has since been commoditised by other firms. The recession has taken out of the business much of the more standard professional work because it could either not compete or did not want to. However, the strategy has been to continue to press the company's creativity. As Porter's work made very clear many years ago, '*innovation is the central issue in economic prosperity*' and the company has never reduced its significant research and development spending. Over the last few years Peter Drucker's view has proved to be true '*innovation is the specific tool of entrepreneurs, the means by which they exploit change as an opportunity for a different business or a different service*' (Drucker, 1985). Whilst people in Property Tectonics have stuck fundamentally to what they are good at, innovation has created opportunities for the delivery of a radically different and new service to the market.

Property Tectonics could not deliver this innovation without relying on a fantastic team of people from within its community and from its supporters outside the company. It now represents one of the best teams of specialists from a wide range of industries and sectors who are willing and able to work together to produce something that is of immense value to their customers, society and future generations.

References

Alvesson, M., Skoldberg, K. (2000) *Reflexive Methodology – New Vistas for Qualitative Research.* Sage, London.
Ashton, K. (2015) *How to Fly a Horse: The Secret History of Creation, Invention, and Discovery.* Doubleday, New York.

Boyer, E.L. (1990) *Scholarship Reconsidered: Priorities of the Professoriate.* The Carnegie Foundation for the Advancement of Teaching, Chicago.

Drucker, P.F. (1985) The Discipline of Innovation. *Harvard Business Review,* August.

House of Lords (2015) *Science and Technology Select Committee Report, The Resilience of the Electricity System.* HL Paper 121. The Stationery Office, London.

Peters, T.J., Waterman, R.H. Jr. (1984) *In Search of Excellence: Lessons from America's Best-Run Companies.* Harper Row, New York.

Porter, M.E. (1985) *Competitive Advantage: Creating and Sustaining Superior Performance.* Free Press, New York.

Schon, D.A. (1983) *The Reflective Practitioner: How Professionals Think in Action.* Basic Books, New York.

Shu-ling, A., Sexton, B. (2009) *Innovation in Small Professional Practices in the Built Environment.* Blackwell Publishing, Oxford.

World Commission on Environment and Development (1987) *Our Common Future.* Oxford University Press, Oxford, p. 43.

Chapter 14
Understanding Value Generation in Complex Urban Regeneration Projects

Carlos T. Formoso and Luciana I.G. Miron
Building Innovation Research Unit, Federal University of Rio Grande do Sul, Porto Alegre, Brazil

14.1 The context: Social housing projects in Brazil

The management of social housing projects is a theme of major social and economic importance in the context of emerging economies. In the case of Brazil, some important changes have happened in the last 15 years. The housing policy has changed and the scale of investment in social housing has increased substantially, compared to the previous decades. For instance, the 'My House My Life' (*Minha Casa Minha Vida*) Programme, currently the most important social housing programme in this country, has delivered nearly three million houses between 2009 and 2014 (Caixa Econômica Federal, 2014). In this country, the target population for social housing programmes are families with a monthly income of up to three minimum wages (around US$ 650). According to Fundação João Pinheiro (2013), this represents around 90% of the Brazilian housing deficit, estimated at 5.9 million homes.

A wide range of new forms of housing provision have been proposed in the last few decades for tackling the housing deficit in Brazil (Keivani *et al.*, 2004). This chapter is focused on integrated housing programmes, which usually have a much broader scope than conventional projects. These integrated programmes provide not only housing units but also other goods and services: road system upgrading, improvement in sewage systems, community services (health, education, professional training; Tillmann *et al.*, 2010). The ultimate aim of this complex combination of products and services is to promote the inclusion of local population in the formal city with the support of community development projects (Minnery *et al.*, 2013). In recent years, some funding programmes have encouraged the development of social housing projects that adopt to some extent this type of integrated approach (Keivani *et al.*, 2004). This is the case, for instance, in highly complex urban regeneration projects partially financed by some international funding agencies.

Future Challenges in Evaluating and Managing Sustainable Development in the Built Environment,
First Edition. Edited by Peter S. Brandon, Patrizia Lombardi and Geoffrey Q. Shen.
© 2017 John Wiley & Sons Ltd. Published 2017 by John Wiley & Sons Ltd.

Integrated programmes usually involve a large number of stakeholders, including different local, state and federal government departments, non-governmental organisations, private companies and the community. This may result in requirement conflicts and in the need to spend much effort managing trade-offs (Formoso *et al.*, 2011). Thus, there is a challenge to improve the project development process in order to deliver a combination of products and services that generates value from the perspective of different stakeholders while emphasising, of course, the needs of target communities.

This paper explores conceptual and practical contributions of value management in integrated social housing programmes that are part of urban regeneration initiatives. The aim of this chapter is to understand the challenges of managing value in highly complex urban regeneration projects. It is based on a set of case studies carried out in the City Entrance Integrated Programme (PIEC) in Porto Alegre, Brazil.

This investigation is concerned with the social dimension of sustainability, which has been recognised as the weakest pillar of sustainable development (Lehtonen, 2004). It points out some opportunities for improving the management of social housing projects so that value generation from the perspective of target communities can be made more effective.

14.2 Management of urban regeneration projects

Previous studies pointed out that traditional project management approaches are not able to cope with the level of complexity that currently exists in many projects (Atkinson *et al.*, 2006; Winter *et al.*, 2006). Traditional project management lies in the strategy of breaking a project into small parts, by defining the activities that are necessary to achieve pre-defined objectives. Even though it is assumed that the project scope is defined through a progressive process of refining objectives and deliverables (Project Management Institute, 2004), the focus of management is mostly on controlling activities and reducing uncertainty that may affect the achievement of expected objectives (Atkinson *et al.*, 2006; Winter *et al.*, 2006). The fundamental problem of such an approach is that it encourages simplifications only useful in ordered circumstances (Snowden and Boone, 2007).

Project complexity may come from different sources (Williams, 2002): (i) structural complexity, which is concerned with the number of steps and interdependences and (ii) uncertainty, which can be related to goals or methods. Structural complexity can be further divided into organisational complexity (i.e. large number of stakeholders), and technological complexity (i.e. large number of interdependent components; Baccarini, 1996).

Urban regeneration projects are usually very complex. Their scope is wide, involving not only the construction of buildings and infrastructure, but often a set of additional actions (services) for generating income, enhancing job opportunities, providing secure forms of tenure and even changing urban governance (Minnery *et al.*, 2013). The number of stakeholders is large, and there may be multiple and conflicting goals. Due to their large scale and long duration, these projects are often highly influenced by economic, social and political factors, including elections and public opinion (Miller and Hobbs, 2005).

Moreover, there is a growing trend of the direct involvement of local communities in decision-making at different project stages, especially when slum upgrading is involved (Patel, 2013), for example, for defining priorities in investment, participative design, self-management of facilities. One particular characteristic of such projects is the target on a community, which needs be mobilised as change agents, requiring some project stakeholders to encourage, facilitate, train, build capacity, and support such transformation (Schilderman and Ruskulis, 2005). Rittel and Webber (1973) pointed out that the nature of the problem frequently changes from the original one along the project, and that there is no stopping rule or ultimate test for the solution adopted. In this context, projects typically have emerging requirements and therefore cannot be regarded as a linear progression from activities to pre-established objectives (Atkinson *et al.*, 2006).

Large infrastructure projects are highly embedded in their contexts. Goals are set as starting points and refined as the project progresses. The project definition and planning processes have many iterative loops and do not follow a linear and continuous progression (Miller and Hobbs, 2005). Organisations must be flexible (Atkinson *et al.*, 2006), decision-making structures decentralised and goals need to be negotiated (Cyert and March, 1963).

Another important criticism to traditional project management approaches is the fact that, even when construction projects are frequently delivered on time and on budget, they may still fail to deliver the expected benefits (Thorp, 1998). According to Winch (2006), the view of value in project management derives from the quality movement, and has indeed contributed to the management of projects by bringing the customer into the perspective. However, this traditional view is narrowly focused on the quality of physical products and does not sufficiently take into consideration the need to generate benefits for the different stakeholders groups (Winter *et al.*, 2006).

Therefore, the emphasis on value generation requires project management to be more strategy-oriented (Görög and Smith, 1999), requiring the regular assessment of benefits and the evaluation of emerging opportunities (Thiry, 2002). This contrasts with the traditional way of assessing house-building projects after delivery, mostly focused on the project's physical products, rather than on the overall impact of the project (Hentschke *et al.*, 2014).

Winter *et al.* (2006) suggest that projects should be regarded as value creation processes, by expanding the meaning of value from the conception, production and delivery of physical products (outputs) to the generation of benefits (outcomes). This is a fundamental change that has been adopted by some innovative value management approaches that have been successfully implemented in construction projects, such as Benefits Realisation (Thorp, 1998), Integrated Project Delivery (AIA, 2007) and Target Value Design (Zimina *et al.*, 2012).

14.3 Value generation

Despite the growing interest in value generation in the literature, the concept of value is often poorly defined, being often misused in the management literature (Khalifa, 2004). In fact, value is a dynamic, multifaceted and complex concept with different meanings according to the context and field of knowledge in which it is used. In Marketing literature, the concept of 'perceived value' by the customer is often used to explain the phenomenon of value creation (Sanchéz-Fernandéz and Iniesta-Bonillo, 2007). This concept is strongly related to the interaction between the customer and the product, and has been used as the starting point for conceptual models that have been proposed to explain value generation.

Kano's model is strongly related to the disconfirmation paradigm, which explains the judgment of satisfaction from the point of view of the customer (Oliver, 1980). Its focus is on meeting and exceeding customer needs: the results of customer's satisfaction (dissatisfiers, satisfiers and delighters) are connected with the fulfilment of basic needs, satisfier needs and attractor or ideal-value needs (Thompson, 1998).

In Monroe's model (Monroe, 1990), value generation is concerned with a trade-off between what the customer receives (benefits) and what is given up to acquire and use a product (sacrifices). Customers' perceived benefits can encompass a range of different meanings such as perceived quality or reliability. Those benefits are assumed to be directly related to product performance, enabling customers to achieve their goals and purposes in use situations (Woodruff, 1997). Perceived benefits are not only the result of product physical attributes, but also of services that are provided – for example, technical support available for a product (Ravald and Grönroos, 1996). Additionally, product acquisition also brings benefits for the customer in terms of symbols that communicate social position and power by means of status, image, exclusivity, respect and comfort (Saliba and Fischer, 2000). Regarding sacrifices, these include the purchase price, exchange costs, start-up costs and post-purchase costs, among others (Saliba and Fischer, 2000).

The mean ends model, originally developed by Gutman (1982), describes how consumers categorise information about products in the memory, with the aim of understanding their choices. The means are the product and service attributes, while the ends are the customer purpose, goal or personal values (Gutman, 1982). This model was extended by Woodruff *et al.* (1993) and Woodruff (1997) by considering not only the perceived value upon purchase, but also the value received during the use of a product. In this new version of the model, value generation is explained by using three hierarchical levels: attributes, consequences and goals. Sets of constructs are defined at each hierarchical level, ranging from tangibles, articulated and objective aspects (e.g. product or service attributes) to a more subtle and intangible level, related to customer goals and purposes.

There is a strong relationship between the perceived value and the customer satisfaction concepts, due to the fact that both of them describe evaluative judgments about the product in use situation (Woodruff, 1997). This relationship is strongly emphasised in Kano's model by connecting the product features to customer satisfaction. Therefore, measures of customer satisfaction are often used as an indicator to understand the customer perceived value.

Figure 14.1 represents schematically the connection between the three conceptual models presented above, which have been used in this chapter to understand value generation in urban regeneration projects. The value perceived by the customer is the ratio of benefits to sacrifices, as defined by Monroe (1990). The generation of benefits

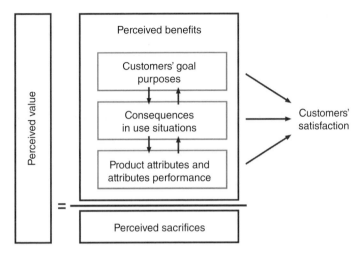

Figure 14.1 Conceptual framework adopted in this study for explaining value generation.

can be understood by relating attributes, consequences and purposes or goals, as proposed by Woodruff (1997). Customer satisfaction is the result of a comparison made by the customer between perceived value with expected outcome, after use of the product (Oliver, 1980).

14.4 Research method

The City Entrance Integrated Programme (*Programa Integrado Entrada da Cidade*; PIEC) started in 2002. It is located in Porto Alegre, the capital of the State of Rio Grande do Sul, Brazil. PIEC can be described as a large urban regeneration programme because it merges four projects for the same target communities: Social Housing, Road Infrastructure, Landscape Improvement and Social Work (including community development, income generation and creation of employment opportunities). Additionally, a fifth project was formally created for managing the PIEC programme, named Project Planning and Control. The original aim of this programme was to improve the living conditions of 3775 families who lived precariously in 22 informal settlements (slums), with minimum displacement of residents. In the first phase of PIEC, which was concluded in 2004, 413 families received new dwellings in three housing estates. In the second phase of PIEC (from 2004 to 2008), 440 families were settled in new dwellings located in two housing estates.

Case study was the research strategy adopted in this investigation, which was divided into three stages. Stage A had an exploratory-descriptive character aiming to understand the programme development process, including the political and institutional background. Data collection was focussed on the perspective of different organisations involved in decision-making. The main sources of evidence were the analysis of design, production control and legal documents, and 16 semi-structured interviews carried out with professionals involved in the conception, design, production and financial management of PIEC projects. During this phase, the main stakeholders were identified and the programme goals (objectives and requirements) were made explicit.

In Stages B and C, the study was focused on the perceived value from the perspective of the final users. Post occupancy evaluations (POE) were carried out in five projects, involving both a survey with final users and direct observation of the housing estates. The users' perceptions on satisfaction, importance and retention were captured by using a questionnaire, which was divided into four parts. The first part addressed the dwellers' profiles, using the same variables employed by the Municipal Department of Housing to identify the families to be benefited, in 2000 and 2001, before the Programme started. The second part contained two open questions, which were used to identify the best and worst of living in the PIEC housing estates, based on the perception of residents. The third part had 24 closed questions with a five-point satisfaction scale concerning the PIEC project attributes, categorised in allotment, housing unit, urban infrastructure, social work and participatory processes. The fourth part explored the housing retention of the target population. It was made up of six open questions and six closed questions concerned with the most important reasons for staying and leaving the PIEC housing units.

Data collection for Stage B was carried out in 2006 and the focus was the 413 families resettled in the PIEC's first stage (Vila Tecnológica, Pôr do Sol and Progresso housing estates). Data collection for Stage C was carried out in 2008, being concerned with the 440 families resettled in the second stage of the Programme (Arco Íris and Santa Teresinha housing estate). Table 14.1 presents the number of dwellings and the sample size for each housing estate.

A Cronbach's Alpha test was used to assess the internal consistency of the questionnaire questions. The values were superior to 0.7, which indicated a good internal consistency (Malhotra, 2004). The best and worst features were analysed and coded according to the same subcategories of the satisfaction questions: allotment (location, neighbourhood, communal areas, safety, parking, costs), housing unit, urban infrastructure, social work and participatory process. The results were quantified by the number of citations from each respondent (up to 5 for both the best and worst features), which provided an indication of the degree of importance. The results of satisfaction were analysed in terms of frequency (percentage). The results related to the housing retention rate (reasons to stay or reasons to leave the housing state) were analysed by ranking.

Table 14.1 Sample size for the five housing estates.

Housing estate	Vila Tecnológica	Pôr do Sol	Progresso	Arco Íris	Santa Teresinha
Number of dwellings	59	130	221	163	214
Sample size	35	56	69	61	63

14.5 Main results

14.5.1 Description of PIEC's development process

The PIEC intervention area covers two full neighbourhoods and portions of other three other neighbourhoods in the northern region of Porto Alegre. This area is divided in two parts, the largest one with 2149 acres and the smallest one with 3 acres (Figure 14.2). The decision to carry out this project was based on problems and opportunities identified by City Council staff. There was a large number of families living in slums in that area, which had a lack of job opportunities, schools and health care services. The infrastructure was inadequate for housing: sewage was not properly collected and treated, and floods were very common in some settlements. By contrast, this area was very close to the city centre and the main transportation systems: the main highway access, a suburban train system, the international airport and the fluvial port.

Most families living in the PIEC area earned between nothing and three minimum wages per month and were entitled to get social housing subsidies. In order to join the Programme, the families had to sign a contract in which they would get the right of use of the house, but not the ownership, and would pay a fairly low occupancy fee (a kind of social leasing). Additionally, those families were encouraged to participate in the Social Work Project, in which there were mechanisms for community participation in decision-making.

A highly participative approach was used in the design phase of PIEC, including a close connection with the City's Participatory Budget. Moreover, a percentage of the funding received was allocated to support social work initiatives within the community: income generation, community development and environmental and sanitary education. The aim of those initiatives was to engage the target community in the programme, encouraging them to remain on the new housing schemes.

The database containing the profile of the beneficiaries of the Programme, created in 2000 and 2001, was used to understand their needs. Based on that information, some additional housing types were proposed: (a) house units for handicapped people, (b) commercial units and mixed units (residential and commercial) for families that had small businesses and (c) possibility of enlargement from a two-floor to a three-floor house. Figure 14.3 presents photos of existing slums before the project started and PIEC housing estates after resettlement.

The organisational structure involved in programme management suffered several adjustments along its implementation, mostly due to the fact that there were changes in funding sources and, consequently, on its scope. However, due to the wide scope and the large scale of the programme, a very large number of stakeholders were involved in all phases. The City Council played a central role: besides being the owner of the project, was in charge of the conception and development of the entire programme, including planning and monitoring the actions to be implemented, signing contracts with funding agencies, hiring external companies involved in project design and execution and management of the housing estates and public spaces after occupation. In fact, several City Council departments and secretaries were involved in the execution of the project. The main ones were: (i) the Housing Department (DEMHAB), in charge of producing

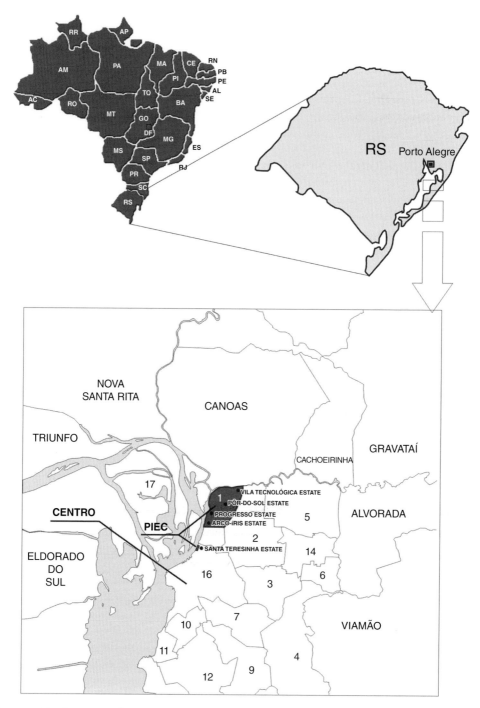

Figure 14.2   Location of PIEC intervention areas in Porto Alegre.

Figure 14.3 Photos of slums (a, b) before and housing estates (c, d) after PIEC interventions. (a) Slum at PIEC area, 2004. (b) Slum at PIEC area, 2005.

(c)

(d)

Figure 14.3 (Continued) (c) Por do Sol project, 2008. (d) Arco Iris project, 2008.

the design of the housing estates and providing social work, (ii) the Department of Construction and Infrastructure (SMOV), in charge of implementing the road infrastructure project, (iii) the Department of the Environment (SMAM), responsible for the landscape improvement project, and (iv) the Department of Industry and Commerce (SMIC), in charge of leading the income generation project. There were also several private companies involved in the project, such as consultancy companies, design firms, construction companies, professional training firms and non-governmental organisations involved in the social work project.

The first phase of PIEC was funded mainly by the *Habitar Brasil BID* Programme, which was jointly financed by the Inter-American Development Bank (IDB) and the Brazilian Government. A more ambitious funding contract was signed with the Financial Fund for the Development of the River Plate Basin (FONPLATA) in December 2003, which became PIEC's main funding agency for the rest of the programme, with 50% of the total investments. There was also funding from BNDES, a Federal Government development bank, CONCEPA, a highway concession company, and directly from the City Council.

Both IDB and FONPLATA played an important role in PIEC's management as they set managerial standards and accountability processes that should be followed. For instance, a percentage of the funding received had to be invested in social work initiatives in the community: income generation, community development and environmental and sanitary education. The aim of those initiatives was to engage the community in the programme, encouraging them to participate in decision-making, as mentioned above.

Another important requirement was that the City Council had to establish an integrated programme management core team, which had project management staff fully dedicated to PIEC, and representatives from eight different departments. This core team was in charge of planning, coordinating, and controlling project actions, as well as preparing three-month progress reports for funding agencies.

An online tool was devised for monitoring the programme progress, making useful information available for all City Council departments involved. The main data available were: (i) status of activities for all projects, including a space to report how problems were being solved, (ii) key performance indicators by project, including the identification of the person responsible for collecting data, (iii) current status of projects, and a comparison to existing deadlines, and (iv) PIEC's overall expenditure and the remaining financial resources available, considering different sources of funding.

14.5.2 Assessment of the project delivery system

As in any complex urban redevelopment project, there were many challenges in the implementation of PIEC. Major adjustments in the programme scope and in the definition of priorities among projects were caused by fluctuations in exchange rates, which reduced substantially the funding from FONPLATA, and by changes in government due to municipal elections, which brought adjustments in the housing policy and also caused the replacement of several team members, especially high-level project managers. Moreover, there were also several problems in the programme implementation that resulted in project delays, such as: the length of time that was necessary to purchase (or negotiate) land for some of the housing estates, the need to remove irregular occupants from areas to be developed and late involvement of stakeholders, such as regulatory agencies, which caused design rework or delays in design approval.

Despite the creation of an integrated programme management core unit and the support of the online tool, there were many problems related to a lack of coordination between projects and collaboration between different organisational units. Interviews with managers indicated that there was much emphasis on measuring the physical progress of individual projects, rather than using the control system to support learning, adaptation to new circumstances and managing the interdependences among activities. As a consequence, tasks that involved more than one department, such as internal approval of decisions, and design changes were very time-consuming. Those difficulties were partly due to the fact that the City Council organisational structure was divided into traditional functional units, and managing projects in an integrated way was new to everyone.

Regarding commercial terms, the City Council had to adopt a traditional lowest-price competitive bidding process to hire external private companies (e.g. contractors, designers, social workers), as established by Federal Law. This delivery process tended to be lengthy and created a barrier for involving some stakeholders in early project stages. Moreover, each project had independent bidding processes, posing additional challenges for their implementation to occur concurrently.

As a result, there were many delays in some of the projects, and several problems related to the lack of synchrony between interdependent tasks were pointed out in the interviews, as illustrated in Figure 14.4. The Social Housing project had a much higher pace than the other projects along a period of 2.5 years. Some Social Work initiatives

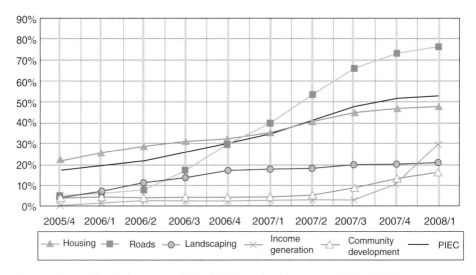

Figure 14.4   Physical progress (%) of PIEC and sub-projects (2005–2008).

(income generation, community development) were particularly affected by the lack of coordination between different projects, since some of the actions were the result of both infrastructure and community engagement, for example, the installation of a cooperative for collecting and recycling garbage. That project was also highly influenced by changes in government that affected community development policies, because some of the actions required subsidies from the City Council (e.g. training courses, creation of small businesses).

14.5.3 Perceived value by the users

At the beginning of the programme, a long-term plan was produced by using a Logical Framework, in which the programme goal, purposes, objectives, expected results and actions to be undertaken were organised in a hierarchical structure. Logical Framework is a tool that is used to establish a logical hierarchy of means by which objectives will be reached. It has been widely used in government programmes for planning actions and outcomes, providing support for project control and evaluation. The general structure of a Logical Framework is a matrix, in which the lines depict project outcomes in hierarchical levels (goal, purpose, results and actions), while columns present the description of activities, indicators, means of verification and assumptions for each level (Australian Government, 2000).

This structure was divided into seven matrices: one that provides an overview of the programme (Figure 14.5), one matrix for depicting the programme purpose, four matrices for detailing the specific projects and an additional matrix related to participatory processes. The programme long-term goal was expressed in a very general way: to improve the quality of living of the population of the PIEC area. The project purpose, the urban restructuring of the northern region of the city, can be regarded as the main consequence of the implementation of the four projects below. At the third level, the aim of each project is defined by a set of expected results. Finally, the results are broken down into actions that should be developed. This structure outlines to some extent the relationships between lower level outcomes (results and short-term outputs) and higher levels outcomes (long-term results), showing some similarities to the conceptual model proposed by Woodruff (1997). Therefore, this matrix should make explicit the actions which contribute for attaining each of the specific project results and achieving the programme purpose and goal, enabling a consistency analysis to be carried out.

Although the Logical Framework was useful for initial planning, it has not been fully implemented. None of the matrices was updated considering changes in the scope of the programme, and some of them were not filled out correctly – assumptions and performance indicators were left blank or poorly defined. For that reason, during this research project, an overall revision of the Logical Framework matrices was carried out, including a refinement of the aims of the programme and actions being undertaken.

Based on that revision, a set of constructs was defined for the evaluation of PIEC. Those constructs were organised in three hierarchical levels (Figure 14.6) according to the programme goal and purpose and the project objectives. At the top level, seven constructs were used for assessing the programme goal: education, income and employment,

PROGRAMME GOAL Enhance the quality of living of the population from northern neighborhoods				
PROGRAMME PURPOSE Urban restructuring of the northern region of the city				
Projects				
Social housing project	Urban infrastructure project	landscape improvement project	Social work project	
			Income generation and employment opportunities	Community development

OBJECTIVES

Enhance the habitability conditions of the population	Improve the road systems in the neighbourhoods	Enhance the landscape of the neighbourhoods	Create alternatives for income generation and employment opportunities for the population	Support community development

RESULTS

1. Areas for the development of the Housing and Income Generation Project 2. Housing interventions and provision of health and education services 3. Families living in the new housing units	1. Road circulation studies 2. Areas available for developing the urban Infrastructure Project 3. Construction of road infrastructure 4. Construction of water flood control and drainage systems	1. Recovery, enhancement and maintenance of recreational areas 2. Landscaping of new open spaces	1. Creation of two garbage recycling facilities 2. Creation of a centre to support regional economic development 3. Creation of product and services cooperative (CONSTRUSOL)	1. Community mobilisation and organisation 2. Actions related to social policies

Figure 14.5 PIEC logical framework overview.

Quality of living of the population of the northern neighbourhoods (Matrix 1)						
Education	Income and employment	Credit access	Retention	Identity	Safety	Appearance
Urban restructuring of the northern region of the city (Matrix 2)						
Spatial orientation		Accessibility and spatial continuity			Centrality	
Project objectives						
Social housing project (Matrix 3)	Urban infrastructure project (Matrix 4)	Landscape improvement project (Matrix 5)	Social work project (community development + income generation and employment opportunities projects) (Matrix 6)		Participatory processes (Matrix 7)	
Quality of the housing unit Quality of the housing estates Quality of urban equipment	Quality of infrastructure	Quality of landscape project	Influence of the social work project		Influence of participatory processes	

Figure 14.6 Set of constructs used in the evaluation of PIEC.

credit access, retention, identity, security and appearance. In the interviews with City Council, the housing retention rate (e.g. the percentage of families that stayed in the housing estates after the intervention) was pointed out as a major indicator of success for the programme. It was assumed that most of the population should remain in the housing estates for the main programme goal to be achieved.

At the purpose level, three constructs were used: (i) spatial orientation, which is related to the ease of moving within the urban space, (ii) accessibility and spatial continuity, which refer to the provision of easy access to specific spaces (housing, recreational facilities, parks), and (iii) centrality, which is concerned with the identification of core spaces that play a major role in meetings and social activities. Finally, two types of constructs were used for assessing the effectiveness of the specific projects and participatory processes: degree of satisfaction and perception of importance by the users.

Some of the results of the programme evaluation are presented below, focusing on the connection between some deliverables (Social Housing and the Social Work Projects) and outcomes (housing retention, income generation and employment opportunities). As the long-term aim of this type of programme is to promote the inclusion of poor communities in the formal city, this analysis must be regarded as a partial evaluation of PIEC, which can be used for providing feedback to some stakeholders.

Table 14.2 presents a comparison of household profiles before (2001) and after (2006 or 2008) the delivery of the new housing estates. Based on that data, some general improvements were identified in all housing estates: (i) increase in educational levels (especially at the secondary school level), (ii) better employment status of family providers (overall increase of formal employment and self-employment; decrease of informal jobs), (iii) increase in the ownership of vehicles. There was also an increase in the relative percentage of women as family providers and in the percentage of families with children, which may be an indirect impact of other improvements: families that have an adequate house and a stable income have better conditions to raise children. The same data also indicates that the Santa Teresinha allotment seems to be substantially different from the other ones. The educational level of the family provider was lower than the average, as well as the level of formal employment. In fact, this was one of the poorest allotments in the PIEC area. There was a large percentage of the families working in garbage collection and recycling, and several problems related to drug trafficking were reported.

Of course, the analysis of household profiles should also consider the housing retention rate, since the improvements in some of the figures might be related to the gentrification phenomenon. In fact, some important changes have happened in the neighbourhood close to the PIEC area, including the construction of a large football stadium and the development of several residential projects for the middle class segment. Those changes made the PIEC area more attractive for the population with a higher income level. Table 14.3 presents the retention rate for the five housing estates. In three of them it was possible to compare that rate at two different points in time (2006 and 2012).

Due to the lack of indicators available on housing retention from other programmes and projects in Brazil, it was hard to assess whether the performance of PIEC housing estates was low or high in absolute terms. On one hand, it is worth mentioning that the initial housing retention rate (above 70%) was much higher than expected by the technical staff of the City Council. Considering that the population had a very low income, many of them expected that a large percentage of families would sell the units informally as soon as they moved in. On the other hand, there was strong evidence of gentrification in the Progresso housing estate: the retention rate reduced substantially

Table 14.2 Change in the profile of families in five housing estates.

PIEC housing estates		First phase						Second phase			
		Vila Tecnológica		Pôr do Sol		Progresso		Arco Íris		Santa Teresinha	
Profile of the head of the family		City C. (%)	POE (%)	City C. (%)	POE (%)	City C. (%)	POE (%)	City C. (%)	POE (%)	City C. (%)	POE (%)
Gender	Female	39.58	48.57	49.48	66.1	52.63	41.17	52.9	57.4	30.3	55.9
	Male	60.41	51.42	50.51	33.92	47.36	58.83	47.1	42.6	69.7	44.1
	Total	100	100	100	100	100	100	100	100	100	100
Education level	Illiterate	8.33	0	2.06	1.79	8.95	4.41	4.6	6.9	13.4	**6.1**
	Elementary incomplete	72.92	71.42	71.13	55.36	**70.5**	55.88	72.4	62.1	72	80.3
	Elementary complete	8.33	5.71	13.40	26.79	10	20.58	11.8	6.9	9.1	4.5
	Secondary	6.25	22.85	12.37	14.29	8.42	19.11	11.2	24.1	5.5	9.1
	Total	95.83	100	98.9	98.2	97.89	100	100	100	100	100
Occupation	Formally employed	39.58	48.57	27.83	37.5	**25.2**	38.24	15.8	37.9	5.6	13.2
	Unemployed	4.66	11.43	7.21	7.14	9.47	14.71	6.6	12.1	0.6	1.5
	Does not work	12.5	11.43	21.64	21.42	17.89	10.29	27.0	19	8.7	17.6
	Informally employed	31.25	5.71	30.92	8.92	28.94	13.24	40.1	13.8	70.8	51.5
	Retired	2.08	2.86	6.18	14.28	9.47	7.35	2.6	5.2	0	5.9
	Self-employed	10.41	17.14	6.18	10.71	8.94	11.76	7.9	12.1	14.3	10.3
	Total	100	97.14	100	100	98.5	100	100	100	100	100
Ownership of vehicle	No	78.69	71.42	82.44	67.85	79.74	73.53	77.6	65.6	38.2	**61.8**
	Car	1.64	0	3.81	0	**9.91**	1.47	6.4	1.7	1.2	0
	Paper collecting trolley	1.64	0	2.29	0	1.29	4.41	0.6	0	56.4	25
	Car or truck	8.2	28.57	11.45	32.14	7.76	19.12	15.4	32.8	4.2	13.2
	Total	90.16	100	100	100	100	100	100	100	100	100
Age	Mean (years)	38.3	39.9	42.7	41.9	38.7	39.36	40.8	41	42.6	38.7

Table 14.3 Housing retention rate for five housing estates.

Housing retention rate	First phase housing estates			Second phase housing estates	
	Vila Tecnológica	Pôr do Sol	Progresso	Arco Íris	Santa Teresinha
2006	77% (3.5 years)	79% (2.5 years)	71% (3 years)		
2008				70% (1 year)	72% (1.5 years)
2013	68% (9 years)	48% (8 years)	24% (8.5 years)		

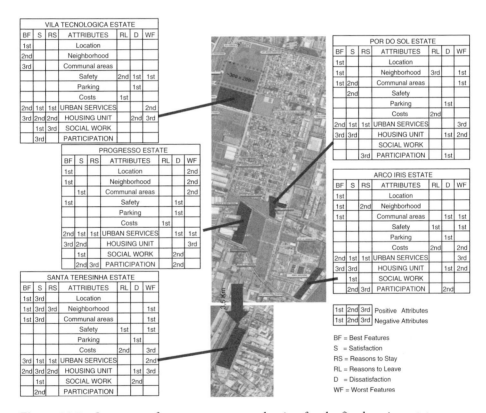

Figure 14.7   Summary of post-occupancy evaluation for the five housing estates.

in 5.5 years, despite the fact that this was the housing estate with the highest degree of satisfaction in 2006.

Figure 14.7 presents a summary of the post-occupancy evaluation of the five housing estates. In all of them, location was pointed out as the best feature – this confirms the importance of keeping the communities near where they used to live. The attributes concerned with urban infrastructure services (e.g. water, sewage, electricity) had the highest level of satisfaction among all categories. The chi-square test identified an association ($p < 0.05$) of these sub-products with the degree of overall satisfaction, which further reinforced this conclusion. Moreover, the supply of water, energy and sewage systems was also extensively mentioned as one of the main reasons for staying in the housing estates. The second most important reason for staying was the relationship with neighbours and the area of the housing unit.

By contrast, the attributes related to the allotment and housing units had in general a higher frequency in the dissatisfaction categories. The most frequent reasons for leaving the housing estates were the occupancy costs (occupancy tax, electricity and water bills) and problems related to the design of the housing unit. It is also worth mentioning that violence and crime also appeared as major reasons for leaving the Arco-Íris and Santa Teresinha housing estates.

Both the Social Work Project and the Participatory Processes had high levels of satisfaction in most attributes. However, none of them were mentioned in the survey as important in any of the housing estates. Indeed, there was a large percentage of missing answers in the evaluation of those attributes, mostly due to the fact that many households had not participated in the actions related to them – some did not even know that these were undertaken.

14.6 Discussion and conclusions

This chapter presents the evaluation of a complex urban redevelopment project, by analysing the project delivery system and assessing the partial results of the programme based on the perception of the final users.

Despite the introduction of some managerial innovations, such as the integrated programme core management team, an online software tool to monitor the programme and mechanisms for the participation of final users in decision-making, there were many challenges in the implementation of PIEC. Some of them were intrinsically related to the scale and complex nature of integrated urban development programmes (e.g. changes in government, combination of different sources of funding), while others can be explained by the underlying theory of traditional project management, in which a certain level of predictability and order is assumed (Snowden and Boone, 2007). In fact, there were many problems related to the lack of coordination between projects and collaboration among different organisational units, and much emphasis was given to the physical progress of individual projects.

This study confirms that the traditional project management approach fails to appropriately deal with the influences of a dynamic social, economic and political context that are typical of urban redevelopment projects. Although more than 10 years have passed since the beginning of the programme, its scope is still being re-evaluated and adapted according to new understandings of priorities and ways to overcome obstacles. As described by Simon (1997), this is a continuous design process of identifying the best possible solution, based on the information available at a given moment in time.

Some improvement opportunities have been identified in the existing programme management system and are summarised below:

1. Make a continuous effort to model user requirements, considering the need to make trade-offs, as well to capture emerging requirements, such as in the Benefits Realisation approach (Thorp, 1998). Those requirements must be clearly connected to the project strategy (goals and purpose);
2. Replace the traditional view of project control, replacing the approach of simply monitoring physical progress (management as adhering) by a focus on the realisation of benefits. This new approach must provide flexibility, so that learning is encouraged (management as learning; Koskela and Howell, 2002), and adaptations are allowed to be carried out, coping with changes in the programme context.
3. Implement approaches that encourage collaborative work between project participants, which is more appropriate for the context of complex projects, as suggested by Williams (2002). A wide range of innovations could be introduced, such as work in multi-disciplinary teams, systematic management of commitments (Isatto *et al.*, 2015), mechanisms for community participation and the use of Building Information Modelling for modelling products and processes.
4. Improve the effectiveness of community development initiatives associated to social housing and urban development programmes. The assessment of PIEC indicated that the importance of the Social Work project was limited, especially due to the lack synchronisation with the delivery of the housing units. Further research work seems to be necessary to identify improvement opportunities in those initiatives.
5. Introduce innovative forms of contracts, which allow the early involvement of stakeholders in the project, and create opportunities for collaborative work, similar to what has been achieved in other countries with the introduction of relational contracts and other similar types of governance instruments (Zimina *et al.*, 2012).

Regarding the assessment of urban redevelopment programmes from the perspective of the final users, this chapter proposed a conceptual model for connecting product and service attributes and values, based on the conceptualisation proposed by Woodruff *et al.* (1993) and Woodruff (1997). At the lowest level of the hierarchy, two main constructs were used to assess products and services: degree of satisfaction and perception of importance. The evaluation of PIEC at that level was divided into four components: Social Housing, Urban Infrastructure, Landscape and Social Work. The second level was concerned with the consequences of the product and service attributes in terms of urban restructuring of the PIEC area, being concerned with three main constructs: spatial orientation, accessibility and spatial continuity and centrality. At the top level, seven constructs were established to express the main benefits of PIEC for the final users, that is, they pointed out how the programme contributes for improving the quality of living of the target community. Those constructs were not identified at the beginning of the programme, but were made explicit in this investigation.

The housing retention construct was emphasised in this chapter, due to its importance for the success of urban redevelopment programmes. The retention rate was relatively high in the first six years of PIEC, but had a substantial reduction in two of the housing estates at its 10th year, indicating a trend of gentrification, probably caused by the fact that the PIEC area became much more attractive in recent years for other housing market segments.

Two concepts that came from the field of Marketing (user perceived value and satisfaction) were useful for creating the logical connection between different hierarchical levels of the conceptual framework. The satisfaction and importance constructs were used for assessing the performance of project attributes. These results, combined with the identification of the main sacrifices and benefits perceived by users and the key reasons for staying or leaving the housing estates, provided some insights on how value was generated in this programme.

References

AIA (2007) *Integrated project delivery: a guide.* American Institute of Architects California Council, Los Angeles.

Atkinson, R., Crawford, L., Ward, S. (2006) Fundamental uncertainties in projects and the scope of project management. *International Journal of Project Management* **24**, 687–698.

Australian Government(2000) *Ausguidelines: The Logical Framework Approach.* Overseas Aid Programme – AusAID, Australian Government, Canberra.

Baccarini, D. (1996) The concept of project complexity – a review. *International Journal of Project Management* **14**, 201–204.

Caixa Econômica Federal (2014) *Minha Casa Minha Vida.* Available at: http://www20.caixa.gov. br/Paginas/Noticias/Noticia/Default.aspx?newsID=904 (accessed 11 November 2015).

Cyert, R.M., March, J.G. (1963) *A Behavioural Theory of the Firm.* Prentice Hall, Upper Saddle River.

Gutman, J. (1982) A means–end chain model based on consumer categorization processes. *Journal of Marketing* **46**(2), 60–72.

Formoso, C.T., Leite, F.L., Miron, L.I.G. (2011) Client requirements management in social housing: a case study on the residential leasing program in Brazil. *Journal of Construction in Developing Countries* **16**, 47–67.

Fundação João Pinheiro (2009). *Déficit Habitacional no Brasil 2007.* Ministério das Cidades, Secretaria Nacional de Habitação, Brasília, D.F.

Görög M., Smith N. (1999) *Project Management for Managers.* Project Management Institute, Sylva.

Hentschke, C.S., Formoso, C.T., Rocha, C.G., Echeveste, M.E.S. (2014) A method for proposing value-adding attributes in customized housing. *Sustainability* **6**, 9244–9267.

Isatto, E.L., Azambuja, M., Formoso, C.T. (2015) The role of commitments for the management of construction make-to-order supply chains. *Journal of Management in Engineering, ASCE* **30**, 92–97.

Keivani, R., Abiko, A., Werna, E. (2004) *Pluralism in Housing Provision in Developing Countries: Lessons from Brazil.* Nova Science, New York.

Khalifa, S. (2004) Customer value: a review of recent literature and an integrative configuration. *Management decision* **42**(5), 645–666.

Koskela, L.J., Howell, G. (2002) The underlying theory of project management is obsolete. In: *Proceedings of PMI Research Conference 2002: Frontiers of Project Management Research and Application,* 14–17 July 2002, Project Management Institute, Seattle, pp. 293–302.

Lehtonen, M. (2004) The environmental–social interface of sustainable development: capabilities, social capital, institutions. *Ecological Economics* **49**, 199–214.

Malhotra, N.K. (2004) *Marketing Research: an Applied Orientation*. Pearson Education, Delhi.

Miller R., Hobbs, B. (2005) Governance regimes for large complex projects. *Project Management Journal* **36**(3), 42–50.

Minnery, J., Argo, T., Winarso, H., Hau, D., Veneracion, C.C., Forbes, D., Childs, I. (2013) Slum upgrading and urban governance: case studies in three South East Asian cities. *Habitat International* **39**, 162–169.

Monroe, K.B. (1990) *Pricing: Making Profitable Decisions*. McGraw-Hill, New York.

Oliver, R.L.A. (1980) Cognitive model of the antecedents and consequences of satisfaction decisions. *Journal of Marketing Research* **17**(4), 460–469.

Patel, K. (2013) A successful slum upgrade in Durban: a case of formal change and informal continuity. *Habitat International* **40**, 211–217.

Project Management Institute (2004) *A Guide to the Project Management Body of Knowledge*, 3rd edn (PMBOK® Guide). Project Management Institute, San Francisco.

Ravald, A., Gronroos, C. (1996) The value concept and relationship marketing. *European Journal of Marketing* **30**(2), 19–30.

Rittel, H.W.J., Webber, M.M. (1973) Dilemmas in a general theory of planning. *Policy Sciences* **4**, 165–169.

Saliba, M., Fisher, C. (2000) Managing customer value: a framework allows organisations to achieve and sustain competitive advantage. *Quality Progress* **33**(6), 63–69.

Sanchéz-Fernandez, R., Iniesta-Bonillo, M.A. (2007) The concept of perceived value: a systematic review of the research. *Marketing Theory* **7**(4), 427–451.

Schilderman, T., Ruskulis, O.E. (2005) *Building Bridges with the Grass Roots: Scaling-up Through Knowledge Sharing*. ITDG Publishing, Bradford.

Simon, H.A. (1997) *Administrative behavior: a study of decision-making processes in administrative organizations*. Free Press, New York.

Snowden, D.J., Boone, M.E. (2007) A leader's framework for decision making. *Harvard Business Review*, November, pp. 3–6.

Thiry, M. (2002) Combining value and project management into an effective programme management model. *International Journal of Project Management* **20**(3), 221–228.

Thompson, H. (1998). What do your customer really want? *Journal of Business Strategy*, July–August, pp. 17–21.

Thorp, J. (1998) *The Information Paradox: Realising the Business Benefits of Information Technology*, McGraw-Hill, Toronto.

Tillmann, P., Tzortzopoulos, P., Formoso, C.T. (2010) Redefining healthcare infrastructure: moving towards integrated solutions. *HERD Journal* **3**, 84–96.

Williams, T. (2002) *Modelling Complex Projects*. John Wiley & Sons, Ltd, Chichester.

Winch, G. (2006) Towards a theory of construction as production by projects. *Building Research and Information* **34**(2), 164–174.

Winter, M., Smith, C., Morris, P., Cicmil, S. (2006) Directions for future research in project management: the main findings of UK government-funded research network. *International Journal of Project Management* **24**(8), 638–649.

Woodruff, R.B. (1997) Customer value: the next source of competitive advantage. *Journal of the Academy of Marketing Science* **25**(2), 139–153.

Woodruff, R.B., Schumann, D.W., Gardial, S.F. (1993) Understanding value and satisfaction from the customer's point of view. *Survey of Business* **29**(1), 33–40.

Zimina, D., Ballard, G., Pasquire, C. (2012) Target value design: using collaboration and a lean approach to reduce construction cost. *Construction Management and Economics* **30**(5), 383–398.

Chapter 15
Integrating Sustainable Urban Development

Stephen Curwell
Heys Environmental, Oldham, OL3 5RL, UK

15.1 Problem realisation

The most important outcome of the United States (US) space programme has been the view of the earth from space (Figure 15.1). This image is one of the most viewed on the internet and has had a profound influence upon how the whole of mankind feels about the Earth: the beautiful blue, but lonely home planet, slowly revolving on a slightly tilted axis on its 'annual' turn around the nearest star – the sun. So fundamental is this time-scale and the way it controls how energy from the sun falls on the surface; it drives the seasonal and daily climate, the weather and carbon cyclical patterns, the 'tune' to which we can observe all natural and human life 'dances'.

The image has also made us recognise the potential fragility of the planetary system and to think more deeply about the ways that human activity can perturb it. Despite the naysayers it is clear that humankind had been damaging the system long before the current concerns over excessive global warming arose. In earlier times effects tended to be more localised and direct, for example, the very poor air quality in the United Kingdom's (UK's) industrial towns caused by the use of coal for heating and power, but we now recognise longer-term effects from this fossil fuel use in the destruction through acid rainfall of large areas of peat in the upland areas of the UK (with an associated additional release of CO_2). However it was not until the problem with ozone depletion and the commensurate danger of loss of ultraviolet protection at the surface caused by indiscriminate release of man-made chemicals – chlorofluorocarbons (CFCs) – that it was clearly demonstrated that human activity can have truly global consequences. This galvanised political opinion to create the first truly international environmental action – the Montreal Protocol, enacted to control the release of CFCs that had been used as propellants in a wide variety of aerosol spray-cans, as refrigerants and as foaming agents in insulation materials. We are now witnessing the increase in skin melanomas as a direct result of this misuse of otherwise valuable chemicals that began in the 1970s and where the US Environmental Protection Agency has advised it may take up to 100 years for the ozone layer to recover. So we have already done lasting damage to the 'system' that

Future Challenges in Evaluating and Managing Sustainable Development in the Built Environment,
First Edition. Edited by Peter S. Brandon, Patrizia Lombardi and Geoffrey Q. Shen.
© 2017 John Wiley & Sons Ltd. Published 2017 by John Wiley & Sons Ltd.

Figure 15.1   The view of the Earth from Space.

maintains us and now it has become accepted, even by the most recalcitrant of nations, that international action is necessary to address global warming as well as a range of other environmental issues.

The potential problems facing us are much wider than that posed by excessive warming of the atmosphere, as difficult as that is to address. The recent Dresden Nexus conference held in 2015 brought together engineers and engineering researchers from all over the globe to address the wide range of current concerns over the planetary 'system' (Costanza and Kubiszewski, 2015) and at which five headlines were noted by this contributor:

1. Four times increase in CO_2 since 1950;
2. 40% more water needed and potentially 50% of mankind in water stress by 2035;
3. 70% urbanisation of population by 2050;
4. By 2100 there will be 11 billion inhabitants on the planet of which seven billion will live in cities;
5. 58% overshoot in resource use.

So we are entering a frenetic hothouse age where there will be a constant trend toward urbanisation and a consequent extension of the overshoot of resource use. The prospect is frightening and one has to ask, where are the other two planets that will be needed to supply these bourgeoning needs?

15.2 Towards a solution

Since the emergence of the 'Club of Rome' and their early concerns over resources, the overall solution(s) mooted to date have been founded on the concept of sustainable development (SD). Early ideas typified by 'Limits to Growth' were static, as illustrated by the three-pillar model of SD (Environmental, Economic and Social dimensions), or the less used or usual four-pillar model that underlay the UNEP's first SD indicator set (Figure 15.2). Although sociologists consider institutions as part of the social domain the four-pillar model is useful because it identifies institutions as a factor in SD and the inertia they present as a potential barrier to progress towards a more sustainable world.

In contrast and with a focus on the urban environment, the former BEQUEST research network in the European Union (EU; Bentevegna *et al.*, 2002) developed a dynamic or 'process' view of sustainable urban development (SUD) that emphasises that there can be no fixed end point or fixed state of SUD and that we need to move from where we are (in cities) through incremental change towards a less resource-intensive situation (less land grabbing, less energy etc.) whilst maintaining a good quality of life (good environment, jobs, income, social contact, culture etc.). In this vision progress towards more SUD is relative, rather than absolute, and assessment has to *integrate* all the four pillars, combining environmental protection with economic and social prosperity through appropriate institutional change. Such processes are not new in urban and operational planning: benchmarking (the situation) at the outset of a change programme and measuring progress over a (long?) timeframe of implementation has long been understood. In its early (possibly the first?) attempt to achieve a common understanding of SUD across professional actors in the EU BEQUEST's early SUD Toolkit in 2001 tried to operationalise this

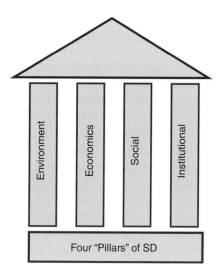

Figure 15.2   The 'Pillars' of sustainable development.

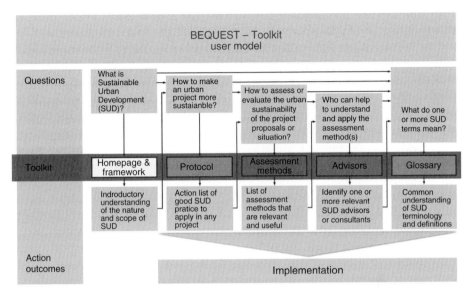

Figure 15.3 Elements of the BEQUEST Toolkit and how to use them.

process (Figure 15.3) and is typical of a large number of other tools that have followed, being based on three central tenets.

The first of these tenets we can call *environmental education*; that is, if we all understand the problem(s) better then we will change our behaviour, for example, by using less energy, using public transport rather than private motor cars, eating less meat, clocking-up fewer air miles (both for our own transport requirements and for the goods and services we consume) and generally adopting a much less resource intensive lifestyle and so on.

The second tenet is consensus, often referred to as a *shared vision* of the problem(s) of the environment, of society, of the Eco-city, of the path to solutions to the current problems, or what is needed for a good life and so on.

Both these remain part of current thinking, for example, Constanza and Kubiszanski (2014) emphasise these dimensions as a critical first step in scenario planning: 'The development of an evidence based understanding of how the world works, combined with a *shared vision* of how we want (or would prefer?) it to work, are powerful tools to tackle even the most complex and recalcitrant of problems'.

The third tenet is *full systems thinking*. Although the concept is usually traced back to Checkland (1999) there is no universally accepted definition of systems thinking, but 'most would agree that it involves thinking in terms of a whole system rather than its parts, focusing on linkages rather than components and observing patterns rather than content' (Alcamo 2015). In the built environment context it tries to map or model the complex interactions and transactions in the city through integrating environmental, economic and social dimensions in order to better understand the current and potential situation of any proposed development. Urban Sim (2015) is an example of a set of advanced software tools that seeks to operationalise this approach.

This chapter seeks to explore if these three tenets still hold true and whether they are adequate when faced with the sustainable urbanisation challenge hinted at above. Will a consensus-based, integrated systems approach move us in a more sustainable direction? To address these questions the potential challenges to systems integration are explored: first, those emerging from the mixed blessings of globalisation and an increasingly interconnected virtual world and the effect this is having on the changing role of cities; second, the relationship between the city, its hinterland and the potential barriers presented by the political and professional systems govern the development of our urban areas.

15.3 *Globalisation and virtualisation*

In an increasingly globalised society what are cities for? Lewis Mumford (1961) in his classic 'A City in History' explains the functions of a city – the market place located at transport junctions, at the crossing of the river, the natural harbour, the pass through the mountains and so on, but in the emerging affluent global knowledge society (KS) where more people have a cell phone than have a toilet (six billion of the world's seven billion people have access to a cell phone and only 4.5 billion have access to a toilet – *Time Magazine* in 2013) and when in 2015 we reached 40% of the world's population being connected to the Internet from a base of 1% in 1995, then these fundamentals are challenged and perhaps are being overtaken by a new set of drivers. The market, commerce and the world of work (and play) are increasingly global, separated from the need for physical proximity. The fundamental need for trade and housing are increasingly taken for granted and are being overtaken by concerns over quality of life and leisure measured in terms of ease of access to a good (natural and urban) and healthy environment as well as to cultural activities on a global scale. All of these are facilitated by good communications: virtual (high-speed Internet) and physical (convenient and cheap air transportation) – making the so-called 'Smart City' the new byword for modernism.

Thus the KS has been an important policy plank in most of the affluent countries. The Lisbon summit held in 2000 began the on-going European policy development towards a sustainable KS in the EU, with an underlying objective of so-called 'soft transformation', that is, an economy based on services rather than the manufacture of goods that supplies growth without the old environmental consequences of pollution, resource depletion and waste. Taken together these changes in society have important implications for urban development. But what does it mean? Will it be Bill Mitchell's e-topian vision of information and communication technologies (ICTs) with the 'intimacy of underwear'? His book (Mitchell, 2000) begins with a requiem for the city as we know it and thankfully some of his worst predictions and concerns do not seem likely to be realised.

Many authors and researchers in urban development and planning have referred to the prospect of the e-agora – a virtual place where consensus over appropriate urban change can be promoted, sought and/or emerge (Figure 15.4); however the jury is out on

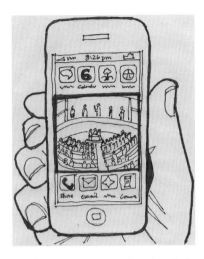

Figure 15.4   The e-agora: a place to integrate virtual and physical space?

whether such a virtual forum can help us to decide what type of (smart? eco?) city we want. But it is important to recognise the link between the emerging KS and more sustainable urban (re)development, that is, the need to integrate the planning and development of virtual space with physical space. This is because the future prosperity of our cities, to attract inward investment and talented people will depend on the provision of a quality environment, measured by a combination of the quality of virtual space, that is, access good quality local information using high speed and advanced communications as well as a good physical environment, home, green-space, workspace and so on, that will support overall wellbeing. There is little evidence of these parallel policy objectives being properly integrated in the planning of the vast majority of our cities in a way that will manage this transformation without major increases in resource usage.

In fact the evidence points towards a migration of talented people towards those centres where such a winning combination has already emerged; London is a good example, putting increased pressure on existing space and infrastructure, mainly falling on the suburban areas and the greenbelt around these cities (Figure 15.5), which is very relevant to the second key area for integration: the relationship between the city and its hinterland.

15.4 The city and its hinterland

What type of (eco-)city do we want? One with increased urban density that is entirely walkable, or one less dense with more green space, its greater space spanned by efficient (non-fossil fuel powered) transportation? In both cases much more could be done to promote 'green' retrofitting of buildings and infrastructure, and for public transport improvements such as those identified by the UK Urban Task Force, once the hierarchical scale of communities is better understood – see Figure 15.6.

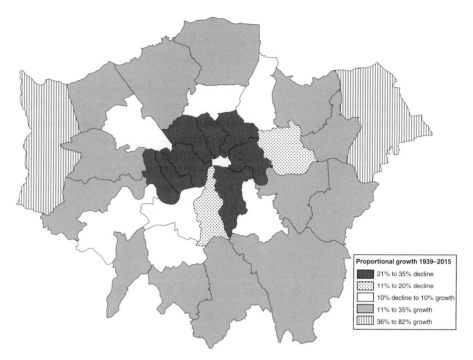

Figure 15.5   London's population growth 1939–2015 (Greater London Authority, 2015).

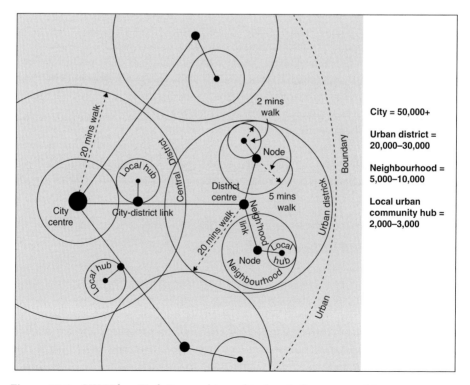

Figure 15.6   UK Urban Task Force – hierarchical scale for communities.

Figure 15.7   Phoenix. Source: Courtesy of Tuca Vieira. Source: Reproduced with permission of Alamy http://www.alamy.com/stock-photo-aerial-sun-city-phoenix-arizona-usa-5722448.html

All these ideas beg the question of how life is changing with respect to the KS and what type of life city residents will seek in future, whether our cities continue to be fit for purpose and how we might adapt them to support a more sustainable KS. One example is Phoenix, Arizona (Figure 15.7) – a city in the desert where everything has to be imported and it is essential to have a car and air conditioning to survive. When this figure is shown in public meetings in Europe people find it hard to understand why such an urban form was ever created but nevertheless development of similar settlements or urban extensions are underway now in the Middle East and other parts of the developing world. Other cities such as Durban, South Africa (Figure 15.8), seems better – close to the centres of food production with better public transportation but exhibiting a huge contrast in wealth between the haves and the have nots. Dealing with such inequalities is among the central SD goals (UNDP, 2015), particularly Goal 11, but it is almost impossible to see how this can be managed without major increase in resource use.

Meanwhile European cities continue to be containers of cultural heritage. Florence, Italy, is many people's ideal city – a beautiful historic city centre ideal for walking in the lovely Mediterranean climate and with a real sense of place which has now almost gone in many other 'modernised' cities. However many of Florence's residents are not so sure because the city is unsuited for many aspects of a modern mobile, ICT-powered society and feel the heritage is strangling modern development which, like in many similar heritage cities, is mainly taking place in the city's hinterland with associated transportation energy use and pollution and loss of agricultural land.

(a)

(b)

Figure 15.8   Durban, South Africa. The gap between rich and poor.

Many of the papers at the recent Berlin Nexus conference mentioned above promote constructive adaption of our cities for a more sustainable future: through environmental and health improvements, additional water production, local food production, alternative energy generation and so on. But the majority of these separate improvements are proposed to be located in the peri-urban area, so the pressure on the immediate city fringe and hinterland is likely to make this the development 'battleground' for the future. How can we fit all this in? Can we find the space? Even if we can, in the vast majority of cities the relationship between the city and its hinterland lacks the integrated planning institutions necessary to control these pressures. Many cities have complex (and dysfunctional?) political structures where historical ward boundaries have little relevance to modern residential communities and transport patterns. It is well understood that the environmental implications of cities are spread over a wide area and some megacities can have a global reach. In the case of water, at the very least planning and pollution control needs to be undertaken over the whole of a river catchment. As can be seen from Figure 15.9, the catchment of the River Severn in the UK includes three cities (Birmingham, Bristol and Cardiff) and 10 other significant settlements from two countries, presenting a real challenge for an integrated systems approach.

15.5 Towards better governance structures

Institutional 'blindness' has been commonplace. A local example from Salford (the joint city with Manchester in the Greater Manchester conurbation made up of 10 metropolitan boroughs) illustrates this well. In the 1980s when a regeneration plan was made to

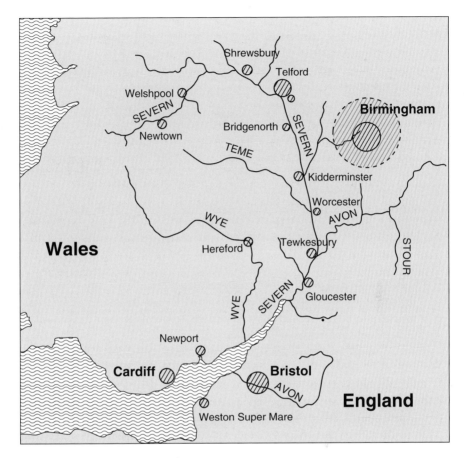

Figure 15.9   River Severn Catchment.

address the serious decline of the original city centre, formerly known as Chapel Street, now Salford Central (Figure 15.10), the proposals failed to show that the area was located just across the River Irwell and thus only a few metres from the central business district of Manchester, which at that time was beginning to boom: a fact that might have been of some interest to an inward investor!

However since then such lessons have been learned and Greater Manchester, now with a population of around 2.7 million, displays admirable institutional development and some of the best examples of cooperation over political boundaries in the UK. In recent years cooperation and integration has continued to develop and in 2011 the Greater Manchester Combined Authority was created with control over economic development, regeneration and transport. The better integrated approach has fostered good progress in waste management (total waste tonnage reduction of over 24% between 2005 and 2010 with the recycling rate up by 36% in the same period) and development of the light rail tramway system to be the largest of all the cities of the UK, with 31.2 million journeys made last year. But why could this cooperation not have happened 25 or even 50 years earlier? The barrier was not only the financial constraint facing the individual

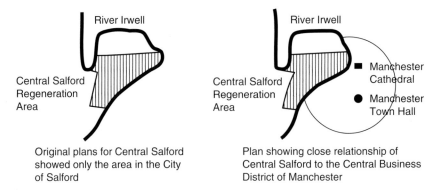

Original plans for Central Salford
showed only the area in the City
of Salford

Plan showing close relationship of
Central Salford to the Central Business
District of Manchester

Figure 15.10   Salford Central regeneration area's proximity to Manchester's central business district.

authorities – new institutional structures were needed with political leadership deploying new skills. Such factors are important to the regeneration of the city, which can now lay claim to be the second most important economic area in the UK outside London with a gross value added of £56 billion.

Can we afford to wait while similar structures and skills are developed in other city regions? If we wish to move more rapidly, nothing less than a radical reorganisation of the way cities *and their hinterlands* are managed and planned is required to enable a whole systems approach to support political decision-making that is more evidence based, more inclusive (through the e-agora?) and more relevant to the emerging needs of citizens who are part of the modern KS, be they resident in the urban core, suburban fringe *or* the hinterland.

Nevertheless even with such radical reorganisation, progress towards more sustainable urban redevelopment solutions is not guaranteed. By this point in time (December 2015) almost every citizen is aware that we can each radically reduce our CO_2 footprint if we consume, drive and fly less. But, as the statistics show, most of us do not choose to reduce our individual demands; and in some areas, such as air transport, demand is rapidly increasing – passenger kilometres have doubled since the mid-1990s (International Civil Aviation Authority, 2105). In fact the low cost air carriers have opened access to air travel to everyone regardless of status or income in an enviably democratic way, but the downside is that northern Europeans now expect to be able to go skiing every winter and to the Mediterranean sun in the summer. It is seen almost as a right. So after 30 years of research and development on the topic of SD this author despairs at this form of denial. It calls into question the first tenet of SD listed above, namely environmental education; that is, if we all understand the problem(s) better then we will change our behaviour. So all decision-makers; the politicians and urban professional actors (planners, urban designers and the construction professions) have all to face-up to the fact that 'information does not necessarily lead to increased awareness, and increased awareness does not necessarily lead to action [these] must be backed up by other approaches' (Collins *et al.*, 2003). There are many reasons for this lack of action, including mixed messages from politicians and confusion created by a range of views and proposals from the 'experts' undermining faith in proposed solutions to urban problems. The wider issue of loss of faith in politics and even in democracy itself is also a factor.

15.6 *Mind the skills gap*

Other major contributory factors include the long-standing professional educational deficit as recognised in the UK's Sustainable Community Development Skill's review, as well as what was christened in the early BEQUEST project as the 'regeneration imperative', a form of skills gap in the political domain.

The UK skills review (DCLG, 2004) identified eight skills areas expressed diagrammatically in what has become known as the Egan wheel, after the chairman of the review (Figure 15.11). However more importantly and in what can be seen as a quite damning indictment of the built environment professions almost 20 years after SD had been recognised, it listed six important areas where professional skills are lacking:

1. Communication between disciplines is not always effective.
2. There are sometimes gaps in the skills, knowledge and understanding needed to make partnership really work.
3. Examples of good practice that do exist are often not shared or even identified, so crucial opportunities to learn from the past are lost.
4. We lack enough skilled people across the professions – architecture, planning, housing and transport (*and we can add water engineers and urban agronomists and ecologists*).
5. We lack people with generic skills such as communication, project management and community engagement.
6. Too many professionals involved in shaping communities work in isolation from one another.

This range of concerns can be summarised simply as an almost complete lack of a joined-up coordinated systems approach! The complete opposite of what seems essential to support SUD and this lack of integration continues as possibly the most significant barrier to progress towards SD in the affluent countries. One could propose, as many have, significant adjustments to the education and formation of the individual professions but something more radical is needed, redefining the concept of urban redevelopment itself and who is responsible for leading it. In an age of community action we need to make much more space for the community to lead the process and define its collective need(s), perhaps in the way proposed in Regenerative Design, which attempts to go beyond environmental protection and simple economic development and seeks to leave the environment (physical, natural, social and economic) in a better, healthier state after an urban intervention. The UK skills review highlights the inability to learn from good practice. Given a choice, professional actors prefer to learn through practical examples, case studies and pilots. There are an enormous number of cases, see the UK Urban Design Compendium (HCA, 2013), but as work by Deakin and others has shown these cases tend to show only one or two good sustainability features and may even have many

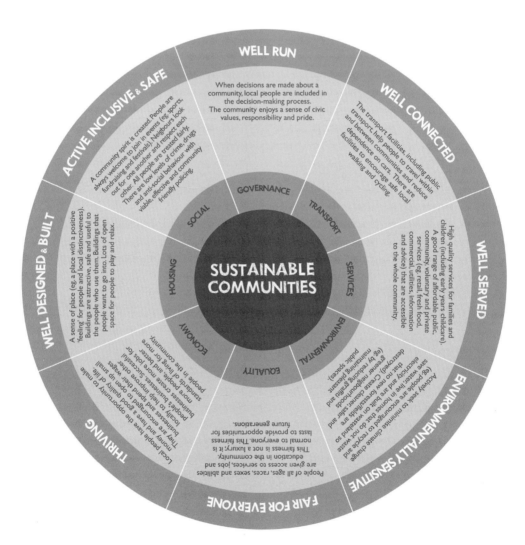

Figure 15.11   The Egan wheel (with the addition of Equity added subsequently).
Source: Reproduced with permission of The Geographical Association.

more that are negative when exposed to an integrated assessment. Professionals need to review these so-called good example case studies with a much more critical eye shaped by the wider systems thinking alluded to earlier in this chapter. Each case study in urban development is so location-specific that it is very difficult and sometimes downright wrong to apply experience from one place in another cultural, environmental or climatic context. So research and practice need to draw out codified learning from previous 'good' examples that has *universal* application.

Case studies are also important in the political arena and can often trigger the regeneration imperative, an ongoing barrier to proper system thinking over urban development in democratic countries. Politicians are driven by the need to show some results (for an investment or a change of policy) within the four- to five-year electoral cycle. Sustainability experts, including the author of this chapter, have railed against such short-sightedness when confronted with the long-time frames (10 years plus) involved in urban development and renewal, especially when hasty, ill-considered actions result in unintended consequences. However with longer experience professional actors can and must begin to accept it as a necessary constraint on urban redevelopment. We have to find ways to work within and perhaps even harness it in the cause of better SUD outcomes – seeking a common vision that can have cross-party political support is one of these ways and regularly updating the vision to respond to changing circumstance is another. This means that professionals need to develop political antennae and tune-up their community and political skills and engage more fully in the political debate over options and potentialities; and again this signals a much deeper engagement with the community as viewed in a very wide sense, not just the residents, but the *whole community system*: residents, business, investors and the banks, social clubs and societies, schools, politicians, transport providers, utility providers and so on.

So, to return to the original question, will a consensus-based, integrated systems approach move us in a more sustainable direction, towards so-called one planet living? Perhaps the answer is a guarded 'yes', but we need to rethink Homer-Dixon (2008) in planning for 'the upside of down' so that good-quality, but less resource-intense lifestyles can emerge. To do this will require the forms of co-production of change implied in the integrated approaches espoused above. The upshot is that professionals have to completely rethink their role and see themselves not just as experts but as community enablers, facilitators and *integrators*. The danger of a whole system approach is that the problem seems to expand exponentially and become so complex as to be unsolvable and there is no denying that modern computer tools can have a role to play here. However the output of such analyses has to be understandable by the non-technical citizen, because key to success is the development of trust between citizens, professional advisors and the politicians. The view of the planet from space, or a video of an iceberg detaching from the ice shelf and crashing into the sea make a much simpler, more powerful message about saving the planetary systems than pages and pages of environmental statistics. So professionals should seek to make the complicated simple and not the reverse. Here again simulation tools and virtual reality can give citizens a better 'handle' to get to grips with complex proposals, but they cannot substitute for sound advice and advocacy. The biggest compliment ever paid to the writer came after a difficult consultation with a community group over an urban design proposal when one resident declared that the solution seemed obvious and did not understand what all the previous fuss was about, which was quite funny really because her comments were not intended as a compliment at all, in fact quite the opposite!

References

Alcamo, J. (2015) *Systems Thinking for Advancing a Nexus Approach to Water, Soil and Waste,* Dresden Nexus Conference Report, Nexus, Dresden.

Bentevegna, V., Curwell, S.R., Deakin, M., Lombardi, P., Mitchell, G., Nijkamp, P. (2002) A vision and methodology for integrated sustainable urban development: BEQUEST. *Building Research and Information* **30**(2), 79–82.

Checkland, P. (1999) *Systems Thinking, Systems Practice.* John Wiley & Sons, Ltd, Chichester.

Collins, J., Thomas, G., Willis, G., Wilsdon, J. (2003) *Demos/Green Alliance: Carrots, Sticks and Sermons: Influencing Public Behaviour for Environmental Goals.* Available at: http://www.demos.co.uk/files/CarrotsSticksSermons.pdf (accessed 22 March 2016).

Constanza, R., Kubiszewski, I. (2015) *A Nexus Approach to Urban and Regional Planning using the Four Capital Model of Ecological Economics.* DNC2015 Position Paper. UNU-FLORES, Dresden.

DCLG (2004) *The Egan Review: Skills for Sustainable Communities.* Department for Communities and Local Government. Available at: http://resources.cohesioninstitute.org.uk/Publications/Documents/Document/DownloadDocumentsFile.aspx?recordId=157&file=PDFversion (accessed 22 March 2016).

Greater London Authority (2015) *GLA Intelligence: Population Growth in London, 1939–2015.* Available at: https://files.datapress.com/london/dataset/population-change-1939-2015/historical%20population%201939-2015.pdf (accessed 22 March 2016).

Homer-Dixon, T. (2008) *The Upside of Down: Catastrophe, Creativity, and the Renewal of Civilization.* Island Press, Washington, D.C.

Mitchell, W. J. (2000) *E-topia.* MIT Press, Cambridge, MA.

Mumford, L. (1961) *The City in History.* Harcourt, Brace and World, San Diego.

Urban Sim (2015) *Urban Sim.* Available at: http://www.urbansim.com/(accessed 22 March 2016).

UNDP (2015) *Sustainable Development Goals (SDGs).* United Nations Development Programme. Available at: http://www.undp.org/content/undp/en/home/sdgoverview/post-2015-development-agenda.html (accessed 22 March 2016).

Further reading

Curwell, S.R., Lombardi, P. (2002) BEQUEST project: methodological framework for Sustainable Urban Development, *Urbanistica* **117**, 22–27 (Italian), 45–50 (English).

Curwell, S.R., Deakin, M., Symes, M. (2005) *Sustainable Urban Development. Volume 1: Sustainable Urban Development: the Framework and Protocols for Environmental Assessment.* Routledge, London

Curwell, S.R., Deakin, M., Vreeker, R. (2008) *Sustainable Urban Development. Volume 3: Sustainable Urban Development: The Toolkit for Assessment.* Routledge, London.

Curwell, S., Hamilton, A., Marshall-Ponting, A., Soubra, S., Vankeisbelck, R. (2004) Towards intelligent cities. In: *e-Adoption and the Knowledge Economy: Issues, Applications, Case Studies* (eds Cunningham, P., Cunningham, M.). IOS Press, Amsterdam.

Curwell, S., Deakin, M., Hamilton, A., Paskaleva-Shapira, K., Soubra, S., Turner, J. (2004) A research roadmap for sustainable information cities. In: *e-Adoption and the Knowledge Economy: Issues, Applications, Case Studies* (eds Cunningham, P., Cunningham, M.). IOS Press, Amsterdam.

Curwell, S.R. (2004) Towards a new social contract. In: *Buildings, Culture and Environment* (eds R. Cole, R. Lorch). Blackwell Publishing, Oxford.

Curwell, S.R. (2004) BEQUEST – an international cross-cultural co-operation and information exchange. In *Buildings, Culture & Environment* (eds Cole, R., Lorch, R.). Blackwell Publishing, Oxford.

Curwell, S.R., Deakin, M., Lombardi, P. (2000) BEQUEST: the framework and directory of assessment methods. *International Journal of Life Cycle Assessment* **6**(4), 373–383.

HCA (2013) *Urban Design Compendium, 3rd edn*. Homes and Communities Agency. Available at: http://udc.homesandcommunities.co.uk/urban-design-compendium?page_id=&page=1 (accessed 22 March 2016).

International Civil Aviation Authority (2015) *Facts and Figures. World Aviation and the World Economy*. Available at: http://www.icao.int/sustainability/Pages/Facts-Figures_WorldEconomyData. aspx (accessed 22 March 2016).

IOER (2015) *Report on the State of the Nexus Approach 2015: Management of Environmental Resources*. Dresden Nexus Conference 25–27 March 2015. Available at: https://www.ioer.de/fileadmin/internet/Oeffentlichkeitsarbeit/Pressemitteilungen/PDF/DNC15_Report_B5_FINAL_WEB.pdf (accessed 22 March 2016).

Chapter 16
Sustainability – The Role of Construction Contracts

Peter Hibberd
Past Chair of the Joint Contracts Tribunal, London, UK

16.1 Introduction

The focus of this chapter is how construction contracts can be used within the procurement process to achieve sustainable outcomes and to look at their effectiveness and limitations. However it is important to place construction contracts within the context of sustainability, not least because one might justifiably ask not only what have contracts to offer but how important are they in the scale of matters related to sustainability.

Sir Crispin Tickell, in his foreword to James Lovelock's book 'The Revenge of Gaia' reiterates that the first requirement is to recognise the existence of a problem regarding sustainability, the second is to understand the problem and draw the right conclusions and the third is to do something about it. Sustainability is now recognised as a problem, although this recognition is still not universal. Furthermore, even if there were such recognition there is still the issue of what is understood to be the problem: defining the problem is an essential requirement of its understanding. It is unclear to what extent this has been achieved and the nature of any agreement on this matter, or indeed whether it can be achieved at all. Therefore it is a moot point as to whether the problem is fully understood. Without understanding the problem it is not possible to draw reliably the right conclusions: they could of course be reached by chance and although this should not be relied upon it cannot be dismissed entirely for, as Camus put it, there is an absurdity in man's futile search for meaning, unity and clarity in the face of an unintelligible world (Camus, 1942).

There are many different views on sustainability which can, and generally do, include the subject of climate change. This linkage is problematic because the cause of climate change is not universally acknowledged. It is argued that the cause and effect is not established and there is still room for debate (Kelly, 2015). (Professor Kelly is Prince Philip Professor of Technology at Cambridge and a Fellow of the Royal Society.) There is a relationship between climate change and sustainability but there is also a clear distinction. One that not only construction practitioners should recognise

---

Future Challenges in Evaluating and Managing Sustainable Development in the Built Environment,
First Edition. Edited by Peter S. Brandon, Patrizia Lombardi and Geoffrey Q. Shen.
© 2017 John Wiley & Sons Ltd. Published 2017 by John Wiley & Sons Ltd.

(as it is important in the context of construction contracts) but everyone, as sustainability is a topic that deserves attention in its own right.

The position on sustainability is quite different in that there is little room, if any, for debate on the need to ensure sustainability (in this narrower sense) because it is self-evident that, in the context of our own planet, most resources are limited and will suffer depletion through use. Nor is there room for debate on the need for the safe disposal of waste or on the emission of pollutants because of their consequences for health as contrasted to any effect they may have on climate. In essence we are proceeding on an empirical basis and one that clouds a legitimate distinction between climate change and sustainability.

Governments should address matters of great concern and, where the matter is not simply domestic in nature, it is absolutely essential that they work with other governments in an attempt to provide a framework to address any such concerns. The Kyoto Protocol and the Climate Change Act 2008 are examples of government action and what could be described as the highest level of intervention into what we do and possibly how it is achieved. Such intervention is intended to be wide ranging and to create a behavioural shift. It is an important tool but one that has significant shortcomings, namely, it may produce ill-defined or inappropriate objectives; the provision of requirements that either widely understate or overstate what is to be achieved; the belief that one nation will interpret its legislation in a different way to another and the lack of appropriate and enforceable sanctions. However, such shortcomings should not prevent the use of this tool because without it one would rely too heavily on the operation of market forces and action stimulated by the occurrence of events that adversely and directly impinge on large numbers of people. Roger Bootle, in a different context, said 'They (the EU) make rules which are supposed to bring benefit without taking account of the effects. Their (sic) inclination is to believe that behaviour is driven by rules. By contrast, economists know that it is driven by incentives' (Bootle, 2015).

The UK Government recognises that point and has sought to improve the sustainability culture of business, through persuasion, through tax and fiscal incentives, in addition to straightforward statutory regulation such as the planning system, or regulations such as the Code for Sustainable Homes (Communities and Local Government, 2006) and building regulations. Although the Code for Sustainable Homes was withdrawn in 2015 it is still relevant as to how one might address construction contracts.

However, there is a risk that some of these approaches are inadequate in that, at best, they deal with minimum requirements and therefore only provide a partial solution. Much more is required and all promoters of buildings and other construction works need to be persuaded that sustainability is not only worthwhile but necessary: it must be embedded in their thinking. Furthermore, there must be much higher regard to regulations covering how a project is built, not just regulations that determine what can be built. Although construction contracts can be concerned to varying degrees with both aspects and may be seen as a lower order of control, they interact with the wider concept of sustainability.

Much of the current process of providing buildings is inherently inefficient and there is a substantial reform process in place in the United Kingdom (UK) that is designed to increase efficiencies in the procurement of construction. This is driven primarily by the desire to produce a given output for a lower price or, to look at it another way, to produce a greater volume for a proportionately lower price, not to address sustainability but it may have a consequential effect. Producing the same output from lower inputs would generally be seen as beneficial in terms of sustainability but that depends upon the nature of those inputs. Consequently, it would be safer to say it *may* be beneficial because alternative material use and alternative processes with lower costs can, and often do, worsen the situation. In other words economic efficiency in terms of cost may not necessarily be a friend of sustainability. Therefore the funder may be presented with a major problem: can a sustainable solution be justified in commercial terms?

Success in optimising performance and output is achieved by bringing together social, economic and environmental sustainability into the right balance. Finding the right balance will arise by seeking to understand the problem that exists and by coming to a proper conclusion. Regardless of the facts, the right balance will vary according to one's perspective and therefore the concept that there is just one right answer appears flawed.

The idea that sustainability can be tackled through construction contracts (which form part of the legal framework in which the building is constructed) might appear ridiculous. This is particularly so when one looks at the spectrum of activity that includes international frameworks, international treaties, domestic legislation (both primary and secondary) and economic instruments, including tax incentives and education. Such measures are clearly of much greater scale and therefore, not surprisingly, will be seen as far more important. However, if tackling sustainability through construction contracts does appear a little weak it would miss the point, which is that a bottom up approach is as valid as a top down approach. Indeed it is unlikely, if not impossible, to achieve the wider goal without engaging individuals at the lower levels of activity. The Strategy for Sustainable Construction (Cabinet Office, 2008) and later publications (HM Government, 2013) recognise this point and that everyone involved in construction has a role to play. How one constructs buildings and how this is controlled by construction contracts is one such approach to sustainability (as compared with climate change – although it may well also impact on that in some small way).

Construction works take place to fulfil the requirements and aspirations of humans. It is a natural consequence of human development, but as populations grow and the need to fulfil those aspirations expands the impact it has becomes more significant. Significant not only in terms of the visual impact it is has on the natural environment but on the environment more generally. The issue of sustainability arises at many different levels and this poses some awkward questions, the answers to which may prove more than merely uncomfortable. It raises huge philosophical questions such as why are we here and to what end, if any, do we progress. What right do we have to do what we do? Should we create different lifestyles? Philosophical questions such as these are seldom addressed when we consider sustainable construction but this is understandable. In whatever we do there is a wider picture, one which we may or may not see, or one perhaps that we choose not to see. In looking at construction contracts one concentrates on a very small part of what we do but that does not mean we are necessarily unaware of the wider picture – although it might. The important thing is that construction practitioners play their part in addressing sustainability because it is fundamental to the way we, and subsequent generations, will live.

It is clear that sustainability is particularly relevant to construction, not least for the reason that the built environment is responsible for nearly half of the UK's carbon emissions, half of its water consumption, one-third of landfill waste and one-quarter of all raw material used in the economy. Not that surprising because construction is a substantial part of the UK economy, consuming vast amounts of resources, both materials and manpower, and contributes around 7% of Gross Domestic Product (GDP) (Trading Economics, 2015).

In looking at any particular aspect of work, however small that work may be, and its effect on sustainability, we are both consciously and unconsciously influencing how we and others think and act. Construction contracts are no different in that respect. In considering construction contracts it is not simply a matter of looking at what the contract states in order to determine what obligations are imposed but more importantly it is about the means by which construction works are procured and how they are reflected in project documents.

Sustainability in construction has a number of different aspects, namely, those concerned with design, construction and operation. Who it is that considers each of those and when they do so will depend upon the procurement process rather than the contract itself. Put another way, the contract simply reflects the decisions which should have been made already. That situation will only arise when participants in the construction process understand what sustainability means in terms of design, construction and operation and act accordingly. Consideration of matters related to sustainability need to be intrinsic and an inherent component of one's thinking – not a separate consideration. Until then, contracts and especially the accompanying guidance on contracts have a very important role – that of making aware and educating.

Some of these general points and others have been more recently reiterated, for instance: 'Sustainable development is a globally recognized goal. However, governments are failing to reach agreement on how this should be achieved. Private actors that are under stakeholders' pressure try to fill this regulatory gap by developing various types of transnational private regulation. However, transnational private regulation suffers from weak legitimacy, questionable effectiveness, and lack of credible enforcement. Since there is a lack of literature and regulation on this topic, companies use sustainable contract clauses without proper knowledge or guidance why and how this should be done and what legal consequences this may have' (Mitkidis, 2015). The Joint Contracts Tribunal (JCT; an organisation founded in 1931 as a contract authoring body and based in London, UK), through its work, has sought to provide an effective means to overcome such shortcomings.

16.2 The JCT consultation

The JCT recognised the importance of sustainability and that this could be tackled in various ways: that was something which it wanted to explore and why it decided in 2008 to set up its own consultation on sustainability and its relationship with construction contracts (JCT, 2013).

The JCT wanted to see if the incorporation of provisions in guidance notes or contract documentation (including the contract conditions) offered the possibility of a more complete solution, whereby the supply chain could be incentivised to improve sustainability by setting down benchmarks that meet the overall sustainability requirements of a particular stakeholder(s) or specific project(s). A further part of the rationale behind that consultation was to bring together in the minds of industry participants the concepts of sustainability and whole life cycle planning and in doing so to try to uncover how they can better tackle and consequently improve the construction industry's overall performance, particularly through contracts, contract documentation and procurement. The underlying question was: 'How should sustainability be addressed as part of a JCT Contract?' (In hindsight, a better question might have been: 'Can a contract address sustainability and, if so, how?)

The output of the initial consultations conducted within the UK was the guidance note on sustainability (JCT, 2011) which was produced with a view to helping practitioners. Although the findings of the JCT consultation and the follow-up work by JCT and its working party have been drawn upon to support the views put forward in this chapter, the views expressed are those of the author unless otherwise stated.

JCT's consultation found that there were diverse views on what constituted sustainability and consequently how to deal with it. Nevertheless, it was clear from the findings that sustainability was a matter of importance for the industry. A substantial majority (84%) of those responding thought that performance could be improved through industry-specific contract documentation but respondents had quite different views as to what type of documents should be used to regulate such matters. There was a belief amongst all respondents that sustainability went far beyond construction contracts and consequently the conclusions reached as to the role contracts could play were markedly different. The wide range of views was partly down to the interpretation of the definition of sustainability. The definition adopted and set out in *'Building a Sustainable Future Together'* (JCT, 2011) is that of the Brundtland Commission, that is, sustainable development is development that meets the needs of the present without compromising the ability of future generations to meet their own needs. It is also probable that the varied views were also influenced by what constitutes a contract. There is a clear and important distinction that can be made between the contract agreement together with the conditions of contract (which comprises a standard form or bespoke contract form) and the other requirements (e.g., specification, schedules etc.) which form part of the documents and are incorporated as contract documents. In the following part of this chapter the term contract conditions apply only to that part of the contract, whereas the term contract will embrace the other incorporated documents as well as the conditions.

Although contract conditions can play an important part they are not necessarily an essential part in setting out and regulating matters related to sustainability. The question for practitioners and clients is not whether they should provide for sustainability but how they should provide for it in the contract. Documents, other than the contract conditions themselves, are thought by many to be the right place to provide for sustainability: such other documents would, in the normal course of events, form part of the tender/bid documents. The minority view is that the contract conditions themselves should be used rather than the other documents. Despite the different views it is evident that a vast majority either already include provisions in its contracts or believe there should be express standard provisions in the contract to govern matters of sustainability.

A small percentage of respondents thought that contract conditions either had no role to play or one that is only marginal in dealing with sustainability. For others the whole process of dealing with sustainability was an inherent part of their work and for a designer an integral part of the project; for them the contract need make no specific reference to sustainability. This is an understandable view but this is still an objective to be fulfilled rather than the situation that applies generally. Awareness of sustainability is a necessary prerequisite for determining how it is to be dealt with. The question for now is whether one should consciously tackle sustainability as a separate exercise and, if so, in what part of the contract. For now it seems we have to think of sustainability as a separate exercise and will do so until such time as it becomes properly embedded in our creative actions. As to which part of the contract, that is an open question but at present there is a continuing trend towards including sustainability provisions in contract documents (not necessarily the contract conditions), with much of this done by reference to other documents: such other documents may not always be incorporated as contract documents.

16.3 Specification or contract conditions

Although nearly all practitioners and building promoters support the proposition that sustainability should be provided for in a construction contract, there is no consensus as to how this should be done. In terms of law it may be said that an express contract provision is superior to the specification. That may be true if the contract condition is a fundamental term (as contrasted with a warranty) because this provides for a stronger remedy in the event of a breach – the ability to terminate the contract where there is such a breach. In other situations the remedy would be damages and these can flow equally from a breach of the contract conditions or a breach of anything contained in a specification or other documents that comprise the contract.

An obligation may be either expressed or implied in a contract, specification or other similar document However, relying on an implied term nearly always raises questions as to applicability and it is far better to use express provisions in whatever documents one chooses for the contract. Terms related to sustainability are not at present generally implied, although over time this may change. What is particularly important in terms of the obligation is that the specification or other document is a contract document or referred to as such and incorporated accordingly. Some provisions related to sustainability may be only incorporated by reference but this is not necessarily a good way of dealing with them as it does not always achieve clarity nor indeed promote awareness and understanding.

In purely legal terms, unless one wants to provide specifically for a stronger remedy for breach, sustainability can be provided for either in the contract conditions or in the specification or indeed both. Notwithstanding this fact, many practitioners (but not necessarily the majority) believe that the contract conditions provide the best means of regulating sustainability, regardless as to whether or not the condition is a fundamental term. This view is no doubt held, in part, in the belief that by doing so it raises the profile of sustainability and therefore helps to educate practitioners and others and to embed the concept in the thought processes.

Sustainability provisions can take the form of either a general contract obligation to comply or in the form of precise technical requirements. This means that both the contract conditions and the specification or other documents may fulfil a purpose; it is a matter of approach. Where such a contract condition is used it is preferable to word it as an obligation to comply with the specific detailed requirements set out in supporting contract documents rather than set out such detail in the contract conditions. The main reason for the inclusion of sustainability provisions in the contract conditions is the prominence it gives; however it is not necessarily the best place to cover detailed technical requirements. The principal reason why JCT chose to incorporate sustainability provisions in its standard form contracts was to raise the prominence of sustainability and hopefully to improve sustainability education.

Perhaps not surprisingly the general view is that contract clauses concerning sustainability must be legally enforceable; after all surely that is what a contract clause is supposed to be: otherwise there is no point because it might be ignored. WRAP makes the point: 'Whilst considering resource efficiency and incorporating it into the procurement process is beneficial, in the absence of a contractual obligation on the suppliers, it is difficult for the Employer to enforce compliance with its required process' (Wrap, 2016b). However with the development of the partnering concept there has been a move towards the inclusion in the contract of non-binding and aspirational provisions. For those who subscribe to the partnering concept, the argument that such provisions are not legally enforceable is countered by the belief that, in the event of failure, other sanctions (if considered appropriate) might apply instead of traditional legal remedies. The most often stated sanction is a loss in continuity of work – conversely this also works as an incentive. The use of aspirational clauses is embraced by some – they are seen as a means to facilitate a shift in what we do rather than an attempt to prescribe what is to be done or achieved. For others there is no place for them in a legally binding document.

Despite the reasons expressed for the inclusion of terms in the contract conditions, the precise terms, if any, that go into the contract conditions as compared with the other documentation that makes up the contract is, as already said, a matter of choice. The actual terms required are dependent principally upon the particular contract that is being considered. For instance, is it between the:

- Client and designer;
- Client and contractor, where the design is already substantially complete and where the contractor has no design responsibility;
- Client and contractor, where the design is already partially complete and where the contractor has some design responsibility;
- Client and design and build contractor;
- Client and design build and operate contractor.

The decision on the procurement of the project will establish the types of relationship that will arise. Procurement, of course, can be approached in many ways and each approach has a number of levels of operation. Some major differences exist within the range of procurement options but there is also much commonality. However, the choice of procurement is not generally determined by any consideration with regard to sustainability but such choice can have a significant effect upon it.

It is probably fair to say that, on a majority of building projects, the design process and the planning of the construction process are given separate consideration and are carried out as separate operations. This has a consequence not only on the outcome of the project, including aspects of sustainability, but also on how sustainability is provided for in the contract. It has been suggested that an integrated approach is desirable and helps overcome this problem (JCT, 2013); also, it has been suggested that some procurement approaches lend themselves more to integration than others. Through effective integration all aspects of the design and the associated construction processes involved with that design are more readily considered together rather than separately. However, the success or otherwise of integration is more dependent upon effective management and leadership than the procurement process itself.

Where the design and construction processes are considered separately in terms of sustainability this will result in:

- The design becoming fixed – the freedom to adopt sustainable construction processes still exists but is limited by the constraints of the design.
- Consideration of the construction processes indicating that sustainability may be better addressed by modifying the design or indeed creating an entirely different design.

Consequently it is unlikely that such an approach will be entirely effective in producing a good sustainable outcome. Where it does produce a good sustainable outcome it is quite likely that reworking of the design will have taken place. That would be an inefficient process and any such process by its very nature is poor in other aspects of sustainability, albeit primarily economic rather than environmental.

Theoretically, as previously alluded to, there should be little or no need in a standard contract to express terms governing sustainability because sustainability should be a normal consideration within the design process and designers should have sufficient knowledge of the construction processes to ensure that a proper sustainable solution is provided. However, in practice, this currently is not the case and, until consideration of sustainability is embedded in the construction industry and it is inherent in its practitioners, the inclusion of sustainability provisions in each of the various contracts of those carrying out design and construction is essential. This applies regardless of the procurement route.

Although it is evident that the approach to procurement can impact on the solution in various ways, including the effectiveness of providing a proper sustainable solution, it is the knowledge and the technical and behavioural skills of the respective players that determine the nature of the solution.

16.4 JCT standard form contracts and sustainability

The principal JCT contracts (which are published by Sweet and Maxwell on behalf of The Joint Contracts Tribunal Limited) for securing sustainability benefits are:

- JCT Framework Agreement 2011.
- JCT – Constructing Excellence Contract 2011 and its associated Project Team Agreement.
- JCT Pre-Construction Services Agreement (General Contractor) 2011.
- JCT Pre-Construction Services Agreement (Specialists) 2011.
- JCT Consultancy Agreement (Public Sector) 2011.

However, all the 2011 (and 2016) editions of JCT contracts (with a few exceptions) contain sustainability provisions in a Schedule to the conditions. To ensure the whole supply chain embraces sustainability and is responsible for delivering a solution it is necessary that sub-contracts and other contracts further down that chain have stepped down into them such sustainability provisions. Everyone in the supply chain is responsible for delivering a solution and needs to embrace all aspects of the concept.

The sustainability provisions contained within the JCT Framework Agreement (which are the same for 2011 and 2016 editions) are set out in 16.5 to 16.7.

16.5 The framework objectives

Clause 5.1 The Framework Objectives are as follows:
5.1.1   Zero health and safety incidents;
5.1.2   Teamworking and consideration for others;
5.1.3   Greater predictability of out-turn cost and programme;
5.1.4   Improvements in quality, productivity and value for money;
5.1.5   Improvements in environmental performance and sustainability and reductions in environmental impact;
5.1.6   Right first time with zero defects;
5.1.7   The avoidance of disputes;
5.1.8   Employer satisfaction with product and service;
5.1.9   Enhancement of the Provider's reputation and commercial opportunities.
Clause 5.2 The Provider's contribution to progress in achieving certain of the Framework Objectives will be monitored and periodically assessed in the manner indicated in Clause 21.

16.6 The provider's supply chain

Clause 10.1 The Provider will endeavour to see to it that all members of his Supply Chain are made aware of, understand and are prepared to embrace and adhere to the principles of collaborative working envisaged in this Framework Agreement. Where practicable and appropriate the Provider will engage members of his Supply Chain on terms which incorporate or reflect such principles.

Clause 10.2 The Provider will, where practicable and appropriate, endeavour to consult with and/or involve members of the Provider's Supply Chain in relation to the following essential aspects of the Tasks:

10.2.1   Design development;
10.2.2   Project planning;
10.2.3   Risk assessment and risk allocation;
10.2.4   Health and safety assessments and planning;
10.2.5   Assessing and improving upon environmental performance and sustainability and reducing environmental impact;
10.2.6   Value engineering;
10.2.7   Change control;
10.2.8   Quality control;
10.2.9   Early warning;
10.2.10   Problem solving.

16.7 Sustainable development and environmental considerations

Clause 16 The Provider will assist the Employer and the other Project Participants in exploring ways in which the environmental performance and sustainability of the Tasks might be improved and environmental impact reduced. For instance, the selection of products and materials and/or the adoption of construction/engineering techniques and processes which result in or involve:

16.1   Reductions in waste;
16.2   Reductions in energy consumption;
16.3   Reductions in mains water consumption;
16.4   Reductions in CO_2 emissions;
16.5   Reductions in materials from non-renewable sources;
16.6   Reductions in commercial vehicle movements;
16.7   Maintenance or optimisation of biodiversity;
16.8   Maintenance or optimisation of ecologically valuable habitat;
16.9   Improvements in whole life performance.

It can be seen that these provisions cover a wide range of matters; not all would be instantly recognisable as pertaining to sustainability, but they are. They either deal with sustainability directly as in Clauses 5.1.5, 10.2.5 and more generally as in Clause 16 but also in the other clauses both directly and indirectly through avoiding wasted effort and through collaborative team working to find improved solutions.

During the JCT consultation and the development of its provisions and guidance note the JCT worked with WRAP. WRAP has produced a significant amount of work, especially in the area of recycling and has also produced its own contract provisions for general resource efficiency (Wrap, 2016b) and for specific components of resource efficiency (Wrap, 2016a). These clauses also illustrate many of the points referred to later.

16.8 *Aspirational or legally binding provisions*

Reference is made above in 16.3 to the use of aspirational clauses and any analysis of the above framework provisions in 16.5 to 16.7 would identify their use. The validity or otherwise of the arguments for using such clauses is a matter for practitioners to decide. However their use in situations where targets are specified, as compared with an obligatory outcome, is understandable. Use of provisions in these circumstances is appropriate. However, it is possible that the use of aspirational clauses will decline over time as experience is gained as to the appropriateness of targets and their measurement because that can lead to specific performance requirements being stated. Clause 21 (Performance Indicators), referred to in Clause 5, is a key point in that certain objectives will be monitored and assessed. It is not expected that monitoring and assessment will apply to all objectives, only to those where performance indicators are stated. Generally, performance indicators are an integral part of a process of continuous improvement but not for use when setting obligatory requirements. Only when there is certainty that an event is possible can any measurable target transmogrify into a requirement that could be legally enforceable.

A fairly typical aspirational clause may include words such as:

'The supplier will assist the employer in exploring ways in which the environmental performance of the works to be constructed might be improved'. Despite specific reference to tangible items and words like 'will assist … in exploring ways' the provision is still aspirational in nature. Although an unwillingness to assist would be a breach, the words are primarily aspirational in nature because the remedy for default is unquantifiable and therefore of little import. Even if such a provision were extended to include reference to reducing environmental impact, as in Clause 5.1.5 above in 16.5, it would remain primarily aspirational.

It is aspirational in that it seeks to improve environmental performance, reduce environmental impact and hence improve sustainability. Its legal enforceability is doubtful, certainly in any meaningful way, because there are no specific requirements: indeed it would be highly questionable that such requirements could be established properly, let alone agreed.

Not only are there no specific requirements, there are no targets: without targets that can be measured readily the provision's effectiveness is limited severely. The use of expert evidence to adduce what would be appropriate targets post facto is not a feasible option. The introduction of measurable targets/performance indicators, as might be used in conjunction with those items to which Clause 16 applies, are essential for providing a meaningful framework for the purposes of continuous improvement but even so still possess limitations because of a vagueness as to what, if any, sanctions might apply. Clearly, the greatest potential for continuous improvement is under long-term procurement arrangements such as framework agreements and the like.

Moving from a target to an obligatory requirement is difficult as few are likely to sign up to any that may be set where there is a lack of benchmarks. The issue of benchmarks will over time be resolved to a large extent by schemes such as the BCIS Benchmark Report run by the RICS; however the bespoke nature of much construction creates a constraint upon its application. We can seek to reduce waste by 'x' or energy by 'y' but, as there is no way of ascertaining how realistic each is or in some instances even controlling what occurs, such provisions will not serve as ones where a legal sanction can be applied properly. However, that is not necessarily the case with regard to other types of sanction. It is one thing preferring a contractor who has previously shown he can achieve or has made good progress towards such targets but quite another securing a legal remedy where there is failure to achieve them. Upon analysis it will be seen that each provision in Clause 16 (referred to above in 16.7) has the potential for establishing targets against which performance can be measured; but as to providing an obligatory requirement that is another matter.

Perhaps the lack of certainty as to legal enforceability is why, in the JCT consultation, little support was found for aspirational provisions. Despite those findings, aspirational provisions are increasingly prevalent perhaps for the reason that there is a high measure of unwillingness to sign up to clauses which are legally enforceable when the basis for establishing a required outcome is unclear – and because there is growing recognition that aspirational clauses do indeed have a very specific role.

One should always be clear as to whether one is using an aspirational or legally enforceable clause. In determining whether a provision in a contract is aspirational, one should ask whether or not the provision sets a specific obligation or target and what sanction, if any, there is where there is a failure to fulfil the obligation or achieve such a target. In those situations where an obligation is set it should be made clear because one that is ill-defined will not necessarily become aspirational in nature but one that remains legally enforceable: following legal proceedings and expert evidence it might establish something somewhat different to that which was anticipated. However, an obligation that cannot be measured objectively will in effect become aspirational as there can be no meaningful contractual sanction.

Despite the reservations expressed by many as to the use of and means to draft clear legally enforceable clauses regarding sustainability there is a contrary view. Legally enforceable clauses are of use and can be drafted where some objective measurement is available and it has been suggested that, for example:

> Building Research Establishment Environmental Assessment Methodology (BREEAM) ratings; Leadership in Energy and Environmental Design (LEED) certification; the Merton Rule (the Merton Rule was a planning policy, developed by Merton Council, which required new developments to generate at least 10% of their energy needs from on-site renewable energy equipment, in order to help reduce annual carbon dioxide (CO_2) emissions in the built environment); Site Waste Management Plan (SWMP; SWMPs are used in the construction industry to plan, monitor and implement actions to manage waste; they were a legal requirement under the Site Waste Management Plans Regulations 2008 but these have since been revoked) and Energy Performance Certificates [Energy Performance Certificates are required for most new buildings as a requirement of the Energy Performance of Buildings (England and Wales) Regulations 2012] can be used.

There are three points here:

> First, specific reference to those measures may feature in the contract, possibly with relevant details in specifically provided contract particulars or alternatively solely in the other contract documents – as detailed requirements may vary significantly trying to enshrine them in standard conditions alone is not a practical proposition.

Second, objectivity in terms of measurement may not be complete – for example, against what is a site waste management plan to be judged. Also a plan is one thing, meaningful deliverables another.

Third, the underlying structure of the scheme and so on may be such that it is not entirely rationale, it may become fixed in time or at worst it is ill-founded, that is, not tackling the cause.

Another problem concerns the fragmented nature of guidance and rating schemes because that makes it difficult for practitioners to know how best to proceed. This is not a criticism because a multifarious approach is quite natural in one's attempt to define a problem and to find a solution, but widely differing approaches do nevertheless form a hurdle for many.

Notwithstanding, it is submitted that the use of such schemes is desirable as a means of changing practice and behaviour so as to make what we do more sustainable. Users should decide what is the most appropriate for the project and specify very clearly what is expected. However, before using any such scheme practitioners should make themselves entirely familiar with all details of the scheme's operation before deciding whether to recommend either a contractual requirement or an aspirational provision.

The initiative for the use of certifiable schemes and the like may arise in a number of ways, for example, through the force of law (both directly and indirectly), by practitioners wanting to be seen as at the forefront of developments or by clients who see both a commercial risk (not doing what others are doing) and an opportunity (providing a competitive edge) in sustainability.

It appears that to date the force of law has been the biggest driver and regulation such as the European Union's Energy Efficiency Directive has been a major motivator. However, the point is made that 'landlords should be prioritising green building improvements to avoid diminishing their properties' future investment appeal' (RICS, 2015), which rightly suggests that consideration of sustainability has a place regardless of legislation. This is absolutely correct because it does. Here we see a commercial issue and we know from experience that commercialism is often the most effective driver of all. The point regarding landlords reinforces a finding of the JCT consultation which stated 'Sustainability objectives are best achieved when the client organisation is committed and takes the lead' (JCT, 2011). It is unlikely that much progress will be made on the form of contract provisions for sustainable outcomes unless clients accept the need. However, it is for professional advisors to point out to clients the potential for sustainable solutions and the part that contracts can play.

It can be seen that standard contract provisions and contract guidance have a role in shaping behaviour and changing practices so as to promote and improve sustainability. External pressures – the client being one such pressure – will impact both positively and negatively. How the forces for improving sustainability will impact on the nature of contracts and contract documentation will depend on such external pressures. It is a two-way process and either way it is necessary for consideration to be given as to how, if at all, the contract conditions make such provision or whether it simply becomes a part of the other contract documentation. The principal factor that will determine this is how the design is developed within the procurement process because the contract reflects that process and needs to provide accordingly.

Many contracts already include performance requirements rather than set out a single design solution. The use of performance requirements is necessary in those instances where the provider is to design/provide a solution and facilitates the possibility of obtaining a number of possible solutions that satisfy such requirements. The use of performance requirements may also maintain a competitive element. It is a system that is in part dependent upon the procurement process but one that works well in those areas where the designer/provider has specialist expertise. It may be that a fixed price can be quoted but where the risks associated with providing a particular solution is high some other basis of payment may be appropriate. Performance requirements are for situations where it is known what is wanted but not necessarily how it is to be satisfied (there being also the possibility of competing solutions), thus providing a legal requirement to perform but not necessarily for a set price.

The use of performance requirements can be extended to sustainability in those instances where the outcome to be achieved can be precisely stated, for instance, by requiring the home to comply with a specified level under the Code for Sustainable Homes (notwithstanding its withdrawal): an approach that can provide an enforceable legal framework. The question then becomes not a legal one but a commercial one, as clients will be asking whether it makes commercial sense to adopt such requirements. So much as to what is deliverable in terms of sustainability is dependent upon the building promoter and it is for this reason that legislation and contract provisions may well play an important part for some time to come.

16.9 The future

If construction is to offer more than a small incremental approach to improving sustainability it will need to address far more than contracts and contract guidance.

Modelling sustainable buildings (facilitated by developments in Building Information Modelling; BIM) will grow rapidly over the next few years and as it does construction procurement will adapt. For some a change in the procurement process will facilitate the development of such modelling and the importance of sustainability is a particularly good reason for this to arise. Changes in procurement will impact on the nature of construction contracts but not necessarily in the way some may anticipate. The traditional type of construction contract will almost certainly still exist for many years to come but other contracts will also emerge – that is, contracts that reflect construction more as a clearly defined manufacturing process yet one that nevertheless facilitates bespoke solutions. Even so this will only go a small way to tackling sustainability because, as previously mentioned, there are much bigger issues. The answers we provide to the philosophical questions referred to elsewhere will have the greater impact.

One of the great challenges for us is to work out the nature of growth that is compatible with sustainability of our environment and indeed the human race. The current form of growth is ultimately incompatible with sustainability, something we are reluctant to accept. Most people see growth as essential as it provides work and the potential for improving living standards. However, the consequences of the current forms of growth on our environment are unwelcome in many ways, not least the fact that they are unsustainable. This poses a rather profound question: how do we really go about tackling the problem of sustainability?

One may ask what this has to do with their everyday involvement with construction. Very little, at one level, because most of the day to day nitty-gritty will continue: business as usual. But at another level it has everything to do with construction because the built environment creates a tension with the natural environment. Not just in terms of land use and its effect on flooding and food production, but also in terms of the use of raw materials, emissions and waste. The creation and location of the built environment also has significant impact because of the logistics and transportation necessary to create it but more importantly for our lives to be maintained thereafter. In terms of growth, most UK political parties, if asked, would say that they wish to see a vibrant construction sector with increased house building and growth in our infrastructure. Most people would agree but how that might be possible in a sustainable way is of course another matter – low carbon construction is only part of the answer (Hibberd, 2010).

Over the next decade or so there will a substantial increase in world population and also a shift in the economic balance between countries; particularly between east and west and between developed and emerging nations. Those changes will create opportunities and change some lives for the better but for others the pressures that will emerge will not only impact badly on them but also on the environment as a whole – our sustainability in anything like what we have become used to will be severely tested. The changing patterns offer opportunities for those businesses that understand the shifts in demand and can cross national boundaries but again these may exacerbate the problem of sustainability rather than address it. In understanding the shifts in demand one must be concerned with their nature and location. The type of work that needs to be done will change. The level and nature of construction activity will certainly change and the proportion of rebuild, renovation and refurbishment must start to increase and the levels of recycling increase if we are to start tackling some of the problems that are before us. There will be an incredibly difficult transition as we start to adjust our wants and our values. Whether it is to realize the opportunities provided by the shifts in demand or just simply to survive, we must start to think differently because clearly there are limits to growth in its current form. However, as it is impossible to see what technologies will be commercially available in 10–20 years' time we have no way of knowing what may be possible: Andrew Smith gives us an insight into the possibilities with biological computing (Smith, 2015), as does the concept of the Internet of Things.

16.10 Conclusion

- There is no single answer as to how we go about tackling the problem of sustainability but the question must remain at the forefront of our minds so that we act in a meaningful way and differently to the way we have done in the past. As we change, the impact upon construction and construction projects will be seen. This change has started and it will gather pace. For some businesses it will be an opportunity, for others it will be their demise. Inevitably, growth will start to be seen differently.

- Promoters of construction should take the lead in sustainability by setting out requirements in their project brief but, where they do not do so, they should be (at the very least) an active participant in the provision of buildings that better meet the objectives of sustainability.
- The procurement process, the nature of integration in that process (especially at the design stage) but more particularly the ability of those charged with that responsibility will greatly influence the nature of any sustainable outcomes. The earlier the supply chain is brought into the design process the better. The greatest benefits with regard to producing sustainable solutions arise at the design stage but only when design and construction are considered together. BIM will assist this process.
- The conditions of the respective contracts and the contracts as a whole will play an important part because there exists a two way process between the development of contracts and those other factors involved in defining and fulfilling sustainability objectives.
- There is no imperative for the inclusion of specific sustainability provisions in the contract conditions because sustainability should be a normal consideration within the design process: designers should have sufficient knowledge of the construction processes to ensure that a proper sustainable solution is provided. However, in practice, this currently is not generally the case. Until consideration of sustainability is embedded in the construction industry (including its clients) and it is inherent in the actions of its practitioners, there are very good reasons for the inclusion of sustainability provisions in each of the various contracts of those carrying out design and construction. That is because in providing such conditions they not only promote sustainability, influence behaviour and educate, they also provide a framework for continuous improvement.
- Although there is an argument to support the view that we should strive to establish legally enforceable conditions governing sustainability, it is a big step from using targets as a driver of continuous improvement to that of setting requirements that must be met.
- Professional advisors are generally judged against a standard of reasonable skill and care and need to be aware that as our approach and understanding of sustainability develops what is considered reasonable will change: the bar as to what is reasonable will rise. The tension that sometimes exists between practitioners and client will likely be more in evidence.
- There is a need to continue to identify credible measurable targets both for specific items and for whole building performance: benchmarking is essential.
- The use of environmental schemes by which to judge projects has merit but it is necessary that practitioners fully understand their operation and limitations, and also ensure their client is on board.
- There is good reason for the inclusion in the specification or other similar documents (rather than in the contract conditions) of the technical requirements related to sustainability. Although, for the present, it is evident that both the contract conditions and the specification and so on have a role in promoting sustainability as well as providing a legal framework.

- How far contracts and contract clauses will change in response to sustainability depends on many things but the more important ones include the legislative process, commercial opportunities and threats, changes in societal values and, of course, the procurement process. Although it has been suggested that it is incentives that create behavioural change, not rules, one must not overlook the fact that they can work together in a classic 'carrot and stick' fashion.
- The fact that the issue of sustainability goes beyond our ken must not prevent us from tackling those problems that we can address, however small they might appear. The knock-on effect of doing so should not be underestimated.

References

Bootle, R. (2015) Viewpoint. *Daily Telegraph*, 28th June, London.

Cabinet Office (2008) People. In: *Strategy for Sustainable Construction*, HM Government, London.

Camus, A. (1942) *Le Mythe de Sisyphus*. Published in English in 1955 by Hamish Hamilton, London.

Communities and Local Government (2006) *Code for Sustainable Homes – a Step Change in Sustainable Home Practice*, Department of Communities and Local Government, HM Government, London.

Hibberd, P. (2010) Redefining Growth. *JCT Newsletter*, April edition, JCT, London.

HM Government (2013) *Industrial Strategy: government and industry in partnership*. Construction Strategy 2025, HM Government, London.

JCT (2011) *Building a Sustainable Future Together – Guidance Note*. Sweet and Maxwell, London.

JCT (2013) *Report on the JCT Sustainability: Lifecycle Consultation*, Sweet and Maxwell, London. Available at: http://corporate.jctltd.co.uk/initiatives/sustainability/ (accessed 23 Mar 16).

Kelly, M. (2015) Comment. *Daily Mail*, 15th March, London.

Mitkidis, K.P. (2015) *Sustainability Clauses in International Business Contracts*, Eleven International Publishing, Utrecht.

RICS (2015) *Modus*, RICS, London, p. 13.

Smith, A. (2015) Weird science. *The Sunday Times Magazine*, 29th March, London.

Trading Economics (2015) *United Kingdom GDP Growth Rate*. Available at: http://www.tradingeconomics.com/united-kingdom/gdp-growth (accessed 23 March 16).

Wrap (2016a) *Contract Clause for Specific Components of Resource Efficiency*. Available at: www.wrap.org.uk/construction (accessed 23 March 16).

Wrap (2016b) *Procuring Resource Efficient Construction: Legal Aspects*. Available at: http://www.wrap.org.uk/content/procuring-resource-efficient-construction-legal-aspects (accessed 23 March 16).

Chapter 17

Transforming Communication and Decision-making Practices for Sustainable Renewal of Urban Transport Infrastructure

Jay Yang[1], Kaichen Goh[2], Geoffrey Q. Shen[3], Dezhi Li[4] and Tan Yigitcanlar[1]

[1] *School of Civil Engineering and Built Environment, Queensland University of Technology, Brisbane, QLD 4001, Australia*
[2] *Department of Construction Management, Universiti Tun Hussein Onn Malaysia, Johor, Malaysia*
[3] *Department of Building and Real Estate, The Hong Kong Polytechnic University, Hong Kong, China*
[4] *Department of Construction and Real Estate, Southeast University, 210018, Nanjing, China*

17.1 Introduction

The twenty-first century is identified as the 'century of cities' as rapid urbanisation becomes inevitable (Landry, 2008). The challenges that cities face nowadays are much broadened and intensified as they become home to more and more of the world's population. By 2030, it is expected that more than 60% of the world population will live in cities (UN, 2013). Urban dispersion in metropolitan areas is inseparably connected with the shift of private mobility from a green transport modes to private cars, as we have seen in the developed countries decades ago and in many developing countries right now. This generates increasing demands on transport infrastructure. The impacts of urban sprawl on the urban infrastructure assets represent complex and very important issues (Klug and Hayashi, 2012).

In Australia for example, the population in capital cities grew by 10.2% from 2007 to 2012, while the rest of Australia was at 6.8% during the same period (ABS, 2014). Because of the geographical dispersion in Australia, day to day lives are heavily dependent upon the distribution of essential services through infrastructure, particularly those supporting transportation (Dur and Yigitcanlar, 2014). Decisions on urban infrastructure development have fundamental influences on the economy, the environment and the long-term prosperity of our society (Jones and Patterson, 2007; Shen *et al.*, 2011).

Following years of inadequate attention, Australia is now facing a massive backlog of infrastructure maintenance and redevelopment (Dollery, 2012; ANIC, 2013). On local

Future Challenges in Evaluating and Managing Sustainable Development in the Built Environment,
First Edition. Edited by Peter S. Brandon, Patrizia Lombardi and Geoffrey Q. Shen.
© 2017 John Wiley & Sons Ltd. Published 2017 by John Wiley & Sons Ltd.

infrastructure alone, the investment deficit is estimated to be between A\$ 12 and 15 billion (RAI, 2012). The Australian governments have realised this importance and are making major investments towards infrastructure. For example, according to the Northern Triangle Infrastructure Plan 2007–2012, the Queensland State Government had plans to invest A\$ 82 billion over 20 years in one region alone to fund transportation, natural gas delivery and water processing projects (DSIP, 2013). This level of investments warrants a closer examination on how urban infrastructure projects can be more sustainable and how they will meet future demands and challenges amid some of the fundamental changes in our society.

Relying on new infrastructure alone is not enough. How to upgrade, rejuvenate and redevelop existing transport infrastructure must also come into the equation. After stipulating the inadequate and aging nature of existing assets, the 2013 Australian National Infrastructure Plan calls for a shift from short-term fixes to long-term, strategic redevelopment (ANIP, 2013). There is a need to better understand how transport solutions can contribute to sustainability and to make smart and well informed decisions with a focus on sustainable deliverables (Jones and Patterson, 2007; Nagpal *et al.*, 2013; Newman, 2014). The sustainable outcome must also be financially justifiable (Goh and Yang, 2013; Yigitcanlar and Teriman, 2014).

Today, urban infrastructure problems have become more pressing, while the capacity to intervene and coordinate responses to these issues is tested increasingly (Yang *et al.*, 2015). High-level demand on project finance, the long-term nature of the work and the large number of public and private stakeholders involved makes decision-making on urban infrastructure renewal a precarious exercise (Surahyo and El-Diraby, 2009; Eames *et al.*, 2013). From the assessment of user needs to the determination of lifecycle costs, communication leading to renewal decisions is often very complex (Nagpal *et al.*, 2013). The global move towards a 'user pays' system and privatisation of infrastructure will inevitably demand more 'user say'. This challenges the conventional approach to engaging stakeholders and making decisions that follows typical dominant modes of public planning, service provision and user consumption (Markard, 2011; Gosse *et al.*, 2013).

Responses to issues of such a scale will not be one-dimensional. Many areas need to be investigated, for example, financial planning, technical innovation, policy-making, environmental concerns and stakeholder engagement. But the aspect that ties many processes, policies and people together is communication and decision-making. The information flow associated with inter-organisational communication can be a key issue. The effectiveness of decision-makers to communicate, evaluate and provide feedback to involved stakeholders can determine how efficiently project goals can be achieved (Alshawi and Ingirige, 2003; Li and Madanu, 2009; Daim *et al.*, 2011). New mechanisms are needed to gain knowledge about stakeholders' needs and emerging financial investment patterns, to embed this information into planning, assessment and decision-making and to facilitate effective communication with all involved parties, including users and the community who are increasingly embracing social media to raise their concerns.

Some research exposed the lack of information sharing and decision-making assistance during urban renewal (Markard, 2011; Cole, 2012; Eames *et al.*, 2013; Newton, 2013). But none has attempted to explore how to provide a positive, tangible communication platform and decision-making environment. There is a need to understand urban density and how it relates to transport infrastructure development and renewal (McIntosh *et al.*, 2014). In highlighting the massive backlog in financing infrastructure renewal, the Regional Australia Institute identified 'a chronic lack of adequate infrastructure finance, planning and management expertise' and 'poor information on the nature of the backlog' (RAI, 2012). It calls for an 'advisory service' and 'consistent national information'. In a United States proposal for transport infrastructure renewal agenda, a group of experts call for 'improved data availability', 'advanced benefit and performance assessment' and 'life-cycle cost-based evaluations' that require effective stakeholder engagement, communication and knowledge-sharing among them (Schofer *et al.*, 2010). Markard (2011) believes the capital intensity, massive investment needs and negative environmental impacts can be motivations for sustainable infrastructure redevelopment. In this context, how to carry out strategic planning, provide communication and make decisions leading to biophilic and resilient renewal of urban infrastructure have very important roles to play and there is a lot to be learned (Beatley and Newman, 2013).

17.2 Aim, objectives and methods of study

With a focus on renewal projects of urban transport infrastructure, the study reported here aims at identifying the key issues involved in the communication and decision-making practices and, through analysing existing literature, investigating possible approaches to achieving sustainable outcomes. The objectives of this study include:

1. Investigate the current situation of developing urban transport infrastructure and identify characteristics and key issues of renewal, with an particular interest in Australian cases.
2. Review previous research in addressing the identified issues.
3. Explore new approaches to improve and potentially transform the existing practices in order to facilitate sustainable renewal of urban transport infrastructure.

The study presented in this Chapter consists of two stages of literature review. The first stage focused on understanding the necessity and characteristics of urban transport renewal, while identifying the key issues of renewal projects. Steps involved in this stage are as follows.

Three electronic journal publication databases were searched first by journal names to identify journals in transport, infrastructure, construction management, urban planning and sustainability. The databases selected were Science Direct, ASCE Library, and Taylor and Francis Online because of their popularity and reputation for data reliability. Subsequently, the authors used keywords to search relevant articles in the identified journals. The keywords included 'urban transport', 'transport infrastructure', 'urban transport renewal' and 'sustainable renewal'. At the same time, to obtain relevant information from more sources, an additional search in the Google Scholar was conducted as well, using keywords 'urban transport infrastructure'. The relevance of all returned results was then evaluated through examining the title and abstract. The next step was to review and analyse the selected articles. Information extracted from the literature was used to portray current situations of urban transport infrastructure renewal; and it provided clues on the characteristics and key issues of urban transport infrastructure renewal.

The second stage literature review was based on the search results of the first stage. Taking on board the key issues identified, the specific aspects that could lead to sustainability acceptance and practice, performance assessment, the engagement and management of stakeholders and the communication and decision-making requirements and tools were investigated. The method used was similar to that of the first stage, but the keywords for the search were set to relate to these specific aspects. The discussion on these aspects led to an exploration for new approaches to the potential transformation of existing practices towards sustainable renewal of urban transport infrastructure.

17.3 Sustainable renewal of urban transport infrastructure

17.3.1 Research on urban transport infrastructure

Infrastructure plays a critical role in providing essential services to our daily life and industrialised societies (Markard, 2011). Urban transport infrastructure facilitates the economic development of cities by connecting workers to their work, delivering raw materials to plants and bringing products to markets (Cervero, 2013). In addition, the development of urban transportation systems has close relationships with urban sprawl and the formation of urban structure (Matsunaka *et al.*, 2013; Velaga *et al.*, 2012). Gordon (2012) states, for example, Australia has a high urbanisation level and this feature further increases the importance of urban transportation in this country. Thus, many of the transport systems in Australia focus on urban transport.

Witkowski (2012) described the composition of urban transport infrastructure by citing Ciesielski *et al.* (1992)'s work. He stated that the urban transport infrastructure consisted of streets, including all permanent facilities serving to control traffic and pedestrians, subway tracks, trains, trams, power supply networks for overhead metro, railways, trams and trolleybuses, power substations (transformers), railway stations and bus stops, car parks, bus and tram depots, garages for local cars and trucks (off the city streets) and cargo-loading facilities. Other studies focused on different elements of the urban transport infrastructure system. For example, Topalovic (2012) analysed the impact of a transit form – light rail transit. The impact analysis concentrated on three aspects, including urban development and land values, health and environmental impact and socioeconomic factors. They also compared light rail transit with other forms of transit, such as rapid bus and local transit schemes, and they concluded that light rail transit should be considered as a viable and desirable transit option for medium sized and growing cities. Cheng and Wang (2011) studied a reconstruction case of an inner city railway station and discussed the method to build an integrated transport hub based on the existing transport infrastructure resources. The increasing number of research studies on urban transport substantiates its topical importance.

With rapid population and economic growth, the demands for urban mobility have largely increased, which was shown by the estimation that about eight billion trips happened each day in cities all over the world (Cervero, 2013). This huge demand generated great pressure on current urban transport infrastructure.

At the same time, various challenges exist in the provision of urban transport (Gordon, 2012). First of all, urban transport infrastructure requires substantial amounts of capital for initial investment, operation and maintenance (Gordon, 2012; Goh and Yang, 2013). The investment on urban transport is typically very resource intensive because of the expense of securing rights of way and the complexity of engineering high-capacity systems in dense areas (Cervero, 2013).

In addition, negative impacts such as congestion, air pollution, reductions in biodiversity, influence on public health and social equity concerns should be carefully addressed in the planning and development of urban transport systems (Velaga *et al.*, 2012). Accordingly, a lot of effort has been made to solve urban transportation problems.

17.3.2 Renewal of urban transport infrastructure

To meet the increasing mobility and accessibility needs, infrastructure renewal, that is, upgrading, rejuvenating, and redeveloping the existing infrastructure is considered a complementary method to developing new transport infrastructure (Black and Schreffler, 2010). Haas (1997) stated that infrastructure maintenance and renewal could result in improved conditions, improved asset value and decreased user costs. The renewal of transport infrastructure was discussed in some studies. Cheng and Wang (2011) explored the method to build integrated transport hub based on the existing transport infrastructure resources, at the same time considering its relationship with the surrounding urban land's development to achieve more intensive land use. The study of Lee and Chan (2008) explored methods to enhance the sustainability of urban renewal projects in the design stage. They identified the critical design factors which can enhance the sustainability of urban renewal projects through a questionnaire survey among 200 stakeholders. In each dimension of sustainability, that is, economic, environmental, and social, several factors were used to reflect its sustainability level. The factors were scored and sequenced by the questionnaire survey respondents based on their contribution to project sustainability. The findings could facilitate the decision-making of local developers, urban designers and government officials during the design of sustainable urban renewal projects. But, except for scoring the factors, this study did not analyse the mechanisms of how these factors impact the sustainability of urban renewal projects, so that recommended methods to enhance or reduce the impacts were missing. To ensure efficient and effective infrastructure renewal, Haas (1997) analysed the required elements for infrastructure renewal and grouped the elements into two categories: (i) policy and political inputs, (ii) management and technical requirements. The policy and political inputs included financing, streamlining of public review, political action and staffing; the management and technical requirements included cost-effective alternatives, skills/education and training, research for better technologies and commitment to implementation. To list the requirements has positive influence on planning and execute the infrastructure renewal. However, all these identified requirements are too abstract and lack concrete implementation methods and measurable criteria.

17.3.3 Sustainability practices in urban renewal

To address the negative impacts of urban transportation, the concept of achieving sustainability in the transportation sector is gaining increasing attention. It has been argued that the transportation sector could make a great contribution to more sustainable cities (Cervero, 2013). Sustainability in the transportation sector is often discussed from three dimensions – environmental, social, and economic. The environmental sustainability in the transportation sector requires the elimination or reduction of negative environmental impacts resulted from the utilisation of petroleum by vehicles, such as the rising greenhouse gases emissions, global temperatures, levels of photochemical smog and particulates in urban environment. Thus, active transport modes, such as walking, cycling and public transit are recommended to reduce the use of cars to alleviate the environmental impacts and improve people's health (Cole *et al.*, 2010; McCartney *et al.*, 2012; Kamel 2013). Urban transport is socially sustainable when mobility benefits are equally and fairly distributed (Cervero, 2013). As for the economic sustainability, it means that resources are efficiently used and distributed in a way which maximises the benefits and minimises the costs of investment in and maintenance of transport infrastructure (Cervero, 2013).

17.3.4 Sustainability assessment of transport infrastructure

Previous research also explored the methods of assessing the sustainability performance of infrastructure projects. Ugwu *et al.* (2006) developed a set of sustainability indicators for infrastructure projects and proposed computational methods and analytical models based on the indicators to appraise the sustainability performance of infrastructure projects. For each project, a sustainability index could be generated to indicate its sustainability performance. To build the models, the 'weighted sum model' technique was used in multi-criteria decision analysis (MCDA) and the 'additive utility model' in analytical hierarchical process (AHP) was applied for multi-criteria decision-making. The appraisal indicators and models guide the translation of strategic sustainability objectives into project-specific concrete actions and have the potential to facilitate more sustainable decision-making in the planning stage. Similarly, Black *et al.* (2002) also investigated the indicators and analytical approaches to assessing the sustainability performance of infrastructure projects, but they focused on urban transportation projects. Their study presented the link between higher-level policy objectives for sustainability and lower-order actions, measurable attributes and performance indicators. This can assist policy makers to propose more sustainable policies. Edum-Fotwe and Price (2009) developed anontology to describe the social dimension of sustainability appraisals within the urban built environment.

Ways to achieving more sustainable outcomes in the transportation sector were also discussed. For example, Lenferink *et al.* (2013) investigated the effects of integrated contracts on the achievement of more sustainable road infrastructure development. The proposed contracting method integrated the design, construction and maintenance stages of the project lifecycle. The study demonstrated that integrated procurement can lead to more sustainable infrastructure development because of the lifecycle optimisation incentives provided by the linked contract stages. Apart from relational contracting, the researchers also recommended green procurement and strategic asset management as strategies to achieve more sustainable infrastructure development. However, little research was directly linked to urban transport renewal works.

17.3.5 Engaging stakeholders for communication and decision-making

The push for sustainability and the complexity of urban transport renewal requires holistic considerations and decision-making between many involved professionals and the community. Literature study identified two issues in this regard. One was the involvement of multiple stakeholders caused by the complexity of both urban renewal and infrastructure development projects, and the other one was a strong demand for associated decision support (Mayer *et al.*, 2005).

Markard *et al.* (2012) discussed the complexity of the sustainability transition of infrastructures. They stated that the transition involved changes in multiple aspects, including technological, material, organisational, institutional, political, economic and sociocultural. In this regard, they encouraged connecting research on sustainability transition with other topics like economic geography, philosophy of science, management, modelling and policy advice. The multi-dimensional feature of infrastructure sustainable transition indicated its involvement of multiple stakeholders, although this research did not include detailed discussion about parties affecting the transition or being affected by it. The involvement of multiple stakeholders has been identified as a feature of infrastructure sectors (El-Diraby, 2013). It has been widely accepted that stakeholders' interests should be dealt with to ensure project success (Achterkamp and Vos, 2008; El-Gohary *et al.*, 2006).

Macharis *et al.* (2012) emphasised the high possibility of disputes happening in transport projects because of the involvement of various social actors. Mayer *et al.* (2005) listed the elements that contribute to the complexity of urban renewal initiatives – the existing urban plan, buildings and constructions, green structures, infrastructures and residents, and they stated that a sustainable design for urban renewal should take all the stakeholders into consideration, that is, people who plan, construct, finance, operate and live in the neighbourhood. Each stakeholder group would strive to achieve their own ambitions and protect their own interests. Thus, there is a need to facilitate the collaboration among stakeholders and to deal with the conflicts.

The agreement among stakeholders could be reached through a collaborative decision-making process (Mayer *et al.*, 2005). However, this has not been easy to achieve. Obstacles included ill-structured problems, lack of information-sharing and communication impediments (Karacapilidis and Papadias, 2001). Various decision support systems (DSS) have been developed to assist decision makers (Bayraktar *et al.*, 2011; Matthews and Allouche, 2012; H. Osman and El-Diraby, 2011; Park and Kim, 2013), but none of the existing DSS is designed for multiple stakeholders and targets urban transport renewal projects.

According to the findings so far, two specific issues – multiple stakeholders' engagement and support for collaborative decision-making – were investigated further and analysed in the next section. Based on the analysis, an approach to facilitating sustainable renewal of urban transport infrastructure was proposed.

17.4 Analysis of key issues in urban transport renewal

17.4.1 Stakeholder management

It has been stated that coordination among project participants has a close relationship with the outcome of a construction project (Jha and Iyer, 2006). To achieve a sustainable built environment, it is essential to reach a high level of integration of disciplinary insights and stakeholders' perspectives (Mayer *et al.*, 2005). In this regard, stakeholder analysis and engagement are two important aspects for achieving higher level of satisfactions.

Stakeholder analysis

Achterkamp and Vos (2008) analysed the existing project management literature related to the stakeholder notion with an aim to investigate the definition and identification of stakeholders. It was demonstrated that an explicit stakeholder classification model and an identification method should be the first steps in stakeholder involvement. However, they found that only a small number of publications defined stakeholders clearly and provided the method to identify stakeholders. As a result of their study, they proposed a role-based stakeholder identification method which could benefit both researchers and practitioners. Yang (2014) stated that the main aims of stakeholder analysis were to identify stakeholders and their interests, prioritise these stakeholders and, subsequently, make appropriate decisions. Two major perspectives were adopted in stakeholder analysis. One was empirical, which relied on project team's or core stakeholders' experiences, and the other was rationalistic, which engaged most of the stakeholders and structures, the real relationships among them. Through the study, the researcher found that the empirical and rationalistic perspectives should be combined to get the most effective results in the stakeholder analysis, depending on resources and the nature of the projects. More practices of these perspectives under various circumstances should be conducted to verify the conclusion and identify more rules to guide practitioners to improve the performance of stakeholder analysis.

Stakeholder engagement

Apart from identifying the stakeholders and analysing their interests, researchers also conducted studies to increase the engagement of stakeholders in the project decision-making processes. EI-Diraby (2013) advocates a mode in which communities lead the decision-making in urban infrastructure with the assistance of information systems. The information system created a virtual organisation which contains all the stakeholders. In the virtual organisation, the customers provide the innovative ideas, public officials support the innovation by explaining and when possible breaking constraints and engineers coordinate and manage ideas. A lot of problems need to be solved before this vision can become a reality, such as how to establish trust and how to open an exchange of ideas and needs between community and public agencies. But it presents a trend for the future, that is, to improve the public engagement in decision-making. Similarly, Chen and Mehndiratta (2007) argued that public participation during the planning of urban transport projects can complement the technical planning process so as to facilitate the generation of widespread distributional benefits and the minimisation of adverse impacts. The public participation processes also increase the chance for vulnerable groups' interests to be considered into the planning process and, finally, public participation results in a better accomplishment of investment goals. Their argument was demonstrated by a case study in Liaoning, China. Through the public participation process, the project shifted focus from major road expansion to secondary road improvements.

As a further step, El-Gohary *et al.* (2006) proposed a more specific tool to facilitate stakeholder engagement. They pointed out that stakeholder involvement was an interdisciplinary domain that refers to many disciplines, so it required a variety of knowledge for project managers to conduct successful stakeholder management. To assist the stakeholder involvement programmes, the researchers developed a semantic model and taxonomy to represent the key concepts underlying stakeholder involvement in public private partnership (PPP) infrastructure projects. The model formed the base for other stakeholder management support tools.

Stakeholder satisfaction

To improve the stakeholders' satisfaction level, Hartmann and Hietbrink (2013) investigated the relationship between stakeholders' expectations, experiences and satisfactions in road maintenance. As a conclusion, the researchers suggested allowing stakeholders to experience the improvements of a maintenance project instead of trying to determine and meet their expectations, because the satisfaction level of stakeholders was usually slightly influenced by their expectations. Li *et al.* (2013) developed a multi-factor hierarchical fuzzy comprehensive model to assess stakeholder satisfaction during public participation in major infrastructure and construction projects. The model not only evaluated the satisfaction levels of individual stakeholder groups, but also assessed the satisfaction of all stakeholders involved. The goal of such a project should be achieving maximised overall stakeholder satisfaction and ensuring each individual group's satisfaction remains above an acceptable level. This research indicated the importance of involving all stakeholder groups, but it did not take consideration of the communication and interaction between different stakeholder groups.

These studies provided theories and methods that can be utilised in the stakeholder management of sustainable urban transport renewal projects.

17.4.2 Decision support

The stakeholders involved in urban transport renewal projects often represent a range of disciplines, priorities and interests. Therefore the management of information, knowledge and expectations as well as the decisions made needs to be a priority (Yang *et al.*, 2015).

Decision support systems (DSS) were developed to provide platforms of communication and management of information. 'Decision support systems (DSS) are computer programs that aid users in a problem solving or decision-making environment. These systems have detailed knowledge, data, models, algorithms, user interfaces, and control mechanisms to support a specific decision problem' (Bhargava *et al.*, 1995; cited in Molenaar and Songer, 2001). Molenaar and Songer (2001) argued that the DSS gets input from the user and then processes the input using analytical tools such as regression models and finally outputs information to assist the user's decision-making process. According to Tsamboulas and Mikroudis (2006), DSS aims at providing the requested information that satisfy the user's needs, through the application of models and/or the assistance of an expert system; and the information is provided in a user-friendly manner. The systems should be able to assist decision-making in a variety of semi-structured and recurring decision situations rather than only be used for a specific specialised study (Power and Sharda, 2007).

Decision support system applications

According to the types of information or assistance provided by the DSS, the DSS were grouped into five categories: model-driven, communications-driven, data-driven, document-driven, knowledge-driven (Power and Sharda, 2007). Model-driven DSS obtain data and parameters from users and input them into the quantitative model(s) that has been embedded in the system, and the output from the model(s) provides decision support to users. Communications-driven DSS derive their functionality from communications and information technologies that are used in the system to support shared decision-making. Data-driven DSS emphasise the access to and manipulation of a large database of structured data. Document-driven DSS utilise storage and processing technologies to provide sophisticated document retrieval and analysis to support decision-makers. Knowledge-driven DSS provide suggestions or recommendations based on knowledge which has been obtained from using Artificial Intelligence and analysing previous data, such as case-based reasoning and Bayesian networks. However, different types of DSS could be included in an integrated DSS. Arnott and Pervan (2005) also discussed the subgroups of DSS, including personal DSS, group support systems, negotiation support systems, intelligent DSS, knowledge management-based DSS, executive information systems/business intelligence and data warehousing. They reported that personal DSS and group support systems were the research focuses and data warehousing was the least published type of DSS.

The contents of different kinds of DSS varied. For example, the data-driven DSS need structured data – precontent, while model-driven DSS require access to models that can be manipulated – content creators. For knowledge-driven DSS, access to knowledge and rules is necessary – metacontent and, for the communications-driven DSS, we need communications capabilities for decision support – content creating and sharing (Power and Phillips-Wren, 2011).

Among the five categories of DSS described by Power and Sharda (2007), the model-driven DSS were discussed most frequently in previous research and have been applied in various areas, including construction and infrastructure development. Techniques used to build model-driven DSS include algebraic models, decision analysis, mathematical programming and simulation. Recently, the latter three are more commonly used than the algebraic models.

Decision analysis

Decision analysis (DA) broadly refers to methods for the evaluation of possible alternative courses of action in a quantitative way (Power and Sharda, 2007). Examples of DA methods include decision trees, decision matrix, influence diagrams, analytic hierarchy process (AHP) and multiple criteria decision analysis (MCDA). Several techniques could be combined to build a decision support model. For example, Wang *et al.* (2013) developed a quantitative model to support the selection of projects for district revitalisation and regeneration. This model utilised several analysing techniques, including the fuzzy Delphi method, interpretive structural modelling and analytical network process, and it considered the benefits, opportunities, costs and risks of different options. Thus, this model transformed complex interaction district reviving factors into a simple quantitative evaluation.

Some advanced techniques were developed to solve construction-related problems. For instance, in order to incorporate various points of view from different stakeholders in the transport projects, Macharis *et al.* (2012) proposed multi-actor, multi-criteria analysis to support transport policy decisions. This analysis methodology visualises the perspectives of different stakeholder groups and structures the discussions. However, the weights of stakeholders were the same in this proposed methodology, which needed to be adjusted when put into practice. It is also suggested to developing the corresponding software to further assist the visualisation of a multi-actor view. Decision analysis software tools which aim at supporting the development of specific DSS applications have been reported. These DSS generator tools include Precision Tree, Expert Choice, Catalyse, Logical Decisions, Super Tree and Tree Plan (Power and Sharda, 2007).

Optimisation techniques aim at providing optimal results for desired decision criteria. Plenty of optimisation-based DSS generator software has also been developed. Examples are the AIMMS modelling system, ILOG optimisation suite and MPL (Power and Sharda, 2007). The methods used to realise optimisation include linear programming, mixed-integer programming and constraint logic programming.

Simulation techniques are used to imitate the behaviour of a human or physical system (Power and Sharda, 2007). The simulation-based DSS often implement the simulation for multiple times and then provide the decision support information based on the analysis of the aggregate results. Several types of simulation have been reported in the literature, including Monte Carlo simulation, traditional mathematical simulation, activity-scanning simulation, discrete simulation, event-driven simulation, probabilistic simulation, process-based simulation, real-time simulation, data-driven simulation, agent-based and multi-agent simulation, time-dependent simulation and visual simulation (Power and Sharda, 2007). Among these techniques, agent-based visual simulations have gained increasing application in recent years. Osman (2012) adopted agent-based modelling to simulate the interactions involved in urban infrastructure management. The agents included in the model were assets, users, operators and politicians, and a detailed behavioural model was established to represent customer perceptions and actions related to infrastructure level of service. Similarly, Tsamboulas and Mikroudis (2006) described a DSS called TRANS-POL which was able to present the impacts of transport policies and projects. With the impact information, users can make wiser decisions accordingly.

Platforms of decision support systems

In terms of DSS development and delivery mechanisms, DSS can be divided into two types: spreadsheet-based DSS and Web-based DSS (Power and Sharda, 2007).

Bayraktar *et al.* (2011) developed a MS Excel-based decision support tool to select the most effective techniques to reach a trade-off between the cost and schedule of a project. According to the user's input about the project characteristics and goals, this tool provides the user with techniques to employ at each stage of the project and the five most effective techniques for the overall project to achieve the desired trade-off between cost and schedule. However, the tool did not provide instructions about the implementation of techniques in different project contexts, such as with different project delivery methods or with contract payment provision. Some of the techniques may not be suitable for certain kinds of projects. Further interaction between user and tool may be required to address this limitation. Another spreadsheet-based DSS was developed by Park and Kim (2013), aiming at facilitating sewer infrastructure management, specifically the selection of pipeline inspection and renewal methods and the estimation of associated costs. This system consisted of a data warehouse, which offered consistent and complete infrastructure data, and decision supporting modules, which specified the decision criteria and provided the user interface. Building on the MS Excel platform ensured a powerful data-analysing ability and also simplicity of system manipulation. But one obvious limitation of this system was that the decision criteria might not be able to cover all possibilities that might have to be refined for some particular cases.

As the Internet has become the primary means of information and data transfer in the world today (Muench *et al.*, 2010), Web-based decision support systems have gained increasing popularity. Web-based DSS not only retains the attributes of single-user DSS, but also increases the accessibility, efficient distribution, effective administration and cross-platform flexibility (Molenaar and Songer, 2001). These benefits can help overcome the difficulties of information sharing and communication among a project team caused by the decentralised nature of the construction industry. All types of DSS, especially communications-driven DSS, can benefit from the application of Web technology. Molenaar and Songer (2001) developed a Web-enabled system to assist the selection of design/build projects in the United States public sector. To enhance urban sustainability, Hamilton *et al.* (2002) developed a Web portal from which users can get advice about how to make urban development projects more sustainable, how to assess the sustainability and whom to contact for further advice. The information was categorised in different modules of the Web portal. A glossary of terms and links to best practice examples were also available to users. However, while this Web portal provided valuable information for professionals, mediators and researchers involved in urban development, more detailed guidance to implement the advised actions was missing. In addition, the Web portal allowed access for users to retrieve information but not add information to the system or communicate with other stakeholders. Osman and El-Diraby (2011) proposed a knowledge-enabled DSS for urban utility route selection. The system created a collaborative semi-automated environment, in which stakeholders can share information. But there has been no further report of applications.

Web technologies facilitate the information sharing among multiple decision makers to some extent, because it increases the accessibility of DSS. Participation of stakeholders and communication among them could be further improved, which may be realised by introducing the concept of social media in designing DSS. Kaplan and Haenlein (2010) defined social media as 'a group of Internet-based applications that build on the ideological and technological foundations of Web 2.0, which allows the creation and exchange of user-generated content'. According to them, there are six different types of social media: collaborative projects, blogs and microblogs, content communities, social networking sites, virtual game worlds and virtual social worlds. Power and Phillips-Wren (2011) explained that '"social media" refers to the use of Web-based and mobile technologies to enhance human communication and create dynamic, interactive dialogues'. Through social media, people can publish ideas and opinions easily without being reviewed, censored or evaluated for quality, and people can also combine, edit, archive and distribute content easily (Power and Phillips-Wren, 2011). This is what would normally occur during the early phases of infrastructure development where various people including the community are engaged.

It was reported that social networking mechanisms can improve the collaboration in construction (Costa and Tavares, 2012); and research about the impact of social media on decision-making has been conducted. Power and Phillips-Wren (2011) demonstrated that the impact of social media on personal and managerial decision-making can be extensive, although the impact could be positive or negative, depending on the adopted specific social media application.

According to Power and Phillips-Wren (2011), Web 2.0 technologies which enable the social media can have significantly positive impact on the design of DSS. Web 2.0 applications are generally superior to the first generation of Web-based DSS applications, because the Web 2.0 technology facilitates information sharing, collaboration and generation and utilisation of collective intelligence, also Web 2.0 technologies may help with managing, accessing and using our decision support content.

Muench *et al.* (2010) presented a Web 2.0-based community where users can create, edit, browse and search site content easily with just a computer, web browser and Internet connection. This online platform aimed at facilitating knowledge transfer within the transportation engineering community. By observing the platform usage, it was indicated that the platform was primarily used as a referencing and learning tool, and the substantial quality content attracted users. However, the collaboration functions were not extensively explored or used, and a means to maintain website currency was needed.

Key issues to achieve good performance of Web 2.0 applications may include: quality of content and community participation. Zhang and El-Diraby (2012) proposed an online portal to facilitate information exchange and knowledge sharing in Architecture, Engineering and the Construction Industry (AEC). This communication system utilised three technologies. First, semantic web technology was used to represent human knowledge, including tacit knowledge; thus a common language for communicating was created. Second, some social web features were adopted in the system to allow people share, reconfigure and generate knowledge easily. Finally, the application of publish/subscribe systems enabled the portal to provide relevant information according to individual interests. This proposed system demonstrated the possible ways for the Internet to assist communication in the AEC industry and subsequently support decision-making.

Banias *et al.* (2011) developed a Web-based DSS to assist the identification of optimal construction and demolition waste management strategy. The Web 2.0 technologies (Javascript/Ajax) were used to design the user interface in order to facilitate interactive information sharing. However, the information sharing was not among different DSS users. The interaction was between the designed DSS and Google Maps or between the user interface and the web server.

Common technologies and phenomena associated with Web 2.0 include: social networking applications, online mapping, portable visual elements, mashups, syndication, tagging, open source, rich Internet applications, Ruby on Rails, AJAX, Flex, Flash, LAMP, web services, virtual worlds and the mobile web (Power and Phillips-Wren, 2011). More studies are needed to investigate the feasibility and performance of applying Web 2.0 and Web 3.0 technologies in decision-making processes in the urban transport infrastructure sector, as well as paying attention to the problems existing in the development of DSS, such as poor identification of clients and users. Arnott and Pervan (2005) found that the identification of clients and users of DSS applications was missing in most research.

More recently, there has been a focus on the capabilities of semantic and distributed search and use of semantic databases, which forms the foundation of Web 3.0 technologies (Yu, 2014). Would Web 3.0 have the potential to overcome some of the limitations identified in previous Web 2.0-based systems and present better potential for engaging people? New research is needed in the space of construction specific applications.

17.5 Findings and discussion

This study first revealed the problems currently facing urban transportation: inadequate capacity to meet increasing mobility needs, general shortage of funding compared to demand and the potential negative impacts on environment and society. Solutions to these problems were also examined. These included the advocacy of efficient and effective urban transport infrastructure renewal and the promotion and implementation of sustainability concepts in the transport sector. However subsequent review found that little research covered these fields directly. Therefore, literature in related areas, such as sustainable urban renewal and infrastructure renewal, was examined to identify the characteristics and issues of urban transport infrastructure renewal projects.

Due to the magnitude of infrastructure projects and the complexity of renewal, especially meeting the challenges of sustainability, many stakeholders need to be involved. This is in contrast to the traditional patterns of planning and delivery initiated and controlled by government. Understanding the interests of all stakeholders, managing their expectations and concerns and achieving overall satisfaction among them should be top of the agenda. Therefore, engaging the stakeholder for involvement and communication and facilitating collaborative decision-making are essential in urban transport infrastructure renewal projects.

Effective communication and decision-making requires, besides accurate information, reliable knowledge, which can be acquired through shared learning and collaboration. In this respect, knowledge-based approaches provide a systematic and collaborative method that can be positioned to manage multiple organisations' and individuals' intellectual assets through facilitating knowledge creation, use, exchange and commercialisation (Dalkir 2005). Knowledge-based approaches (including computer-supported collaborative decision support systems that facilitate the solution of ill-structured problems by a set of decision makers working together as a team) present the potential for dealing with complex issues such as the redevelopment of existing urban transport infrastructure (Karacapilidis and Papadias 2001; Cole 2012; Comes *et al.* 2012). Eames *et al.* (2013) reiterate the need 'to develop the knowledge and capacity to overcome the separation between the "what" and "how" of urban scale retrofitting in order to promote a managed social–technical transition'. Doing so, they believe, can facilitate systemic transformations that are critical for achieving sustainability. However, achieving social–technical transition is full of challenges.

Newton (2013) believes that a significant hurdle to more intensive development is community support. With community participation, formulated policies and decisions might be more realistically grounded in community preferences, the public might become more sympathetic evaluators of the tough decisions that government administrators have to make, and the improved support from the public might create a less divisive, combative populace to govern and regulate (Irvin and Stansbury 2004). This is particularly true when dealing with transport infrastructure renewal issues because of the many interaction points with the community on multiple scales over a long lifespan. However, thus far, such collaborative decision practice in infrastructure projects has not been widely explored and followed.

Collaborative decision-making is a challenging task that demands mutual understanding, agreement and support between stakeholders. It requires the sharing of capacities, responsibilities and risks, as well as business benefits. The renewal of transport infrastructure also demands intensive, cross-disciplinary interactions. Therefore, collaborative decision-making will need to explore the inherent links and develop innovative approaches to assemble knowledge and communicate project information to all involved in a digestible and transparent way (Gudes *et al.*, 2010).

To enhance the involvement of stakeholders and facilitate collaborative, well-supported decision-making, applicable stakeholder management strategies and a specific design of decision support systems (DSS) need to be highlighted. There should be renewed focus on identifying stakeholders, analysing stakeholders' interests, improving stakeholder engagement and assessing stakeholder satisfaction towards sustainable goals and performances in the specific urban transport sector. The importance of engaging stakeholders in the decision-making processes is widely recognised.

The definition and categorisation of DSS were studied. The DSS were classified into model-driven, communications-driven, data-driven, document-driven and knowledge-driven, according to how the DSS provided decision support. Then, commonly used decision support techniques for model-driven DSS and their application examples were investigated, including decision analysis, optimisation and simulation. These techniques were used to process the input data from users and to output relevant information to support decision-making. It was also found that DSS typically relied on two means of providing user interfaces for inputting and retrieving data. These two means were spreadsheets and the Web. Web-based DSS are quickly gaining popularity because of their easy accessibility to multiple users in different locations.

As the decisions of infrastructure upgrade and renewal intertwine with emerging socioeconomics as well as technical forces such as sustainability, globalisation, e-society and knowledge economy, a social media-facilitated communication environment can provide important platforms for stakeholders and the community at large to share ideas and explore win–win decisions through a well-connected and knowledgeable process (El-Diraby, 2013). In this context, applications of social media and Web 2.0 and Web 3.0 technologies in decision support can provide easy means for information exchange and knowledge sharing and, in the case of Web 3.0, more user-oriented search and knowledge distribution. They are most likely to contribute to the holistic and collaborative decision-making required in the renewal projects for urban transport infrastructure. Such applications also have the potential to allow people to harness collective intelligence and co-develop knowledge-based products to drive business and enter global market places (Hendler and Berners-Lee, 2010).

This study did not find any existing attempts at utilising the above-mentioned tools for urban infrastructure development, particularly in Australia. The industry sector-specific, real-world needs of information sharing and knowledge management among key stakeholders need to be encapsulated and presented through appropriate communication means and protocols for decision support. Achieving a holistic and mutually beneficial decision-making environment should be a priority, while testing the feasibility of Web based communication platform compatible with social media is also important. This will help unite all involved stakeholders, such as governments and the general public, developers and users, planners and contractors, financiers and the operators. It will also support the sharing of the increasing volume of information and knowledge for sustainability and renewal works. Through new research works in these areas and information dissemination, it may be possible to influence people's perceptions, transform obsolete practices and highlight new directions for the infrastructure sector to work together, to reduce risks, maximise efficiency and deliver sustainable products and services.

17.6 Conclusion

This chapter presents the results of a study on the key issues involved in urban transport infrastructure renewal and, in response to the identified issues, a further study on the investigation of possible approaches to changing current communication and decision-making practice in order to achieve sustainable outcomes. These studies are based on a review of existing literature on a global scale with particular reference to a number of Australian cases.

The involvement of multiple stakeholders, increasing pressure to delivery sustainable facilities and services and a strong demand for decision support were identified as key issues of urban transport infrastructure renewal. To address these issues, collaborative and strategic planning, stakeholder engagement through communication and holistic decision-making are highlighted strategies. Communication portals and decision support systems have been developed and tested for applications in sectors other than infrastructure construction. How to adopt applicable theories and design appropriate tools is yet to be explored.

Web 2.0/3.0 technologies have the potential to deliver a communication and decision-making environment suited for multiple stakeholders and multi-criteria decision-making that is common in the urban infrastructure sector. This will be conducive to reaching identified stakeholder management goals through widespread communication. Open and holistic decision-making is another major criterion in this regard.

This research has identified that, in spite of considerable coverage of the methods and approaches for developing computer-based decision support applications, little has been made specifically available in the infrastructure space, particularly in Australia. Further work is needed to identify the specific industry requirements and mechanisms for the adaption of emerging technologies, such as Web 2.0/3.0, through new dedicated research with the involvement of urban transport industry partners.

References

ABS (2014) *Article 3218.0 – Regional Population Growth, Australia, 2012.* Australian Bureau of Statistics. Available at: http://www.abs.gov.au/ausstats/abs@.nsf/Products/3218.0~2012~Main +Features~Main+Features?OpenDocument#PARALINK10 (accessed 18 November 2015).

Achterkamp, M.C., Vos, J.F.J. (2008) Investigating the use of the stakeholder notion in project management literature, a meta-analysis. *International Journal of Project Management* **26**(7), 749–757.

Ahuja, V., Yang, J., Shankar, R. (2010) IT enhanced communication protocols for building project management. *Engineering, Construction and Architectural Management* **17**(2), 159–179.

Alshawi, M., Ingirige, B. (2003) Web-enabled project management: an emerging paradigm in construction. *Automation in Construction* **12**(1), 349–364.

ANIP (2013) *June 2013 Australia National Infrastructure Plan.* Infrastructure Australia. Available at: http://www.infrastructureaustralia.gov.au/coag/files/2013/2013_IA_COAG_Report_National_ Infrastructure_Plan_LR.pdf (accessed 20 November 2013).

Arnott, D., Pervan, G. (2005) A critical analysis of decision support systems research. *Journal of information technology* **20**(2), 67–87.

Banias, G., Achillas, C., Vlachokostas, C., Moussiopoulos, N., Papaioannou, I. (2011) A web-based decision support system for the optimal management of construction and demolition waste. *Waste Management* **31**(12), 2497–2502.

Baum, S., Kendall, E., Muenchberger, H., Gudes, O., Yigitcanlar, T. (2010) Geographical information systems: an effective planning and decision-making platform for community health coalitions in Australia? *Health Information Management Journal* **39**(3), 28–33.

Bayraktar, M., Hastak, M., Gokhale, S., Safi, B. (2011) Decision tool for selecting the optimal techniques for cost and schedule reduction in capital projects. *Journal of Construction Engineering and Management* **137**(9), 645–655.

Beatley, T., Newman, P. (2013) Biophilic cities are sustainable, resilient cities. *Sustainability* **5**(8), 3328–3345.

Bhargava, H.K., Power, D.J., Sun, D. (2007) Progress in Web-based decision support technologies. *Decision Support Systems* **43**(4), 1083–1095.

Black, C.S., Schreffler, E.N. (2010) Understanding transport demand management and its role in delivery of sustainable urban transport. *Transportation Research Record, Journal of the Transportation Research Board* **2163**, 81–88.

Black, J., Paez, A., Suthanaya, P. (2002). Sustainable urban transportation: performance indicators and some analytical approaches. *Journal of Urban Planning and Development* **128**(4), 184–209.

Byrnes, J., Dollery, B., Crase, L., Simmons, P. (2008) Resolving the infrastructure funding crisis in Australian local government: a bond market issue approach based on local council income. *Australasian Journal of Regional Studies* **14**(2), 167–175.

Cervero, R. (2013) *Transport Infrastructure and the Environment: Sustainable Mobility and Urbanism*. IURD Working Paper 2013–03, IURD, New York.

Chen, W., Mehndiratta, S.R. (2007) Planning for laobaixing: public participation in urban transportation project, Liaoning, China. *Transportation Research Record Journal of the Transportation Research Board* **1994**, 128–137.

Cheng, P., Wang, Z. (2011) Explore the integration of urban transport infrastructure and land development. Illustrated by the case of conceptual urban design on reconstruction of Shapingba railway station. *Chinese and Overseas Architecture* **4**, 023.

Ciesielski, M., Gługiewicz, Z. (1992) *Gospodarowanie w transporcie miejskim*. Wydawnictwo Akademii Ekonomicznej w Poznaniu (in Polish).

Cole, R., Burke, M., Leslie, E., Donald, M., Owen, N. (2010) Perceptions of representatives of public, private, and community sector institutions of the barriers and enablers for physically active transport. *Transport Policy* **17**(6), 496–504.

Cole, R. (2012) Regenerative design and development: current theory and practice. *Building Research and Information* **40**(1), 1–6.

Comes, T., Wijngaards, N., Hiete, M., Conrade, C., Schultmann, F. (2012) A distributed scenario-based decision support system for robust decision-making in complex situations. *International Journal of Information Systems for Crisis Response and Management* **34**(4), 17–35.

Costa, A.A., Tavares, L.V. (2012) Social e-business and the satellite network model: Innovative concepts to improve collaboration in construction. *Automation in Construction* **22**, 387–397.

Daim, T., Ha, A., Reutiman, S., Hughes, B., Pathak, U., Bynum, W., Bhatla, A. (2011) Exploring the communication breakdown in global virtual teams. *International Journal of Project Management* **30**(1), 199–212.

Dainty, A. (2008) Methodological pluralism in construction management research. In: *Advanced Research Methods in the Built Environment* (eds A. Hnight, L. Ruddock). Wiley/Blackwell, Oxford.

Dalkir, K. (2005) *Knowledge Management in Theory and Practice*. Elsevier, Oxford.

Dollery, B., Kortt, M.A., and Grant, B. (2012) Harnessing private funds to alleviate the australian local government infrastructure backlog. *Economic Papers: A Journal of Applied Economics and Policy* **31**(1), 114–122.

DSIP (2013) *Northern Economic Triangle Infrastructure Plan – Progress Report 2009–2010*. Department of State Government, Infrastructure and Planning, Queensland Government. Available at: http://www.dsdip.qld.gov.au (accessed 18 November 2015).

Dur, F., Yigitcanlar, T. (2014) Assessing land-use and transport integration via a spatial composite indexing model. *International Journal of Environmental Science and Technology* **12**(3), 803–816.

Eames, M., Dixon, T., May, T., Hunt, M. (2013) City futures: exploring urban retrofit and sustainable transitions. *Building Research and Information* **41**(5), 504–516.

Edum-Fotwe, F.T., Price, A.D.F. (2009) A social ontology for appraising sustainability of construction projects and developments. *International Journal of Project Management* **27**(4), 313–322.

El-Diraby, T. E. (2013) Civil infrastructure decision-making as a chaotic sociotechnical system: role of information systems in engaging stakeholders and democratizing innovation. *Journal of Infrastructure Systems* **19**(4), 355–362.

El-Gohary, N.M., Osman, H., El-Diraby, T.E. (2006) Stakeholder management for public private partnerships. *International Journal of Project Management* **24**(7), 595–604.

Goh, K.C., Yang, J. (2013) Importance of sustainability related cost components in highway infrastructure: perspective of stakeholders in Australia. *Journal of Infrastructure Systems* **20**(1), 04013002.

Gosse, C., Smith, B., Clarens, A. (2013) Environmentally preferable pavement management systems. *Journal of Infrastructure Systems* **19**(3), 315–325.

Gudes, O., Kendall, E., Yigitcanlar, T., Pathak, V., Baum, S. (2010) Rethinking health planning: a framework for organising information to underpin collaborative health planning. *Health Information Management Journal* **39**(2), 18–29.

Gordon, C. (2012) Financing and managing urban transport. In: *Urban Infrastructure: Finance and Management.* (eds K. Wellman, M. Spiller), pp. 225–258. Wiley/Blackwell, Oxford.

Haas, R. (1997). VIEWPOINT: infrastructure renewal requires more than money, political will, and commitment. *Journal of Infrastructure Systems* **3**(2), 55–58.

Hamilton, A., Mitchell, G., Yli-Karjanmaa, S. (2002) The BEQUEST toolkit: a decision support system for urban sustainability. *Building Research and Information* **30**(2), 109–115.

Hartmann, A., Hietbrink, M. (2013) An exploratory study on the relationship between stakeholder expectations, experiences and satisfaction in road maintenance. *Construction Management and Economics* **31**(4), 345–358.

Hendler, J., Berners-Lee, J. (2010) From the semantic web to social machines: a research challenge for AI on the world wide web. *Artificial Intelligence* **174**(2), 156–161.

Irvin, R.A., Stansbury, J. (2004) Citizen participation in decision-making: is it worth the effort? *Public Administration Review* **64**(1), 55–65.

Jha, K.N., Iyer, K.C. (2006) Critical determinants of project coordination. *International Journal of Project Management* **24**(4), 314–322.

Jones, P., Patterson, J. (2007) The development of a practical evaluation tool for urban sustainability. *Indoor and Built Environment* **16**(3), 255–272.

Kamel, M.A. (2013) Encouraging walkability in GCC cities: smart urban solutions. *Smart and Sustainable Built Environment* **2**(3), 288–310.

Kaplan, A.M., Haenlein, M. (2010) Users of the world, unite! The challenges and opportunities of social media. *Business Horizons* **53**(1), 59–68.

Karacapilidis, N., Papadias, D. (2001) Computer supported argumentation and collaborative decision-making: the HERMES system. *Information Systems* **26**(4), 259–277.

Kietzmann, J., Plangger, K., Eaton, B., Heilgenberg, K., Pitt, L., Berthon, P. (2013) Mobility at work: a typology of mobile communities of practice and contextual ambidexterity. *Journal of Strategic Information Systems* **3**(4), 282–297.

Klug, S., Hayashi, Y. (2012) Urban sprawl and local infrastructure in Japan and Germany. *Journal of Infrastructure Systems* **18**(4), 232–241.

Landry, C. (2008) *The Creative City*. Earthscan, London.

Lee, G., Chan, E. (2008) Factors affecting urban renewal in high-density city: case study of Hong Kong. *Journal of Urban Planning and Development* **134**(3), 140–148.

Lenferink, S., Tillema, T., Arts, J. (2013) Towards sustainable infrastructure development through integrated contracts: experiences with inclusiveness in Dutch infrastructure projects. *International Journal of Project Management* **31**(4), 615–627.

Li, T.H.Y., Ng, S.T., Skitmore, M. (2013) Evaluating stakeholder satisfaction during public participation in major infrastructure and construction projects: a fuzzy approach. *Automation in Construction* **29**, 123–135.

Li, Z., Madanu, S. (2009) Highway project level life-cycle benefit/cost analysis under certainty, risk, and uncertainty: methodology with case study. *Journal of Transportation Engineering* **135**(8), 516–526.

Macharis, C., Turcksin, L., Lebeau, K. (2012) Multi actor multi criteria analysis (MAMCA) as a tool to support sustainable decisions: state of use. *Decision Support Systems* **54**(1), 610–620.

Markard, J. (2011) Transformation of infrastructures: sector characteristics and implications for fundamental change. *Journal of Infrastructure Systems* **17**(3), 107–117.

Markard, J., Raven, R., Truffer, B. (2012) Sustainability transitions: An emerging field of research and its prospects. *Research Policy* **41**(6), 955–967.

Matsunaka, R., Oba, T., Nakagawa, D., Nagao, M., Nawrocki, J. (2013) International comparison of the relationship between urban structure and the service level of urban public transportation– a comprehensive analysis in local cities in Japan, France and Germany. *Transport Policy* **30**, 26–39.

Matthews, J., Allouche, E. (2012) Fully automated decision support system for assessing the suitability of trenchless technologies. *Journal of Pipeline Systems Engineering and Practice* **3**(2), 55–64.

Mayer, I.S., van Bueren, E.M., Bots, P., van der Voort, H., Seijdel, R. (2005) Collaborative decision making for sustainable urban renewal projects: a simulation-gaming approach. *Environment and Planning B: Planning and Design* **32**(3), 403–423.

McCartney, G., Whyte, B., Livingston, M., Crawford, F. (2012) Building a bridge, transport infrastructure and population characteristics: explaining active travel into Glasgow. *Transport Policy* **21**, 119–125.

McIntosh, J., Trubka, R., Kenworthy, F., Newman, P. (2014) The role of urban form and transit in city car dependence: analysis of 26 global cities from 1960 to 2000. *Transportation Research Part D: Transport and Environment* **33**, 95–110.

Molenaar, K., Songer, A. (2001) Web-based decision support systems: case study in project delivery. *Journal of Computing in Civil Engineering* **15**(4), 259–267.

Muench, S., Mahoney, J., White, G. (2010) Pavement interactive: pavement knowledge transfer with Web 2.0. *Journal of Transportation Engineering* **136**(12), 1165–1172.

Nagpal, M., Kortt, M.A., Dollery, B. (2013) Bang for the buck? An evaluation of the roads to recovery program. *Economic Papers: A Journal of Applied Economics and Policy* **32**(2), 239–248.

Newman, P. (2014) Density, the sustainability multiplier: some myths and truths with application to Perth, Australia. *Sustainability* **6**(9), 6467–6487.

Newton, P. (2013) Regenerating cities: technological and design innovation for Australian suburbs. *Building Research and Information* **41**(5), 575–588.

Newton, P., Newman, P., Glackin, S., Trubka, R. (2012) Greening the greyfields: unlocking the redevelopment potential of the middle suburbs in Australian cities. *World Academy of Science, Engineering and Technology* **71**, 138–157.

Osman, H. (2012) Agent-based simulation of urban infrastructure asset management activities. *Automation in Construction* **28**, 45–57.

Osman, H., El-Diraby, T. (2011) Knowledge-enabled decision support system for routing urban utilities. *Journal of Construction Engineering and Management* **137**(3), 198–213.

Park, T., Kim, H. (2013) A data warehouse-based decision support system for sewer infrastructure management. *Automation in Construction* **30**, 37–49.

Power, D.J., Phillips-Wren, G. (2011) Impact of social media and Web 2.0 on decision-making. *Journal of Decision Systems* **20**(3), 249–261.

Power, D.J., Sharda, R. (2007) Model-driven decision support systems: concepts and research directions. *Decision Support Systems* **43**(3), 1044–1061.

RAI (2012) *Catalysing Local Infrastructure Renewal*, Regional Australian Institute. Available at: http://www.regionalaustralia.org.au (accessed 1 November 2013).

Saunders, M., Lewis, P., Thornhill, A. (2009) *Research Methods for Business Students*. Pearson Education, Upper Saddle River.

Schofer, J., Evans, L., Freeman, M., Galehouse, L., Madanat, S., Maher, A., McNeil, S., Myers, J., Peskin, R., Wlaschin, B. (2010) Research agenda for transportation infrastructure preservation and renewal: conference report. *Journal of Infrastructure Systems* **16**(4), 228–230.

Shen, L., Wu, Y., Zhang, X. (2011) Key Assessment Indicators for the sustainability of infrastructure projects. *Journal of Construction Engineering and Management* **137**(6), 441–451.

Shim, J.P., Warkentin, M., Courtney, J.F., Power, D.J., Sharda, R., Carlsson, C. (2002) Past, present, and future of decision support technology. *Decision Support Systems* **33**(2), 111–126.

Stokman, F.N., Van Assen, M.A., Van der Knoop, J., Van Oosten, R.C. (2000) Strategic decision-making. *Advances in Group Processes* **17**(1), 131–153.

Surahyo, M., El-Diraby, T.E. (2009) Schema for interoperable representation of environmental and social costs in highway construction. *ASCE Journal of Construction Engineering and Management* **135**(4), 254–266.

Topalovic, P., Carter, J., Topalovic, M., Krantzberg, G. (2012) Light rail transit in Hamilton: health, environmental and economic impact analysis. *Social Indicators Research* **108**(2), 329–350.

Tsamboulas, D.A., Mikroudis, G.K. (2006) TRANS-POL: a mediator between transportation models and decision makers' policies. *Decision Support Systems* **42**(2), 879–897.

Ugwu, O.O., Kumaraswamy, M.M., Wong, A., Ng, S.T. (2006) Sustainability appraisal in infrastructure projects (SUSAIP): Part 1. Development of indicators and computational methods. *Automation in Construction* **15**(2), 239–251.

UN (2013) *World Population Policy Report*. Department of Economic and Social Affairs Population Division. United Nations, New York.

Velaga, N.R., Beecroft, M., Nelson, J.D., Corsar, D., Edwards, P. (2012) Transport poverty meets the digital divide: accessibility and connectivity in rural communities. *Journal of Transport Geography* **21**, 102–112.

Wang, W.-M., Lee, A.H.I., Peng, L.-P., Wu, Z.-L. (2013) An integrated decision making model for district revitalization and regeneration project selection. *Decision Support Systems* **54**(2), 1092–1103.

Witkowski, K. (2012) The solutions for improving the urban transport system based on resident surveys. *Management* **16**(1), 131–145.

Yang, J. (2014) An investigation of stakeholder analysis in urban development projects: empirical or rationalistic perspectives. *International Journal of Project Management* **32**, 838–849.

Yang, J., Yuan, M., Yigitcanlar, T., Newman. P., Schultmann, F. (2015) Managing knowledge to promote sustainability in Australian transport infrastructure projects. *Sustainability* **7**(7), 3132–8150.

Yigitcanlar, T., Teriman, S. (2014) Rethinking sustainable urban development: towards an integrated planning and development process, *International Journal of Environmental Science and Technology* **12**(1), 341–352.

Yigitcanlar, T. (ed.) (2010) *Sustainable Urban and Regional Infrastructure Development: Technologies, Applications and Management*. IGI Global, Hersey.

Yigitcanlar, T. (2008) Public oriented interactive environmental decision support system. In: *GIS and evidence- based policy making* (eds S. Wise, M. Craglia), Taylor and Francis, London, pp. 347–366.

Yu, L. (2014) A web of data: towards the idea of a semantic web. In: *A Developer's Guide to the Semantic Web* (L. Yu), Springer, Heidelberg, pp. 3–21.

Zhang, J., El-Diraby, T. (2012) Social semantic approach to support communication in AEC. *Journal of Computing in Civil Engineering* **26**(1), 90–104.

Chapter 18

Rethinking the Role of Time in Sustainable Urban Development

Manila De Iuliis
Municipality of Santo Stefano al Mare, 18010 Santo Stefano al Mare, Italy

18.1 Introduction

Time and sustainable development are inextricably entwined. Assumptions about how long a development is expected to be sustainable, or over what period an issue is to be considered, are at the heart of sustainability. Scientists, governing bodies and planners make decisions within the context of an assumed time period. How long this time period should be is a question of great importance.

There is a variety of views of the time horizons and time dimensions related to sustainable development. This is due to the multifaceted character of reality, which is defined by a set of different but interrelated aspects. Sustainable development deals with environment, economy, social integration, equality, politics, personal and collective well-being, safety, cultural identity and background. All these aspects are fields for scientific investigation defined by proper rules, norms, issues and dimensions. Each of them has proper time horizons and dimensions, which appear to be independent from one another. For these reasons, an integrated approach to sustainable development is needed.

There is a wide literature on *time and sustainability* or sustainable development, but it is quite difficult to find papers, books or reviews dealing with time in sustainable development or defining what *sustainable time* means. This is despite the importance of a time dimension to the whole subject. To bring these two concepts together, time and sustainable development, implies an underpinning into complex and partly undiscovered fields.

Sustainable development is a process of change. Over what time sustainable development is to be achieved is a crucial and not yet answered question.

Future Challenges in Evaluating and Managing Sustainable Development in the Built Environment,
First Edition. Edited by Peter S. Brandon, Patrizia Lombardi and Geoffrey Q. Shen.
© 2017 John Wiley & Sons Ltd. Published 2017 by John Wiley & Sons Ltd.

18.2 Why time?

Time has been the subject of a great number of studies in science, mathematics, philosophy, anthropology, sociology, literature, poetry and fine arts. Its application to urban planning discipline is still in its infancy (Brandon and Lombardi, 2005). Defining the term 'time' is not an easy exercise. Saint Augustine in his *Confessions* stated, 'What is Time then? If someone asks to me I cannot explain' (Augustine, 1991). The *English Dictionary* (Collins, 2000) defines time as 'the continuous passage of existence in which events pass from a state of potentiality in the future, through the present, to a state of finality in the past'. Since ancient Greece, time has been considered as a fundamental characteristic of everyday life, defined by *Aion*, the eternal and sacred time, and *Chronos*, the ordinary time. These two different aspects of time have influenced many further theories giving time different meanings. In the sixth century B.C., the Athenian statesman Solon considered time as a *judge* – able to discover and avenge any act of injustice. In the same period, Hesiod saw time as the *moral order of the universe*, giving an account of man's decline from a primaeval golden age. Anaximander and Heraclitus extended the concept of justice to the whole universe by asserting that 'to him (time) everything that happens in the natural world is rational through and through and subject to a rigid norm' (Whithrow, 1989). Later, the Pythagoreans considered time as the *soul of the universe* – its procreative element. The meaning of time has often been connected with the meaning of human life and soul. Time has been considered as a fundamental characteristic of human experience despite the lack of evidence that we have a special sense of time as we have of sight, hearing, touch, taste or smell. Why then concern oneself with time? It is because time is part of our life and of our identity. Durkheim asserted that time is embedded in social life, and that it is a social category of thought (Lucas, 2005).

Time is a fundamental characteristic of human experience. The personal experience of time is always of the present, and the subjective idea of time comes from reflecting on this experience. Through the flowing of time, experience of everyday life turns into memory, which is part of personal background and identity. Past, present and future are three temporal horizons characterising man's experience of everyday life.

Memory, identity and background are grounding concepts in urban planning. All human settlements (cities, villages etc.) are rooted in time. The Latin phrase *Ab Urbe Condita* represented a year-numbering system used by some ancient Roman historians to identify particular Roman periods. The English translation is 'from the founding of the City (Rome)' and it expresses the deep connection existing between the founding of the city and the counting of time. In Varro's point of view, time started with the foundation of Rome on 21 April 753 B.C. This indicates that, in ancient civilisations, time started with a city foundation. From that date, past, present and future existed as interconnected horizons.

The evolution of the spatial urban structure has always reflected the passing of time. Time is perceived through change occurring within the spatial urban character which, through centuries, becomes a palimpsest. The sense of personal and collective identity is rooted in this palimpsest as the historical evolution of urban structures.

Space and time are related through change. Plato asserted that time and the universe are inseparable, as time does not exist in its own right but is a characteristic of the universe.

The founding of a city was a sacred ritual grounded in time. In ancient civilisations, the city was founded around a sacred place called *the centre* whose archetypal image was the cosmic mountain, the eternal tree or the central pillar sustaining the planes of the cosmos. Mircea Eliade asserted that 'in cultures that have the conception of three cosmic regions – those of Heaven, Earth and Hell – the centre constituted the point of intersection of those regions. It is here that the break-through on to another plane is possible and, at the same time, communication between the three regions… Hell, the centre of the Earth and the door of heaven are all to be found, then, upon the same axis, and it is along this axis that the passage from one cosmic region to another is effected' (Eliade, 1991). The centre was the zone of intersection between the higher (divine) world, the terrestrial world and the subterranean (infernal) world. In the oriental religious tradition, many cities were conceived as being in the centre of the world. Babylon, for example, was considered a *gate of the gods*, for it was there that the gods came down to earth. The summit of the cosmic mountain was considered as the navel of the earth, the point at which creation began. An ancient rabbinical text affirms, 'The Holy one created the world like an embryo. As an embryo proceeds from the navel onward, so God began the creation of the world from its navel onward, and from thence it spread in different directions' (Eliade, 1991). The creation of man took place similarly from a central point, 'Adam was created at the centre of the earth, on the very same spot where later on, the Cross of Jesus were to be erected' (Eliade, 1991). The existence of a sacred place, the so-called *centre*, was a grounding in building the system of orientation that was proper to each inhabitant. The personal and collective image of the city was built around the *centre*, which was a symbol of the community identity. Personal and collective identity and sense of orientation are grounded in spatial and temporal dimensions. As Kevin Lynch asserted, 'The need to recognise and pattern our surroundings is so crucial, and has such long roots in the past, that this image has wide practical and emotional importance to the individual' (Lynch, 1960). The city is a continuous evolving city rooted in time and changing within space. Like that of Irene, 'it is a city in the distance and if you approach, it changes. For those who pass it without entering, the city is one thing; it is another for those who are trapped by it and never leave. There is the city where you arrive for the first time; and there is another city which you leave never to return. Each deserves a different name; perhaps I have already spoken of Irene under other names; perhaps I have spoken only of Irene' (Calvino, 1997). The symbol of the centre is rooted in time, and it is part of the personal identity and sense of orientation.

The definition of the existing man–environment relation is crucial in solving the question related to time and sustainable development. Sustainable development is a question of time, in particular it is a question of the increasing distance between biological and anthropic time.

18.3 Planning with time

The term 'planning' refers to a wide range of activities designed to ensure that desired goals are achieved in the future. These goals include environmental protection, urban development, economic activity, social justice and so on. Sustainability planning means 'to bring about a society that will not only exist but thrive far into the future.' The word 'sustain' indicates an expanded time horizon to be considered in the planning processes.

Urban structures depend on the environment in physical, economic and social terms. The connection between subjective harmony (human equilibrium and satisfaction) and the temporal equilibrium of the surrounding environment (natural and built ones) indicates *temporal coherence* as the leading concept (De Iuliis, 2010).

Cities are grounded in time. They are characterised by discordant rhythms having their genesis in the accidental intersection of time and space. Cities are *experienced* in everyday life. Through individual and collective experience, cities evolve. Cities are like cultural texts enclosing a wide range of interrelating symbols and meanings, 'broad fashion as a space in which there is a weaving together of symbols to create an irreducible plurality of meaning. It is a signifying practice that abolishes the distinction between writing and reading, production and consumption. A text does not occupy space as does a work on the library shelf, but is a field within which there is an activity of production, of signification' (Duncan and Duncan, 1992). An *urban text* is a physical structure, a combination of signs, monuments, buildings, streets and so on, which is represented in maps, planning documents, real estate publications, as well as films, music, art, literature and other cultural forms (Gottdiener and Lagopulos, 1986). The citizens' experience of the urban context is an interactive process of coding and decoding of these signs and symbols (Stevenson, 2003). Roland Barthes argues that 'the urban text is one where unstable and transient signifieds are continuously being transformed into signifiers – forming an infinite chain of metaphors whose significance is always retreating or becomes itself a signifier' (Barthes, 1970). It means that all users of the city *write* their own relationship with the urban space in highly idiosyncratic ways. Experiencing the urban space means *writing* and *reading* the *urban text* by modifying it through action. Action causes change; and change is related to time by *motion*, which is the passage from a *before* to an *after* moment. The urban context is a *cultural text* rooted in time. For this reason, planning, as a multifaceted discipline, requires an approach to time as a leading factor of the urban evolution.

Spatial and environmental planning are caught in a process of change. Planning is a task that up to now has been geared toward defined circumstances that are fixed in the future. This traditional sense of planning is now replaced by actor-centred, process-oriented approaches; and planning has assumed a strategic character. Because of its dealing with change, sustainable planning should rediscover time as a connecting link, as mediator between nature and culture, between economy, ecology and social space. The concept of change as driving for urban evolution suggests that of *transitions*, which are 'liminal spaces of possibility... in transitional situations space and time come to be more densely compressed' (Hofmeister, 2002). The concept of transition indicates the passage from a situation *before* change to another situation *after* change. Through the succession of transitional moments, the urban context evolves by changing. Evolution is a historical-formative process, and planning is the instrument of this process. Planning with time implies the abandonment of the principle of *separation* that became dominant during the Enlightenment, which saw nature being reconstructed with the aim of 'separating that which is combined and homogenising that which is separate' (Beck, 1996). Following these principles, planning was a conscious, socially controlled means of organising space by creating *islands*; everything had its time, and everything had its space. Given that time is the leading factor for urban evolution, the planning approach should be integrated in order to take into consideration all those aspects and all those temporal dimensions, which define the urban system. The concept of the *diversity of time* is an important aspect in planning discipline. Thinking about temporal diversity involves thinking about the switching between different forms of time. Bernard Albert, in a report on the Ninth Conference of the Tutzing Time Ecology Project (April 2000) entitled 'Temporal Diversity', provided the following grid of mapping temporal diversity (Albert, 2002):

- The fundamental dimensions or elements of time were the moment/instant, duration/extension and temporality/change.
- The forms of time were designated as beginnings and ends, pauses and transitions, as well as tempo and repetitions.
- Time patterns were considered to encompass specific arrangements of forms of time such as rhythm (repetition with variation, thus allowing for change), metronomic beat (precision, repetition of exactly the same, that is, without change) and simultaneity.
- Time structured were denoted processes that have evolved into temporally ordered events.
- Time Gestalten (forms) were formulated as context-dependent ensembles of interdependent temporal patterns, forms of time and interactive processes that are specific to personal, social, cultural and natural systems.
- *Timescapes* was earmarked as the overarching term in the debate; the tapestry that weaves together all the elements, forms, structures, processes and systems outlined above. As such, it embraces the general and specific products and processes of time, being and becoming. Timescapes have to be understood in conjunction with their spatial and material context, and they have to be appreciated as inescapably contextual and perspective-dependent.

The above grid suggests time as *contextualised*. The temporal aspect of the urban evolution is not an a priori character, which is to be fixed outside of the evolving process of the urban context. Time is rooted in the urban space, and the urban space is rooted in time. Planning for sustainability requires the analysis of the symbiotic relation existing between urban space and formative time.

Planners are resorting to the dimension of time. Chrono-urban studies are starting to emerge as a sub-discipline of urban planning.

The development of the chrono-urban studies and the adoption of time-oriented programmes indicate an increasing interest in time as a grounding aspect in everyday life.

In a time-oriented approach, the first task for urban and environmental planners should be to observe time in space. In particular, it should be to observe social/historical time (time related to social interaction and human evolution) in its connection with biological time (time of nature). The relation between historical time and biological time and, in particular, the discrepancy existing between them are at the core of sustainable planning. As suggested by Prof. Enzo Tiezzi, of the University of Siena, historical time and biological time follow different rhythms and have different time horizons (Tiezzi, 2005). The different and contrasting temporal character of the social and natural environments is the main problem facing sustainable planning. Differences in time horizons make it difficult to decide for a shared direction to take in order to plan a sustainable urban future. Nevertheless, time is a driving aspect in urban planning; and it cannot be ignored.

Dealing with time in planning procedures is not an easy task. All the theories, which flourished around the term 'sustainable development' have suggested two basic and shared principles (Hofmeister, 2002):

- The principle of use-integration, which is based on an understanding of space in the unity of economic space, socio-cultural and ecological living space;
- The principle of the preservation of long-term use options, which are based on the requirement of justice within and between generations;

Planning for sustainability involves several interacting aspects, which follow different rhythms and have different time horizons.

Given that the evolution of the urban context is defined by a succession of temporal phases, related *transitions* (passage from one temporal phase to the following one) mark changes occurring within places in the urban space.

Planning for sustainability implies planning with time. Planning with time implies dealing with change and the impacts it causes.

In everyday language, an *impact* is the effect of a specific *cause*. An impact is any alteration of environmental conditions or creation of a new set of environmental conditions, adverse or beneficial, caused or induced by the action or set of actions under consideration (Rau and Wooten, 1979). More particularly an impact 'can be described as the change in an environmental parameter over a specific period and within a confined area, resulting from a particular activity compared with the situation which would have occurred had the activity not be initiated' (Wathern, 1992). Impacts can be direct or indirect. The direct ones fall on the environment as the result of the project input; the indirect ones are generated by activities resulting from the project.

Impacts are to be measured with relation to time. Among all techniques that have been developed on impact assessment, none of them has a properly considered time factor.

Time and space are two main aspects in urban planning. They have a complex meaning and structure. Both in spatial and in temporal terms, scales are various. The spatial scale may correspond with a farm, village, town or a city, region, country and so on until the entire world has been considered. The difficulty is that all scales are interlinked.

Time scales play a crucial role in urban planning. Establishing time scales within a social urban system is not an easy task (Bell and Morse, 1999):

- Different systems may require different time scales.
- Different components of sustainability in the same system may be measured by different time frames.
- Important is the choice of the starting point (need of a reference point).
- It is important to establish where the length of time is to start.

Planning for sustainability requires an integrated approach to time. Cities are at the core of sustainable development. Time is a driving aspect in sustainable urban planning.

18.4 Time as a linking factor. Hermann Dooyeweerd's philosophy of the law idea

Herman Dooyeweerd was a Dutch philosopher. He was born on 7th October 1894 in Amsterdam. His thought developed in a particular historic and social context, characterised by a rapid proliferation of special sciences. His being a philosopher depended on his interest and awareness of his surrounding reality, not merely as a spectator, but as someone with a more interactive role.

Dooyeweerd considered reality as an integrated system of mutual relations, in contrast with the Greek thinking and Western culture point of view.

The philosophy of the law idea was conceived as a way to investigate the complex and multi-aspectual character of reality. In the introduction to the first volume of his masterwork '*A New Critique of Theoretical Thought*', Dooyeweerd provides a clear description of his concept of reality, 'If I consider reality as it is given in the naive pre-theoretical experience, and then confront it with a theoretical analysis, through which reality appears to split up into various modal aspects then the first thing that strikes me, is the original indissoluble interrelation among these aspects which are for the first time explicitly distinguished in the theoretical attitude of mind' (Dooyeweerd, 1983a). Reality is conceived by Dooyeweerd as multi-aspectual, described by the set of 15 modalities given in Table 18.1.

A *modality* can be defined as an irreducible area of the functioning of a system. It is characterised by a nucleus of meaning, which provides it with an internal order named *sphere sovereignty* and with a set of laws by which it is governed, enabling entities to

Table 18.1   List of modalities.

Modality	Nuclei of meaning
Numerical	Numbers
Spatial	Continuous extension, pure space
Movement	Pure movement
Physical	Energy, mass
Biological	Life function
Sensitive	Senses, feelings
Analytical	Discerning of entities, logic
Historical	Formative power
Communicative	Informatory, symbolic representation
Social	Social intercourse, social exchange
Economic	Frugality, handling limited resources
Aesthetic	Harmony, beauty
Juridical	Retribution, fairness, rights
Ethical	Love, moral
Creedal	Faith, commitment, trustworthiness

Source: Lombardi and Basden (1997). Reproduced with the permission of Springer.

function in a variety of ways. In '*A New Critique of Theoretical Thought*', Dooyeweerd asserted that 'the modal aspects in their functional structure are consequently the determining, necessary conditions of all modal individuality in which temporal reality reveals itself within the law-spheres concerned. For this reason they can be called the modal a priori conditions of all individuality of meaning. This cosmic state of affairs is founded in the temporal world-order, which also determines the possibility of our experience. We can experience the modal aspects both in the pre-theoretical and in the theoretical attitude only in their temporal coherence, according to the foundational and the transcendental direction of time' (Dooyeweerd, 1983b).

The concept of time is fundamental in Dooyeweerd's philosophy of reality. In the '*New Critique of Theoretical Thought*' he wrote, 'The Idea of cosmic time constitutes the basis of the philosophical theory of reality in this book. By virtue of its integral character it may be called new. According to this conception, time in its cosmic sense has a cosmonomic and a factual side. Its cosmonomic side is the temporal order of succession or simultaneity. The factual side is the factual duration, which differs with various individualities.' (Dooyeweerd, 1983a). In Dooyeweerd's philosophy, time is *cosmic*, an integral conception enclosing the conditions of being and becoming, but not limited by them.

Cosmic time is experienced by a human being in everyday life. Experience of time is possible mainly because of the *feeling of time* that allows human beings to become aware of a more complete form of time, not just as it appears as measured by clocks or calendars. Within cosmic time, Dooyeweerd makes a distinction between *law side* and *entity side*. According to the law side, cosmic time is a structural time – an order embracing the entire temporal reality as defined by the 15 modalities. It is an invariant cosmic time structure within which all modalities and all individuality – structures (events, things, societal relationships etc.) are defined. According to the entity side, cosmic time is *duration*, a continuous mutual fusion of moments, events and so on (Dooyeweerd, 1983a).

In Dooyeweerd's philosophy, time is a very deep concept. It plays an important role in giving coherence to the modal aspects of reality, and it is fundamental in everyday human experience. Dooyeweerd asserted that 'Cosmic Time is the medium through which the meaning totality is broken up into a modal diversity of aspects' (Dooyeweerd, 1983a). He used the simile of the prism that splits light into distinct colours; time is the prism that splits light up into distinct aspects. Time, as disclosed by Dooyeweerd in his philosophy, can give meaning to the whole reality, embracing all aspects.

Following Figure 18.1, Time links modalities in a succession of anticipation and postication moments (before and after moments). This suggests each modality (each aspect of reality) contains echoes of the previous ones and is contained in the following ones. This indissoluble link is provided by Time.

According to Dooyeweerd, time is horizon and duration at the same time. Such a conception is of great importance, and it opens to an undiscovered, uncertain, wide and fascinating field.

Time is a fundamental characteristic of human experience. It is the bedrock of the social and cultural evolution of human civilisations since their dawning until today. Dooyeweerd has provided useful indications on the role of time within reality, by

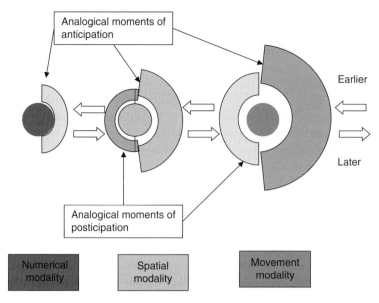

Figure 18.1   Temporal modal order. How time links modalities. Source: De Iuliis (2010).

structuring an ordered and integrated model. Following these indications, it is possible to come up with interesting and fruitful results in the practical application of Dooyeweerd's theory on urban planning procedures.

18.5 The grave of time. Why current planning approaches fail

Planning is a discipline, not a science. Because of the multi-aspectual character of the subject of analysis (urban contexts and, more in general, anthropic spaces), planning processes require the application of a wide range of notions belonging to the different fields of science. As suggested above, time is a pivotal aspect in urban development but its application to urban planning is still at its infancy.

In the synthesis report on the global consultation on addressing inequalities (UNICEF/UNWomen, 2013; p. 9), it is asserted that 'Transformative change towards a more equal and inclusive world and the eradication of poverty in all its forms, will depend on coherent global and national policy action in and across the economic, social, environmental and political domains'. The executive summary of the sixth EU Report on economic, social and territorial cohesion (European Commission, 2014b; p. xxix), recognises that 'This report comes out at the start of a new seven-year programming period for cohesion policy, when the situation in the EU is diametrically different from what it was at the start of the previous period in 2007. There is a time lag between the moment an investment is made and the time when its impact can be measured'. In the introduction to the EU Communication titled '*The Urban Dimension of EU Policies – Key Features on an EU Urban Agenda*' (European Commission, 2014a) it is declared that EU policies need to be better adapted to the urban realities where they will be implemented.

It is recognised that a poor and sectoral response to past EU urban policies have been registered. In the Report titled '*State of the Union and Key Challenges for Europe's Future*' (Emmanoulidis and Ivan, 2014), the Director of Studies at the European Policy Centre asserts 'In this unprecedented situation, there was no textbook that European and national decision makers could turn to for advice and guidance on how to react to these complex and interwoven crises. There are several doubts as to whether the EU and its members will be able to manage the process of growing global interdependencies and connectivity' (p. 9).

Why is it that urban policies at the European level have not been able to launch the ship of Sustainable Development? One possible reason is related to Time or, to be more specific, it is related to our inability to deal with the different time horizons that characterise all aspects involved in Sustainable Development. In current policies and planning tools, time is normally reduced to a 'schedule'. Deadlines, time optimisation, timetable are the most commonly used terms in urban management and urban policy. Urban planning discipline lacks an integrated temporal approach and tool that could help governments in finding possible solutions for a sustainable future of cities. Current policies are based on sectorial approaches without taking into value the epochal form of time. That's why they fail in providing concrete response to complexity.

The future of built environments is affected by uncertainty due to rapid change. According to Tarnawska and Rosiek (2015), the world population in 2050 is expected to increase to 9.3 billion, most of which will be absorbed by urban areas. We are becoming a city planet (Brand, 2011). Urban areas are crucial for improving sustainable living and human quality of life.

To address sustainability we need a systemic approach as, following Aristotle, 'the whole is greater than the sum of its parts'.

Sustainable development deals with complexity. According to Holland (2014), complexity 'once an ordinary noun describing objects with many interconnected parts now designates a scientific field with many branches'.

Complex does not necessarily mean complicated but it is very difficult not to complicate things when the connection between Time and Sustainable Development raises so many unanswered questions.

How can people, businesses and institutions plan for the future when they do not know what tomorrow will bring?

According to van der Duin (2007), futures research and planners should adopt an approach having the following characteristics:

- Holistic; future is uncertain by nature, and it indicates that it is (or will be) more than the sum of its constituent parts. The future is not simply a calculus.
- Interdisciplinary; futures research focuses on a wide range of subjects and fields of investigation, which are open interrelating systems.
- Multidisciplinary; the future ought to be viewed from many different perspectives, with a search for a workable and valid integration between these perspectives.
- Transdisciplinary; future research might become a discipline crossing and combining tools and knowledge of different disciplines.

Planning for Sustainable Development in an uncertain era requires a deep focus on the future. It is certainly a long-term issue but it needs to be reconciled with short-term policies (European Commission, 2014).

For sustainable development to be multidisciplinary, reconciling all the temporal dimensions involved is of great importance.

Schwartz (1996) suggests rehearsing the future as a way to reduce uncertainty. He affirms that 'In the real world, you do not know ahead of time which scenario will take place, but you prepare…, and then train yourself tools for one or two small details so that you can recognise the full play before you are called upon to act'.

The human ability to imagine the future is necessary for planning for the future.

18.6 Summary

This chapter suggests some key considerations which can be summarised as follows:

- *Sustainable development requires an integrated systemic approach* to the notion of built environment. The complexity of sustainable development resides in the number of aspects involved, and in the difficulty of dealing with them in a systemic way.
- *Time is a leading factor in urban planning and development.* Time plays an important role as a structuring element in urban reality. Cities are like palimpsests, and they need an integrated approach rooted in time in order to be fully analysed.
- *The philosophy of the law idea developed by H. Dooyeweerd suggests a set of aspects that are descriptive of reality.* It provides a multidisciplinary and systemic approach to urban planning.

The investigation of the concept of time is a difficult task. Although there has been great interest in time by many authors over the centuries, who have written and theorised on it, time has remained a stranger. Fraser (1987) wrote 'the passage of time is intimately familiar; the idea of time is strangely elusive'.

18.7 A future challenge

Today long-term thinking seems to be impossible to our eyes, nevertheless, it is necessary as never before.

Planners and decision-makers are required to consider time not just as a measure for scheduling activities, rather as a creative tool for building images of possible futures.

To do this and successfully cope with uncertainty, a change of perspective is necessary. This chapter suggests the following challenge for the future: the finding of the so-called Archimedean Point, an external and fixed point from which to objectively observe the world as a whole and learn from its dynamics. It is the basis for decision-making, particularly when dealing with complexity. It is the vantage point for planning discipline, which could consider the subject of analysis (human settlements) as the result of a multi-aspectual evolution, being rooted very far in time.

Rethinking the role of time in sustainable urban development can help in finding it.

References

Albert, B. (2002) Temporal diversity. A note on the Ninth Tutzing Time Ecology Conference. *Time and Society* **11**(1), 89–104.

Augustine (1991) *Confessions* (ed. H. Chack). Oxford University Press, Oxford:

Barthes, R. (1970) Semiology and the Urban. In: *The City and the Sign: An Introduction to Urban Semiotics* (eds M. Gottdiener, A. Lagopoulos). Columbia University Press, New York.

Beck, R. (1996) Die Abschaffung der Wildniss. Landschaftsasthetik, bauerliche Wirtschaft und Okologie zu Beginn der Moderne. In: *Naturlandschaft-Kulturlandschaft. Die Veranderung der Landschaft nach der Nutzbarmachung durch den Menschen* (ed. W. Konold). Ecomed, Landsberg/Lech, pp. 27–44.

Bell, S., Morse, S. (1999) *Sustainability Indicators: Measuring the Immeasurable*. Earthscan, London.

Brand, S. (2011) *The Salt Summaries. Seminars About Long Term Thinking*. Long Press Now, San Francisco.

Brandon, P., Lombardi, P. (2005) *Evaluating Sustainable Development in the Built Environment*. Blackwell, Oxford.

Calvino, I. (1997) *Invisible Cities*. Vintage, London.

Collins (2000) *English Dictionary*. Harper Collins, Glasgow.

De Iuliis, M., Brandon, P. (2012) The time horizon in the evaluation of sustainable development. *Journal of Civil Engineer and Architecture* **6**(3) 334–343.

De Iuliis, M. (2010) *A Dooyeweerdian Approach to Time in Sustainable Development*, PhD thesis, University of Salford, Salford.

Dooyeweerd, H. (1983a) *A New Critique of Theoretical Thought*, vol. **1**. Paideia Press, Ontario.

Dooyeweerd, H. (1983b) *A New Critique of Theoretical Thought*, vol. **2**. Paideia Press, Ontario.

Duncan, J., Duncan, N. (1992) Ideology and bliss: Roland Barthes and the secret histories of landscape. In: *Writing Worlds: Discourse, Text and Metaphor in the Representation of Landscape*. (eds T. Barnes, J. Duncan). Routledge, London.

Eliade, M. (1991) *Images and Symbols*. Princeton University Press, Princeton.

Emmanoulidis, J.A., Ivan, P. (2014) *State of the Union and Key Challenges for Europe's Future*. In: *AAVV Challenge Europe. Challenges and New Beginnings: Priorities for the EU's New Leadership*, European Policy Centre, Issue 22. Available at: www.epc.eu/…/pub_4855_challenge_europe_issue (accessed 12 December 2015).

European Commission (2014a) *The Urban Dimension of EU Policies – Key Features of an EU Urban Agenda*. Available at: http://ec.europa.eu/regional_policy/sources/consultation/urb_agenda/pdf/comm_act_urb_agenda_en.pdf (accessed 1 August 2015).

European Commission (2014b) *Investment for Jobs and Growth. Promoting Development and Good Governance in EU Regions and Cities*. Sixth Report on Economic, Social and Territorial Cohesion, Brussels, Directorate-General for Regional and Urban Policy. Available at: http://ec.europa.eu/regional_policy/cohesion_report (accessed 12 December 2015).

European Policy Centre (2014) *Challenge Europe. Challenges and New Beginnings: Priorities for the EU's New Leadership*. Available at: http://www.epc.eu/pub.php (accessed 4 November 2014).

Fraser, J. (1987) *Time the Familiar Stranger*. University of Massachussetts Press, Amherst, Mass.

Gottdiener, M., Lagopulos, A. (1986) *The City and the Sign: An Introduction to Urban Semiotics*. Columbia University Press, New York.

Hayward, P. (2007) Inside the foresight mind. In: *Knowing Tomorrow? How Science deals with the future* (ed. P. van der Duin). Eburon, Delft.

Hofmeister, S. (2002) Intermediate "time-spaces": the rediscovery of transition in spatial planning and environmental planning. *Time and Society* **11**(1), 105–130.

Holland, J.H. (2014) *Complexity. A Very Short Introduction*, Oxford University Press, Oxford.

Jaffe, S. (2015) A tale of one city? *Nation* **300**(6), 20–24.

Lombardi, P.L., Basden, A. (1997) Environmental sustainability and information systems. *System Practice* **10**(4), 473–489.

Lucas, G. (2005) *The Archaeology of Time*. Routledge, New York.

Lynch, K. (1960) *The Image of the City*. MIT Press, Cambridge, Mass.

Rau, J.G. and Wooten, D.C. (1979) *Environmental Impact Analysis*. McGraw-Hill, New York.

Schwartz, P. (1996) *The Art of the Long View. Planning for the Future in an Uncertain World*. Doubleday, New York.

Smith, P.F. (1973) City as organism. *Ekistics* **35**(209), 238–239.

Sotarauta, M. (2005) Shared leadership and dynamic capabilities in regional development. In: *Regionalism Contested: Institution, Society and Governance* (eds H. Halkier, I. Sagan), Urban and Regional Planning and Development Series. Routledge, New York, pp. 53–72.

Stern, N. (2015) *Why Are We Waiting? The Logic, Urgency, and Promise of Tackling Climate Change*, MIT Press, Cambridge, Mass.

Stevenson, D. (2003) *Cities and Urban Cultures*. Open University Press, Philadelphia.

Sneddon, C., Howarth, R.B., Norgaard, R.B. (2006) Sustainable development in a post-Brundtland world. *Ecological Economics* **57**, 253–268.

Tarnawska, K., Rosiek, J. (2015) The Jessica initiative: an instrument for urban sustainable development. Examples of urban regeneration in Silesia (Poland) and Central Moravia (Czech Republic). *Comparative Economic Research* **18**(2), 119–138.

Teece, D.J., Pisano, G., Shuen, A. (1997) Dynamic capabilities and strategic management. *Strategic Management Journal* **18**(7), 509–533.

Tiezzi, E. (2005) *Tempi Storici, Tempi Biologici. Venticinque Anni Dopo*. Donzelli, Roma.

UNICEF/UNWomen (2013) *Global Thematic Consultation on the Post-2015 Development Agenda. Addressing Inequalities*. Synthesis Report of Global Public Consultation. Available at www.worldwewant.org (accessed 12 December 2015).

van der Duin, P. (ed.) (2007) *Knowing Tomorrow? How Science Deals with the Future*. Eburon, Delft.

Wathern, P. (1992) *Environmental Impact Assessment: Theory and Practice*. Routledge, London.

Whithrow, G. (1989) *Time in History: Views of Time from Prehistory to the Present Day*. Oxford University Press, Oxford.

Chapter 19
Suggestions for Future Sustainability: Philosophical and Practical

Andrew Basden

Business School, University of Salford, Salford, M5 4WT, UK

19.1 Sustainability

Sustainability is a complex issue, as shown by the diversity of topics covered by the other chapters in this volume. This is shown pictorially in Figure 19.1, which summarises this author's understanding of the main issues that seem central to the message of each chapter.

In Figure 19.1, the house with a person inside represents a building of any type with its inhabitants. The built environment is composed of many such buildings, along with their people and with natural things, depicted by trees. 'CC' represents climate change, with an arrow, its emissions. The person on top of the house represents the client in a construction project, and the person with a hammer represents construction. The thick-lined individual depicts those who think about, research or plan these other activities, with the think-cloud representing that thinking, researching, planning and their themes, worldviews or specific topics. An arrow between people represents discourse or participation. Arms outstretched in front of people denotes an interest in values. A rectangular box represents a tool, usually ICT. The long arrow from left to right represents time.

In brief, this author's understanding of what is important in each chapter is as follows. Brandon (Chapter 1) refers to all the chapters to discuss broad themes relating to sustainability, including worldviews, ICT, practice and time, ending with a set of values. Biscaya and Aouad (Chapter 7) present a utopian vision of smart technologies that, they believe, will help address future challenges. Cooper (Chapter 5) charts the history of sustainable urban development over the last 15 years, with particular reference to the BEQUEST network, and makes suggestions for how it should develop in future. Curwell (Chapter 15) aims at integration in our thinking and views. De Iuliis (Chapter 18) discusses the time element in sustainability in depth. Du Plessis (Chapter 3) argues broadly that we need a new worldview and especially a transformation of the self. Fernando and Alzahmi (Chapter 9) argue that we need tools for collaborating on disaster risk. Formoso and Miron (Chapter 14) discuss how values may be managed in

Future Challenges in Evaluating and Managing Sustainable Development in the Built Environment,
First Edition. Edited by Peter S. Brandon, Patrizia Lombardi and Geoffrey Q. Shen.
© 2017 John Wiley & Sons Ltd. Published 2017 by John Wiley & Sons Ltd.

Figure 19.1   A depiction of built environment sustainability issues discussed in the other chapters.

complex urban regeneration projects. Hibberd (Chapter 16) discusses how sustainability might be embedded into construction contracts, rather than being seen as an optional extra. Kocaturk (Chapter 10) discusses challenges in designing for sustainability and especially the multidisciplinary values that impinge on it. Lombardi and Sonetti (Chapter 4) emphasise the insufficiency of simple models and the need for new paradigms for resilience. Mok and Shen (Chapter 12) discuss stakeholders engaging about values. Mole (Chapter 13) reflects on the experience of one consultancy business in sustainability. Newton (Chapter 6) discusses a virtual reality tool to facilitate for wider participation in development. Perera and Victoria (Chapter 8) discuss how carbon emissions might be managed in the construction industry, both embodied and operational carbon. Ratcliffe (Chapter 2) argues that thinking about and planning cities of the future require a multi-aspectual approach. Sarshar *et al.* (Chapter 11) discuss one case of moving towards a 'smart city' using technology and community involvement to reduce carbon footprint. Yang *et al.* (Chapter 17) discuss the sharing of ideas in transport projects and how social media technology might foster this.

There is considerable diversity, not only among issues, but also among types of issues: buildings, the built environment, cities, nature, carbon footprint, construction processes, building ownership, project management, discussions, plans and planning, participation, analyses, research, theories, worldviews, beliefs, history and time. All are important for sustainability or resilience. Among all these issues and types of issue there are connections, which also provide links among the chapters, sometimes explicit but often less so. This is the complexity that is sustainability.

19.1.1 The challenge

How can all this be holistically understood, to guide and inform our practice? How can we bring together such a disparate set of issues? One answer is to reduce and ignore certain issues as 'unimportant' but in sustainability, with its integrated interdisciplinarity (Boden, 1999), that is not an option because justice must be done to all the issues without ignoring or reducing the importance of any. To view all the issues through one lens, such as that of economics or a functionalist approach, is also inappropriate, since such reductionist methods cause many important issues to be overlooked. Such approaches tend to downplay normativity and the structural element, so a socio-critical approach might be justified. However, such approaches tend to focus on the theme of emancipation, which privileges the human over the non-human.

To do justice to sustainability, both in theory and practice, requires a future-proof understanding of sustainability that incorporates normativity and social structures but is sensitive to all issues, including non-human ones.

19.1.2 The need for philosophical thinking

Such diversity as sustainability urges on us requires philosophical thought. Whereas the sciences each concern themselves with single aspects of reality, philosophy concerns itself with how these aspects relate to each other. To Hart (1984), philosophy is the integrative discipline, and Strauss (2009) calls it 'the discipline of disciplines'. All science and research rest on philosophical assumptions: we cannot begin to form scientific theories until we have selected a way in which reality is meaningful to us – physical, biotic, social, economic and so on.

Philosophy however does not need to be abstract or abstruse. In *Systemic Intervention*, Midgley (2000) offers reasons why philosophy is necessary when – and especially when – considering practice:

- Philosophical assumptions can be used to justify (and critique) practice.
- Philosophy can be used to help define alternatives, and explain why they should be considered.
- Philosophy can assist debates about methodology, and help us discuss and select guidelines for practice.
- Philosophy can help critique and justify intuitive notions and ethical stances in scientific methodology.
- Philosophy helps us see practice in a different light – as Peter Brandon discovered with the philosophy introduced below!
- Philosophy reveals why different approaches are incompatible and cannot simply be 'compared' (an example Midgley gives is of utilitarian and rights-based approaches to managing the National Parks in the USA).

Each of these is important in the research and practice in sustainability. Not only can philosophy help with each, but how we approach each will be deeply influenced and constrained by a philosophical stance, often without our being aware of it. Philosophical interest in the importance of sustainability is scarce, except as a special topic. One reason for this is that most philosophies have hindered thinkers from taking the relationship between human and non-human as seriously as we need to.

19.1.3 Problems with much philosophy

The hindrance comes from philosophy's role in forming the way we presuppose the world to be. To risk oversimplification: Greek philosophies tended to denigrate the material realm, except perhaps as something to form categories about, mediaeval Scholastic philosophies denigrated nature and the secular, except as an aid to the sacred, and most philosophy since the Renaissance has centred on the human, especially human freedom, with Kant introducing the 'Copernican Revolution' that makes human consciousness dominant (c.f. Chapter 3). A few philosophies, such as naturalism, go to the opposite extreme, coercing us to reduce the human to mere natural processes. In all these, the relationship between the human and non-human, which is so important in sustainability, has always been skewed one way or the other by prior presuppositions. Though some contemporary thinking might seem to recognise the relationship more, most do so by explaining it solely via one of its aspects, such as separation (Heidegger), power (Foucault) or communicative action (Habermas). Most philosophy, recent or ancient, tends to direct our thinking along certain channels, which usually means we fail to do justice to other issues.

The challenge is: how can we do justice to the diversity of issues that are meaningful to sustainability, both human and non-human together, without either unwarrantedly ignoring any, or else descending into confusion?

One philosophy that might help us is that of Herman Dooyeweerd (1894–1977), a Dutch thinker of the mid-twentieth century.

19.2 Dooyeweerd's philosophy

This section briefly lays out several themes of Dooyeweerd's philosophy (Dooyeweerd, 1955, 1979), tailored to sustainability of the built environment and making reference to the various chapters of this book. A fuller account of Dooyeweerd's ideas may be found in Basden (2008).

Dooyeweerd sought to understand rather than reduce diversity as it 'speaks to us' within our everyday experience, and especially to understand the coherence that characterizes everyday experience. Though his main work preceded current concern for sustainability, it provides a promising approach, by which human and non-human may be considered with equal dignity, and the coherence between human and non-human understood in all its diverse aspects, such as the physical (climate change), biological, economic or social.

Dooyeweerd's philosophy is founded on very different presuppositions than are those mentioned above and, though initially largely confined to the Netherlands, his ideas are attracting increasing interest throughout the world and in many fields of interest. These include information systems and sustainability (Lombardi and Basden, 1996), with Brandon and Lombardi (2005) initiates a systematic debate about how Dooyeweerd's ideas might be useful for the latter in the urban context.

To Dooyeweerd, philosophy itself must be understood in the context of everyday experience (of which 'practice' is part). So, though philosophy might help us reflect on practice, as Midgley (2000) says, it can never sit as judge over practice, and indeed must itself always be judged by everyday practice. That is the attitude we will take here.

19.2.1 Human and non-human

The first and perhaps most fundamental point is that thinking about sustainability requires a conceptual framework that applies equally to both the human and the non-human, the natural and cultural, with equal aplomb. All three of the Greek, Scholastic and Humanist strands of philosophy tend to place humanity at one pole of a dualism and non-human reality at the other.

By contrast, Dooyeweerd saw all Reality as Being and Occurring by virtue of what he called a '*law side*' of reality, which pertains for both human and non-human equally, though in different manners. This is converse to the *fact side* or *subject side*, which is all that actually exists and occurs, both human and non-human together. Both human and non-human are subject to the same laws, and hence cannot be pushed to opposite poles.

19.2.2 Diversity and aspects

The law side is diverse, constituted of a number of distinct '*law spheres*' or *aspects*. Each law sphere provides fundamental laws of various kinds that govern the activity of all reality, such as mathematical, physical, biotic, psychological, technical, social, economic and ethical laws. In the 'early' or 'pre-human' spheres (aspects), like the physical, the laws are largely determinative but, in later ones, like the social, they allow freedom and are seen as normative in that they distinguish what is good for reality from what is harmful.

Insofar as sustainability may be seen as concerned with the whole of reality, both human and non-human, Dooyeweerd's notion of law spheres might help us understand its diversity, and in a way that incorporates some innate normativity. For example, what climate change emissions results from construction, as discussed by Perera and Victoria (Chapter 8), involves both (non-human) physico-chemical activity and (human, social) decisions of what is constructed and the taking of responsibility for these; Dooyeweerd enables us to consider the laws (determinative or normative) for all these within the same conceptual system, by means of his delineation of fifteen distinct law spheres or aspects.

The word 'aspect' is usually preferable to 'law sphere' since much of our discussion is about ways in which reality may be viewed as meaningful. Just as in architecture, an aspect in Dooyeweerd's sense is a way of viewing things, but Dooyeweerd extends this from buildings to all reality. Each aspect is an irreducibly distinct way of viewing, experiencing and understanding reality, as well as being a law sphere, each being as important as all the others.

The 15 aspects or law spheres Dooyeweerd delineated are shown in Table 19.1. 'Kernel meaning' indicates the way in which the aspect enables situations, things and functions to be meaningful in everyday experience and also in research, 'Potential good' indicates the benefit that the aspect can bring to reality and contribute to sustainability if reality functions in line with its laws. Examples of how each might be relevant to sustainability are given in column 4, some drawn from Brandon and Lombardi (2005).

Dooyeweerd believed that the kernel meanings of the aspects are the same across all cultures (the table entries only partially express them). Moreover, they are grasped by intuition better than by theoretical thought. This opens up a greater possibility of cross-cultural understanding, which is a concern of Yang *et al.* (Chapter 17).

Though irreducible to each other, each aspect depends on others. For example, language and social activity can never be reduced to each other, yet social activity cannot function without language, and language would be almost meaningless if not serving social activity. So it is in sustainability: how we function in one aspect eventually has impact on others.

The physical functioning of the environment is affected by functioning in other aspects, for example when tree roots crack rocks, or when businesses extract physical materials to employ as resources. Which physical materials we extract are determined by our economic choices, which are in turn influenced by our aesthetic choices (as in leisure shopping), which in turn are influenced by our aspirations (pistic aspect), which are mediated through the media (lingual functioning). The care with which we extract materials is determined by ethical attitudes. With that example, we see that even an

Table 19.1 Dooyeweerd's aspects.

Aspect	Kernel meaning	Potential good (examples)	Sustainability (examples)
Quantitative	Amount	Reliable quantity	Measurement
Spatial	Continuous extension, space	Simultaneity, continuity	Geography
Kinematic	Movement: 'flowing and going'	Dynamics	Movement of CO_2; Transport
Physical	Forces, energy, matter	Irreversible persistence and causality	Climate change
Biotic	Life	Organisms sustained in environment	Ecological health
Sensitive	Feeling, response, emotion	Interactive engagement with world	
Analytical	Conceptualising, clarifying, categorising and cogitating	Independence from the world; Theoretical thinking	Clear thinking, analysis
Formative	Formative power (deliberate shaping)	Achievement, construction, innovation; technique, history, culture, technology	Construction; working to reduce CO_2 emissions
Lingual	Symbolic signification	Articulation of intended meaning	Information dissemination; good conversation
Social	Social interaction	Togetherness, institutions	Friendliness
Economic	Frugal management of scarce resources	Sustainable prosperity	Conservation
Aesthetic	Harmony, surprise, fun	Munificent delight	Enjoyment for all
Juridical	Due; appropriateness; rights, responsibilities	Justice for all	Laws, government
Ethical	Self-giving love	Extra goodness, beyond the imperative of due	Generous attitude
Pistic	Vision, aspiration, commitment, creed, religion	Courage, hope; openness to the Divine; change in direction of society	Hope, vision

apparently simple physical activity involves many aspects; Dooyeweerd's aspects offers us the ability to separate out these tangled issues so as to consider them.

Though aspects up to the lingual are concerned with the functioning of individual entities, those from the social onwards are concerned with social activity, and the juridical, ethical and pistic aspects are concerned with societal structures and activity. Juridical societal structures are those of the state and politics; ethical societal structures are attitudes that pervade society; pistic societal structures are the prevailing beliefs and unwritten assumptions and presuppositions that deeply influence our functioning in all other aspects. There is, however, also an individual form of functioning in each of the post-social aspects; for example, economic functioning of carefully managing resources can be undertaken by each individual and by organisations as part of a market. In the pistic aspect we see this dual functioning as that of Western society, including a belief in and commitment to the supremacy of the individual human being, while that of any one individual being their individual beliefs and, perhaps, the courage to hold contrary beliefs. This provides a basis on which the individual and the social may be understood together as all part of one systemic picture. We will return to this below.

Note that Dooyeweerd was self-critical about his suite of aspects: it 'can never lay claim to material completion' (Dooyeweerd, 1955) but should expect to be constantly revised. Yet, as Basden (2008) argues on both practical and philosophical grounds, it is probably the best suite of aspects currently available to us.

19.2.3 Towards an understanding of sustainability

Every thing or situation potentially exhibits every aspect and is subject to the laws of each aspect. This includes sustainability, especially of the urban environment (Brandon and Lombardi, 2005). For example the built environment is meaningful spatially, bioti-cally, socially, economically, lingually, physically and so on. It is subject to spatial laws in relation to neighbouring areas that exist simultaneously with it, biotic laws in its ecology, social laws of being together (e.g. politeness), economic laws in how resources are managed, lingual laws that enable and guide discourse, and especially physical laws by which climate change emissions are generated.

Functioning in each aspect can bring beneficial (good) repercussions and, from the biotic onwards, the possibility of detrimental (evil) repercussions. As Table 19.1 shows, each aspect provides the potential for a different kind of good to be manifested in reality. For example, the physical aspect makes causality and persistence possible, without which biotic functioning would not be possible. The biotic aspect makes the organism possible, the psychic gives interaction, the analytic aspect gives conceptual-ization and analysis and so on up to the pistic aspect, which makes commitment and courage possible.

Inspired by Brandon and Lombardi's (2005) ideas, Vandevyvere (2011) has expended and developed them to provide a philosophical–cultural framework for assessing sustainability.

19.2.4 Sustainability as harmony

The difference, in Dooyeweerd's understanding, is that human beings can function differently in certain spheres of this meaningfulness and law, to which we now turn.

Generally, functioning well in an aspect, in line with its laws, has positive (good) repercussions, which are summarised in Table 19.1, while going against its laws has neg-ative (evil) repercussions: in the social aspect, treat someone as a friend and they will cooperate; treat them as an enemy and they will not. Repercussion chains might occur; for example, if contractors function justly (juridical aspect), the client receives their due; if the client functions justly, the inhabitants receive their due; if inhabitants function justly, the built environment/community receives its due; if that functions justly, nature and planet receive their due and are not harmed. Sustainability thus involves all levels and, in his chapter, Hibberd discusses the first of these but possibly also the wider implications for the rest.

However, is not sustainability more than juridical? Does it not involve all aspects, including the biotic, the social, the economic, the ethical and so on? Dooyeweerd did not use the term 'sustainability' but he held that, for full 'prosperity', 'wellbeing' and so on, we should function positively in all aspects in a way where all aspects work in harmony with each other, as do players in an orchestra. Basden (2008) employs the Hebrew word *shalom* (or the Arabic word *salaam*) to denote this multi-aspectual harmony in life and existence.

The main suggestion in this part of the chapter is that sustainability may be seen as multi-aspectual harmony. Hence sustainability in the built environment requires, and results from, functioning well in every aspect. For example, both capitalist and Marxist approaches over-emphasise the economic aspect to the detriment of others, and this jeopardises sustainability. Some aspects operate over short timescales, some over longer ones. The latter include the juridical aspect (of legal and political structures), the ethical aspect (of prevailing attitudes that gradually spread) and the pistic aspect of deeply assumed beliefs, aspirations and commitments. This offers a useful way of understanding not only the general concept of sustainability but also specific functions that result in good or ill at all timescales.

Resilience, as discussed by Lombardi and Sonetti (Chapter 4) requires this multi-aspectual harmony. Two things jeopardise sustainability: (i) going against the laws of any aspect and (ii) giving too much emphasis to one aspect and ignoring others.

19.2.5 Values

This provides a way of understanding values; each value that we find meaningful is likely to be centred on an aspect, or perhaps a combination of a couple of them. For example, economic value is what helps us manage resources better, biotic value is what helps life, social value is what improves relationships. No kind of value can be reduced to any other.

In this volume, Mok and Shen (Chapter 12) are interested in stakeholders engaging about values. Formoso and Miron (Chapter 14) are particularly interested in managing value in urban regeneration projects and for this they need to understand 'value generation' and to be sensitive to values held by those who live there as well as city planners and owners. Each group of stakeholders is likely to find different aspects of importance as values: for example economic values to city planners and owners, but social and biotic values to inhabitants, with pistic values important to both sets but in different ways, such as religious beliefs to inhabitants and reputation of the city to planners. The Dooyeweerdian harmony of the law spheres, which Basden (2008) calls *shalom/salaam*, might offer a means of value sharing, not by lowest common denominator, but to enable all parties to see why values held by parties might be important in the wider picture.

19.2.6 Thinking about sustainability

Sustainability is thought about during analysis, planning and research. Dooyeweerd's suite of aspects can be employed during analysis to separate out meaningful issues in a way that transcends the interests or biases of analysts (Ahmad and Basden, 2013). For example, we may separate the economic from the biotic issues in sustainability, the lingual from the social and the analytical from the formative; and yet the inter-dependency among aspects means we must consider them all together. This is particularly useful for interdisciplinary research, which is vital for sustainability (Brandon and Lombardi, 2005; Strijbos and Basden, 2006).

The activity of thinking, analysing, researching and theorising, which several authors in this volume discuss, has the analytical aspect at its core, and this targets other meaningful aspects of the world. Cooper learns lessons from research that has taken place. Fernando and Alzahmi (Chapter 9) recognise that several aspects are meaningful targets during risk analysis, especially the social, economic, biotic and physical. Yang *et al.* (Chapter 17) wish to promote sharing, including harmony across cross-cultural situations, which might be facilitated if analysts attend to the kernel meanings of aspects, since these pertain across cultures.

Research involves a special kind of thinking, which aims at greater generality and reliability of knowledge: theoretical thought. Contrary to traditional assumptions, Dooyeweerd maintained that theoretical thought is never neutral but is driven by pre-theoretical beliefs about what is meaningful – prefiguring more recent thinkers like Habermas and Foucault. He carefully argued this both historically by an extensive, immanent survey and also philosophically by transcendental critique; this critique occupies most of Volume I of his *magnum opus* (Dooyeweerd, 1955). He identified three pre-theoretical roots underlying theoretical thought:

- What is deemed meaningful to study is a pre-theoretical choice and commitment (for example in this book, Biscaya and Ghassan's focus in Chapter 7 is on a technological tool).
- How we integrate distinct rationalities (e.g. economic and social rationalities) is a human responsibility, not a mechanical–logical operation; this is the concern of this chapter's first proposal.
- On what basis the community of discourse believes it is valid to critique proffered ideas depends on deep presuppositions about how reality is meaningful (e.g. this often involves the presumed tension between nature and humanity); this is the concern of this chapter's second proposal.

Dooyeweerd believed that these three are necessary for any research or philosophy but are too often hidden in presuppositions. He suggested that self-critical explication of these pre-theoretical factors can facilitate mutual understanding and discourse between disparate paradigmatic views. This might help in two ways.

First, because they are ways in which reality is meaningful, Dooyeweerd's aspects can enrich individual research projects. Two examples: (a) By referring the Seven H's in Brandon's contribution (Chapter 1) to different aspects, they can be philosophically grounded and the links between them be readily explored. (b) More elaborately, Dooyeweerd's aspects might assist Fernando and Alzahmi (Chapter 9) in disaster risk assessment by: (i) helping to focus on distinct types of risk (physical, biotic, psychological, social, economic, etc.) during risk analysis and evaluation, (ii) offering a 'comprehensive theoretical framework' they call for and (iii) providing a basis for sharing understanding in multi-agent situations, where each agency has its own aspect of primary interest but can acknowledge the aspects of other agencies. The reader is invited to consider how each of the other chapters, or papers outside this volume, might be similarly enriched.

Second, Dooyeweerd's aspects can situate the contributions in a work of this nature, painting the kind of holistic–harmonious picture that Brandon (Chapter 1) calls for. Table 19.2 summarises, for each of the chapters of this book, which aspect of sustainability each finds it meaningful to study or discuss. The first column contains the author together with this author's understanding of what is meaningful in their chapter. To aid clarity, four different activities are distinguished, in columns 2–5 of the table:

- Aspects of living in a built (and any other) environment;
- Aspects of the process of construction or procurement of that environment;
- Aspects of discoursing about sustainability;
- Aspects of thinking about any of that (research, planning, theories, worldviews).

This provides an opportunity to integrate the ideas in all the disparate chapters of this work, into a single picture that we might call 'sustainability'.

This analysis reveals several things in an indicative way. One is that all four activities are represented here, though some more than others. Another is that, within each activity, there is little duplication of aspects, suggesting that this work contains a reasonably broad range and good balance. Even the technical tools are for different things. Yet another is to see which aspects are missing, such as the social or economic aspects of construction. This can guide us towards how an even more complete picture of sustainability might emerge from this work, by deliberately considering the missing aspects in each activity.

19.2.7 Human functioning in sustainability

All four activities listed above should function well in every aspect: living in a built environment, constructing or procuring the built environment, discoursing and participating in the built environment and thinking about the built environment (analysing, researching, planning, holding worldviews). Each activity is considered in turn as multi-aspectual human functioning.

Thinking about sustainability (column 5) has been discussed above.

In *living in a built environment* no aspect is necessarily more important than any other. Nevertheless, each aspect may be studied separately, as several chapters in this work do. Mole (Chapter 13) is particularly interested in energy, which is primarily the physical aspect of living in a built environment, but also involves the psychic aspect of people

Table 19.2 Aspects on which the chapters focus. Chapter numbers are given in parentheses in column 1.

Chapter authors and main interests (chapter number)	Aspects of living	Aspects of construction, procurement	Aspects of dialogue or discourse	Aspects of analysis, planning, research, views
Brandon: Broad themes and history (1)				Aesthetic (harmonisation)
Biscaya and Aouad: Smart technologies to meet future challenges (7)		Pistic (Utopian vision); formative (tool)		
Cooper: History of research into built environment (5)				Formative (history)
Curwell: Integrated thinking and views (15)				Aesthetic
De Iuliis: Sustainability and time (18)	(Time: beyond aspects)			
Fernando and Alzahmi: Tools and so on for collaborating on disaster risk (9)				Formative (how-to)
Formoso and Miron: Managing values in urban regeneration projects (14)		Ethical		
Hibberd: Embedding sustainability in construction contracts (16)		Juridical		
Kocaturk: Multidisciplinary values in design (10)		Formative (design)		Pistic
Lombardi and Sonetti: Multiple states of resilience (4)	Aesthetic (diversity, coherence)			
Mole: Giving energy advice in practice (13)		Formative (design)	Lingual (advice), physical (energy)	

Table 19.2 (Continued)

Chapter authors and main interests (chapter number)	Aspects of living	Aspects of construction, procurement	Aspects of dialogue or discourse	Aspects of analysis, planning, research, views
Newton: Tools for public participation (6)			Lingual (discourse), social (participation), formative (tools)	
Perera and Victoria: Carbon emissions from the construction industry (8)		Physical (CO_2); formative (controlling)		
Du Plessis: We need a new worldview (3)				Pistic
Ratcliffe: Future-orientation in planning (2)	Multiple			Juridical (due to future)
Sarshar et al.: Smart cities (11)	Physical (CO_2)			Formative (technology), social (participation)
Mok and Shen: Stakeholders engaging about values (12)			Ethical	Social
Yang et al.: Social media tool to foster sharing of ideas in transport projects (17)		Social (sharing), formative (tool), aesthetic (harmony)		

feeling warm, the economic aspect of saving energy and the social aspect of neighbours. Population is an important factor in sustainability worldwide, as discussed by Perera and Victoria (Chapter 8); this is a quantitative aspect with economic overtones. Sarshar *et al.* (Chapter 11) are concerned about carbon footprint of cities (physical aspect) with juridical responsibility. Lombardi and Sonetti (Chapter 4) argue that simple models, which recognise only a few aspects, are not sufficient, while Ratcliffe (Chapter 2), in his five 'crucibles', actually separates out many of those mentioned here (social, spatial, formative, aesthetic, juridical, lingual, economic, ethical and pistic aspects of living in cities) and argues that we should do justice to all of them, which is a juridical aspect of the planning process.

Other human activities that we have identified here do often have one aspect that is of primary importance in making each meaningful; Dooyeweerd called this the *qualifying aspect*: the formative for construction, the lingual for discussion and the analytic for thinking about sustainability, though all the other aspects are important for its full potential.

Constructing the built environment is qualified by the formative aspect. Thus, Kocaturk (Chapter 10), interested in part of the activity of construction itself (design for sustainability), focuses on this qualifying formative aspect. However, since for construction to be fully sustainable all other aspects are also important, Kocaturk also discusses the analytical aspect of comparing actual performance of buildings with that predicted. Other authors discuss yet other aspects. Perera and Victoria (Chapter 8) are interested in carbon emissions from construction worldwide (which is the physical aspect) and managing it (formative aspect). Hibberd (Chapter 16) is possibly the only author in this volume who focuses on a juridical aspect, contracts that encourage sustainability. Those three also involve the social aspect of people working together and, of course, the economic aspect of management of resources.

This gives a picture in which all these aspects – analytical, formative, juridical, aesthetic, social and physical – are important when considering construction for sustainability. There are yet others, such as biotic, the ethical (especially when constructing in downtrodden communities or developing countries) and the pistic (the overall meaningfulness of construction). Insofar as each aspect indicates the core interest of a discipline (Basden, 2010), Dooyeweerd thus provides a basis for bringing many disciplines and their professions in construction together when considering sustainability.

Discussions about sustainability in the built environment, including by planners, is qualified by the lingual aspect, but again all aspects are important as content of the discussions. Mok and Shen (Chapter 12) emphasises both the ethical aspect in his discussion of stakeholders engaging about values and the social aspect of engagement. Kocaturk (Chapter 10) is particularly interested in the diversity of values (beliefs about what is important: pistic aspect) that impact on design. Mole (Chapter 13) discusses giving advice especially about design (formative aspect). Newton's (Chapter 6) discussion of tools for participation covers not only the lingual aspect, but also the formative aspect of tools and the social aspect of participation. The idea of smart cities, discussed by Sarshar, Ianakiev and Stacey (Chapter 11), tries to unite technology with community participation (formative, social aspects) to reduce the carbon footprint of the life of a city (physical aspect).

In Chapter 1, Brandon tries to incorporate all these human activities in his broad themes and history. He is aware of all Dooyeweerd's aspects and, in fact, came to see aspects as 'a way of thinking'. There may have been a mutually reinforcing cycle here, between valuing interdisciplinarity and seeing things with a suite of aspects that are intuitively grasped in both theory and practice.

This demonstrates the integrative capability of Dooyeweerd's aspects. With them we can conceptually separate out the issues that are meaningful and place them all within a wider picture. This in turn makes it possible to identify common interests and links. It also demonstrates the stimulatory capability in revealing issues that might otherwise be overlooked.

19.2.8 Worldviews

In this volume, both Lombardi and Sonetti (Chapter 4) and du Plessis (Chapter 3) argue that we need a new worldview or paradigm. Du Plessis is particularly exercised by the divides left by the Enlightenment: between individual and community, body and soul, interior and exterior. From where can we get changed worldviews? In some sustainability and environmental circles, there is an ideological dogma that we should decentre the human, reacting dialectically against the destructive, ugly dominance of humanity especially since the Enlightenment. It sees anthropocentrism as an evil to be overcome and those who question it as heretics. As a result, many in the wealthy world, especially the United States and Australia, have reacted against this, to see environmentalism itself as an evil that prevents the poor from achieving their material aspirations.

Most of the chapters in this work seem to range somewhere around the middle between the two extremes. Dooyeweerd's analysis of ground-motives (Dooyeweerd, 1979) accounts for how such divides arose and gained a hold on contemporary thinking. They are not themselves fundamental, Dooyeweerd argued, and hence may be overcome if we take a ground-motive in which diversity of meaningfulness is important.

Ratcliffe (Chapter 2) calls more specifically for future-orientation through 'enlightened city leadership' and 'strategic urban foresight'. Curwell (Chapter 15) calls for more integrated views covering multiple factors. Kocaturk (Chapter 10) calls for recognition of multidisciplinary values (= multi-aspectual) in design.

These are more nuanced, integrated and future-oriented than dialectical reactions are, and Dooyeweerd offers a basis for them. Each worldview, he suggested, elevates one aspect, usually to a dominant position in which other aspects become ignored. So a more integrated worldview may be seen as recognising the equal importance of all aspects (which is why Dooyeweerd spoke of the aspects as earlier–later, rather than lower–higher). Dooyeweerd's philosophy might offer a framework for disclosing which aspects are being undervalued or elevated in discourses around, or action towards, sustainability and for rectifying such imbalances.

19.3 The longer view

19.3.1 Time and progress

As several of the chapters argue, sustainability cannot be divorced from time. But what is time? Dooyeweerd believed that time itself exhibits all the aspects and that all aspects of time need to be recognised. 'Clock' time is physical time and cannot be prioritised over psychological time (our feeling of time), nor historical time, governed by the formative aspect as the moving-forward to human-shaped events, nor biological time, which is cycles of birth, growth, maturity and death.

All aspects of time are important in sustainability and, in her PhD thesis, De Iuliis (2010) made an extensive exploration of Dooyeweerd's ideas of time in relation to sustainability. Her chapter here (Chapter 18) builds on this, to especially consider the longer term.

Long-term issues like sustainability refer to the pistic aspect. While most other aspects are concerned with processes and how repercussions arise from our functioning, the pistic aspect is also concerned with beginnings and ends, all with the meaningfulness of all the processes taken together. Though many processes contribute to sustainability, sustainability as such is long term. Moreover, if someone challenges us with 'Why bother with sustainability?', this is a pistic question to do with ultimate meaningfulness over the entire existence of sustainability from beginning to end. Reference to other aspects, such as the economic or biotic, do not suffice.

How does sustainability relate to 'progress', especially of technology or economy? Progress, to Dooyeweerd, is more than technical or economic; it is the opening up of the potential of aspects and is closely related to science and the disciplines. For example, the potential of the formative aspect was opened up by tools, techniques and technologies, while the potential of the lingual aspect was opened up by writing, film and now ICT.

The opening up of an aspect is achieved by generating knowledge of aspectual law, both theoretical and experiential, and involves both delving into the depths of the aspect and being stimulated by application to other aspects, during which the echoes of those aspects are revealed. The discussion of processes for assessing disaster risks in Chapter 9 by Fernando and Alzahmi is a good example of opening up the formative aspect of achieving something, which then opens up the social aspect of collaboration. Research contributes to this opening process in all aspects but it is itself an opening up of the analytic aspect, and so it is important that Cooper (Chapter 5) traces the history of the idea of sustainable development and makes suggestions for its future.

ICT may be seen as opening up the potential of the lingual aspect (e.g. with the World Wide Web and social media). This is why it is important to consider information-based tools in relation to sustainability, as Biscaya and Ghassan (Chapter 7), Newton (Chapter 6) and Yang *et al.* (Chapter 17) do in their discussions on simulation tools, techniques for analysing big data, tools to encourage participation and social media as a tool for sharing ideas and perspectives.

Drawing on Dooyeweerd, Schuurman (1980) argues that this opening process is guided by the norms of aspects and that the opening of any one aspect should never be guided by its own norms but should serve the norms of all other aspects. The goal of national economies, for example, should never be merely to achieve growth in GDP but should be to facilitate development of other aspects of society. Similarly, though technology can be developed initially under its own dynamic, it must someday serve other aspects or else it becomes sterile. Such sterile thinking might also be indicated by Utopian views of technology, which can be found in Chapter 7. Only when the opening of each aspect facilitates others, is sustainability assured, especially over the long term. This implies responsibility. This is, perhaps, a theme that could be developed further in relation to sustainability to ensure that no one aspect is developed just for its own sake, so as to dominate others.

19.3.2 Humanity's mandate with respect to the rest of reality

The opening up of the potential of various aspects gives human beings enormous power – for either good or ill. Dooyeweerd held that humanity has a mandate to open up the potential of all the aspects in harmony, for the good of the whole of temporal reality, non-human as well as human, and to do so with wisdom, humility and courage.

To date, via the sciences and disciplines, humanity has opened up a number of aspects. The opened-up formative aspect, in the shape of technology, multiplies the power of achievement (of good or ill). The opened-up lingual aspect means the spread of knowledge, beliefs and attitudes. The opened-up social aspect means we work together more effectively – but it also magnifies groupthink. The opened-up economic aspect increases efficiency. The opened-up aesthetic aspect gives us more delights to seek after. As the human population has burgeoned, the amount of good we can bring, or damage we can do, to the world has increases enormously.

To Dooyeweerd, this power imparts responsibility to ensure it is wielded in a way that fulfils the norms of all aspects (Schuurman, 1980). Sadly, for most of its history, humanity has done the opposite. On the one hand, sections of humanity have often elevated an aspect as of supreme importance, suppressing and ignoring others; common examples include elevating technology, economy or religion at the expense of other aspects. On the other, humanity has used the opened potential to serve its own ends, especially the ends of the wealthy and privileged. Both ways undermine sustainability.

Some might try to react against the elevation of one aspect by drawing attention to another aspect and, in turn, elevating that aspect. This has been particularly true in the environmental movement (Basden, 1999). However, this reactive, dialectical approach has seldom proven effective in bringing sustainability about, because sustainability requires all aspects to be practised well. Those who react against the techno-economic system, for example, might produce good ideas but are usually ineffective since they deny themselves the good that technology and economic functioning (careful management) can bring.

By contrast, Dooyeweerd tries to recognise the unique power and contribution of every aspect and how the aspects work together. Not only can his philosophy account for the failure of the others, in terms of aspects they ignore, but it can also chart a route to a more integrated approach in which we aim at harmony among the aspects.

19.3.3 The first proposal

The above collection of suggestions for how Dooyeweerd's philosophy can assist our thinking and practice within sustainability can be embraced within a single proposal: that Dooyeweerd's philosophy provides a sufficient basis for researching, understanding and planning for sustainability, on which extant discourses about sustainability may be integrated.

It has been shown how Dooyeweerd's philosophy is able to address issues in sustainable or resilient urban living, in construction, in ICT tools to help sustainability and in thinking about sustainability within planning or research.

All these contribute to what Dooyeweerd sees as humanity's mandate to open up the potential of each aspect with responsibility for the rest of temporal reality. Many share his view, but Dooyeweerd also provides an ideological, moral and philosophical foundation for it, which most others lack. His notion of law side brings human and non-human together. His notion of aspects provides a non-reductionist basis for addressing diversity in a way that includes meaningfulness and provides a normative thrust. His suite of 15 aspects provides a conceptual tool for separating out the diverse issues that are important in sustainability, in a way that none is elevated over others, so that harmony may be maintained. The aspects cover both human and non-human issues, at individual, social and societal levels. His critique of theoretical thought provides a basis for thinking about sustainability, in both research and planning, and a framework within which extant research may be seen as part of a whole picture.

Dooyeweerd might not provide answers, but he offers a framework within which we can at least do four necessary things: (i) highlight aspects that have been or are being overlooked, (ii) understand the role of every aspect in sustainability and thus encourage us to act without fruitless reaction, (iii) understand the power of humanity in all this and (iv) highlight and direct the responsibility of humanity in all its activities in the built environment.

19.4 The importance of attitudes and beliefs to sustainability

It is being increasingly argued that the problem of sustainability (including climate change) will not be properly addressed until and unless the self is changed, as du Plessis put it in Chapter 3. Ratcliffe (Chapter 2) argues that getting people to change (their minds) is one our biggest challenges. How is this to be achieved? That is the question with which Brandon (Chapter 1) challenges us.

Dooyeweerd would predict that, though all these have a part to play, education, politics, the economic system and technology are not sufficient. Between them, they do not exhaust all the aspects. The ethical and pistic aspects are particularly important and necessary, as prevailing values, attitudes and beliefs, because these impact the functioning in all other aspects via inter-aspect dependency mentioned earlier and are aspects that are particularly important for our sense of self.

19.4.1 The ethical aspect: self-giving and sacrifice

The ethical aspect suggests that sustainability will not be achieved while society and individuals are driven primarily by attitudes of self-interest or self-protection. It will only be achieved once the attitude that pervades society (and is held among many individuals and especially opinion-formers) is one of self-giving, willing sacrifice, vulnerability, repentance ('I was wrong') and forgiveness. Their opposites include self-centredness, reluctance to sacrifice, self-protection, self-justification and continual rehearsal of wrongs. Such attitudes are seldom visible but deeply influence our lifestyles and, in the public sphere, our political, economic, social and other decisions.

The ethical aspect can predict some of the things within its own jurisdiction that are necessary to make real progress on sustainability. However, except when speaking in weak generalities, such predictions take on a moral tone that can offend, such as emanates from strident environmentalists. The ethical aspect would predict that the prosperous sectors of the world must be willing to forego some of the comforts, conveniences and pleasures they currently enjoy that undermine sustainability in their embodied or operational carbon; at the same time, the developing sectors of the world must no longer aspire to those sustainability-undermining kinds of prosperity, which have been globally promulgated by an affluence-driven media, but aim for sustainable prosperity. The prosperous sectors must acknowledge the harm they have done, without excuse and without expectation of return, and eschew their harmful ways, while the developing sectors must forgive, without demand for reparations.

Inter-governmental climate agreements are full of self-protective clauses. Dooyeweerd would suggest these go against the norms of the ethical aspect and thus undermine and jeopardise the achieving of sustainability. It would take unusual courage – especially in a media-dominated democracy like those of the United States and Europe – to appear to be giving away one's own national advantages.

Does that sound impossible? Where does such courage come from? When focusing on the ethical aspect alone, it is impossible because the courageous motivation that this requires does not lie in the ethical aspect, but rather in the pistic aspect.

19.4.2 The pistic aspect: beliefs, commitments, courage, religion, ideology

The pistic aspect suggests that sustainability will not be achieved without challenging and renewing people's faith, beliefs, vision, mindset, worldview, aspirations, expectations, view of what is meaningful in life and direction of life. Commitment is important, as Mok and Shen (Chapter 12) argue, and Dooyeweerd extends this to courage to take radically ethical attitudes, standing out against prevailing attitudes and beliefs.

Historically, it is in religions and ideologies where the pistic aspect has been most active because these concern the deepest beliefs, aspirations and commitments. (The differences between religion and ideology are not discussed here.)

For the economic aspect there is a discourse around the processes and possibilities of specific economic systems, such as capitalist or Marxist, and how they relate to sustainability (e.g. Patel, 2011). For the social aspect, likewise. However, for the ethical and pistic aspects there is very little discourse around how the processes and possibilities of specific systems of ethics or beliefs relate to sustainability. Discussion of ethics and faith related to sustainability has been in general terms – such as which values and beliefs we should hold towards the earth. However, what specific ethical, religious or ideological ideas have to offer in pursuit of sustainability has been seldom discussed. This is what will be attempted here, very briefly.

The reason for this is complex, but much arises from what Dooyeweerd called the Scholastic ground-motive, which dominated mediaeval thought and still influences thought to this day: a presupposition that the sacred and the secular should be kept in different compartments. Religious faith and morals are now presumed by many to be a purely private matter, subject only to personal choice, and their specific content is of little material significance in most academic fields. September 2001, perhaps, forced some to question this presumption but religion is now seen by some as fundamentally evil, rather than as something that might positively contribute. Indeed, pistic without ethical can be sectarian and dangerous, and ethical without pistic can be weak and ineffective. So it is important to consider these aspects together, along with their interactions with other aspects.

It is time to consider the dynamics of how particular religions or ideologies might help or hinder sustainability. Hereafter '*pistic system* (of thought and practice)' will be used instead of 'religion' or 'ideology'. Each pistic system or version thereof offers not only a set of values and beliefs, but also a view of how (or whether) the Divine acts with humans and the world towards some ultimate good, plan or story, and the relationship between humans and the world. Insofar as sustainability may be viewed as a broad good, plan or story, such views must be relevant.

19.4.3 Discourse on beliefs, values and attitudes

One example is now charted of how a pistic system might transform the inner selves of people towards sustainability, that with which this author is most familiar: a version of Christianity. Whether examples can be found in other religions or ideologies is not discussed here; study of for example Buddhism is recommended. The reader should be aware that what follows expresses a personal interpretation and commitment.

Very few discussions have occurred on how versions of Christianity specifically affect sustainability, environment or nature. One is White (1967), who argued that mediaeval Christianity was the root 'cause' of our 'ecological crisis'. According to White, this version of Christianity separated humanity from the rest of creation and aspired to control rather than contemplation. At the end, White advocates an 'alternative Christianity', based on the ideas of Francis of Assisi, who treated animals and the earth as equal with humans.

While White's criticism of mediaeval Christianity is worthy of consideration and response, it should not be used, as it has sometimes been over the past four decades, to exclude consideration of the potential that Christianity might offer in achieving the change of self that is required for sustainability. White's argument is poor, with sudden unwarranted jumps and a polemical style that he fails to justify. What he calls 'Christianity', against which his polemic is aimed, is in fact a limited kind – the mediaeval, Scholastic sort we have referred to above – and he largely ignores Protestant, Reformed and Pentecostal versions. Dooyeweerd's (1955) critique of the Scholastic position is more detailed and nuanced, arguing that it cannot be truly called 'Christian' and that it is actually the subsequent Humanist view, rather than any Christian view, that places humanity at the apex. While White's proposal of a Franciscan approach is interesting, it is too brief to let the reader judge whether or how it is likely to work, especially given that White remarks that Francis ultimately failed.

Though White (1967) does discuss the dynamics of a specific pistic system in relation to ecology, it is negative and historical rather than looking for positive future-oriented contributions.

The Papal Encyclical *Laudato Si* (Francis, 2015) also briefly mentions some of the dynamics of its pistic system, such as a 'need to experience a conversion or change of heart' and 'the effects of their encounter with Jesus Christ' (Francis, 2015, p. 159) and also some tenets Francis of Assisi held, more deeply than White does. However, the link between the dynamics of this encounter and sustainability is weakly drawn, with change of heart treated as mere aspiration. Even though it recognises that a change of heart must be a community as well as an individual conversion, how this occurs in relation to sustainability is not discussed in enough detail. That conversion will lead to sustainability is more assumed than discussed and, like most other discussions, this document gravitates towards merely setting out a set of attitudes or values that we as humans 'ought' to adopt, such as 'loving awareness' or developing our 'God-given capacities' (Francis, 2015, pp. 160–161). The document might usefully stimulate a change of values about the rest of creation (or sustainability) among the large number of Roman Catholics. It is less useful, however, as a contribution to the discourse around sustainability itself.

It is within sustainability discourses themselves that discussion is needed about the dynamics offered by specific pistic systems. One that might do this is Prince Philip and Mann (1989). Recognising the importance of pistic functioning, Prince Philip invited five of the world's major religions to Assisi in 1984 to present their attitude to nature. He was disappointed that what was presented by the Christian churches was little different from that of the Jewish religion – nature belongs to God, so we ought to respect rather than plunder it.

So he instituted a Consultation on *The Christian Attitude to Nature* during the late 1980s, to which this author was invited to contribute. The outcome was published (Prince Philip(and Mann 1989), going beyond the Jewish ideas in several ways, by adding the activity of Jesus Christ and the Spirit of God. Despite its establishment origins, the document contains some radical ideas. The following briefly summarises and paraphrases what the Consultation found, supplemented, expanded, updated with material from other sources and applied to an historical example.

19.4.4 The dynamics in one Christian view

The specifics of this pistic system are briefly as follows. Jesus Christ (whom Christians see as God manifest in human form) makes it possible to become acceptable to God as an unmerited gift, rather than as a reward for religious practice or ethical uprightness. If a person accepts this gift, the Holy Spirit (of God) begins to dwell in their deep inner self and starts a transformation process. Depending on the extent to which the person freely cooperates with the Spirit of God, the person is transformed deeply inside. Things become meaningful to them in new ways, with different aspirations and so on (pistic aspect), combined with a self-critical and self-giving attitude (ethical aspect). This in turn transforms functioning in other aspects, as expressed by the early Christian thinker, Paul, as 'the fruit of the Spirit': love, joy, peace, patience, kindness, goodness, faithfulness, gentleness or humility, self-control. This is an attitude towards 'the other' – including both human and non-human. According to this version of Christianity, it is solely the Spirit of God that accomplishes this and provides courage to stand against prevailing views and to persevere, rather than laws, education, politics, economic incentives and so on – these play a supporting role.

The impact of this can be not just on the person, but also on their community and society. To the extent that such people allow the Spirit of God to change their lifestyle, values and worldview and to prompt them to courageous yet self-effacing action in the *agora* (public space), others around them can be affected, – grassroots, politicians, opinion-formers and so on. Bodies of knowledge as developed by the sciences and professions can also be impacted.

There have been several incidents of this occurring on a wide scale in recent history, one being the abolition of the slave trade. This was seen by Metaxas (2007) as much more than a change in policy and laws; it was a change in foundational attitudes and beliefs in society (collective ethical and pistic functioning). At that time, most people assumed that slavery was part of the 'natural order', essential for their growing economy and necessary for the war against France. Yet the change happened: not only did laws change, but slavery was no longer believed in as necessary or good.

The reasons it occurred are many, and contributions from functioning in all aspects and at all levels of society must be recognised. However, it is the specific content of the pistic system of the kind of Christianity that William Wilberforce and his colleagues experienced which must be seen as crucial. It gave a clear vision (Metaxas, 2007) to William Wilberforce and to various Wesleyan and Calvinist believers of the time, along with the courage to persevere even though often resisted and sometimes derided by society at large; see for example Clarkson (1836).

19.4.5 Application to sustainability

Metaxas (2007) remarks that the change that the slave-trade abolitionists sought of the British people was as radical as asking people today to give up driving cars (or trucks). Yet it happened. It happened because of their sustained commitment (pistic functioning) and willingness to sacrifice for the sake of good (ethical functioning).

Is it possible that something similar could occur in relation to sustainability, given for example that transport is a major contributor to climate change emissions? It is challenging, but not impossible, if the pistic dynamics outlined above are valid, because it addresses people's aspirations, expectations and attitudes. Various authors (Prince Philip and Mann, 1989; Basden, 1988; Campolo, 1992) apply the fruit of the Holy Spirit specifically to attitudes to the natural world, for example:

- Love, including of the natural world, and hence a desire to cherish and protect it;
- Peace, including with the natural world, and hence an active sacrificial desire to prevent its destruction;
- Patience, including with the speed at which the natural world works, which can act as a curb on unbridled competition;
- Self-control, including resisting the pressure to maximize profits and being content with 'enough' instead [c.f. Simon's (1956) 'satisficing'].

At the individual level, a person changed by the Holy Spirit aspires less to self-centred conveniences, comforts, fashions or pastimes that undermine sustainability and begins to find their enjoyment and achievement via other, more sustainable, means. For example people might not only choose to walk or cycle rather than jump in the car (kinematic aspect), not only choose to holiday and find their leisure locally (aesthetic aspect) rather than involving air travel, not only privilege local and organic food (biotic aspect) and require less of it (economic aspect), but also be willing to sacrifice such things as convenience and habit (ethical aspect). They will think such things through critically (analytic aspect).

At the community level, conversations (lingual aspect) might focus less on the self and more on the other (ethical aspect), and collective action might be taken (social aspect). The changed person has the courage to be different from others, even when derided, and has the persistence and commitment to continue despite adversity. It has been found that a greater sense of responsibility to 'the other' (human and non-human) begins to pervade organisational and business life, affecting the ecological footprint.

At the level of society the changes affect societal structures, which, as we saw in the abolition of the slave trade, includes policy, pervading attitudes (self-giving rather than self-protection) and prevailing beliefs that give courage to act and sustains perseverance in the case of resistance.

That is the potential – and there are some historical precedents for it.

19.4.6 The second proposal

The second proposal is that the specific content of pistic systems (religions or ideologies) needs to be discussed as part of the discourse around, or action towards, sustainability and not just relegated to 'religion'.

It is not sufficient to discuss only faith or ethics in general; the discussion needs also to include the dynamics offered by specific pistic systems and their effect on functioning in all aspects, at all levels. This discussion needs to take account both of specific pistic theory (which is often expressed as 'doctrine' in religious practice) and of historical cases in which it has been worked out. The example of the abolition of the slave trade, and the change in societal beliefs that attended it, was examined in an indicative rather than exhaustive way to show the operation of one version of Christianity. That example and its pistic theory deserve more investigation within the discourse of sustainability, rather than in the discourse of religion. So do examples and pistic theory from other pistic systems.

19.5 *Conclusion*

Two proposals have been made. The first is that Dooyeweerd's philosophy can help us understand sustainability as multi-aspectual functioning and values and can offer a practical conceptual framework for evaluating and guiding towards sustainability. Sustainability itself is seen as the state in which individuals and society function well in every aspect.

It has been shown how the importance of each of the chapters in this book may be affirmed by reference to Dooyeweerd's suite of aspects and situated according to the aspectual contribution to sustainability each might offer.

The second proposal begins with Dooyeweerd's ethical and pistic aspects, because our pistic functioning deeply influences our functioning in all other aspects. However, it can be considered separately from Dooyeweerd's aspects, since it goes beyond aspectual functioning to consider the dynamic activity of the Divine alongside humanity and the world. It suggests that, in addition to trying to advocate general attitudes, values or beliefs, those concerned with sustainability and with our ecological crisis in general should seriously discuss the dynamics offered by specific pistic systems (religions or ideologies). One religious theory has been examined as an exemplar, a version of Christianity that understands the role of the Spirit of God to transform the hearts of people, communities and society.

I am not hereby trying to promote (one version of) Christianity, and I would welcome discussions of a similar kind in other pistic systems. The discussion of this version of Christianity is offered as an exemplar, as a possible template for discussion of other faiths and ideologies. The challenge is to find an alternative way of effecting the deep transformation of the self that du Plessis (Chapter 3) and Ratcliffe (Chapter 2) believe is necessary, a change in pistic orientation which will deeply influence the functioning in all other aspects that pertain to sustainability. Research is needed on this – but it should not take too long.

References

Ahmad, H., Basden, A. (2013) Down-to-Earth Issues in Information System Use. *Proceedings of the Pacific Area Conference on Information Systems*, Paper 191.

Basden, A. (1988) *Ecological Enterprise*, Industrial Christian Fellowship, Birmingham.

Basden, A. (1999) Engines of dialectic. *Philosophia Reformata* **64**(1), 15–36.

Basden, A. (2008) *Philosophical Frameworks for Understanding Information Systems*, IGI Global, Hershey.

Basden, A. (2010) On using spheres of meaning to define and dignify the IS discipline. *International Journal of Information Management* **30**, 13–20. ((For full paper see http://aisel.aisnet.org/ukais2009/10 (accessed 1 January 2016)].

Boden, M.A. (1999) What is interdisciplinarity? In: *Interdisciplinarity and the Organisation of Knowledge in Europe* (ed. R. Cunningham). Office for Official Publications of the European Communities, Luxembourg, pp. 13–24.

Brandon, P.S., Lombardi, P. (2005) *Evaluating Sustainable Development in the Built Environment*, Blackwell Science, Oxford.

Campolo, T. (1992) *How to Rescue the Earth, Without Worshipping Nature: A Christian's Call to Save Creation*, Word Publishing, Milton Keynes.

Clarkson, T. (1836) *The History of the Rise, Progress and Accomplishment of the Abolition of the African Slave Trade by the British Parliament*, John W. Parker, London.

De Iuliis, M. (2010) *A Dooyeweerdian Approach to Time in Sustainable Development*, PhD thesis, University of Salford, Salford.

Dooyeweerd, H. (1955) *A New Critique of Theoretical Thought*, vols I–IV (1975 edition), Paideia Press, Jordan Station, Ontario, Canada.

Dooyeweerd, H. (1979) *Roots of Western Culture; Pagan, Secular and Christian Options*, Wedge Publishing Company, Toronto.

Francis (2015) *Laudato Si (a reprint of the work of Franciscus)*, Libreria Editrice Vaticana, Vatican City, Rome.

Hart, H. (1984) *Understanding Our World: An Integral Ontology*, University Press of America, Philadelphia.

Lombardi, P., Basden, A. (1996) Environmental sustainability and information systems: the similarity. *Systems Practice* **10**(4), 473–489.

Metaxas, E. (2007) *Amazing Grace: William Wilberforce and the Heroic Campaign to End Slavery*, Harper Collins, New York.

Midgley, G. (2000) *Systemic Intervention: Philosophy, Methodology and Practice*, Kluwer/Plenum, New York.

Patel, R.N. (2011) Crisis: capitalism, economics and the environment. *Undergraduate Economic Review* **8**(1), 3.

Prince Philip, Mann, M. (1989) *Survival or Extinction: A Christian Attitude to the Environment*, authored by Prince Philip, HRH The Duke of Edinburgh and The Rt. Rev. Michael Mann, Michael Russell Publishing, Salisbury, for St. George's House, Windsor Castle.

Schuurman, E. (1980) *Technology and the Future: A Philosophical Challenge*, Wedge Publishing, Toronto.

Simon, H.A. (1956) Rational choice and the structure of the environment. *Psychological Review* **63**(2), 129–138.

Strauss, D.F.M. (2009) *Philosophy, Discipline of the Disciplines*, Paideia Press, Grand Rapids.

Strijbos, S., Basden, A. (eds) (2006) *In Search of an Integrative Vision of Technology: Interdisciplinary Studies in Information Systems*, Kluwer/Springer, Amsterdam.

Vandevyvere, H. (2011) How to cut across the catch-all? A philosophical–cultural framework for assessing sustainability. *International Journal of Innovation and Sustainable Development*, **5**(4), 403–24.

White, L. (1967) The historical roots of our ecological crisis. *Science*, **155**, 1203–1207.

Index

Future Challenges in Evaluating and Managing Sustainable Development in the Built Environment,
First Edition. Edited by Peter S. Brandon, Patrizia Lombardi and Geoffrey Q. Shen.
© 2017 John Wiley & Sons Ltd. Published 2017 by John Wiley & Sons Ltd.